American Radio Networks

ALSO BY JIM COX AND FROM MCFARLAND

Sold on Radio: Advertisers in the Golden Age of Broadcasting (2008)

This Day in Network Radio: A Daily Calendar of Births, Deaths, Debuts, Cancellations and Other Events in Broadcasting History (2008)

The Great Radio Sitcoms (2007)

Radio Speakers: Narrators, News Junkies, Sports Jockeys, Tattletales, Tipsters, Toastmasters and Coffee Klatch Couples Who Verbalized the Jargon of the Aural Ether from the 1920s to the 1980s — A Biographical Dictionary (2007)

The Daytime Serials of Television, 1946–1960 (2006)

Music Radio: The Great Performers and Programs of the 1920s through Early 1960s (2005)

Mr. Keen, Tracer of Lost Persons: A Complete History and Episode Log of Radio's Most Durable Detective (2004; softcover 2009)

Frank and Anne Hummert's Radio Factory: The Programs and Personalities of Broadcasting's Most Prolific Producers (2003)

Radio Crime Fighters: More Than 300 Programs from the Golden Age (2002; softcover 2009)

Say Goodnight, Gracie: The Last Years of Network Radio (2002)

The Great Radio Audience Participation Shows: Seventeen Programs from the 1940s and 1950s (2001; softcover 2009)

The Great Radio Soap Operas (1999; softcover 2008)

American Radio Networks

A History

JIM COX

McFarland & Company, Inc., Publishers
Jefferson, North Carolina, and London

All photographs are supplied by Photofest.

LIBRARY OF CONGRESS CATALOGUING-IN-PUBLICATION DATA

Cox, Jim, 1939–
American radio networks : a history / Jim Cox.
p.   cm.
Includes bibliographical references and index.

ISBN 978-0-7864-4192-1
softcover : 50# alkaline paper ∞

1. Radio broadcasting—United States—History.   I. Title.
PN1991.3.U6C63   2009   384.540973—dc22   2009019995

British Library cataloguing data are available

©2009 Jim Cox. All rights reserved

*No part of this book may be reproduced or transmitted in any form
or by any means, electronic or mechanical, including photocopying
or recording, or by any information storage and retrieval system,
without permission in writing from the publisher.*

On the cover: Edward R. Murrow, on *Years of Crisis*,
CBS Radio, 1951 (CBS/Photofest); Background ©2009 Shutterstock

Manufactured in the United States of America

*McFarland & Company, Inc., Publishers
Box 611, Jefferson, North Carolina 28640
www.mcfarlandpub.com*

For Irene Heinstein
Investigator Extraordinaire

Acknowledgments

It's getting to be a habit, but one that I trust will continue. Intrepid researcher Irene Heinstein is due sizeable credit for some of the factual details in this book. A tireless stalker of the unknown, she never quits until she ferrets out the most obscure matter, tracking it with a vengeance. Never have I witnessed such tenacity in exploring every lead until she has finally put her finger on an elusive detail that makes a piece complete. You are as fortunate to read her results as I am to have a colleague possessing such wide-ranging ability and dedication. You and I are genuinely blessed by Irene's involvement in the mix.

Another gallant performer, to whom an earlier text was dedicated, is Doug Douglass. Quietly, unobtrusively, he routinely ships me items that have caught his eye which he thinks will be interesting, provocative or helpful in my pursuits. Often they are all of the above. I've been grateful for his friendship for a long while, leaning on Doug for all sorts of New York–area data that would escape my notice without his attention to detail.

Herb Squire manifestly contributed to this tome, too, and I am happy to recognize his participation. I'm always happy to express thanks on behalf of many hobbyists to an assemblage of dedicated vintage radio servants who profoundly impact this venture with their involvement in sundry communications media. Among their number are Jim Adams, Frank Bresee, Bob Burchett, Steve Darnall, Jack French, Tom Heathwood, Jay Hickerson, Walden Hughes, Ken Krug, Patrick Lucanio and Chuck Schaden. They continue to inspire me to press on.

To my lifelong partner, Sharon Cox, I shall ever be grateful. She lends me to these projects and provides the constant encouragement I need. I'm also thankful to other family members who share me in these efforts.

And finally, to all of you who profess a concerted passion for radio, I am grateful. It is you who keep my spirit—as well as old time radio itself—alive.

Contents

Acknowledgments	vi
Preface: Fascination	1
1—The Net Rewards of Radioland: With the Twist of a Wrist	3
2—The Proceeds of Experimentation: Getting Ready to Play for Real	8
3—National Broadcasting Company: The House That Sarnoff Built	16
4—Columbia Broadcasting System: The House That Paley Built	45
5—Mutual Broadcasting System: The Network for All America	72
6—American Broadcasting Company: A Nobleman's Dream	89
7—The Regional Hookups: Local Radio Gone Wide	101
8—Washington Watchdogs: Safeguarding the Airwaves	116
9—Remuneration: The Hardest Nut to Crack	122
10—Czar Wars: The Empire-Builders Fight Back	132
11—Halcyon Days: A Showtime Sampler	139
12—Sight Radio: No Renaissance for Imagination	169
13—The Spinmeisters: Rancor Among the Ranks	178
14—Raconteurial Resurgence: The Spielers Have Their Say	184
Epilogue: When You Wish Upon a Star	188
Appendix—Ex Chains: Webs of Extinction	191
Chapter Notes	203
Bibliography	215
Index	219

Preface
Fascination

It was fascination that drove me to finally surrender to my inner thoughts and set down on paper an inspiration that had been swirling in my mind for ages—a history of the commercial broadcast radio networks in 20th century America. Anybody who has read anything I've written knows that this author takes a shine to practically anything about history, whatever the form, whether it's a place, a person, or a passion.

The pages of this tome are occupied by my lifelong infatuation with radio—and particularly, and unabashedly, with *network* radio—the old-fashioned kind that extended its borders to ours, wherever they might be. Sprinkled in are liberal dashes of personalities and places from which it emanated. I hope, whether you relish history or generally accept it only in meted doses, this will be a gratifying trip. We'll wander down memory lane together through encounters with the nation's first mass communications medium that connected us all to uniform brainwaves at the same instant. Only the "pictures" were left to personal interpretation. May this be a pleasant as well as an edifying journey for everybody who reads these words.

The book begins with the gifts that network radio bestowed on all of us followed by a look at a trial-and-error epoch in which the foundations were laid. There are probes into a distinct quartet of major players in the aural broadcasting arena during network radio's golden age (its outer limits are, for our purposes, considered to extend from the mid–1920s to the early 1960s). There's a focus on the regional chains that dotted America's landscape. The book encounters Big Brother, the underwriting for ethereal services, the manipulations of a couple of industry gurus, and an exhibition of some of the fare that made the aural medium so incredibly indispensable. Finally, this work explores the impact of television, turntables, troublemakers, and talk on audio transmission. It concludes with an appendix surveying some of the noteworthy chains that once prevailed alongside the foremost transcontinental webs.

A disclaimer is in order before proceeding: I have diligently sought to give you an error-free text from start to finish. Be aware that it isn't going to happen. "There is no such thing as the perfect book," a publisher informed me matter-of-factly before I penned my original broadcasting volume. That bromide, received many years ago, should be carved in stone. I've proven its accuracy with every successive effort. Despite the admission, I think I'm gradually gaining on it, finding fewer mistakes with every added volume. (This is my 18th book, all but four pertaining to broadcasting.) Nevertheless, if you discover an error (and I'll bet you will), in spite of every painstaking effort that several trained proofreaders have made to the contrary, blame me. I take full responsibility; and be assured the mistakes grieve me more than they do you. Maybe some will say: "I know he *tried* to get it right." As Lily Tomlin's brat character Edith Ann might add, "And that's the truth!"

In the meantime, the story of radio—and particularly *network radio*—is a fascinatingly provocative romp in the annals of mass communications. While you encounter some of the basic information that those of us may already know (including you, dear reader) who are on the fringes of this alluring business, you'll probably cultivate a whole lot more that went on behind the microphones that you hadn't experienced until now.

It's a captivating province. I hope I've made it tempting for you. I'm glad you've come along for the ride.

1

THE NET REWARDS OF RADIOLAND
With the Twist of a Wrist

Can there be any room to doubt the phenomenal consequences which occurred when the human voice, frequently augmented by reverberations of disparate proportions, permeated the ether in synchronized form for the very first time? Far-flung points were suddenly, swiftly, concurrently bound together, an event that indelibly altered the landscape of mass culture on the planet forever.

For the first time in global history, what informed and amused us was profoundly affected by technological advancements that had gradually made their way to the forefront. The discovery and application of those innovations were largely unknown to human beings from the beginning of time. Not until multiple factors coalesced in the final decades of the nineteenth century, allowing deeply-hidden mysteries to unravel at a rapid pace, did we substantiate their existence and enormous possibilities—confirmation at last of what may have been inklings in many minds for centuries.

Harnessing electric power, transitioning a manual labor force into one that commanded power-driven machinery, pervasive socioeconomic and cultural shifts, and many other performance revolutions occurred. Transpiring in an epoch of innovative thinking, they led to vastly improved communications that resulted in mechanisms like the invention of the telegraph (1844) and telephone (1876).

That spirit of eternal optimism persisted unabated as intrepid pursuers of countless persuasions—zealous dreamers, really—continued to press for more and better ways to breach the chasms that still separated mankind. Heinrich Hertz, Guglielmo Marconi, Nathan Stubblefield, Reginald Fessenden, Lee de Forest, Edwin Armstrong, Frank Conrad and legions of equally visionary thinkers made worthy contributions to deliver a breakthrough that could be attributed to so many. A new means of transmitting sound across long distances was the outcome, one by which man would receive endless hours of refreshment for minimal cost with the twist of a wrist.

Thus, in the early decades of the twentieth century, the denizens of this world became an infinite unseen audience in widely diverse locales, able to share in comparable opportunities by grasping the same matter at the same time. It was a marvel that had never been encountered in such extensive proportions. And after its implementation, life on the earth as it had always been lived was destined to never be quite the same again. Radioland was connected!

An early outgrowth of this broadcasting phenomenon was the fulfillment of a concept that allowed people who lived in multiple communities to participate in common programming efforts, albeit vicariously. This occurred even though they frequently were separated by substantial geographical terrain.

In practice, productions generated by an originating unit were beamed not just to those living nearby in possession of receivers (radio sets) but to those who also tuned in to one or more distant "relay" stations. These outposts might be situated in remote settings, where the fare was picked up by listeners dwelling within those far-off provinces. Theoretically, a single programmer could transmit specific programming to scores or even hundreds of added broadcasting facilities. Local outlets could make matter for broadcast available to audiences of pretty formidable sizes. This was something new: all of the recipients were tuning in to the same sequence at the same time.

Such networking, sometimes dubbed "chain broadcasting," was simplistically classified as "simultaneous broadcasting of an identical program by two or more connected stations."[1] In a government-sanctioned document issued in the early 1940s, this pithy portrayal aptly characterized the form's extended scope.

> The growth and development of chain broadcasting found its impetus in the desire to give widespread coverage to programs which otherwise would not be heard beyond the reception area of a single station. Chain broadcasting makes possible a wider reception for expensive entertainment and cultural programs and also for programs of national or regional significance which would otherwise have coverage only in the locality of origin. Furthermore, the access to greatly enlarged audiences made possible by chain broadcasting has been a strong incentive to advertisers to finance the production of expensive programs.[2]

The inception of the National Broadcasting Company in 1926, the country's initial transcontinental hookup, encouraged its parent firm to project a "great force for the cultural improvement of the American people."[3] Time bore out that its mission, also shared by a couple of formidable competitors, was achieved.

There were still more sterling treasures emanating from this interconnection of stations and the programming it projected to the American people, all worthy of tallying.

Network radio provided more than the obvious advantage of a channel that has allowed us all to be a part of a synchronized audience for the unremitting ebb and flow of current events; and definitely more than intrinsic values like edification, inspiration, diversion and recreation. Network radio brought us together for countless high moments in the nation's passage, including some very bright and some very dark hours: declarations of war and truce-signings signaling their conclusion; the first landing on the moon; terrorist attacks and the fallout they precipitated; assassinations; political conventions and inaugurations; the passing of notables of contrasting persuasions—performers, artists, educators, sportsmen, heroes and public service officials; scholastic achievements; World Series, Super Bowl and Final Four matches; parades and holiday celebrations; stock market rallies and declines; the implications of international newsmakers and events; plus a plethora of assorted occasions that have captured our spirit and stirred our interests and imaginations.

A farsighted governmental troupe, writing more than seven decades ago, cited some imperative underpinnings for sanctioning chain broadcasting: "The organization of transmission facilities in networks of stations is ... indispensable in times of national emergency, such as a widespread catastrophe, a national financial crisis, or the advent of sudden attack, because it is only through such organization that there can be efficient mass communication on a regional and national scale."[4] How often has the veracity of that declaration been witnessed? Our guess is, many more times than we can possibly begin to recall.

Their assessment continued: "Competitive networks if properly operated are not only sound but also essential in the scheme of American broadcasting ... they have rendered meritorious service to the public."[5] Yes they have. And network radio has given us so much more.

It altered the listening patterns of the homeland. With the arrival of chain broadcasting, local stations which dominated the dial, particularly in hamlets and villages and along rural countrysides, no longer possessed uncontested monopolies over the ether in the communities they covered. By the late 1920s, web-linked outlets presented more sophisticated fare, technically-advanced stuff that was usually originated at a trio of New York–based flagships: WEAF (the National Broadcasting Company's Red network), WJZ (NBC's Blue web) and WOR, later WABC (the Columbia Broadcasting System).[6]

In satisfying a widely diverse clientele tuning in across the nation, the networks were obliged to air programming that had broad appeal and offered first-rate talent. The chains regularly made available series which would have been next to impossible for independent outlets to present on a consistent basis. Instead of sometimes providing untrained amateur singers, comics and instrumentalists, these webs routinely gave listeners the superstars of their day—Howard Barlow, Ben Bernie, Major Bowes, Walter Damrosch, Vaughn DeLeath, Jessica Dragonette, Ernie Hare, Ted Husing, Al Jolson, Billy Jones, Vincent Lopez, Will Rogers, Paul Whiteman and many more of their reputed ilk.

> Outside of the large theatrical centers, the pitiful lack of talent available to station program directors made such a system of broadcasting essential if a public attracted to radio by its novelty, was to be held. Programs—and not just broadcasts—had become the lifeblood of the industry. So, overnight, the Baron Munchausen of Jack Pearl; the warblings of Ethel Shutta and Ruth Etting; the hilarious comedy of Ed Wynn and Milton Berle were no longer the peculiar property of Broadway. Radio gave them to the nation.[7]

Beyond the normal fare, the webs beamed unrestrained events from widely diverse locales, special occasions that begged national approbation. The response from audiences was clear: by the mid 1930s, an extraordinarily high 88 percent of all radio listeners favored network programming over whatever was being generated by their unaffiliated counterparts.[8] In most places, there would be just as strong a collective endorsement in the 1940s and at least early 1950s.

From a business standpoint, network radio also delivered unlimited access. The chains made it possible for marketers of many persuasions to reach across vast expanses of topography with their promotional plugs. Until then—beyond simple word of mouth—sales agents had relied almost entirely on print advertising in newspapers, magazines, posters, billboards, road and barn signs, handbills and direct mail. Network radio proffered the ability to access the majority of the country with single announcements on the same day and, perceptually, in a more personal way. As vendors applied sophisticated electronic technology—something to which most recipients were heretofore unaccustomed—they created quite a stir. For a while, at least, many of those listeners really didn't want to miss any of it as they hung on every word.

As a result, advertising agencies—the middlemen of commercialization—proliferated. It was they that inspired, sold, wrote, produced and delivered not only the promotional plugs but, in a brief while, most of the programs in "package" form (including talent, content and oversight). Chain broadcasting was a burgeoning endeavor that continually opened new doors to sideline ventures and entrepreneurial free spirits.

Soon audience measurement systems sprang up. This spinoff venture gave advertisers, agencies and networks reliable clues about how many—and who—tuned into their airwaves wares. Suddenly, too, there was a need for artist bureaus and talent agencies to populate the webs' programming requirements.

More posts were created and rapidly proliferated. On the administrative side, there were appeals for executives, producers and directors. On the talent side, there were expanded calls for actors, comedians, announcers, emcees, instrumentalists, vocalists, composers, consultants, advice-givers, sportscasters, newscasters, panelists, writers and numerous other professionals. On the support side, new hires were summoned as engineers, sound effects techs, production crew helpers, facilities managers, tour guides, studio ticket distributors, crowd controllers, clerical staffers and on and on. As chain broadcasting flourished, so did the occupations as an escalating new industry tested arenas, broadly diversifying into untested domains.

Of course, the financial implications of this phenomenon resulted in profound effects on commerce outside those production centers. The manufacture and sales of radio sets alone multiplied in spades. A large chunk of that good fortune could be directly attributed to the fans' response to the level of artistry and programming content afforded by the major webs.

By 1932, one out of three American homes boasted a radio receiver; that percentage surged steadily until nine out of 10 U.S. domiciles exhibited at least one radio set a decade and a half later.[9] And concurrently, millions of residents displayed multiple sets in their homes and workplaces. By the late 1940s, many of those same people drove radio-equipped vehicles. Within a decade legions of them toted lightweight hand-held portable transistor radios wherever they went, still another innovative offshoot.

Aside from that, network radio saw new state-of-the-art broadcasting facilities erected to accommodate the trade's growing needs. That generated significant infusions of cash in local economies. Studio and office furnishings, equipment and supplies, technical paraphernalia, musical instruments, food and beverage units, utilities, transportation, tax revenues, licenses, legal retainers and sundry other supplies and services benefited from the growth of radio.

On yet another front, the economic dependence of the network affiliates on those chains is clearly evidenced. In a 1937 study nearly a third (32.11 percent) of the typical web station's revenues at mid-decade was directly attributable to chain-derived programming.[10] In some cases it was enough of a decisive edge to prevent a local station from operating at financial losses. Perhaps even more impressive, however, is data like this: in a survey of U.S. outlets conducted in 1935—including those linked to chains and those that weren't—the network affiliates earned nearly three-fourths (74.53 percent) of the gross receipts of all commercial broadcast operations. And if that isn't convincing enough of the power they held, that year (1935) the affiliates acquired 86.18 percent of national and regional non-network business and 56.08 percent of local business.[11]

Typical revenue earnings for chain-fed outlets in all classes of stations (local, regional and clear channel) averaged $201,030 in 1935. (Keep in mind that this is still in the depths of the Great Depression fostered by the collapse of the stock market.) At the same time, independent (non-network) stations in that categorical trio earned on average $36,710.[12] Could there be any doubt that connecting with a network, at least during radio's golden age, was a fast track to prosperity and influence among the outlets that were fortunate enough to be so ensconced?

Let it be noted that network affiliates of every class were usually situated in the most desirable markets. That was viewed as a substantial bonus to the chain-fed outlets. One authority affirmed that network ties still appeared to exert a stronger influence in attracting national and regional non-network business to an outlet. Other factors like power and—probably more importantly—location in a market affected average local time sales of different classes of stations.[13]

Meanwhile, the networks themselves were also scoring astonishing bottom lines. NBC raked in a profit of nearly $2.2 million in 1930.[14] While in 1935 local radio stations generated almost $56.3 million (52.3 percent) in total estimated broadcast advertising revenues—including time sales and programming fees—the webs accounted for another $30.1 million (28.1 percent).[15] Beyond that, direct charges for talent, programs and miscellaneous (each major net operated its own artist bureau, harvesting added revenues) contributed another $21 million (19.6 percent). The aggregate exceeded $107 million in trade that year.

Could AT&T, which owned New York's WEAF, have ever dreamed of such imposing feats when it sold its pioneering operation for a cool million just nine years earlier? And, as it turned out, the halcyon days of radio were still in the future—when billions of dollars would be realized—enough to finance the birth of television and continue to provide a tidy profit for the aural side of the house.

We've explored some of the positive influences resulting from the growth of network radio, including social, cultural and economic factors. But beyond those dynamics, it could have been left to an erudite media observer to enumerate the most comprehensive and compelling rewards that web broadcasting has derived for the countrymen.

> Perhaps the most significant influence of radio ... was the effect its programming was having upon the homogeneity of the nation. The United States had always been afflicted by sectional, regional, and cultural differences which kept it from becoming a fully united nation. Historical events, linguistic idiosyncracies [sic], and cultural differences all testify to the heterogeneity of the country.... Network broadcasting transmitted a single standard. The same announcers were heard coast-to-coast; celebrities became nationally known; the values and attitudes projected in radio dramas were heard by millions in every part of the country.
>
> Network radio increased the similarity among Americans because it communicated the same stimuli throughout the nation. It developed a national constituency for its programs and commercials. In doing so it had to avoid offending sectional or regional differences. Forced to find the common denominator among all groups within the United States, radio became the thread that tied together all people. More than print or film, politics or laws, radio united the nation.... In a single stroke network radio standardized, entertained, informed, and educated its mass audience.[16]

In "Liberty Tree," poet Thomas Paine declared: "Let the far and the near all unite with a cheer."

Here was a country standing on the precipice of swiftly developing communications breakthroughs. It was also a nation fit to be tied. Americans everywhere could hardly believe their ears when network radio accomplished that feat at last, a reality prompting transcontinental celebration. Stepping into a void that had existed since the beginning of time, chain radio was the first medium to give us an instant easy-to-use process for embracing a scattered nation simultaneously, all with merely the twist of a dial or the punch of a button.

The citizenry quite understandably leaned heavily upon network radio in the medium's halcyon days between the 1920s and the 1950s. It was a highly dependable source of much of peoples' diversification and illumination. For a very long while it occupied the leading edge of achievements in the broadcasting industry.

Network radio's venerable traditions now exist in a legacy left to contemporary communications that succeed it in reaching—and unifying—the masses.

In that undertaking, in that day, there was absolutely no equal.

2

THE PROCEEDS OF EXPERIMENTATION
Getting Ready to Play for Real

While the benefits had been understood and pervasive acclaim was accorded to American chain broadcasting by the mid 1930s, networking had almost fallen beneath the bureaucrats' radar during the industry's nascent phase. Authorities charged with its oversight had completely ignored this development (web transmission) that was to dominate broadcasting for decades. Not until Congress—in something of an afterthought—added a single line to the Radio Act of 1927 was there any hint of networking's potential influence on this promising, rapidly burgeoning commercial enterprise.

The postscript advised that members of the newly-appointed Federal Radio Commission were, henceforth, charged with making "special regulations applicable to radio stations engaged in chain broadcasting." Until that juncture, joint public commercial service of the airwaves and its proliferating impact hadn't seemed particularly worthy of Officialdom. That would all change, of course, as keener insights prevailed and as more and more Americans became convinced of just how multidimensional, advantageous and utterly indispensable chain broadcasting was speedily becoming.

The earliest efforts to relay a radio program from one site to another appear to have been remote reports—often conducted under the most trying and primitive of circumstances—from sports events such as baseball, football and basketball matches. Dispatched over telephone lines, sometimes mere scores and at other times vague depictions of what occurred on an athletic field could be reported. Dozens of similar circumstances surface in the accounts of radio historiographers. Of course, those attempts were but stopgap measures before presenting live, protracted transmissions. Logically, it would seem that those archaic efforts might have prompted a few visionaries to step forth within the industry. Possibly they did whet some appetites for broadcasting whole programs of assorted varieties to joint audiences in far-flung locales.

There were more instances of programming from isolated spots in those early days, too.

Shortly before Christmas 1921, impresario Vincent Lopez appealed to WJZ listeners from his embedded venue at the Hotel Pennsylvania's Grill Room in New York, asking them to telephone for reservations for his outfit's supper-club show. "The flood of incoming telephone calls knocked out one of midtown Manhattan's major telephone exchanges," declared one correspondent. Beyond the fact that Lopez delivered the first of zillions of remote band pickups on the ether, here was an indication that radio could be a useful tool in persuading the public to respond to its sales plugs. This could be useful knowledge for the inevitable future deliberations on how broadcasting was to be underwritten.

In another prelude, during the following year (1922), the Radio Corporation of America and Westinghouse Electric and Manufacturing Company jointly opened a radio studio in the Waldorf-Astoria Hotel. It was connected with the WJZ transmitter in Newark by direct wire.

Call it *satellite broadcasting* if you will (although not under the more common application of that term we usually think of today); such evidence suggests that the possibility of generating live programming from atypical sites was gradually evolving into a crescendo. With a little ingenuity, this could be turned into something pretty big.

Enter the long distance hookups.

The thought of connecting two or more outlets for airing features in tandem surely had occurred in more than one somebody's mind fairly early in broadcasting's life. Isn't it true that when the pioneer explorers reached a coastline they wondered among themselves what was beyond the oceans? The same principle applies here. Those early dreamers wanted to exceed the grasp they had already attained—to reach beyond where they were. On the ether, if multiple outlets could be linked together, they reasoned, a single show could be beamed to many more listeners than those confined to the geographical purview of a lone station's transmitter. Looking at it a different way, what investor doesn't want to gain greater profits from a venture if there's a method to achieve it without adding insurmountable undue risk?

J. M. Mathes, whose advertising agency was instrumental in launching *The Eveready Hour* for the Eveready Battery Company over New York's WEAF on December 4, 1923, was among those seeing visions of grandeur in chain broadcasting. Mathes "hit upon the idea of a network which would permit entertainers in New York to be heard in various parts of the country by means of telephone lines connecting various stations with the New York outlet."[1] Somehow he had missed the obvious detail that—about a year before—web radio already had become an established fact. Nevertheless, on February 12, 1924, *The Eveready Hour* auditioned via an existing WEAF-WJAR linkage connecting New York and Providence, Rhode Island. Acclaimed there, the series was soon dispatched to a 12-station hookup as far west as Chicago.

"For the first time, the bright stars of the New York area were being heard throughout the country," insisted one wag. Featuring the Browning King Orchestra (named for a local clothier) and dazzling singers of that day, *The Eveready Hour* had "hit" written all over it. A second modern pundit obsessed: "Judged even by today's standards, it [the show] would not be found wanting."

Between 1919 and 1926—an interval prior to the launch of America's first permanent coast-to-coast broadcasting endeavor (the National Broadcasting Company, instituted in late 1926)— a handful of commercial concerns with disparate interests took more than passing notice of ethereal activity.

The American Telephone & Telegraph Company (AT&T) and its manufacturing supplier Western Electric (WE)—an appendage of AT&T—were at the vanguard of what became branded as the Telephone Group. The General Electric Company (GE), Radio Corporation of America (RCA) and Westinghouse Electric and Manufacturing Company (WEM) found a satisfying comfort level in partnership as the Radio Group.[2] GE and RCA fabricated the radio apparatus while WEM retailed it. Therefore, all had vested interests in broadcasting's well-being and promising future.

One of the visible offshoots of the appeal to these entrepreneurial corporate players was demonstrated when AT&T, GE, RCA and WEM went on a station-construction spree. It would take backers of their magnitude, or perhaps a prosperous individual or cluster of investors, to underwrite operations on any grand scale.[3]

In that period, before the inception of aural advertising of any serious substance, there was little anticipation that broadcasting itself would produce any direct income. Indeed, initial broadcast rates were set so low—WEAF charged $35 an hour—that as late as 1924 that station's officials petitioned audiences to "contribute as much as you can" to assist in signing top-flight talent. The donations received were so trifling, nevertheless, that they were returned to the benefactors.[4]

RCA appropriated $100,000 annually to its airwaves operations that included a trio of stations. Two were in New York. RCA purchased partial interest in WJZ in 1923 with a format characterized as "light" and "popular." It opened WJY, depicted by its so-called "quality" programming that stressed culture and edification. A third outlet, WRC, also constructed in 1923, served listeners in the District of Columbia.[5]

In the meantime, in July 1922, AT&T opened WBAY in New York only to find that reception tanked; its transmitter had been erected in a mammoth steel-framed facility-lined metropolis, a "no-no" officials instantly concluded. Rapidly correcting their fiasco, on August 16, 1922, AT&T followed up by introducing WEAF to New Yorkers.[6] That effort not only proved successful but gained steady approbation. It boasted what was, for its time, state-of-the-art studio gear coupled with a superior transmitter. In the days, months and years immediately ahead, WEAF was to acquire momentous advantage that netted it almost invincible prestige: it unquestionably became the focal point of much of radio's most eminent program originations, a facet to be borne out in detail a little later.

The subject of selling advertising time on the air affords an opportunity for a provocative discussion. Stemming from WEAF's foray into the field when it was but a dozen days old, it has direct implications for the larger industry. So many times WEAF surfaced at the crossroads of whatever happened of prime import in those days in Radioland, often branding its mark upon the medium as a permanent consequence. Its sales orientation proved no exception.

There are some credible indications that WEAF's initial paid commercial — actually, an infomercial, as it aired for 10 minutes — wasn't really radio's first commercial after all. In the decades since, WEAF's pitch has been widely accepted by many, and generously touted as the "authentic original" by numerous media historiographers, although it isn't necessarily so.[7] The plug occurred between 5:00 and 5:10 P.M. on Monday, August 28, 1922, as a shrouded voice identified only as "Mr. Blackwell" (H. M. Blackwell) was recognized by WEAF announcer Vischer Randall.

Blackwell dispatched a lengthy discourse about residential apartment dwelling in Jackson Heights. The promo purportedly netted the station $50 (or $5 per minute) for the use of its airwaves, paid for by the underwriting realtor, the Queensboro Corporation. In a rambling exposition, the firm's spokesman surmised:

> It is fifty-eight years since Nathaniel Hawthorne, the greatest of American fictionists, passed away. To honor his memory the Queensboro Corporation, creator and operator of the tenant-owned system of apartment homes at Jackson Heights, New York City, has named its latest group of high-grade dwellings "Hawthorne Court."
> I wish to thank those within sound of my voice for the broadcasting opportunity afforded me to urge this vast radio audience to seek the recreation and the daily comfort of the home removed from the congested part of the city, right at the boundaries of God's great outdoors, and within a few minutes by subway from the business section of Manhattan. This sort of residential environment strongly influenced Hawthorne.... He analyzed with charming keenness the social spirit of those who had thus happily selected their homes....
> There should be more Hawthorne sermons preached about the utter inadequacy and the general hopelessness of the congested city home. The cry of the heart is for more living room, more chance to unfold, more opportunity to get near the Mother Earth, to play, to romp, to plant and to dig.
> Let me enjoin upon you as you value your health and your hopes and your home happiness, get away from the solid masses of brick, where the meager opening admitting a slant of sunlight is mockingly called a light shaft, and where children grow up starved for a run over a patch of grass and the sight of a tree....
> Friends, you owe it to yourself and your family to leave the congested city and enjoy what nature intended you to enjoy. Visit our new apartment homes in Hawthorne Court, Jackson Heights, where you may enjoy life in a friendly environment.[8]

There were four additional commercial messages for tenant-owned garden apartment living aired at the same cost-per-unit rate, plus a $100 evening treatise espousing a comparable theme.[9] Those plugs proffered a rather dry delivery in somewhat less-than-urgent appeals for response. Commenting on the outcome of Queensboro's groundbreaking efforts, a critic protested: "The truth is that talk alone—unless it be on an absorbing subject—seldom does a good selling job."

At the same time, Queensboro's landmark promotions established a pattern for more commercial messages that soon followed: labeled "talks" by media observers, each one of the nascent pitches normally adopted the 10-minute time formula established by Queensboro. Several underwriters followed suit. Jumping into the fray over WEAF were outfits like American Express Company; Gimbels, Hearn's and Macy's retail merchandising emporiums; Gillette Safety Razor Company; radio manufacturer A. H. Grebe; Haynes Motor Car Company; the William H. Rankin advertising agency; Shur-On Optical Company; the pharmaceutical firm of E. R. Squibb and Sons; Tidewater Oil Company; and the Young Men's Christian Association.

Responding to public and government sentiment, WEAF officials cautiously navigated the waters of pioneer broadcast advertising. Policing its own commercial announcements by limiting them to an indirect approach which could be judged as only mildly persuasive, in April 1923, the station set down some regulatory guidelines.[10] For several years, it methodically adhered to them in deciding whether to accept or reject commercial sponsorship.

In addition to forbidding pricing references in the commercials it carried, AT&T—WEAF's creator and owner in the experimental phase—also nixed package descriptions, sales arguments and offering the public product samples. Cigarettes and toothpaste were on a list of commodities that fixated broadcast executives due to their "personal or offensive nature." WEAF's earliest policies disallowed paid promotions on Sunday. (For a moment, imagine applying that rule to today's broadcast and cable networks, eliminating the stupendously lucrative revenues they derive on TV's most watched night of the week.) Such banishments, which appeared to tarnish rather than brighten advertising's potential, undoubtedly found their way into successor radio chains that emerged not long after those warnings were written.

Meanwhile, a stellar media scholar observed that the advertising later aired by NBC pursued a natural progression from its embryonic WEAF cradle, terming those commercials "brief, circumspect, and extremely well-mannered." Some traditions carried a long shelf life. Make no mistake: a new die had been cast when WEAF started turning the ether into a profit-making zone. Once again the New York station was at the forefront of a practice that has endured down through the ages.

At this juncture we'll introduce an aside that mustn't be missed if what transpired a little later is to be fully understood. It pertains to a series of documents signed between 1919 and 1921 involving the discoveries and inventions of several parties. Those pacts assigned to an aggregate of American enterprises the rights to manufacture, sell, distribute and apply various communications components.[11]

The accords, among other things, had a profound impact on the power and control of the airwaves during the fledgling days of broadcasting. Beyond that, and of still greater significance, they perceptibly altered the fate of aural transmissions in the United States by powerfully influencing broadcasting's course well beyond the experimental epoch.

> A. T. & T. had financed much of early radio experiment in the hope that radio might be profitably adapted to the telephone system, and as a result held many vital, basic patents necessary to the manufacture of both receivers and transmitters. In 1920, A. T. & T. licensed General Electric, RCA and Western Electric (and later extended the agreement to include Westinghouse) to use these patents in the manufacture of radio equipment. In return, these manufacturers agreed that A. T. & T. should have the sole right to operate a toll station. So while WEAF and its telephone network sold time on the air long before 1926, WJZ, the RCA station, and its network could broadcast only sustaining programs.[12]

Under the patent agreements endorsed by all the parties, the Telephone Group (AT&T, WE) maintained exclusivity in three domains:[13] (1) manufacture and sale of radio transmitters for broadcasting applications; (2) sale of advertising time, popularly labeled *toll broadcasting*, classified in the same vein as long distance or toll telephone calling; and (3) providing the hardware to connect outlets for multiple (network) broadcasting efforts.

Each of these points eventually frustrated members of the Radio Group (GE, RCA, Westinghouse), who ultimately found themselves at cross purposes with the Telephone Group.[14] The objectors countered that: (1) only patents pool members could make and sell radio receivers; (2) any station could recover costs via advertising underwriters; and (3) radio outlets could be unified by any method that would do the job. There were various attempts to reconcile the differences between the two factions, which were making advancements through various experimentations. Their discoveries were to markedly impact the humble beginnings of chain radio.

Just 26 months after Pittsburgh's KDKA (owned by Westinghouse) aired the infamous Harding-Cox presidential election returns on November 2, 1920, a broadcasting precedent was set.[15] On January 4, 1923, New York's WEAF generated a feature that was dispatched over telephone lines to Boston's WNAC more than two hundred miles away for airing simultaneously. While the endeavor consisted purely of a five-minute saxophone solo, it qualifies as the foundational "network" broadcast.

The experiment wasn't duplicated for another five months. On June 7, 1923, four outlets fused their programming skills to bring it about. Along with WEAF and KDKA, the mix united Chicago's KYW and Schenectady's WGY. That same summer, sustained (continuous) network broadcasting arrived for the first time as some WEAF series were dispatched to WMAF in South Dartmouth, Massachusetts, for a three-month trial. This experiment, too, could be deemed successful.

There was much more like it coming down the pike. Over the next three years, AT&T, which owned WEAF and had also constructed WCAP in Washington, D.C., in 1923, frequently connected those dual outlets for network transmissions.[16] The pair formed the nucleus of a budding, ambitious AT&T hookup that was a foretaste of things to come. Chain broadcasting had definitely gained a foothold and was about to realize greater visibility than most observers had likely begun to project, one from which there would be no retreat.

The Telephone Group had ambitious plans for airing several orations by U.S. President Warren G. Harding during the warm months of 1923. But Harding turned ill while on a Western swing in late July and by August 2 he was dead.

Two days hence Texans and Missourians and lots of people living nearer the District of Columbia heard his successor, Calvin Coolidge, tell Congress of his agenda via a hastily arranged audio extension. In early 1924, AT&T launched a transcontinental tie-up by incorporating San Francisco's KPO into its diffusion. On October 24, 1924, the Telephone Group put together another nationwide combo, linking 22 stations for an address by Coolidge to the U.S. Chamber of Commerce. On that occasion, the president was received by an audience of 18 million, a summit never previously surmounted.

But even that pinnacle faded during his inauguration to a full term on March 4, 1925. From coast to coast, an estimated 23 million Americans sat mesmerized beside their radio sets. Most of them were witnessing something of remarkable import they hadn't experienced before, eavesdropping on history while they listened to the leader of the free world being sworn into office.[17] Considering that there were just 114 million Americans alive then, it appears that—for the very first time—an incredible one in five denizens may have heard the nation's chief executive take the oath that day.[18] Only a handful, limited to Washingtonians exclusively, might have heard Harding's acceptance speech in 1921. No similar instance was transmitted even locally by commercial radio before that.

Coolidge, incidentally, had acquired the nickname "Silent Cal," so branded for being a man of few words. Radio appeared to flatter his flat, soft cadence, however. A *New York World* journalist conjectured that—despite a personal appearance that was also perceived as fragile—Coolidge's audio inflection undoubtedly projected him to triumph over a couple of challengers in the 1924 presidential campaign. Indisputably, he was the first of the U.S. presidents to utterly embrace and benefit from the inception of network radio, even while it was still in its most lowly manifestation. In five-plus years as president (1923–1929), he delivered about 40 radio speeches. "He had little to say," maintained one scholar, "and said it well."

While the Telephone Group put together more than a score of outlets for a transcontinental web during the Coolidge presidency, an impressive challenge, the Radio Group was similarly engaged. Twenty-six affiliates comprised the enduring Telephone chain established in 1925 with WEAF as its nerve center. Its line feed extended as far west as Kansas City's KSD.[19]

On another frontier, the Telephone sector was also selling advertising time at $2,600 an hour for programs disseminated on a basic link of 13 outlets.[20] In so doing, it earned roughly $750,000 annually in gross revenues.[21] That triumph was forgotten in the not-too-distant future: after successor NBC was organized, it raked in almost $3.4 million in its first 13 months, and $90 million in only its fifth year.[22] What a gravy train!

Although the Radio Group's efforts were noticeably muted against the quality and quantity of its principal rival, it made valiant strides at stringing together a handful of stations. With WJZ as its chief originating point, the Radio Group's net was heavily concentrated in the Northeastern United States. In numbers, that web didn't begin to approach the considerable outlets amassed by its Telephone competition.

More importantly from a commercial standpoint, however, was a persistent, thorny issue of major differences in sound quality between the dual systems. The Radio Group experienced dismal success in attempting to reach sound parity. Because the Telephone Group maintained exclusivity (translated "supremacy") in exploiting its circuitry—and tightly controlled to whom it rented its wires—the Radio Group was sometimes frozen out of markets altogether. Keep in mind that all of the parties had signed those infamous patent agreements a few years earlier.

The Radio aggregate turned to Western Union's telegraph wires to transmit its aural features. Unfortunately, low fidelity broadcasts accompanied by loud hums typically characterized the system. Telegraphy's dot-and-dash schematic using wire that wasn't insulated and was predisposed to atmospheric and human-generated electrical intrusion proved a poor conductor of the spoken word and instrumental sound. Particularly was this so when compared to the clarity offered by telephone line transmissions. The bottom-line result was substantial loss of public confidence in the Radio Group's broadcasting capabilities, including listeners and potential affiliates. This just wasn't a satisfactory fix for the Radio Group's business model. Yet, in the formative period of network radio, it was the leading alternative to telephone wires in transmitting most broadcast shows over great distances.

At the same time, in 1923–1924, Westinghouse was relying on shortwave transmissions to connect Pittsburgh's KDKA with satellite outlets at Cleveland, Ohio (KDPM), and Hastings, Nebraska (KFXX). KDKA was even able to relay programs for rebroadcast to a Manchester, England, station during those same years. One reporter obsessed that this method didn't provide lasting reliability or meet sound quality expectations either.[23]

Parenthetically, lest the reader be misled into thinking AT&T was the Big Bad Wolf and RCA (the leader of the Radio pack) was altogether Lily White, let's clarify the situation by interjecting that—as Gilbert and Sullivan maintained in *HMS Pinafore*—things are seldom what they seem. Eventually the industry recognized that RCA held certain monopolies of its own that stemmed from the infamous accords of 1920–1921. Furthermore, in 1923, Congress ordered the Federal Trade Commission (FTC) to probe RCA for possible antitrust law violations. A year afterward, the FTC brought complaints against eight firms including RCA.[24]

After so long a tiff, however, in 1925 the contending Radio and Telephone blocs finally agreed to binding arbitration to settle their enduring disputes. Following months of hearings, the chosen mediator subsequently favored the Radio Group's stance on virtually every count. As a result, AT&T's perceptible domination of America's broadcasting commerce was thwarted. Shortly before this occurred, on May 15, 1926, AT&T established an ancillary unit, Broadcasting Company of America (BCA), and shifted its network operations there. One informant affirmed: "The stated purpose of this transaction was to recognize the growth of the radio operations and the special issues related thereto, but subsequent events make it clear that the disposition of the radio assets was also a fact."

In the meantime, the impasse between opposing parties was amicably settled with a complex tri-part contract effective July 1, 1926. The document's intent was to delineate the specific tasks of radio and telephone welfare, and it did so thusly: (1) The evolving realities of broadcast communications netted a redefinition of licensing agreements that had been penned a half-dozen years earlier; (2) AT&T was awarded what amounted to total control over wire interconnections linking the radio outlets; and (3) AT&T agreed to abandon radio ownership for a period of at least eight years and in doing so it sold WEAF to RCA for $1 million effective November 1, 1926; if AT&T should violate the eight-year rule it was to forfeit $800,000 of the purchase price.[25]

Together with its partners GE and Westinghouse—as part of that sweeping agreement—RCA not only acquired control of AT&T's flagship station originating a great deal of sterling programming, it gained unlimited access to the rest of AT&T's long established hookup.[26] RCA underwrote 50 percent of the WEAF purchase price of $1 million while GE contributed 30 percent and Westinghouse supplied the remaining 20 percent. That turned the entrepreneurs into more than mere cooperating decision-makers, for now they were true financial partners with a commitment to spur their purchase into doing well.[27]

The $1 million, incidentally, denoted a generous bonus over what radio stations were then selling for. It mirrored WEAF's imposing stance in the trade, including its admission to AT&T's greatly enhanced transmission wires. There was speculation that $800,000 of the purchase price represented goodwill and access to those lines.[28] The lines fashioned the major artery of NBC's soon-to-be dual webs (Red and Blue) for the next 15 years. With the exception of only a few instances where those lines didn't exist or weren't reachable, RCA exclusively relied upon AT&T for its radio communications.[29]

"By withdrawing from actual broadcasting," noted a source spelling the narrower focus of AT&T, "it would be able to make available to networks at profitable toll charges its meshwork of lines and concentrate entirely upon the telephone business," a seemingly winning formula.[30]

With prominent network ownership guaranteed, it was then GE, RCA and WEM holding the whip hand in American broadcasting. That triumvirate was free all of a sudden to sell advertising time to potential sponsors to help in recouping their steep financial investment. Henceforth, they would take aggressive efforts to turn the venture into a profit. But the magnitude of their stunning results might have indicated that almost nobody connected with the sale could have projected the stupendous outcome that RCA, in particular, would reap across six decades of broadcasting ownership.

Like the Telephone Group had done in creating the Broadcasting Company of America not long before, the Radio Group formed a separate component to manage the operations of its soon-to-be burgeoning network commerce. While a pair of networks was already operating, the Radio Group was—in reality—giving birth to a new commercial enterprise. It established the National Broadcasting Company (NBC) on September 9, 1926. The following month, RCA assigned the rights to purchase BCA to NBC. In November, NBC paid $1 million to AT&T and assumed operating WEAF. All of it marked the end of an era in broadcasting as the pioneer stage in network development concluded. AT&T relinquished the reins to the Radio Group that it had so tightly held until then.

"The air of distinction and vision which NBC managed to impart to its operation in its formative months was an extraordinary phenomenon," claimed a respected sage who catalogued the era of ethereal history. "It left little room for doubt that broadcasting was in the best possible hands."[31] Exuding an aura of wonderment, NBC president Merlin Aylesworth suggested to a congressional panel that "the enormous power concentrated in the hands of a few men controlling a vast network of radio stations" was due "the consideration of statesmen." To their credit, in those days the NBC brass believed so strongly in the stewardship of their task that they created an ad hoc council composed of 15 to 20 prominent citizens (the number varied sporadically) for the purpose of hearing appeals that could "be carried over the heads of the operating executives." It must have been a welcome gesture by any who doubted where all of this was going. As recently as 1929, chairman Owen D. Young insisted that NBC's aim "has never been to make money, but rather to offer programs of such varied interest that our people could not afford to miss them."[32] Imagine such a practice ruling the fate of the major radio and TV webs in the modern era!

For a few years, until May 23, 1930, NBC was to be jointly controlled by GE, RCA and WEM. On that date, GE and Westinghouse bowed out, selling their shares of NBC stock to RCA. NBC became a wholly-owned subsidiary of RCA.

The experimental phase of network radio, then ended, could be compared to major league baseball's spring training. Once it was over, it was time to get serious—and play for real.

3

NATIONAL BROADCASTING COMPANY
The House That Sarnoff Built

Although the National Broadcasting Company (NBC) of contemporary times rather blithely and infrequently points to 1926 as its year of origin, any who have read this far know that its historic lineage is traceable more than four years earlier. Indeed, while the country's foremost transcontinental web may have experienced its licensed corporate naissance in 1926, its true genesis—where it was already doing essentially the same thing it did as NBC—is vested in a couple of foregoing radio stations.

WBAY, the first in the line of antecedents, went on the air in downtown New York in July 1922, emitting an incredibly weak signal. To their dismay, its operators found that a conurbation rife with high-rise steel towers did not offer an ideal setting for projecting radio broadcasts. WBAY's benefactor, the American Telephone & Telegraph Company (AT&T), was closely monitoring all of this with disappointed yet resolute eyes. That entrepreneur vowed to take the necessary steps to beef up its investment's poor reception quality at once.

After swiftly pronouncing final rites for WBAY, AT&T committed its capitalistic spirit and innovative style to a second attempt: it started over with another transmitter situated atop the multi-storied Western Electric (WE) building. While WE and AT&T had merged three decades before, they might have been deemed by some as co-conspirators in this venture where they were eventually labeled by insiders as the "Telephone Group." This resulted after broadcasting's leading commercial interests shook out in a couple of distinct factions; the other was dubbed the "Radio Group." (Particulars are delineated in Chapter 2.)

Briefly, AT&T had been in business under sundry monikers since shortly after Alexander Graham Bell (1847–1922) exhibited his invention of the telephone in 1876. AT&T subsequently gave birth to the American telephone monopoly, the Bell System.[1] The Bell System was exploiting technologies to diffuse voice- and music-grade audio over short and long distances, employing both wired and wireless applications. WEAF was to provide a laboratory venue for those R and D pursuits.

Western Electric, meanwhile, extended from 1856 under varied appellations. In its first quarter-century, it manufactured typewriters, alarms, and lights, and supplied telegraph operator Western Union with equipment. Western Union withdrew from the telephone arena in 1879 and AT&T acquired Western Electric two years later. From 1881 to 1995, WE supplied its parent with apparatus for telephone connections and was the Bell System member companies' purchasing agent.[2]

In contrast to its dismal and disappointing initial attempt to launch a flourishing radio station, AT&T was triumphant in its second try. WEAF—the new kid on the Gotham block as of August 16, 1922—became a colossal success. It was instrumental in launching "network" radio, a participant in early experiments involving two or more outlets connecting by wire for single transmissions over protracted distances. Perhaps more importantly, that lone station actively reflected the direction of web diffusion—and possibly the whole specter of broadcasting itself. In network radio's embryonic era, WEAF was categorically the brand's most influential model. As the crown jewel of the National Broadcasting Company hookup, it may have come to symbolize as well as dominate the ether for a few years.[3]

From these humble beginnings, NBC emerged as the trade's original juggernaut. Not only did it inspire competitors, the web possessed an innate ability to taunt and thwart them as it applied tenacity to its advantage again and again. Credit the deep pockets of the Radio Corporation of America (RCA)—and its backer, General Electric—with an indomitable will to not only succeed but to utterly dominate the hill. If vanquishing its archrival, the Columbia Broadcasting System (CBS), was a byproduct of its business pursuits, then so be it.[4] (This compelling topic receives more reflection and interpretation in Chapter 10.)

> NBC, like RCA, was born with a silver spoon. It had behind it the wealth of huge corporations. It entered the world at a moment of business affluence. Godfather-sponsors stood ready with rich gifts.
>
> It had a promising commercial purpose—played down in public announcements—but along with this it had a service to perform, for which it was uniquely equipped. It could speak at once to east and west, city and country, rich and poor. Awareness of this touched off expressions of idealism that matched the euphoria of the first year of broadcasting. NBC seemed a child of destiny. That there was, or might ever be, conflict between the commercial purpose and the destiny of service did not apparently occur to those who brought NBC into the world.[5]

RCA and its early partners were committed to doing whatever it took, including spending anything deemed necessary, to give the American public first-rate entertainment. In doing so, it kept a faithful crowd of generous proportions coming back to imbibe at its perennially springing fountain. With a few exceptions, for a long while in that gritty quest (extending into the late 1940s), NBC was probably perceived as broadcasting's unparalleled leader. Its achievements were almost always worthy of emulation, as others regularly nipped at its heels but seldom overtook it throughout the 1930s at least.

NBC's formation, as previously noted, stemmed from WEAF's successful attempts to share its programming with other stations through a hookup put together by AT&T. The experimental webs persisted from 1923 through 1926 until AT&T sold WEAF to the Radio Group for $1 million.

The year 1926 was fundamental in the chronicles of network broadcasting. One by one, pieces of a large jigsaw puzzle fell into place, culminating with the launch of NBC late in the year. In abbreviated mode, its action-packed sequential plot advanced like this:

- May: AT&T turns its broadcast properties into a quasi-autonomous auxiliary, the Broadcasting Company of America.[6]
- July: Radio and Telephone clusters finally settle their long running internal strife in the market by inking a trifocal accord; AT&T agrees to bow out of radio station operations to concentrate on transmission of radio programming generated by station owners RCA and others.
- September: RCA and partners establish the National Broadcasting Company (September 9).
- October: RCA assigns the rights to buy the Broadcasting Company of America to NBC.
- November: NBC purchases WEAF from AT&T (November 1) and begins recurring broadcasting on NBC Red, the old AT&T station hookup (November 15).
- December: NBC announces that a second network, identified as NBC Blue, the tie-up fostered by WJZ, would begin operating January 1, 1927.

The night of November 15, 1926, was, of course, the most important of that imposing commencement year. But before we examine it in depth, let's momentarily recess to introduce a handful of pivotal figures that dominated the landscape during the initiation of NBC.

No one fills the role of that period's chief architect more strategically than international financier-industrialist Owen D. Young. He climbed the corporate ladder of General Electric to become first overseer of the Radio Corporation of America. Born October 27, 1874, at Van Hornesville, New York, Young grew up on a dairy farm in the rural upstate, earning a law degree at Boston University in 1896. He practiced law in Boston from 1896 to 1912 and became GE's general counsel in 1913. Elected a vice president of the firm soon afterward, Young was its chairman by 1922, a post he occupied until his retirement in 1939.

Starting with Woodrow Wilson in 1919, and at the request of five U.S. presidents, Young rendered public service through sundry appointments. They included developing plans to stabilize the German economy and direct German reparations after World War I. With the intent of preventing American patents from passing to European control while intensifying the country's international communications, Wilson asked Young to organize what resulted in the Radio Corporation of America in 1919. Overlapping a noteworthy interval at GE, Young served the RCA board as chairman from 1920 to 1929 and chairman of its executive committee from 1929 to 1933. As a derivative, this plurality revealed just how much NBC mattered to RCA: the dual jurisdiction appreciably underscored RCA's depth of commitment to its fledgling broadcasting empire.

As much as anyone and maybe more, Young possessed a vision for turning limited, pioneering, experimental radio chains into quality transmissions with transcontinental range. Amassing a formidable cache of skilled artisans for his executive management staff, he allowed his subordinates plenty of support and latitude. Young inspired his leadership team to extend their grasp well beyond a smallish hookup principally focused on the Northeastern U.S. quadrant. He also fostered an environment that urged them never to be satisfied with anything less than excellence. All of this helped turn NBC into a hardy competitor that often led the triumvirate of national broadcasters. Young lived to see the glory years of NBC Radio and a respected shift into television. *Time* magazine's "Man of the Year" for 1930 died on July 12, 1962, at Saint Augustine, Florida.

Young had encouraged the advancing careers of several key players in the formative years of NBC Radio. Among the innovative thinkers he gathered about him were Edward J. Nally, David Sarnoff and Merlin H. Aylesworth.

Both Nally and Sarnoff were officers at American Marconi Company before Young brought them to RCA in 1919 as president and commercial manager respectively. American Marconi had some implications in the founding of NBC. Communications history buffs might find the backdrop compelling.[7]

Edward Julian Nally was born April 11, 1859, at Philadelphia and was already 60 when he assumed the helm as first CEO at RCA. He filled that role in 1919–1923 and was, for two years, managing director of RCA's Paris-based international relations unit. Retiring in 1925 with a half-century tenure in communications, Nally was widely hailed in the trade as "the grand old man" of wireless telegraphy. He persisted as an RCA director from 1920 to 1950.

Launching his career at 16 in 1875 at St. Louis as a $13-a-month Western Union messenger, like RCA chairman Owen Young, Nally lived to witness the early years of television. In fact, he fashioned it as "the world of tomorrow" in live comments telecast by NBC during the World's Fair in April 1939, limited to New York environs. Nally died at Bronxville, New York, on September 22, 1953.

His career took him from messenger to progressively more and more responsibility, running Western Union's western division out of Chicago in 1892 with authority over 22 states. Moving to New York in 1906, he became a vice president and director. As a visionary, Nally is cited as having recommended that Western Union's idle wires be used profitably for sending night letters following the business day. He resigned from the firm in 1913 to join American Marconi as vice president, general manager and director. Nally took an active role in developing radio transmissions linking the United States with Japan, Europe and South America.

As mentors, Owen Young and Ed Nally took under their wings protégé David Sarnoff, who was painstakingly groomed for the fundamental leadership posts he occupied during much of his life. He was born at Uzlian in the Russian province of Minsk on February 27, 1891; his classic rags-to-riches tale is extensively demarcated in Chapter 10. Suffice it to say that—after coming through the ranks of American Marconi—on December 1, 1919, in RCA's early weeks, Sarnoff was appointed the new firm's commercial manager. By 1922, at 31, after having spent half his life in the field, he was elected a vice president.

Sarnoff's star rose rapidly; more than anyone, he exhibited hands-on control not simply at NBC's launch but through more than four successive decades. Elected RCA president in 1930 and chairman of the board in 1947, his influence was paramount over the NBC Radio and Television chains from their dawn to his retirement in 1970 at 79. Death overtook him in New York on December 12, 1971.

Merlin Hall ("Deac") Aylesworth was offered the presidency of NBC Radio in 1926, a post that was to pay him $50,000 annually. He was serving a public utility troupe at the time and was without professional skill in communications. When approached by Owen Young, perhaps to his own amusement, he remarked that he didn't even own a radio. "We'll send you one," Young assured, to which Aylesworth answered: "I still don't understand why you want

David Sarnoff, a hard-driving immigrant from Russia, was an office and delivery boy for the Marconi Company at first, then rose to head the most powerful communications enterprise on the planet. Here Sarnoff demonstrates some of the primitive telegraph apparatus that inspired him early to communicate with the world.

me." Young replied: "Look, Deac, you've visited practically every community of more than 10,000 people in the country. So you know people.... As a network we must give listeners what they want.... We've got to make it a great public service."[8] Aylesworth accepted without further hesitation.

Nevertheless, he somehow let the name "American Broadcasting Company" slip through his hands when a minor operator offered the rights to it. Aylesworth was savvier the next time around when the "National Broadcasting Company" became available; it seemed cogent for a web whose parameters were expected to embrace the entire country.

Born July 19, 1886, at Cedar Rapids, Iowa, Aylesworth earned a law degree from the University of Denver and another at Columbia University. In a colorful, multidimensional occupational journey, he practiced law in Colorado from 1907, was chairman of the Colorado Public Utilities Commission from 1914 to 1926, counsel for the Utah Power and Light Company in 1914–1919 and managing director of the National Electric Light Association from 1919 to 1926.

Joining NBC as first president in 1926, Aylesworth was instrumental in defining and maturing the competing Red and Blue webs. He also led the NBC affiliates to quadruple in number while cultivating an auxiliary list of independent outlets that sporadically carried NBC programming. After a decade of guiding the network's direction, Aylesworth resigned in 1936 to become president and chairman of Radio-Keith-Orpheum Corporation. A year afterward he joined the management team of the Scripps-Howard newspaper chain. From 1938 to 1939, he published *The New York World-Telegram*. He returned to practicing law at the start of 1940, that time in New York. Aylesworth died at 66 on September 30, 1952, in Gotham. Assessing his tenure at the helm of NBC in that strategic period, author Ben Gross wrote in *I Looked and I Listened* in 1954: "If there is one man who may be said to have 'put over' broadcasting with both the public and the sponsors, it is this first president of NBC."

On November 1, 1926, this handful of principals and their contemporaries brought the National Broadcasting Company into being. The new entity was launched with significant fanfare in a four-hour star-studded gala broadcast live from the Waldorf-Astoria Hotel on November 15.[9] Sparing little expense, the evening's event dipped into the fledgling web's coffers to the tune of $50,000. "Hardly a cent," affirmed president Aylesworth to one author. The performers gave their services, and advertisers would underwrite it all in the future based on what they had witnessed that night.

It was a black tie, formal occasion that drew a crowd of 1,000 guests to the hotel's Grand Ballroom. An observant scholar depicted the celebrated invitees as something more than a throng of mere mortals, indeed, composed of "captains of industry and finance, stars of the music and theater worlds."

A dashing Aylesworth was master of ceremonies for a program that included well-known instrumental ensembles, vocalists and humorists of the day. "Think of it!" he cried. "Ten or maybe twelve million persons may be hearing what takes place in this ballroom tonight." To demonstrate the effectiveness of radio's access, there were a few remote pickups from distant places, too—a Chicago soloist, Mary Garden, performing "Annie Laurie"; a witty Will Rogers, speaking from Kansas City, mimicking President Calvin Coolidge. Impresario Walter Damrosch was at the podium as the New York Symphony played and the New York Oratorio Society sang. Participants enjoyed the music of Edwin Franko Goldman's band, the singing of Metropolitan Opera star Titta Ruffo and the comedy duo Weber and Fields. From detached locations, they heard dance bands under the tutelage of impresarios Ben Bernie, Vincent Lopez, George Olsen and B. A. Rolfe.

NBC officials had lined up a couple of dozen outlets in the East and Midwest—connected by 3,600 miles of special telephone cable—to carry its inaugural ball. They included:

WEAF, New York	WJZ, New York
WCAP, Washington	WTAM, Cleveland
WJAR, Providence	WBZ, Springfield
WEEI, Boston	WBZA, Boston
WFI/WLIT, Philadelphia	WWJ, Detroit
WTIC, Hartford	WOC, Davenport
WCAE, Pittsburgh	KDKA, Pittsburgh
WGN/WLIB, Chicago	KYW, Chicago
WSAI, Cincinnati	KSD, St. Louis
WGR, Buffalo	WCCO, Minneapolis
WCSH, Portland	WDAF, Kansas City

Of course, nobody could imagine the extent to which all of this NBC folderol would lead—locally, regionally, nationally, globally, and into the stratosphere! In time those unassuming origins would expand through advancing technologies into television, satellite, audio and visual taping, Internet, digital and infinite added derivatives, some of which haven't yet been announced. After that inaugural occasion, incidentally, Aylesworth admitted to a reporter somewhat sheepishly that most of the four-hour marathon's celebrated artists had donated their performances as opposed to being paid in exchange for the hype surrounding the kick-off spectacular. No matter. It had to be a good deal for everybody connected with that incomparable—and never before witnessed—venture.

Within a matter of weeks following its colossal bash NBC revealed in newspaper accounts that, effective January 1, 1927, it would unveil no less than a second network. This one was to be based on the old hookup of the Radio Group with the bulk of its programming originating at WJZ. Recall that this system had relied on the less-than-satisfactory sound quality dispatched through Western Union's rented telegraph lines. Of course now—since the newly revised patent agreements that displaced AT&T as a broadcaster, and with that firm's much more sound-effective telephone wires available—it was an easy step for the RCA-GE-WEM combine to switch to AT&T linkage.

The premiering ethereal feature, on New Year's Day of 1927, was Graham McNamee's play-by-play coverage of a Rose Bowl gridiron match. Aired live from California, Alabama opposed Stanford (and as luck would have it, the outcome resulted in a 7–7 tie). While there were only six affiliates carrying that game, it was still the start of a broadcasting (and sportscasting) heritage that continues on both radio and television in the modern age.

To distinguish between its dual chains, NBC identified one as the Red (WEAF) hookup and the other as the Blue (WJZ). How the color-coding came about remains a mystery, although there are multiple theories. In one, AT&T engineers supposedly kept the web routings separate on a U.S. map by coloring the circuits for one red and the other blue. In another, pushpins of the two hues on a map identified the cities reflecting the outlets of the pair of webs. Other hypotheses have been advanced but none validated. Suffice it to say that the origins weren't predominant—the verbal identifications were rapidly integrated into the listeners' minds and served to distinguish between the pair.

Looking at it from an operational standpoint, there were some differences in the double chains, nevertheless. From the outset it must have appeared to faithful members of those nets' audiences that—if a difference existed in the quality of material aired on the Red and the Blue— there seemed to be a categorical edge of favoritism toward the Red. Was there? Time would inevitably tend to bear out that supposition, for in the early 1930s it was apparent that NBC devoted most of its first-rate star-studded hours, at least in primetime (although that term hadn't yet been applied), to airing on the Red chain.

Second-tier talent and more erudite programming (e.g. panel discussions, educational and cultural fare) almost automatically went to the Blue chain.

It was common for shows to debut on the Blue Network and then transition to the Red Network to reach that network's larger audiences. Some of those shows included *The Jack Benny Program* (1932), *Fibber McGee & Molly* (in 1935), *The Bob Hope Show* (in 1935 and 1937), and *Information, Please!* (in 1938).[10]

Discontent with the manner in which NBC was managing the Blue Network in relation to the Red Network was evident in letters and memorandums sent to NBC. A letter dated June 28, 1934, from station WSYR in Syracuse, New York, complained that the Blue Network was being neglected in favor of the Red Network.[11] On September 18, 1935, the Blue Network sent a memorandum complaining that it was being denied access to World Series broadcasts,[12] followed soon after by a letter dated October 5, 1935, from Hearst Radio complaining in general about the weak quality of the programming on the Blue Network and in particular about the transfer of *Amos 'n' Andy* and the Al Pearce programs to the Red Network.[13] One in-house memorandum from February 1937 was so caustic that the author's name was removed.[14]

Until the late 1930s, the Blue commanded fewer stations than the Red. The Blue also offered many sustaining shows. It did so for a couple of reasons: (1) its often lower-power stations weren't as attractive to sponsors as those of the Red strain, which frequently were clear-channel, high-powered outlets in a given market carrying the Red's prestigious fare, thereby diminishing the income of any nearby Blue stations; and (2) sustaining shows were viewed as a public relations gesture that offset the culturally deprived but more popular menu provided by the Red stations.

All of it hearkened back to the experimental radio chains as WEAF and the Telephone Group proffered an image of venerated shows carried over the sound quality of telephone wires. WJZ and the Radio Group, in the meantime, fostered an image of an also-ran, seemingly attracting less desirable or leftover features transmitted by less-than-satisfactory telegraph lines. Lest the reader wonder about bias, this isn't meant to disparage either web during the rudimentary days of radio or later when NBC operated two chains. Instead, to many people's perceptions, it was a fact that one of the chains invariably outranked the other on several fronts.

Interestingly, in their heyday NBC affiliation contracts did not specify with which chain (Red or Blue) a station was to be linked, even when an outlet could be clearly identified with the basic Red or basic Blue hookups. "NBC has the power to shift a station from the far more remunerative Red network to the less remunerative Blue network or vice versa at any time, regardless of the station's wishes," a Federal Communications Commission (FCC) interpretation postulated.[15]

Despite alleged favoritism, at least from the listeners' perspective, the watchdogs nevertheless concluded:

> The Red and Blue networks are not separate business enterprises, nor are they even two distinct operating divisions or departments within NBC. All its property, including studios, offices, and equipment, is equally and interchangeably available to both the Red and Blue networks. NBC announcers, musicians, talent, and engineers are used interchangeably; and, with two exceptions, no distinction is made in the duties of NBC personnel either in New York or in the field.
>
> One exception is the sales department. A special division to promote Blue network sales was established in this department in 1938, and in December 1940 ... the department itself was split into two sections, one for each network. At the same time, the program department was similarly split.[16]

Long before all of this transpired, however, a multiplicity of moves took place that shaped the character of NBC during its fledgling years. Almost immediately some fundamental programming directions were set in stone. Walter Damrosch was hired as musical overseer, KDKA's

Frank Mullen was deputized to create an NBC farm service, and ad man Frank Arnold was appointed liaison with the environment of big business, working in a glorified time sales capacity as director of development.

Such activity was matched by comparable surges at upper corporate levels. The infamous patents possessed by RCA, which had earlier resided in impasse territory, were instantly thrust into a tangle of relationships with other domains—automobiles, film, phonographs, theater, vaudeville. Deals and mergers followed in rapid succession. Broadcasting, led by NBC, was having a cumulative impact on other spheres, paving the way for new alignments. The moves that filled the years 1927–1929 were as impressive as the moves made by Owen D. Young in 1919–1921. They also stirred visions of wealth and grandeur, so much so that rumor mounted on rumor, energizing an already quickening stock market ascent. In that delirium, radio stocks were among an advantaged sector.

There was also at least a third NBC hookup. The Pacific Coast Network, sometimes identified as the Orange Network, was established April 5, 1927, prior to AT&T extending broadcast wires to connect the West Coast with the Midwest and East. Under-capacity of long lines and prohibitive telephone costs meant generating features in San Francisco over NBC affiliates KGO and KPO. The pair furnished program wares to a chain of seven West Coast outlets extending from Seattle to Los Angeles. The tie-up was created as much for sales generation as for program production.

Actually, truth be told, in many cases it wasn't original material being performed in San Francisco at all. It had usually already aired on the Red or Blue chain back East, then scripts and accompanying sheet music were dispatched by Railway Express from New York or Chicago to San Francisco, where live productions were recreated by West Coast actors and musicians. That patchwork maneuver lasted only until late 1928, when AT&T finally made transcontinental broadcast wires available at affordable rates. NBC was able to furnish coast-to-coast programming on both the Red and Blue on a sustained basis for the first time, eliminating the need for West Coast personnel to fill the daily schedules.

In October 1927 headquarters of NBC and operations for both WEAF-Red and WJZ-Blue were joined in new quarters on four floors of a 15-story edifice at 711 Fifth Avenue. Eight studios with sophisticated soundproofing, half of those two stories tall, permitted concurrent broadcasting, recording and rehearsal. But the new facilities were only temporary: soon there was widespread talk of moving into a central structure in midtown New York known as Rockefeller Center. It was an articulation of buoyancy in the midst of the nation's severest economic depression that led some to brand the entire edifice Radio City.

> There was no grander sign that radio was here to stay, and that New York was the heart of this fabulous activity, than the structure that ascended, with grace and power, seventy stories high on Sixth Avenue between Forty-ninth and Fiftieth Streets. Plans for Rockefeller Center were unveiled in March 1930, and on 4 June of that year the Radio Corporation of America agreed to develop the entertainment areas of the complex. A lease was signed on 29 October 1931, and the RCA Building—the hub of what everyone called Radio City—was occupied during the autumn of 1933. It housed the Red and Blue Networks of NBC and their local flagships, WEAF and WJZ.[17]

NBC's new showpiece headquarters provided growing room for two burgeoning networks in state-of-the-art studios and supplementary facilities. All of its functions, apart from the transmitters for the two Big Apple outlets, were now housed under one roof. The inaugural broadcast aired from Radio City on Saturday, November 11, 1933, over the combined Red and Blue webs from 8 to 9 P.M. Eastern Time.

To be inclusive, any narrative about NBC must make reference to its identifying chimes that were rung at the close of aural features and which may still be heard sporadically today

Photographed from an aircraft in the summer of 1933, the soon-to-be-occupied 70-story RCA Building was an imposing addition to New York's midtown Manhattan Island skyline. Rising to a height of 850 feet, the white Indiana limestone edifice set the architectural parameters for successive ones added to the Rockefeller complex. Its jagged form follows zoning regulations then in place. The RCA structure housed headquarters of the parent firm as well as its ancillary National Broadcasting Company. Two years after General Electric purchased RCA in 1986, the tower was dubbed the GE Building. In the lower right center sits the 31-story RKO Building and the Radio City Music Hall.

over NBC Television and MSNBC cable network (on the latter in modified five-note form). While the inspiration for the three-note (G-E-C played on the scale) chimes isn't confirmed, the resonance was heard regularly over Atlanta's WSB, an NBC affiliate.[18] During a Georgia Tech football game, when the chimes rang, someone at NBC in New York—then airing the game on its hookup—sat up and took notice. The web had been seeking an identifiable aural symbol. It requested the privilege of adopting those three notes. WSB granted permission and NBC began applying that din in 1931. So important was it to the web as time elapsed, in fact, that the "NBC chimes" eventually became the first audio sign registered by the U.S. Patent and Trademark Office.

Richard H. Ranger of the Rangertone Company mechanized the chimes in 1932. In addition to registering instant identification with listeners, they sent a low level signal of constant amplitude heard by myriad switching stations manned by NBC and AT&T engineers. In so doing, the chimes became a system cue for switching different stations between the Red and Blue feeds.[19] Due to concerns of offending commercial sponsors by cutting off their programs in mid-sentence, the mechanized chimes were invariably rung by an announcer who pushed a button to activate them. To avoid just such calamities, they were never set to an automatic timer, although some weighty exchanges on the topic ensued between engineers and program staffers during network radio's heyday.

Administratively, meanwhile, in 1930, GE and WEM—which had partnered with RCA in 1926 to launch NBC—decided to formally transfer their perceptibly limited participation in the day-to-day operations of the network to RCA. On May 23, RCA acquired the NBC stock previously owned by GE and WEM. Two years later, those allies bowed out entirely. RCA assumed total control and made the National Broadcasting Company, Inc., its operating subsidiary. The die was cast for determining NBC's fate for the next half-century.

Let us examine the question of numbers of affiliates, a topic that has been alluded to already. In its first full year, 1927, NBC boasted that 28 stations had joined its ranks. Of those, 22 exclusively subscribed to Red programming while the remaining six received Blue features. While the overall figures steadily increased, the pattern of Red dominance persisted until the first year that the net's combined activity surpassed 100 affiliates (1937), having attracted 111 by then. That same year also denoted an aggressive push that allowed the Blue programming to be heard on more outlets than the Red: the result was 33 Blue, 30 Red and 48 independent stations occasionally carrying one or more Red or Blue shows.[20] It was the model that continued for the remaining years that NBC controlled both networks.

NBC Radio reached a peak of 225 stations in 1941, its highest number during the proverbial golden age, and a pinnacle it would not return to for three decades (1971). In the final year (1941) prior to the separation of the two webs, there were 92 Blue outlets, 74 Red and 59 alternates carrying some NBC features.

By maintaining two affiliates in most of the larger metropolitan centers, NBC maintained a decided advantage over the other webs as well as local independent stations. Few independents, for example, could afford to adequately compete against NBC, as it programmed one affiliate against the other and pursued competitive price-cutting.[21]

Interestingly, once television became an established commodity that shared the ether with radio, the number of local outlets carrying NBC Radio proliferated instead of withering as one might generally anticipate. From 1953 forward, only once did the total fall below 200 stations (1957, with 199). The numbers reached phenomenal summits by the 1980s. In 1983, 370 affiliates carried at least some NBC programming, most likely news-on-the-hour, followed by 389 in 1987, 475 in 1988 and 478 in 1986. There were logical explanations for the increase, much of it due to NBC joining other major chains in that era creating specialized webs that appealed to narrowly focused local broadcasters. That topic will be addressed in greater detail later.

When contrasted with its major rivals CBS, MBS and eventually ABC, NBC's station lineup in the golden age continued to prosper, reflecting a strong position in the industry. Although the smaller chains could claim more actual affiliates carrying their wares—especially MBS ("This is Mutual, the network for *all* America," its announcers were fond of proclaiming) that reached more than 500 stations in the decade extending from 1948 to 1957—there is a not-to-be-missed caveat among the numbers.

It's noteworthy that NBC and CBS, in particular, usually drew the most prestigious and normally most powerful wattage stations in major metropolitan centers. More than 51 percent of total watts of unlimited airtime outlets was allocated to NBC affiliates (Red and Blue outlets combined) in 1938. At the same time, CBS claimed more than 35 percent of the total, with the remaining 14 percent divvied up among MBS and NBC-MBS and CBS-MBS combos. As a result, the two leading rival chains consistently reached far larger audiences than the smaller, generally less generously endowed stations. The latter group often proffered only 5,000 or 10,000 watts of power and were often related to one or the other also-ran webs. A host of MBS and ABC stations turned up in the smaller communities, hamlets and rural territories, too—places that simply couldn't command 25,000- and 50,000-watt transmitters.

Furthermore, by 1938, the four networks (including NBC Red and Blue, CBS, and MBS) had affiliated with 50 of the 52 clear-channel stations in the United States.[22] A federal inquiry conducted in that pre–ABC, late–1930s epoch concluded: "By and large, the stations associated with Mutual are less desirable in frequency, power, and coverage."[23] All of it made a huge difference in perception, in audience size, in web ties and in amounts advertisers were willing to spend in given markets. The big audiences that popular chain-fed shows drew were magnets for local advertisers, significantly boosting local affiliates' bottom lines. Consequently, NBC and CBS—including the networks and the stations they owned or operated—controlled more than half the business of the trade by the 1940s with MBS commanding just two percent of net time sales.[24] The disparities could hardly be any more pronounced.

NBC introduced exclusivity provisions into its contracts with affiliates in 1936. Stations were prohibited from supplying facilities to any other major web. Until that juncture, NBC's contractual obligations with its affiliates were written annually. Beginning then, however, agreements were drawn to engage the stations for five-year periods while binding NBC to just one year.[25]

As broadcasting matured, NBC opened its own talent bureau early in 1927 to furnish artists for its and other broadcasters' programming needs. The unit managed concert singers, thespians, interlocutors, wordsmiths and others connected with broadcast performances. By 1928, that entity brought in slightly more than $1 million in gross receipts. Less than a decade later, the figure exceeded $6 million (1937), including $306,099 derived from Civic Concert Service, Inc. The web acquired half interest in that agency in 1931 and full ownership in 1935. Civic Concert organized and managed music performance courses across the nation, reaching into 77 cities in 1938. By November 1, 1938, NBC's talent service was managing in excess of 350 artists. Nevertheless, an inquisition into the chain's artist bureau operations by Big Brother underscored some sobering concerns about the arrangement.

> As agent for artists, NBC is under a fiduciary duty to procure the best terms possible for the artists. As employer of artists, NBC is interested in securing the best terms possible from the artists. NBC's dual role necessarily prevents arm's-length bargaining and constitutes a serious conflict of interest. Moreover, this dual capacity gives NBC an unfair advantage over independent artists' representatives who do not themselves control employment opportunities or have direct access to the radio audience. Many of these independent artists' representatives have complained to the [Federal Communications] Commission of NBC's unfair control over the supply of talent and have filed briefs.... This problem will receive ... continuing attention ... and may warrant further inquiry.[26]

By 1934, NBC added a transcription service to its affiliates and independent stations providing large discs featuring prerecorded material. The discs were actually produced by the RCA Manufacturing Company, another ancillary of the parent firm, although NBC negotiated sales transactions with diverse commercial parties.

In a tri-pronged pursuit, the network (1) established a library service (dubbed Thesaurus) that offered an assortment of transcribed musical selections leased or licensed to individual stations, enabling them to produce programs by only adding local messages; (2) created customized recording services that embraced shows produced by NBC, by sponsors or advertising agencies—"complete packages" dispatched to stations and commercial sponsors; (3) recorded shows while they were aired live for rebroadcast at a later time. By 1938, the NBC-RCA combo accounted for about $1.3 million of the annual projected transcription business in the U.S., which was then less than $5 million total. Thus, NBC was among the trade's largest suppliers, and possibly its largest.

The chain was also purchasing some of those outlets carrying its shows, owning them outright (known in the trade as O and Os, owned and operated stations). This became common practice in the trade, not limited to NBC, although that web initiated the strain. By 1933, NBC owned 10 stations, seven 50,000-watters and nine licensed for unlimited time on the air (Chicago's WENR was the exception). The complete list, including their year of acquisition and power, included:

Affiliate	Acquired	Watts
WEAF, New York	1926	50,000
WJZ, New York	1922	50,000
WRC, Washington	1923	5,000
WTAM, Cleveland	1930	50,000
KOA, Denver	1930	50,000
KGO, San Francisco	1930	7,500
WMAQ, Chicago	1931	50,000
WENR, Chicago	1931	50,000
KPO, San Francisco	1932	50,000
WMAL, Washington	1933	5,000

NBC additionally signed management contracts with two licensees to "program" five outlets owned by them, including operating those stations, in 1932. The five were WGY, Schenectady, licensed to General Electric Company, and four owned by Westinghouse Electric and Manufacturing Company: KDKA, Pittsburgh; KYW, Philadelphia; WBZ, Boston; and WBZA, Springfield, Mass. All except the last broadcast at 50,000 watts; WBZA aired synchronously with WBZ at 1,000 watts. The programming and management of those stations raised eyebrows under provisions of the Radio Act of 1927, however. Consent of the Federal Radio Commission (FRC), which regulated the broadcast industry at the time, had never been sought nor obtained. In January 1940, when the applications for renewal of the licenses were reviewed at a hearing, those management contracts were rescinded. The five stations entered into new agreements as affiliates of NBC as a result.

From a business standpoint, the National Broadcasting Company, Inc., and its counterparts were formed as money-making enterprises, pure and simple. Not only recouping its investment in the high profile auxiliary it created but additionally turning it into a profitable cash cow had been among parent firm Radio Corporation of America's chief intents since Day 1. The fact that NBC could serve as a laboratory for some of RCA's projects—and generate sales of some of its products—added value to the purchase. Frankly, unlike some of the operators of broadcasting ventures in the pre-network era who performed in the arena without regard to profit, RCA expected to make a killing off of NBC. The realization in time of what they had, however, became so incredibly extraordinary that possibly no one could have anticipated the stupendous results.

With the exception of its first 14 months of operations, extending through 1927, NBC earned substantial profits every year for many years. Revenues from time sales after discounts and before agency commissions of nearly $7.3 million in 1928 netted earnings of $427,239 that year. Contrast that with figures posted for 1940. In only a dozen years, revenues were almost $41.7 million (nearly six times what they were in 1928) with that year's proceeds exceeding $5.8 million (nearly 14 times the earlier share).[27] The original investment in WEAF ($1 million) and leasing AT&T wires (about $1 million annually) paled by comparison, especially when weighed against the potential for so many fruitful years out into the future.

Not counting on-air artists, there were 1,359 NBC staffers in 1931. That year the Red and Blue chains featured 256 special events, carried 159 incoming international programs originating at 34 sites, and aired 19 appearances by the U.S. president, 24 by cabinet members and 65 by members of the U.S. Congress.

The standing of NBC in the province of broadcasting cannot be fully comprehended nor accurately assessed without some awareness of the history and activities of its parent firm, the Radio Corporation of America. It should be understood that NBC at that time was but one offshoot of an immense corporate behemoth. RCA straddled the fields of communications, radio apparatus manufacturing and entertainment. One source branded RCA "a giant, industrial octopus" and intimated it possessed "tentacles" that ranged far and ran deep. Organized in Delaware on October 17, 1919, a full year before the commencement of radio broadcasting, as already noted RCA was established by the General Electric Company to assume commerce of the American Marconi Company. When federal operation of radio stations terminated, RCA embarked on activities that were to turn it into the incontestably foremost American radio communications firm.

Under 1920 cross-licensing agreements, RCA became sole sales agent for radio receiving sets manufactured by both GE and Westinghouse. The proliferation of broadcasting in turn magnified the demand for sets. While RCA's gross sales were under $1.5 million in 1921, in 1922 they were almost $11.3 million, an increase of about 7.5 times the earlier revenues.[28] Two years later (1924) gross sales reached $50 million, strong indicators about the growing interest in radio's impact on daily living.[29] By 1926, RCA proclaimed it was the largest distributor of radio receivers on the planet and granted licenses to a number of radio set manufacturers.[30] Concurrently, it persisted as a major set distributor also.

RCA diversified early into many other amusement arenas that gainfully multiplied what might be perceived as a formidable throttlehold on the flourishing performing arts. As a primary distributor of radio receivers, holding thousands of patents in the realm, RCA entered the sector of vending combined radio-phonograph players. Initially it worked with Brunswick-Balke-Collander Company, and later with the Victor Talking Machine Company, and ultimately acquired Victor in 1929, when it was already the dominant phonograph and phonograph record manufacturer.[27] The progression into phonograph commerce afforded a leg up in the transcription and talent source sectors: RCA Victor artists broadcast over NBC and made RCA transcriptions while NBC performers recorded for RCA Victor. The upshot substantially benefited RCA and its auxiliaries, giving the conglomerate a striking competitive advantage over other broadcasters, radio parts and receiver-makers and rival phonograph and phonograph recording producers.

In another entertainment sector, RCA's entry into movie-making, at first via RCA Photophone and then through Radio-Keith-Orpheum Corporation, was a step-by-step process, too, similarly enriching its position in added domains. By the early 1930s, with patents, managed artists, manufacturing plants, distribution facilities, personnel, experience and financial strength, RCA was occupying the catbird seat, defying most challengers in a burgeoning trade. RCA had no hesitation or difficulty, for instance, about entering newly created openings like frequency modulation (FM) broadcasting when it was patented in 1933, or television, which began to seem like a viable diversion after it was introduced during the 1939 New York World's Fair. RCA's competitive advantage discouraged many neophytes, in fact, from pursuing similar dreams in territory already occupied by RCA, where it either had subjugated its rivals or seemed to be well on its way to doing so.

All of this, plus RCA's exploits into international radio circuitry, maritime communications, manufacturing subsidiaries, technical education, laboratories and research organizations underscored an indisputable perception of NBC's viability as leader in radio broadcasting—for a long while at least. The chain's role in its sphere was comparable to its parent firm's in the broader context.

Of four national webs existing by 1940, NBC owned two. Roughly a quarter of all local U.S. stations, applying almost half of the total nighttime power, were NBC affiliates. If broadcasters needed transcriptions, NBC made them. If they needed talent, NBC hired them and offered to manage them as their agent in personal appearance and radio work. Together with Broadcast Music, Inc., the web diversified into musical copyrighting.

All of it dovetailed into what Americans were hearing on the ether and signified the depth and breadth of a corporate leviathan that possessed infinitely deep pockets and an insatiable desire to do more than prevail—to utterly dominate its competition. That was the corporate mindset during radio's golden age, and NBC was swept up in it as a small but significant portion of RCA's global operations.

Turning now for a while to its programming, NBC—as CBS, acting independently but similarly—majored in the early years on dance band music. The three webs (NBC Red and Blue and CBS) aired an aggregate 14 such weekly shows in the 1930–1931 season, and by 1933–34 they carried a combined 24 dance features, improving the total to 26 shows a year later. The trio of chains proffered 70 name bands for their 1939 summer schedules with MBS adding still more to that number. Big-band remotes from hotels, restaurants, supper clubs, auditoriums, terraces, roof gardens and other venues proliferated. By the number of hours it filled, dance band music was typically the most popular fare in primetime and in after-hours, although the designation "primetime" hadn't yet come into vogue.

Early in the 1930s, meanwhile, the action took a definite swing from the reticent orchestral fare that had dominated much of the 1920s agendas to "name" personalities generally plucked from vaudeville and now headlining their own shows. It was a new trend, and American listeners were quick to register their approval.

On June 15, 1931, NBC president Merlin H. Aylesworth rather pompously boasted that NBC "holds its network stations together only by the superiority of its network program service and by the demand of listeners for NBC network programs." But when a new chain, MBS, entered the marketplace in 1934, NBC abandoned its reliance upon program superiority and listener demand and removed its stations from competition through five-year exclusive contracts modeled after one designed by CBS.

That isn't to suggest that NBC relaxed its programming standards, certainly. Indeed, the net persisted in offering much of the available superior talent that could be amassed for radio consumption. Fred Allen, Jack Benny, Edgar Bergen and Charlie McCarthy, Milton Berle, Les Brown, Eddie Cantor, Dennis Day, Jimmy Durante, Phil Harris and Alice Faye, Bob Hope, Gordon Jenkins, Al Jolson, Groucho Marx, Billy Mills, Bill Stern, Rudy Vallee, Fred Waring, Meredith Willson, Ed Wynn and others became enduring members of an almost impenetrable NBC primetime family, pillars of the House that Sarnoff built. Seemingly loyal to a fault, they never wavered in their steadfastness—not, at least, until CBS's Bill Paley found a way to attract a host of them to the competition.

Along with its glittering headliners, NBC proffered a list of longstanding audience favorites that kept legions coming back for another dip at the well: *The Adventures of Ozzie and Harriet, The Aldrich Family, The Band of America, The Bell Telephone Hour, The Breakfast Club, The Chamber Music Society of Lower Basin Street, A Date with Judy, Dragnet, Father Knows Best, The Fitch Bandwagon, Fibber McGee & Molly, Grand Ole Opry, The Great Gildersleeve, Meet the Press, The Metropolitan Opera, Monitor, The National Farm and Home Hour, One Man's Family, The Railroad Hour, Truth or Consequences, The Voice of Firestone, X-Minus One.* It was none too shabby what NBC's zealous passion and RCA's financial backing could provide.

There were a handful of signature occasions in which network radio performed extraordinarily well, sometimes capturing the imaginations of throngs of Americans by taking to them celebrated events that they had never before witnessed. For example, on June 11, 1927, aviator Charles Lindbergh returned from his solo flight across the Atlantic Ocean. That occasion was turned into the first majestic multiple-announcer aircast. Spaced along a ticker-tape route lined with cheering crowds of spectators, interlocutors from an NBC inventory of professionals—

with names that were becoming household words in American domiciles—were passing the air spotlight to one another much like a flaming torch as listeners to 50 stations followed the dramatic action. It was stuff like that which fed a media frenzy and sold more and more radios. NBC, of course, was at the forefront of numerous magnificent events like it, being the only broadcaster at the time with the capacity to provide such comprehensive eyewitness accounts (to say nothing of the receiving sets so many were hearing them on that previous spectacles sold).

The network's most important innovation of the era, nonetheless, was its decision to put on a couple of white guys pretending to be black guys and let 'em dialogue with each other nightly in characteristic Negro dialect while mired in zany incidents. The depiction was launched as *Sam 'n' Henry* over Chicago's WGN on January 12, 1926, by Freeman Gosden and Charles Correll. The black figures those white boys portrayed turned into a laugh riot that quickly drew the rapt attention of listeners tuning in across the miles, well beyond the shores of Lake Michigan. People of multiple ethnic backgrounds loved the good-natured fun that exuded from their calamitous situations. When the pair shifted to the Windy City's WMAQ on March 19, 1928, they renamed their aliases *Amos 'n' Andy*, two black boys from Atlanta who moved north to seek their fortunes.

Gosden and Correll were the ones finding the fortunes, however; when Pepsodent toothpaste offered them $100,000 annually to perform their shenanigans in nightly quarter-hour installments over NBC, seemingly all of America—including black and white fans—could hardly get enough of it.[32] Respected radio historian John Dunning lauded theirs as "the most popular radio show of all time" while inveterate addict Calvin Coolidge left orders at the White House that he wasn't to be disturbed while *Amos 'n' Andy* was on the air. Movie theaters, restaurants and shops interrupted their normal fare to pipe in the live broadcasts to their establishments so patrons wouldn't miss an episode of their favorite series. Factories altered shift changes to accommodate it, and in so many other ways life in the United States ground to a virtual standstill for a few minutes every weeknight in the early years of the Great Depression. Millions with little to laugh about roared appreciatively, smitten by antics that, according to Dunning, "held the hearts and minds of the American people as nothing did before or since."[33]

Those blackface sensations were once again reminders to audiences that NBC was at the forefront of novel programming concepts that enthralled legions of listeners. It became a tradition that the chimes chain proudly bore as radio grew up, advancing through halcyon years with an incredible amount of network broadcasting's stupendous fare.

Some of those sterling programs leaned far and away from the tricks exhibited by *Amos 'n' Andy* and their cohorts, appealing instead to a more urbane, sophisticated, erudite audience. David Sarnoff for one classified himself in that category, an ultra-cultured individual who preferred listening to opera as opposed to the trendy comedians that populated his web on so many nights of the week. While laughter paid the bills and did so handsomely, Sarnoff never was particularly friendly with the likes of Fred Allen, Jack Benny and Bob Hope. They may have underwritten the salaries of many in Sarnoff's employ but he was more impressed by the fact that their being at NBC allowed his dual chains to program countless cultural series—many sustained without sponsorship—the programming he himself preferred. It was Sarnoff who pushed for a great philharmonic orchestra conducted by none other than Arturo Toscanini, the famed Italian impresario whom he coaxed out of retirement. Credit the RCA chairman with many of the upscale offerings that pleased a clearly defined posh segment of American society.

It was seldom that NBC could be considered a laggard in any aspect of innovative radio broadcasting. But that did happen on rare occasions. One of those provinces in which NBC started late—and, over the course of a quarter-century, demonstrated difficulty in catching up (although there were some notable exceptions to that blanket assertion)—was in the field of news. America's forerunner in netcasting frequently found itself playing second fiddle in a highly competitive market orchestrated and dominated by rival CBS. In time the latter advanced a roster of names of news jockeys with impeccable credentials that were lauded by scholars as unsurpassed in their ability to obtain and deliver the news, and even to analyze it. With Edward R. Murrow as the legendary guru of the breed, the CBS stalwarts included Charles Collingwood, Douglas Edwards, Allan Jackson, Larry LeSueur, Robert Pierpoint, Eric Sevareid, Lowell Thomas (after an early start at NBC), Dallas Townsend, Robert Trout and others of their exalted rank.

In a move of one-upmanship designed to protect their own financial interests, in the spring of 1933, a trio of foremost newsgathering organizations—Associated Press, United Press, and International News Service—ended all dispatches to the radio networks. Placed at a crossroads, the big chains could persist in giving little more than a passing nod to news, or go after it aggressively themselves. While NBC's initial attempts could be considered anything but forceful, it laid some groundwork for establishing a newsgathering organization that was to eventually extend to the ends of the earth.

Though small, its effort delivered surprising results. "Because of its leading position, NBC probably had less incentive than CBS toward reckless adventure," one analyst advanced. Its pursuit focused on one man, Abraham A. Schechter. Though young in years—born August 10, 1907, at Central Falls, Rhode Island—Schechter had prepared himself for just such a tactical opportunity as he was thrust into at NBC. He had reported for *The Providence Journal* and *The New York World* and been a New York editor for Associated Press before his hire at age 24 as NBC's director of news and special events.

While churning out publicity for the Red and Blue chains in 1932, he evolved into a one-man corporate news division. He occupied space in a joint carpentry shop-storage room at 711 Fifth Avenue, actually a minuscule broom closet ventilated only by an airshaft. (Can Brian Williams even begin to imagine those conditions?) "Each evening Schechter would pick wood shavings from his hair and head home to listen to Lowell Thomas, the authoritative newscaster with his worldwide sources," a media historiographer noted.

In his strategic post, Schechter revealed just what an individual possessing a telephone—his lifeline to the world—could achieve. For a decade, he gathered news tips supplied by publicity agents working for NBC affiliates around the country. Prompted by those bits of data as well as what he read in the newspapers, he placed phone calls everywhere seeking follow-up details. Almost anybody, he discovered, accepted a telephone call "from NBC." Many times his efforts paid off handsomely, allowing him to scoop the newspapers and news service organizations that had rebuffed his employer.

Becoming the darling of the press agents, he rewarded tipsters with tickets to Rudy Vallee broadcasts, a prize placed in inestimable regard in that day. He fed enough material to Lowell Thomas (then an NBC property) to fill a quarter-hour each evening while saving a few choice morsels for the gossip-mongering Walter Winchell on Sunday nights.

Suffice it to say that the one-man groundbreaking newsgathering operation Schechter mustered established NBC as a serious player on new turf, ultimately leading to a global newsgathering team that included wizards of electronic journalism like Morgan Beatty, Pauline Frederick, H. V. Kaltenborn (a transplant from CBS), Herbert Kaplow, Irving R. Levine, Merrill Mueller and more. As for Schechter, he moved on to the U.S. Office of War Information in 1942, was a vice president at MBS (1945–1950), and returned to NBC at mid-century. At that time he helped create *Today* for its television network, serving as first executive producer in 1950 to 1952. From 1952–1973, Schechter ran his own PR shop, and succumbed to death at 81 on May 24, 1989, at Southhampton, New York.

In the twilight years of a great radio network, meanwhile, between 1955 and 1975, NBC's

Monitor multiplied the traditions Abe Schechter set into motion. Preceded by a couple of warm-up acts in the 1953–1955 epoch in the form of *The Road Show* and *Weekend* magazine experiments, *Monitor* was a news junkie's paradise. Much of that marathon swirled about news and public affairs, current events, and interviews with eminent figures from diverse configurations. At the same time it supplied remote pickups from newsmaking occasions that transpired while the show was airing live. In that context, NBC far outweighed its audio opponents by offering virtual round-the-clock newsbreaking reportage, a precursor to the cable video news chains that dotted the ethereal landscape in the decades thereafter.

NBC also instigated some brilliant concepts in documentaries in this era, such as its award-winning *Biography in Sound*. Appearing late in radio's heyday, the show's roots were embedded in a collection of more than 150,000 recorded bits of trivia that NBC journalist Joseph O. Meyers amassed from 1949. In those 1954–1958 broadcasts, producer Meyers profiled renowned individuals via a series of sketches followed by interviews with people linked with his subjects. The headliners were chosen from diverse breeds, including some arresting icons like Franklin P. Adams, Winston Churchill, Leo Durocher, F. Scott Fitzgerald, George Gershwin, Ernest Hemingway, Gertrude Lawrence, Sinclair Lewis, Joe Louis, Connie Mack and Carl Sandburg. Once again, even as it was then fading fast, NBC Radio's news division was taking a mighty stand, leaving the folks at home with a generally favorable impression of its concerted efforts over the past quarter-century.

Long before those days, however, there was the separation of the Red and Blue webs. There's no other way to sum it up: that landmark episode dealt a staggering blow to the senior Sarnoff and his comrades. They had fought vigorously, valiantly, doggedly to prevent it. While they had already divided the company into separate subsidiaries in 1940 just in case they had to appeal (NBC Red Network, Inc., and NBC Blue Network, Inc.), there is evidence that—until the bitter end of a hard-fought struggle—they believed the courts would rule in their favor. But the appeal failed. Accepting the inevitable finally came only when they were given no alternative. While awaiting the final outcome, in January 1942, the two webs formally divorced their operations.[34]

We won't belabor the complexities of the FCC's ultimatum here; it would take many pages to examine the underlying issues as well as the arguments proffered by the Federal Communications Commission that NBC crushingly dominated the broadcasting trade (which it did). As a result of its intensive hearings and follow-up investigation, conducted from 1938 to 1941, the FCC in practice ordered NBC to divest itself of one of its two webs—and to own no more than one station in any single market. The intent was to reduce the company's unfair advantage over competitors, potential competitors, advertisers, talent and all other broadcasting commerce. That, in a nutshell, was the outcome of a directive issued on May 2, 1941, by the FCC. When the Supreme Court sided with the FCC in 1943, the string had run out for NBC. The FCC's order was to shake up the industry and present unmistakable lingering effects on broadcasting that extend into contemporary times.

NBC acquiesced to the ultimatum by putting its less powerful and less popular chain, the Blue web, up for sale. Within two months of the Supreme Court's May 1943 rendering, RCA announced that the Blue had been sold to a cash buyer. Candy magnate Edward J. Noble (Life Savers confections) purchased it for $8 million.[35] Following mandatory hearings, the FCC approved the sale in mid October 1943, changing the ownership of New York flagship station WJZ, Chicago's WENR and San Francisco's KGO, and divorcing the Blue Network, Inc., from NBC/RCA. In mid 1945, the "new" chain took on a new identity: the American Broadcasting Company (ABC).[36]

The Blue network had time sales of $24.6 million in 1943, the year it was divested. Under a new owner, the following year its sales improved to $41.3 million, a 67 percent increase.[37]

While equal footing might never have been expected to occur with its long established opposition, the future of ABC at that juncture seemed viable.

In addition to the personalities already outlined who formulated NBC's direction from conceptualization through the web's first decade, others appeared to fill the empty shoes of the hardy pioneers. A quartet who made more than passing impressions consisted of Niles Trammell, John F. Royal, Sylvester L. (Pat) Weaver and Robert W. Sarnoff. A succinct introspective into each man will reveal the level of proficiency that NBC maintained while attracting to its management team individuals with vision, competency, creative genius and knack for securing their employer's future.

Niles Trammell, NBC's third president, was born July 6, 1894, at Marietta, Georgia. Following service in World War I, he joined RCA in San Francisco. Favorably viewed by David Sarnoff, Trammell moved to NBC in 1928 as a salesman. The following year he was assigned to Chicago as vice president of NBC's central division, a post occupied for a decade. During his tenure in the Windy City, Trammell was responsible for premiering NBC features like *Amos 'n' Andy*, *Fibber McGee & Molly*, *Lum and Abner* and *Ma Perkins*. He also signed entertainers Phil Baker, Eddie Cantor, Al Jolson and Ed Wynn to the NBC roster.

By 1939, Trammell was in the home office in New York as a vice president. He was elected president the following year. In 1949, he became chairman of the board at NBC. A statement he made that year alluding to the advance of television onto radio's turf has been repeated often by radio historians: "Within three years, the broadcast of sound or ear radio over giant networks will be wiped out." In three years (1952), Trammell resigned at NBC to accept the presidency of Biscayne Television Corporation in Miami. He died March 28, 1973, at North Miami, Florida. His prediction of 1949 never literally came true, although radical changes in how radio was to be available to the masses lurked in the wings.

John Francis Royal came out of vaudeville to join the network. Born at Cambridge, Massachusetts, on July 4, 1886, he grew up to become Harry Houdini's press agent before running Keith-Albee theaters in Boston, Cincinnati and Cleveland. And in the latter city, he found radio, or vice versa, where he managed the powerful NBC Red affiliate WTAM. So endowed was WTAM with Midwest underwriters and so independent-minded was its ownership in clearing time for NBC series that the New York brass arrived at the conclusion it should buy out WTAM's owners. In doing so, NBC not only fully controlled a respected outlet in a lucrative market but also acquired Royal in the transaction. Making what turned out to be a prudent decision, NBC officials summoned Royal to Gotham as the network's vice president.

While NBC enjoyed a head start in plucking first-rate vaudevillians from that venue to regularly or occasionally appear before its microphones, CBS had begun to seriously chip away at its dominant position in that province. A media observer depicted Royal's response to the challenge in typical vaudeville tradition. "He saw the NBC-CBS situation in terms of competing marquees," the analyst conjectured. "He watched the marquee across the street. Any strong move called for a similar but more spectacular countermove."[38] Cited was a litany of actions taken by CBS with reactions by NBC in quests to trump its opposite number. In the latter 1930s, Royal's provocative pursuits followed earlier revelations by CBS in the areas of Shakespearean plays, symphonic music, educational documentaries, poetry reading, prestigious original dramas and so forth. Whenever CBS made an impressive announcement, media observers could anticipate a similar message from NBC within a short while.

Royal died at 91 in New York City on February 13, 1978.

Sylvester Laflin (Pat) Weaver, Jr., was the closest thing NBC witnessed to a true creative genius, undoubtedly so prior to the arrival of some inspired TV pacesetters in the final decades of the 20th century. Born at Los Angeles on December 21, 1908, Weaver was responsible for programming moves in two mediums that often have been cited for novel brilliance. Reporting his death at 93, *The New York Times* dubbed him "the most important innovator in television programming." It might have been difficult to argue otherwise.

After getting into radio as an announcer following graduation magna cum laude from Dartmouth College in 1930, he shifted between stations until he landed a stint managing a San Francisco outlet. Weaver joined the Young & Rubicam advertising agency in 1935, subsequently managed advertising at the American Tobacco Company (Lucky Strike, Pall Mall, Herbert Tareyton, et al.), and served in the U.S. Navy 1942–1945. Following the war he returned to Young & Rubicam as vice president for radio and television. In 1949, Weaver made the transition that was to establish him as an icon in American entertainment programming development.

He joined NBC that year as vice president in charge of television, and his creative instincts coupled with demonstrated ability thrust him into the president's office in December 1953. In the interim, the boy wonder busied himself by launching several features that were to make indelible impressions on broadcasting. On his first day on the job in 1949, he rescinded a cancellation order for *Meet the Press*, airing on radio then and presently TV's longest-running news forum. At a time when TV sets were an uncommon opulence in American domiciles—with the trade run like radio as sponsors produced and controlled their own shows—Weaver successfully contended that national chains should produce the shows and sell

Winning the Sylvania Television Award for "outstanding contributions to creative television techniques" was one of the copious honors accorded Sylvester L. (Pat) Weaver, Jr. (at left), during his turn running NBC. The trophy was presented by broadcaster Deems Taylor, awards chairman, on November 29, 1955.

commercial time to advertisers. (On that, he was in full harmony with CBS mogul William S. Paley.)[39]

Weaver commissioned NBC spectaculars: 60, 90 and 120 minute live specials like *Peter Pan* starring Mary Martin and Gian Carlo Menotti's *Amahl and the Night Visitors*, the first opera custom-built for video. His wife, actress Elizabeth Inglis, termed him "a great idealist" who viewed TV as a way to introduce the common man to culture. "He put on opera for the first time because he said the man in the street ... wants to hear anything and he doesn't have the money," she affirmed. "His plan was that everybody should have access."[40]

Weaver was credited with debuting a plethora of innovative projects for NBC-TV. Among his brainchildren were *Today, Tonight, Home, Wide Wide World* and more. Two of his series, of course, persevere more than a half-century after their inception, offering no sign of fading while still mesmerizing audiences in large quantities every weekday.

His greatest contribution for radio was the epic *Monitor*, an ambitious unstructured magazine classic that aired 40 hours every weekend from its start. It persisted for two decades (1955–1975) in abbreviated segments while some prophets claimed it "saved a network from extinction." Whether it did or not is for conjecture, but it staved off the inevitable in the late 1950s while attracting legions of fans and advertisers to NBC. Listeners were drawn by its immediacy, novelty, resiliency and portability. Presenting snippets of mostly three minutes' duration tops, its concept fit well into the growing impatience fans harbored for formulaic material while fitting precisely into the trendy lifestyles of Americans on the go. *Monitor*'s durability was a testament to Weaver's ingenuity in establishing a method to inform, amuse and sustain with grand diversity.

To keep things in their proper perspective, it should be noted that not every Weaver notion turned out as charmingly. The most colossal failure laid at his feet occurred on NBC Radio in 1955–1956. When Weaver and his protégés cleared NBC's daytime schedule of nearly every longrunning soap opera, quiz, music and variety feature — disrupting the housewives' loyalties to a pattern NBC had followed for decades — it found little favorable reception to a copycat version of *Monitor* bearing the soubriquet *Weekday*. A five- to six-hour daily magazine debuting on November 7, 1955, stemming from the phenomenal success of *Monitor*, simply fell on deaf ears and was off the air in a matter of months. With years of traditions by then irretrievably broken, NBC found itself languishing in the cellar of discontent Monday through Friday during the sunlight hours. And with its *Weekday* series a washout, millions permanently threw in the towel, having discovered other pursuits in the interim. The miscalculation was costly: it was turf NBC would never again dominate. Within weeks after *Weekday*'s departure, Weaver followed suit.

According to newspaper accounts, "His greatest power over network programming came when Mr. Weaver was NBC's president, a job he was forced to relinquish in 1955 to Robert Sarnoff, the son of Gen. David Sarnoff, the head of RCA."[41] Wrote another: "Mr. Weaver was pushed out as NBC president in 1955 by Robert Sarnoff, son of David Sarnoff — the head of NBC's parent corporation, RCA."[42] Although Weaver was named NBC chairman on relinquishing the presidency and CEO post, he labored between two Sarnoffs — papa, chairman of parent RCA, and son, president and CEO of NBC. While Weaver continued to receive plaudits for his dazzling achievements (e.g., in April 1956, the Newspaper Guild Press Club cited him "for creating new programming ideas and methods for bringing new excitement into television," one of numerous honors[43]), there were published rumors that he was not a happy camper.

In one revealing sidebar, when Weaver arrived at his inaugural meeting as chairman of NBC, he reportedly noted — smiling — that RCA chairman David Sarnoff had seated himself at the head of the table.[44] Weaver exclaimed, "Why, General, that's my seat!" The elder Sarnoff obligingly vacated the chair. A few months afterward, Weaver was looking for work.

At a board meeting about eight months after being kicked upstairs, on September 7, 1956, derision erupted when Weaver announced he couldn't abide by some aspects of projected management reorganization. To everyone's utter surprise, even though rumors had circulated for months, he suddenly resigned in protest. Within days more loyalists (one with 30 years' tenure at NBC) quit. Much of this exhibition, which NBC and RCA preferred to keep a lid on, spilled out onto the pages of the nation's daily newspapers. In the 1960s, Weaver joined Subscription Television, Inc., a pay cable TV venture that ultimately failed. He was a media consultant thereafter. He died at 93 at Santa Barbara, California, on March 15, 2002, having never regained anything closely resembling his brief turn at Camelot.

Robert W. Sarnoff was the eldest of a half-dozen sons of David Sarnoff, the RCA chairman. When the younger Sarnoff was elected president of NBC and subsequently its chairman, of course the water cooler conversations in Rockefeller Center were abuzz with the inevitable whispers of favoritism and nepotism. Some branded him the "crown prince" and there was talk by naysayers of a "Sarnoff dynasty." But if one of his dad's biographers is to be believed, he earned the right to hold his offices through solid understudy and hard work, not purely ambition and kinship.

Born July 2, 1918, in New York City, Robert Sarnoff was equipped with a Harvard degree and a year of Columbia law school. He focused on broadcasting with the Coordinator of Information (later Office of Strategic Services) followed by a stint as a naval communications officer during World War II. Joining Cowles Publishing afterward, he worked a year at one of its newspapers, *The Des Moines Register and Tribune*, before shifting to its *Look* magazine staff in New York.

Obviously restless, disenchanted with print media as a profession and—perhaps influenced by his father's forthrightness—in 1947, he decided television stood on the threshold of being the nation's chief news, amusement and advertising source. He also believed he should be identified with it. The younger Sarnoff discussed his convictions with a chum, Frank Mullen, executive vice president of NBC. In January 1948, Mullen hired him as an account executive (time salesman) at NBC. Though Sarnoff the elder supposedly conveyed unease, he didn't interfere in their arrangement.

Some time later Sarnoff the younger transferred to TV network programming and production. His dad's deep passion of two decades had been to see video developed to overtake audio, and the newer medium was on the brink of doing so right then. Meanwhile, Robert Sarnoff's star rose quickly. Elevated to vice president over the NBC film

Robert W. Sarnoff, the eldest of six sons of Radio Corporation of America chairman David Sarnoff, was hired by NBC in 1948. He was a quick study and rose to top positions, but following his father's passing, it all began to unravel.

unit in 1952, he was named executive vice president of the company the following year. By the end of 1955, he was NBC president. "The younger Sarnoff has inherited his father's zest for battle," wrote newspaperman Jack Gould in reporting Robert's ascension to the presidency.[45] But Robert wasn't done by a long shot; by 1957, he was chairman, holding the same post his father held at parent RCA.

Elected president of RCA in 1965, Robert Sarnoff was named CEO two years afterward. When his ailing father retired from the chairmanship, in the wings was a gentleman-in-waiting who had been groomed for the post for more than two decades. As he stepped into that role in 1970, he may have anticipated a durable tenure befitting a Sarnoff. But he soon learned that life does not favor every man equally. In fact, by Sarnoff standards, Robert's occupancy was fairly brief.

It coincided with some nasty economic reverses that soured any legacy he might have been favorably credited with. Some of the disarray was hung squarely around his shoulders. An ill-timed, ill-prepared folly into computers and abandonment of the pursuit in 1971 cost the company almost a half-billion dollars. Investors and directors took Robert Sarnoff to the woodshed for it. Hard times led the firm to curtail its quests into space activities to converge most of its energies on electronics. Meanwhile, Sarnoff carried the company into widespread diversification, allowing it to invest heavily in domains far from its core business. It included publishing (Random House), vehicle renting (Hertz), chicken farming (Banquet Foods), carpet-making (Coronet) and greeting cards (Gibson) among others. To some it seemed reckless and irresponsible, and he was criticized sharply for it.

In that same time frame, hoping to find some relief for the bottom line, Sarnoff shopped NBC Radio and the subsidiary's owned-and-operated radio stations. He was unsuccessful in securing a buyer for the total package, nonetheless. Signaling trouble to the public, meanwhile, NBC canceled its two-decades-old *Monitor* in January 1975. In rapid succession, it offered continuous news feeds starting in June 1975 (*News and Information Service*) for 55 minutes 24–7 to any station that subscribed, including non-affiliates, watering down the pure-bred product. Few bit the bait, however, and that dismal failure was rescinded in less than two years. All of it portended bad tidings and must have been interpreted by close industry watchers as cries of desperation.

In an attempt to turn the situation around and put a positive spin on their intents, the RCA directors abruptly fired Robert Sarnoff in late 1975. Perhaps a blessing was that his father didn't live to see it, nor most of the debacle that befell the mighty corporation he had given his life to; he died in 1971. And finally, after 49 years, a Sarnoff was no longer involved in steering NBC or its parent organization. The year 1975 marked the passing of a torch. Robert Sarnoff lived to be 78 and died in New York on February 22, 1997, after battling cancer for 16 years.

If the divestiture of one of its dual webs had been a bitter pill for NBC executives to swallow in the first half of the 1940s, there was a second capsule they had to digest in the latter half of the same decade that must have made them candidates for gall bladder surgery and removal. It swirled about the antagonism that persistently languished just beneath the surface in dealings between NBC and archrival CBS. On rare occasions its unsightly head emerged in public. Actually, the enmity appeared about as pronounced between the two men running those broadcast empires as it did between the networks themselves. NBC/RCA's David Sarnoff and CBS's William S. Paley loved nothing better than to spar with their opposite, unless it might be winning a game of one-upmanship. And in winning, it was icing on the cake to those tycoons if—while the victor collected his spoils—the other could be humiliated in public. More details of their rigorous sporting are reported in Chapter 10.

Having lost some crucial battles to Sarnoff and NBC over several years, Paley was biding his time, lying in wait for the right opening to strike his opposite number with a devastating blow. At last he saw it. He made his move in the late 1940s on finding not only an opportunity to trump his old nemesis but to potentially cart away enough venerated NBC talent to preserve the future of his first broadcasting love—CBS Radio. What Paley didn't fully realize then but in time would come to witness was that the deals he made proved even more injurious to NBC than he had first imagined: they packed the CBS lineup with popular performers to headline the latter's early television years, giving it a decided edge on its competition. How could it get any better than that?

Paley's first acquisition brought NBC's *Amos 'n' Andy* to the CBS fold in September 1948 for $2 million, paid to Freeman Gosden and Charles Correll. Subsequently, in strikingly similar 1948–1949 deals, Paley enticed legendary entertainers Jack Benny, Edgar Bergen, George Burns and Gracie Allen, Ozzie and Harriet Nelson, Harold Peary and Red Skelton to CBS, all from NBC. To their number he added ABC's Bing Crosby and Groucho Marx.

It was a coup d'état on a massive scale, carried out so suddenly that insiders labeled the raids "Paley's Comet" for their velocity.[46] It was "the biggest upheaval in broadcasting since Paley bought CBS in 1928," a Paley biographer assessed.[47] The action reformulated the programming agendas of two radio webs for the remainder of the medium's golden age. It guaranteed CBS a strong showing for a few more years, even as television was rapidly encroaching on its turf. For the first time in two decades, CBS had larger audiences than NBC. At the start of 1950, CBS owned 80 percent of network radio's top 20 Nielsen-rated shows.[48] The mayhem banished NBC to little more than also-ran status, and certainly so until *Monitor* arrived in 1955 to rejuvenate a formerly prestigious chain that had been on a markedly downhill slide. In addition to losing so many of its listeners, NBC suffered a $7 million ad revenue loss in a single year.[49] Yikes! The grand net that had been at the vanguard of radio's quintessence could seemingly do very little but lick its wounds for a while.

The raids heralded a new order that Paley had been experimenting with of late: wresting programming power away from the advertising agencies and returning it to the audio webs where it had resided until those leading broadcasters relinquished it to the ad packagers in the early 1930s. The nets would regain control over their only product and retain it from then on. At the time, having accomplished that turnaround feat, CBS boasted that—of 29 programs it owned outright—the available commercial time on all of them had been fully sold to sponsors.[50] It wasn't a bad spot to be in at the middle of the 20th century.

For five years, meanwhile, NBC's aural landscape was almost completely devoid of its usual deputation of fêted favorites following the striking blow of Paley's Comet. An attempt to restock its long-envied, then-desolate Sunday night schedule with a 90-minute glitzy showcase headlined by actress Tallulah Bankhead, *The Big Show* (1950–1952), ultimately proved futile. Touted as "radio's last big show," its production ceased several weeks before the second season was to end with NBC astonishingly $1 million in the hole. Theorized one wag: "*The Big Show* had its moments, but *The Jack Benny Program* rolled along on CBS, as consistently brilliant and funny as ever. The moral, perhaps, is that brilliance and genius cannot be bought, that a buckshot approach never works, and that most good things come finally from a single inspired source."[51]

"How could you do this to me?" was about all that Sarnoff could muster to Paley once the dust of the raids settled. While NBC had prevailed in a lot of skirmishes and key battles over the years, it was plain to most media observers that CBS had won the decisive (and what proved to be, final) war (of decisive consequence).

In spite of its many celebrated programming triumphs of the 1940s and the strong fare it presented to waiting Americans every week in recurring time frames during the halcyon era of the 1940s, NBC suffered a couple of very bad falls that decade. And—despite a few isolated bright spots now and then as the 1950s emerged (e.g. *Biography in Sound, Dragnet, The Six Shooter,*

X-Minus One), like Humpty Dumpty, all the king's horses and all the king's men couldn't put Humpty together again.

The handwriting on the wall pertaining to network radio's eminent extinction (or at least, devaluation) must have become clearer to Sarnoff and his henchmen sooner than it did to Paley and his tribe. It was Paley, you recall, who still believed in radio. In the 1950s, he stood tall against affiliates clamoring for reduced chain features so they could sell time more profitably at home; he also stood up to leaders within his own camp who saw TV as the viable wave of broadcasting's future. Sarnoff, of course, had been planning for that unimpeded eventuality in the late 1920s and worked tenaciously at it through video experiments for years. At the same time, he visualized RCA-manufactured TV sets occupying the living rooms of millions of American domiciles.

Network radio's sagging fate can be blamed on a number of factors that are explored elsewhere in this volume. But in the rapidly declining environment in which its management found itself as the 1950s arrived, some responded well while others folded their tents and ran up the white flags. With nothing to lose, MBS continued to produce its normal fare of programming, at least until mid-decade, having no TV network to dilute its predominantly dramatic features. CBS persevered to the end, being the last of the major chains to maintain as much of its schedule intact as it possibly could, with many of those shows airing on a sustaining basis. In spite of a strong effort early in the 1950s to reverse some of its audience erosion (such as by returning daytime soap operas to the lineup after nearly a decade's absence), ABC, meanwhile, found it was too little too late and gave up on serious program development and innovation.

Regrettably, NBC—now badly wounded (though not mortally so)—made a decision to provide little more than the status quo in the 1950s. With the few stunning programming exceptions alluded to earlier, NBC was on auto-pilot in the final decade of the golden age. It appeared to be maintaining the fort while continuing to put something on the aural ether every day. Sarnoff's commitment and heart were bound to TV, and there seemed few vestiges left of a once-creative highly regarded radio production department. Sure, somebody showed up each day to throw a few switches and put prerecorded programming on the airwaves. But in many cases it gave the impression of a lackluster effort, signifying most of what listeners would experience from NBC until it finally passed into the great Valhalla of the radio webs.

As the medium's golden age passed, one sage, Matthew J. Culligan, an NBC vice president—a man plainly close to the scene—allowed: "Radio didn't die. It wasn't even sick.... The public didn't stop loving radio despite TV. It just started liking it in a different way—and radio went to the beach, to the park, the patio and the automobile.... Radio has become a companion to the individual instead of remaining a focal point of all family entertainment. An intimacy has developed between radio and the individual. It has become as personal as a pack of cigarettes [*sic*]."[52]

An apostle of Pat Weaver, Culligan bought the whole load. Yet his logic appeared reasonable and sound. NBC and its counterparts must appeal to the listening audience in a different way if they were to remain viable, attracting patrons that had something to sell as well as those who were available to buy. The mechanized quarter-hour, half-hour and hour-long shows weren't working for advertisers or audiences any longer. Weaver predicted the change by the start of the 1950s; a decade hence, radio executives had all the evidence they needed. Radio had become fluid as disc jockeys occupied the airchairs that comics, live vocalists and actors previously inhabited. NBC could be a part of the change or be swept aside. How would it answer that daunting dilemma?

As the other networks had been doing for some years, NBC joined them in continuing to program five minutes of national and international news every hour. In NBC's case, it chose to go head-to-head at the top of most hours with CBS for the same audience. For the most part the last remaining vestiges of the well-known names reporting from the NBC trenches during the golden age stayed by the stuff during the early decades of the post-golden epoch.

And like most of its transcontinental competitors, NBC offered its affiliated stations a number of pithy special features throughout the weekday. Following CBS's insertions under the label *Dimension* in 1962, NBC clustered a round of these under the *Emphasis* banner in 1963. ABC followed suit the same year proffering *Flair Reports*, five-minute capsules heard multiple times daily.

From October 1966 through December 1982, NBC offered its listeners one of the most durable features to air in the last half of the 20th century. *Second Sunday* was a 55-minute documentary programmed on its namesake day every month. To have prevailed 16 years, it had to be a well done fan favorite.

In the early 1970s, during a sweeping nostalgia craze, the web experimented by returning to the airwaves a fictional dramatic series that was exceedingly popular in the 1950s. *X-Minus One* had been pulled from the schedule 15 years earlier. NBC got the notion that a new age band, as well as those from past generations that had heard it originally, would appreciate hearing those transcribed tales once more. All went well until NBC officials began to mess with it, big time. While the reprised show aired monthly—the same pattern applying concurrently to *Second Sunday*—unfortunately for everybody who might have loved it (especially any diehard sci-fi fans), NBC shifted *X-Minus One* into myriad timeslots without prior announcement. Not only that, listeners never knew which day it would air: sometimes Saturdays, sometimes Sundays. Serious potential audiences for the show must have felt disenfranchised as they diligently sought to "run across" it. Is that any way to attract a permanently loyal base?

Consequently, despite pleas from the series' original announcer, Fred Collins—who had returned to make new introductions to old narratives, also asking fans to write in and "tell us how you like it"—there weren't enough who located it regularly and wrote in to make a difference. The trial went down in flames, ending March 22, 1975, less than two years after its experimental launch. It was unfortunate and hinted that there might have been troubles at the commanding spaceship. There were, of course.

Having canceled *Monitor* in early 1975, on June 18 of that same year, NBC launched the *News and Information Service* (NIS) over 33 stations. Its structure supplied subscribing outlets with up to 55 minutes of news and features every hour 24–7 minus a few hours on Sunday. In the remaining five minutes of each hour, a station could carry *NBC News on the Hour*, of course, cutting the local staff to a bare minimum. The chain didn't really care if the outlets airing NIS were NBC affiliates: the web said it must have 150 subscribers to make it work. But NIS aired in only 62 markets when it, too, was pulled from the ether in less than two years on May 29, 1977. Stations carrying it in some of the larger markets were forking over monthly fees of $10,000 to the network, one report acknowledged.[53]

NBC Radio's next major venture was in air-testing a one-hour taped Willie Nelson concert on February 9, 1979. Officials had observed that ABC gained a substantial following with a younger crowd in the mid 1970s by offering some live-on-tape music specials. After a heavily promoted Nelson outing drew a respectable response, NBC introduced *The Source*, a youth-oriented audio web, on May 28, 1979. It intended to offer similar fare on an ongoing basis. In addition to its transcribed concerts, in every hour the chain provided two minutes of reports on topics of interest to youth. The feeds were programmed 24 hours daily beginning September 1, 1979. They were indeed one of the few prevailing success stories as NBC changed hands on a couple of occasions in the mid to late 1980s.

On November 2, 1981, NBC jumped into the all-night world of words by offering its listeners *Nighttalk*. For two hours beginning at 10 o'clock Eastern Time, financial wizard Bruce Williams addressed the money concerns of callers to his live show.[54] That was followed by three hours of banter concerning listeners' psychological issues with resident therapist Sally Jessy Raphael.

In the meantime, one wag cited multiple advantages to local radio stations that participated in such programming arrangements. "NBC Radio..., can get "big name" guests that a station in a smaller market couldn't attract on its own. Affiliates are thus persuaded to join the NBC TalkNet in order to boost their own image by being able to advertise a personality on a talk show that their listeners would not otherwise be likely to get a chance to call and speak with."[55] In addition, overnight network programming allows individual stations to cut their expenses by reducing the number of staff needed during those hours. For the network itself, more affiliates means a larger potential market for advertisers, allowing it to charge a higher price for commercial minutes.[56]

Widespread acceptance of *Nighttalk* by the nation's insomniacs and others that worked at night led NBC to form *Talknet* in April 1982. From darkness to dawn, beginning as early at 7 P.M. Eastern Time, it featured those same personalities plus some new ones (Bernard Meltzer, Harvey Ruben) airing their multi-hour shows via satellite distribution. *Talknet* was to continue to the mid 1990s, even after NBC Radio transitioned into new hands twice in the 1980s.

NBC observed a watershed on December 31, 1982. That day it ended the news-and-features format it had pursued since the end of radio's golden age. After more than two decades, in one fell swoop the web scrubbed virtually all of its daily audio visitors and weekend public affairs programming. Gone from the schedule were Joyce Brothers' *Ask Dr. Brothers*, Roger Mudd's *Here and Now*, Mike Jensen's *The Jensen Report*, Gene Shalit's *Man About Anything*, Willard Scott's *Willard's Weather*, and the durable documentary *Second Sunday*.

At that juncture, all that was left of NBC Radio as an audible entity was *NBC News on the Hour*, a few two-minute weekday *Comment on the News* bits, *Talknet*, and *Meet the Press*, an aural rebroadcast of the TV forum airing every Sunday. Nothing more. Just 14 months before, on October 31, 1981, NBC beat its collective chest touting that it was airing "the first live network radio drama in a quarter of a century." The occasion was a broadcast of "A Halloween Story" for a special *All Star Radio Theater* performance. But from the close of 1982, it appeared clearer with each passing season that there would be an unavoidable end to it all one day.

When Robert Sarnoff was relieved of duty as chairman of RCA in 1975, it was a sad omen: if anybody needed one, it was yet another nail in the coffin of chain radio, a reminder that the remnants of a once robust aural broadcasting empire had been not only eclipsed but was vanishing from the scene, never to recover any of its former glory. RCA persisted in floundering for a decade at the hands of multiple successors until late 1986, when General Electric bought it and along with it, NBC, in a $6.28 billion pact.[57] Ironically, GE was the firm that had given life to RCA in 1919.

> In many ways the story of RCA is the story of David Sarnoff. His drive and business acumen led to RCA becoming one of the largest companies in the world, successfully turning it into a conglomerate during the era of their success. However in 1970, now 79 years old, Sarnoff retired and was succeeded by his son Robert. David Sarnoff died the next year; much of RCA's success died with him.
> During the 1970s, RCA Corporation ... became increasingly ossified as a company. Under Robert Sarnoff's leadership, RCA diversified far beyond its original focus on electronics and communications [and was] plagued by financial problems. Robert Sarnoff was ousted in a 1975 boardroom coup by Anthony Conrad, who resigned a year later after admitting failing to file income tax returns for six years. Despite maintaining a high standard of engineering excellence ... ventures such as the NBC radio and television networks declined....
> This eventually led to RCA's sale to GE in 1986 and its subsequent break-up.[58]

After its purchase, RCA simply ceased to exist as a separate identity.[59] Yet that requires some clarification, particularly if one visits the appliance sections of mercantile stores today and is suddenly confronted with the initials RCA burnished on modern clock-radios, MP3 players and other electrical devices—goods still being manufactured now that bear the long-familiar nomenclature. RCA is currently a trademark applied by the French outfit Thomson SA which produces consumer electronics like televisions, DVD players, VCRs, direct broadcast satellite decoders, camcorders, audio equipment, telephones and numerous accessories. It is also used by Sony BMG Music Entertainment, which owns the RCA Victor and RCA Records labels. The two firms purchased those assets from GE and maintain their manufacturing operations outside the United States. Popularity, quality, innovative engineering, styling and moniker combine in perpetuating the RCA sobriquet among buyers in modern times.

The destiny of NBC Radio fared no better than the fate meted out to RCA. One of new NBC president Robert C. Wright's initial decisions was to once again hang a "For Sale" sign on the radio chain—a path Robert W. Sarnoff had trod unsuccessfully about 15 years earlier. Wright, of course, a product of the mid 1940s, may have had little appreciation for NBC as a listener or, obviously, for radio itself, although he was infatuated with television. Repeating a time worn axiom, he was willing to put all of his eggs in one basket. Could he and the Sarnoffs possibly have been cut from the same cloth? It certainly seems they could have been at least distantly related.

Wright had joined General Electric as a staff attorney in 1969 but left that employer twice—from 1970 to 1973, and again from 1980 to 1983. Otherwise, he held assorted managerial positions at GE leading to a appointment as president and CEO of NBC, Inc., when GE acquired RCA. He would later be named chairman and CEO of NBC and vice chairman of GE (2000) and chairman and CEO of NBC Universal, Inc. (2004–2007). It was strictly a business decision, then, when he announced in July 1987 that he had a buyer for the radio division. At the time, NBC Radio, *The Source* and *Talknet* supplied programming for more than 700 stations; all were divorced from the TV web (and industry) that the original brand had financed heavily in the 1930s, 1940s and 1950s.[60]

New York–based Westwood One, a communications conglomerate focused on syndicated programming services that were pitched to youthful listeners, was the proud owner of NBC's audio division for $50 million. The transition took place August 26, 1987. It must have been a slap in the face to any who knew the particulars and cared for NBC. Just two years earlier, Amway Corporation fetched $30 million from Westwood One for MBS, a Johnny-come-lately upstart web formed in 1934, some eight years after pioneer NBC's inception.[61] Throughout its life, prestige-, program-, personality- and profit-wise, MBS seldom held a candle to NBC. Were NBC and its entourage worth but a mere 66.67 percent more than MBS? (The difference would be reduced to just 28.2 percent if a higher purchase figure of $39 million reported for MBS is accurate.) Borrowing from Marcus Antonius' eloquence in William Shakespeare's epic *Julius Caesar*, it was perhaps the "most unkindest cut of all."

Meanwhile, NBC president Wright hadn't quite completed his obliteration of the final remnants of an illustrious broadcasting prodigy. He subsequently sold the eight NBC owned-and-operated radio affiliates piecemeal—five of those to Emmis Broadcasting Corporation. Their historical legacies met untimely ends, too: after 66 years, for instance, the web's flagship outlet (which had operated under the call letters, in order, WBAY, WEAF, WNBC, WRCA and WNBC again over its long existence) was an Emmis property in 1988. It hastily dropped NBC's enduring programming traditions to become an all-sports broadcaster locally in metropolitan New York.[62]

> In its final moments, WNBC's life flashed before its ears. "The First 66 Years" was a sixty-six minute show that few other stations could attempt....[63] Once again, by transcription, Vincent Lopez, Rudy Vallee, the Silver Masked Tenor, Amos 'n' Andy, and Fred Allen were heard from Radio City. Mae West reprised the performance that had caused any mention of her name to be

banned from NBC. Pearl Harbor, D-Day, the death of FDR, the assassination of JFK—all reminded listeners that this was once the station that millions were likely to tune to first at a time of crisis, and stay with the longest. For one more time there were Toscanini, Tallulah, Imus, and the words of Mister Blackwell of the Queensboro Corporation urging tenement dwellers to come out to Jackson Heights.

At 5:30 P.M. on 7 October 1988, WNBC signed off forever. WFAN would move down from 1050kHz to air its all-sports programming (and Don Imus) at the superior 660 spot. The Radio City studios had been dismantled, old equipment and memorabilia picked clean by staff and visitors. At its last sign-off, WNBC had been reduced to two model RE-20 microphones. As Alan Colmes delivered the final farewell, in the background a little xylophone rang three times.[64]

Colmes, given the privilege of signing off the station forever, spent the last afternoon interviewing WNBC alumni in person or by telephone. Among them were Ted Brown, Bill Cullen, Wolfman Jack, Ed McMahon, Bruce Morrow, Gabe Pressman and Buffalo Bob Smith. "I listened [to WNBC] since the mid–50s," said Colmes. "I was a toddler and Bill Cullen did the morning show. Today I'm getting an opportunity to interview and meet my radio heroes, the people who gave me my inspiration to be in this business."[65] It was a day of rejoicing tinged with sadness for about 60 staffers then looking for work.

Owen D. Young, Edward J. Nally, David Sarnoff, Merlin H. Aylesworth and others of their ilk who were present at the baptism of that enduring institution, NBC, might have been gagging even in death. "It's hard to even think about, because NBC, after all, was the leader," opined longtime NBC network announcer Del Sharbutt. NBC had been feted over the years with almost 1000 Emmy medals (more than any other network) and more than 100 prestigious George Foster Peabody honors. All of that would mean little to an industry then on life support. The pioneering radio network and its GE/RCA stakeholders was, at that instant, out of the radio business altogether. The final ax had swung.

In 1993, Westwood One engaged Infinity Broadcasting, owned by CBS, in managing its radio chains. In addition to its original Westwood One program service launched in 1975, plus the acquisitions of MBS and NBC, the company added CBS Radio News, CBS MarketWatch.com Radio Network, Fox News and CNNRadio—all audio news services—to its portfolio. Thus, in the 1990s, three of the four radio chains that had served the nation since transcontinental networks were formed, and all staunch rivals for most of their histories, were under the same umbrella. Only ABC, begun as the Blue chain of NBC, persisted independently of the other three.

By 1999, recalled one informant, "NBC is essentially gone ... as Westwood discontinues use of the 'brand name.' Most regular network operations ended in 1999, with some weekday morning programming surviving into 2000."[66] Early in the 21st century, that source claimed that while GE still licensed the NBC nomenclature to Westwood, "it is not promoted heavily." While that may be, there are still areas of the country in which denizens can tune in regularly to pithy national and international newsfeeds under the guise of NBC.

By mid 2008, Westwood One continued to offer radio stations a service it labeled *NBC News Radio*. It's advertised as "the only radio network with newscasts fully anchored by top television news talent," including NBC and MSNBC news anchors and reporters (as this is written in late 2008) Brian Williams, Ann Curry and Lester Holt. One-minute newscasts are provided on the hour weekdays from 6 A.M. to 10 P.M. Eastern Time and at 50 minutes past every hour weekdays from 6:50 A.M. to 9:50 P.M. Eastern Time. The reports airing at 50 minutes past the hour are replayed on the hour. *NBC News Radio* also presents simulcasts of breaking news events from both television webs.

This would hardly be imaginable to NBC News icons of an earlier age like Morgan Beatty, Alex Dreier, Pauline Frederick, H. V. Kaltenborn, Irving R. Levine, Robert McCormick, Henry J. Taylor, John W. Vandercook and their skillful voice-oriented colleagues. And what of the "one-minute network" being exclusively devoted to news if viewed from the perspectives of entertainers Fred Allen, Eddie Cantor, Phil Harris, Bill Stern, Rudy Vallee and a host of other key NBC properties?

News was, of course, but a slice of a representative day in the life of the dominant, all-powerful, all-pervasive NBC Radio. Now proffering no more than 17 scattered minutes of original material on a typical weekday—accompanied by utter (and deafening) silence on weekends—contemporary NBC Radio pales in comparison to the hours of amusement and information it afforded listeners back in the day. With as many as 100 broadcast hours of programming per week then compared to 17 minutes now, it begs the question: does the diminished schedule even mildly hint at how little our powers of concentration are able to focus for extended time periods in the modern era?

Regardless of that issue, in the meantime consider this possibility: David Sarnoff—who would be the first to admit he was never a radio man, yet was irrefutably a company man—has almost assuredly got to be turning over in his tomb.

4

COLUMBIA BROADCASTING SYSTEM
The House That Paley Built

The origins of the Columbia Broadcasting System (CBS) are couched in victrolas and fiascoes, rescues and cigars, copyrights and rebuffs. Its start was far more complex and colorful than that of its most formidable competitor, the National Broadcasting Company (NBC). It possibly dates to the fourth annual meeting of the National Association of Broadcasters (NAB) in September 1926—the precise year and month that NBC was initiated, coincidentally.

Promoter George A. Coats, a prosperous paving equipment manufacturer who began to smell money in radio, addressed credibly 30 delegates to the NAB gathering. Incensed by the American Society of Composers, Authors and Publishers (ASCAP), Coats' specific issue was the radio trade's heavy reliance on ASCAP artists for which he paid hefty talent fees. He urged the broadcasters to form their own entity to license performers and thereby avoid the costly sums they were shelling out to the ASCAP. The issue was emblematic of the impasses for which the NAB was founded three years earlier in 1923, as it sought to defend its own territory against an encroaching ASCAP federation. It would do so by directly confronting the organization on such matters.

Not 30 days following that fourth meeting of the NAB, member Arthur Judson of New York City participated in a series of high-level conversations that undeniably and powerfully impacted broadcasting's future forever. Born February 17, 1881, at Dayton, Ohio, he was to eventually become America's most recognizable, most potent concert manager. Judson had anticipated becoming a violin virtuoso in younger days but it never happened for him. Subsequently, he turned his attention to the details of managing other artists. In the formative years of the NAB, Judson was the refined manager of the Philadelphia Orchestra. Just as importantly and potentially more lucratively, he simultaneously operated a musicians' booking enterprise.

At 19, Judson was dean of the music conservatory at Denison University, a post he occupied for seven years, 1900–1907. While living in New York in 1915, he was tapped to manage the Philadelphia Orchestra. During his heyday in the early 1930s, Judson concurrently managed the Philadelphia contingent to 1936, plus the New York Philharmonic Symphony to 1956, along with a couple of seasonal music series: Lewisohn Stadium summer concerts on the campus of City College of New York and Robin Hood Dell East musicales in Philadelphia's Fairmount Park. Judson was also president of the Columbia Concerts Corporation, headed a different concert promotional outfit under his own moniker, remained the second largest stockholder of CBS shares and—in 1938—became sole owner of Columbia Records.

In the meantime, Judson was a dominant figure at Columbia Artists Management from its inception in 1932. When the feds began to probe the concert trade in 1941, seeking to eliminate monopolies, CBS sold its interest in the outfit to Judson and a few partners. The unit was renamed Judson, O'Neill & Judd and continued furnishing talent for CBS, NBC and local stations. Judson remained in that pivotal spot until October 9, 1963, when he resigned under a cloud at 82. A few weeks later, he formed a new concert management venture without direct ties to CBS. He died at 93 in Rye, New York, on January 28, 1975.

Judson knew little of the ethereal environment just developing in 1926 but was anxious about its potential implications on the concert market from which he drew his livelihood. The rise of a well-heeled underwriter, Radio Corporation of America (RCA) that emerged in the midst of that milieu, stirred him to investigate attentively.

He called upon RCA's David Sarnoff, then in the throes of organizing the future NBC, with a proposition for furnishing talent to ensure "cultural quality" and "adequate compensation" for artists performing on the air. He outlined his plan for an agency to supply polished professional talent to NBC at fees "sufficient to make it worth while and yet not ruin the business." Sarnoff asked for a written document that would spell out Judson's ideas in order for any action to be taken. Judson provided it a short time later. "Sarnoff read the plan with great interest and said that if it was within his power when he got his chain organized ... he would certainly put me in charge of the programs and of supplying the artists."[1]

When the initial announcement of NBC's creation was revealed to the public, Judson anticipated a call from Sarnoff. It never came. By then, in September 1926, Judson had summarily formed the Judson Radio Program Corporation. He let the matter slide until early January 1927. NBC had just announced that there would be a second chain aligned with the already existing one (the Red and Blue webs), adding still more urgency to the issue swirling in Judson's mind. Yet there was still no word from Sarnoff. The pressure mounting, Judson—accompanied by his confidante and comrade George Coats, for any moral support that might be required—called on Sarnoff again. Inquiring what was to be done with his proposal, the NBC emissary, then a vice president, replied: "Nothing." Taken aback, Judson admonished indignantly: "Then we'll organize our own chain!" The air in the room was fairly bristling. Sarnoff scolded: "You couldn't do it. I've just signed a contract to take a million dollars' worth of long lines from the telephone company. Even if you had a broadcasting station you couldn't get any wires."

Their dialogue initiated one of the great droll scenarios in U.S. corporate history. In January 1927, Judson and Coats persisted by launching United Independent Broadcasters Association (UIB), and persuading Major James Andrew White, an RCA castoff, to join their select little circle. White's history offers a colorful case study in itself.

Born in New York City on August 8, 1889, he died at 76 in May 1966. White maintained an active presence in radio until he turned 40 on May 1, 1930, thereby finishing 20 years' service in the medium. He worked for American Marconi Company beginning in 1910, eventually becoming its public relations director. Then he helped launch a trio of radio stations: WDY, Roselle Park, New Jersey; WJZ, Newark/New York; and WRC, Washington, D.C. White was also a veteran editor of *Wireless Age* and a pioneer sportscaster, although he was eclipsed in time by some younger lions like Norman Brokenshire, Ted Husing and Graham McNamee. In time White became the first president of the Columbia network, and later its managing director. He remained a CBS stockholder in retirement.

A fourth member of that intrepid panel of original maverick crusaders was a patron of the arts as well as a well-heeled heiress, Mrs. Christian (Betty Fleischmann) Holmes. When she learned of the group's financial plight, she contributed $6,000 to underwrite the hunt for affiliates. Some additional bail-out investments she supplied soon brought Holmes' early beneficence to $29,500.

A series of crucial rescues began to occur with her transactions, making it an even more incredible story. A media wag compared those rescues involving several parties to a Horatio Alger saga: "At desperate moments a mysterious rich person would turn up." There were numerous instances of the salvation of a network when everything was going awry.

Coats launched a search for stations that could be enticed to join their fledgling operation by approaching two Philadelphia siblings who jointly owned the city's WCAU: Leon Levy was a dentist and his brother Isaac D. (Ike) Levy was an attorney. Signing them for a guaranteed $500 payment from UIB weekly in exchange for airing 10 hours of UIB programming, Coats moved on. In all, he corralled a dozen outlets for a hookup with shows originating at New York's WOR.[2] UIB would re-sell the time to advertisers and create programming to fill those 10-hour allotments.[3]

The aggregate weekly commitment of time charges was $6,000. Of course, UIB had not yet taken in a dime from an advertiser, nor did it have staff, program talent or an estimate of American Telephone & Telegraph (AT&T) line charges—and not even any lines. Reacting skeptically, AT&T opted to deny UIB's use of its wires, convinced the operation was an unsound business risk. If approved, of course, it would have also potentially provided stiff competition for NBC, a principal patron of AT&T's long line services.

Judson and his UIB pals had no bona fide attraction toward running a radio web either. Their real interest was in supplying programming and personalities. In the early part of 1927, they diligently looked for the right person to manage the affair. Serious consideration was given to individuals at companies like Atwater Kent, Paramount Studios, Victor Talking Machine and Columbia Phonograph Record.

In the phonograph trade, meanwhile, rumors circulated that RCA, parent of NBC, was about to merge with the Victor Talking Machine Company. The latter outfit was in dire straits thanks to technological obsolescence and radio competition. At about the same time, Victor's chief rival, Columbia Phonograph Corporation, gained warm fuzzy feelings for United Independent Broadcasters Association. With 16 stations (none west of the Rockies) having signed on the dotted line and a weekly commitment of $8,000 for time alone, UIB was definitely in a bad way. Could their common plights by alleviated by merging their broadcasting and record-player interests?[4]

Columbia and UIB decided to go for it in an attempt to bail out one another. While retaining their independent corporate identities, the duo signed an agreement on April 5, 1927, creating the Columbia Phonograph Broadcasting System, Inc. (CPBS). Columbia instantly infused UIB with $163,000 in cash, precisely what Judson and his compatriots needed to keep afloat at the moment. The record-presser, at the same time, gained operational control of the radio network. That included the station-network appellation. Columbia hoped that would translate into increased sales of recordings and phonographs. CPBS signed a pact with Judson Radio Program Corporation to supply talent for 10 hours of programming weekly at about $10,000 per week. Unofficially, that put Judson and company in charge of the new chain's programming division.

The original 16 CPBS stations included:

> WOR, Newark WEAN, Providence
> WNAC, Boston WFBL, Syracuse
> WMAK, Buffalo WCAU, Philadelphia
> WJAS, Pittsburgh WADC, Akron
> WAIU, Columbus WKRC, Cincinnati
> WGHP, Detroit WMAQ, Chicago
> KOIL, Council Bluffs KMOX, St. Louis
> WOWO, Fort Wayne WCAO, Baltimore

CPBS collaborated with AT&T that summer to firm up a deal to use its wires for transmitting the programming. After several postponements, the new chain finally debuted. An entry in *This Day in Network Radio* describes the watershed event in radio broadcasting:

> CBS premiers Sunday, Sept. 18, 1927 as Columbia Phonograph Broadcasting System; chain VP Maj. J. Andrew White master of ceremonies for inaugural with 22-piece symphony conducted by Howard Barlow, Metropolitan Opera Co. cast in "The King's Henchman"; New York Philhar-

monic, Philadelphia Symphony Orchestra featured same day; 16-station hookup originated at Newark WOR (replaced by New York WABC in 15 months); hookup went east to Boston, west to Council Bluffs, north to Detroit, south to St. Louis.[5]

That debut was an orchestra fantasy written and narrated by composer-critic Deems Taylor. In "What We Thought of the First Columbia Broadcasting Program," *Radio Broadcast* reported in its December 1927 issue, some three months after the fact: "Probably not a dozen people in the country ... heard it. No one not paid to do so, as we are, could have survived it.... Our stomach is still unsettled." With reviews like that one, if commonplace, Columbia needed help on more fronts than purely financial.

H. C. Cox, identified as president of the Columbia Broadcasting System, said in an advance story appearing on premier morning in *The New York Times* that "more than one hundred artists participating in a six-hour program replete in variety" would titillate those with radio receivers. But after losing $100,000 in its first month when advertising sales failed to reach projections, Columbia decided to opt out of its contract at the end of 30 days (a provision stated in writing already), leaving UIB's original partnership once more holding the bag.

A desperate Arthur Judson turned again to the well-heeled dowager who had earlier pulled him out of the fire, Betty Holmes. Learning that she was aboard an ocean liner somewhere in the Atlantic, he anxiously cabled her. By wire, she came to his aid again, immediately making available another $45,000. It was enough to cover whatever outstanding debts the web had rung up with the telephone company. Parenthetically, there's little reason to fret about Mrs. Holmes' checkwriting activities: she reportedly sold her stock sometime later for $3 million, a none-too-shabby return on her investment.[6]

After paying off AT&T, Judson faced Columbia Phonograph president H. C. Cox, who for a brief while presided over both the broadcasting and record manufacturing operations. Cox had obviously enjoyed watching Judson squirm through all of this. It was a proud moment for him, and he took some special delight in telling Judson, "Now the network belongs to us." Judson had not yet revealed his latest escapade. "Not so fast," he remarked. "Well," was Cox's retort, "you can't pay your telephone bill, so it all belongs to us." "I'd like to show you something," Judson responded. Reaching into his pocket he produced an AT&T receipt showing that the transmission firm had been paid in full.

Cox was bowled over in surprise. When he recovered, in exchange for 30 hours of broadcasting time and $10,000, he relinquished all of Columbia's shares in the network and stepped aside.

Cox wasn't quite as shrewd as his post possibly required. Shortly before this, but within the same time frame while running Columbia Phonograph, he was heavily influencing the programming decisions at CPBS. While Cox occupied his fleeting capacity with the network, Judith Waller, station manager at Chicago's WMAQ, called on him in New York. She came to the Big Apple on a shopping trip, in fact, hoping to find a web for one of her station's properties, *Amos 'n' Andy*, to give them greater exposure. She recalled their conversation that day about like this:

> Cox: What is it you're trying to get us to buy, Miss Waller?
> Waller: A daily blackface act.
> Cox: Well, we have *Moran and Mack* in New York.
> Waller: This isn't a *Moran and Mack*. This is not a song and dance act. This is a continued story.
> Cox: Miss Waller, do you mean to tell me that you believe an act can go on a network at the same time every day in the week, five days in succession?
> Waller: Yes, I believe that.
> Cox: I think you'd better go back to Chicago. It's very plain to see that you know nothing about radio.[7]

Amos 'n' Andy, of course, was snapped up by NBC and became, according to historian John Dunning, "the most popular radio show of all time."

It was aural broadcasting's good fortune that creator-writer-producers Elaine Carrington, Frank and Anne Hummert, Irna Phillips and many more of their stripe—all having bought into the serialized story line—were never influenced by Cox's limited thinking. The same could be said for weekday show folks like Tommy Bartlett, Bob (Elliott) and Ray (Goulding), Rosemary Clooney, Bing Crosby, Bob Crosby, Arthur Godfrey, Robert Q. Lewis, Art Linkletter, Curt Massey and Martha Tilton, Don McNeill, Jack Smith, Fred Waring and scads of others. If they had believed what the temporary titular head of CPBS avowed, the medium might have been bereft of a whole lot of first-rate entertainment.

Arthur Judson's next appeal for a lifeline of support was presented to an affluent Philadelphia contractor-sportsman, Jerome H. Louchheim, a pal of WCAU's Ike Levy. Born in the City of Brotherly Love on November 24, 1873, Louchheim died there at 71 on April 4, 1945. In between, from 1893 to 1933, he worked for firms that excavated large tracts of land and built railroad tunnels and subways. With four decades of experience, he organized a partnership with similar pursuits, Louchheim, Brown & McDonough Construction Company. On the side, he owned and bred race horses, always hoping to enter a winner in the Kentucky Derby, a prize that habitually eluded him. Louchheim was, in addition, a director of several banks and commercial institutions.

Over the outspoken protests of his attorney, who strongly counseled against it, Louchheim wrote Arthur Judson a check and temporarily took control of the broadcasting business. An obituary later labeled him as "one time chairman of the board of the Columbia Broadcasting System," which was true, although it may not have been expressed then in those precise terms. The Levy brothers, incidentally, also bought in as shareholders. The trio provided a combined $135,000 on that occasion.[8] That rescue assured UIB it could pay its AT&T obligations for several months into the future.

A consensus to rename the network Columbia Broadcasting System took effect November 19, 1927, with UIB and CBS coexisting side by side.[9] Meanwhile, Louchheim, demonstrating both occupational acumen and political savvy, renegotiated the affiliates' contracts with the web. The chain would pay only for sponsored shows while airing sustained programs without any dollars changing hands. NBC, to the contrary, was charging its member stations for every feature, underwritten or not.

Furthermore, in frequent trips to Manhattan, Louchheim and Ike Levy helped pioneer announcer White, a key UIB player, to attract to the network such leading advertisers as Bromo-Seltzer, Chrysler, Dodge and *True Story* magazine. Yet the promise of a solution quickly faded as most advertisers turned to a far more alluring NBC. As indebtedness piled up, more cash transfusions were needed. New stock was issued several times as Louchheim came to the rescue again and again. By the middle of 1928, CBS was in debt to the tune of $1 million, about half of it owed to Louchheim. As if that wasn't enough bad news, Louchheim suffered a hip fracture that summer and, for multiple reasons, decided to pull out of the venture entirely. Before doing so, he urged Ike Levy to "Get Leon to go to New York and assume the presidency of CBS." Leon Levy declined, preferring the City of Brotherly Love as his permanent residence.

Needing programming for WCAU, Ike Levy immediately sought a replacement. He found one in the work of Samuel Paley, a Russian Jewish immigrant born December 15, 1874, who through sheer ingenuity, commitment and hard work had built an impressive cigar-manufacturing empire in Philadelphia employing hundreds of workers. His daughter, Blanche, coincidentally, had wed Leon Levy. Sam Paley proposed that his son, William, might be an alternate solution to Ike's dilemma. Actually, prior to Jerome Louchheim's entry into the financial picture, Sam—with the blessing of both Levy and Louchheim—had mentioned the notion of managing the upstart broadcasting business to Bill Paley. "I don't want anything to do with this pipsqueak radio network—this phony chain," the younger Paley reportedly replied.[10] Yet, at that moment, he seemed to be waiting in the wings.

In one of its initial time sales, CBS contracted with the Paleys' Congress Cigar Company through that firm's youthful vice president and advertising manager, William S. Paley. Congress bought a series of 26 shows, *The La Palina Smoker*, to promote its La Palina cigars.[11] Debuting in 1928, in rapid succession sales of the La Palina brand perked up dramatically. Young Paley had introduced a provocative "Miss La Palina" who sang and quipped with male smokers. Sales of La Palinas doubled in four months, surpassing a million cigars daily. *Fortune* termed it "one of radio's earliest spectacular achievements." So astounded were the Paleys with the turn of events, in fact, that William S. Paley committed $45,000 to the audio enterprise. Then he got busy with homework.

Canvassing Manhattan ad agencies about radio's financial prospects, he learned that most were cool to the idea of any long-term growth potential. Yet, trusting minority opinions and his own instinct, with the concurrence of his father, who recruited some added investors within the Paley ranks, young Bill decided to put half his fortune into the venture. "I had about a million dollars of my own and I was willing to risk any or all of it in radio," he allowed.

On September 25, 1928, three days before his 27th birthday, Bill Paley paid $417,000 for a 41 percent share of UIB-CBS stock. Ike Levy owned another 20 percent. The remainder of the stock was held by Paley kin, Louchheim, Judson and Holmes. The Paley family, including Bill, held 50.3 percent of the new web's shares, giving them controlling interest. Of course, all were looking to Bill to make good on their tenuous investments.

William S. (Bill) Paley could be calm, cool and collected. At times he could just as readily be cantankerous, cunning and careless. As chairman (and majority stock owner) of the Columbia Broadcasting System, his post afforded him opportunities to talk softly, labor quietly and gain what he ultimately desired—if he couldn't get it any other way—by brandishing a big stick.

According to one source, "He planned to take a six-month leave of absence from the cigar company, get CBS-UIB in better shape, and then go back to selling cigars." But it didn't work out that way. Three weeks into it young Paley was so entranced by the prospects of his new venture that he couldn't let it go. As it turned out, of course, he was to run it for decades, still holding the reins as chairman of the board at his death in New York at 89 on October 26, 1990. Sam Paley, Bill's father, on the other hand, was a director of the broadcasting enterprise for some years before his own death at 88 on March 31, 1963, in Palm Beach, Florida.

Just who was this intrepid young amateur entrepreneur who took it upon himself to commit his family fortune to an upstart challenger with a litany of broken promises in its epigrammatic history? And more importantly, who in his right mind would be willing to go up against the powerful, prosperous, prevailing principal of the industry, NBC, with the bold commitment of RCA's enormous resources and resolve behind it?

William S. Paley, it would turn out, was a brash playboy, then depicting an image that characterized him throughout his life that he seemed to enjoy. He was a man willing to take risks and he liked a good fight, frequently demonstrating a highly competitive nature. That regularly led him into frays with his opposite number, RCA chairman David Sarnoff, who kept a large hand in the affairs of subsidiary NBC. While both men were Jewish by ancestry, Sarnoff was proud of it while Paley tended to routinely hide his heritage. The two sparred tenaciously to secure their respective operations, and loved nothing better than pulling a fast one on their chief opponent. Yet they could work together to stave off potential governmental intrusion when the industry's collective interests were being challenged by interfering watchdogs.

Sarnoff was the dignified, cultured corporate executive displaying a marked sophistication in his business dealings, also considered by colleagues to be distant, unapproachable and aloof. Paley, on the other hand, preferred the popular, flamboyant lifestyle, was more open to input by trusted confidantes (whether he accepted their observations or not) and routinely surrounded himself with beautiful women in the midst of a fast-paced social life. Born January 28, 1901, in Chicago, he spent most of his career on securing the prosperity of CBS, Inc.

The Paley family's original monetary commitment to CBS increased by another $1.2 million within a few months. Added investments shored up America's second broadcasting domain, including the purchase of network flagship station WABC in New York.[12] Those call letters were altered to WCBS at 10 p.m. on Saturday, November 2, 1946. CBS relied on WOR as its originating outlet until WABC was acquired.

> When WOR refused to clear additional time for the CBS network, WABC stepped in to become the second affiliate, a move it hoped would justify a power increase. For a few weeks in 1928, WABC was the CBS station on Sunday, Tuesday, and Thursday, with WOR carrying the network on the other four days, but soon WOR dropped CBS completely.
>
> In November 1928, Columbia offered to buy either of its New York area affiliates, and President William S. Paley negotiated with both [A. H.] Grebe [WABC owner] and Bamberger [WOR dry goods store owner]. WOR's facilities were superior, but Paley chose the less-expensive WABC, and in December the Atlantic Broadcasting Company became a subsidiary of CBS. The sale price was $390,000, though the appraised value of the studios and transmitter was just $130,000.... Among the assets were goods [Grebe] accepted as payment from sponsors: jewelry, kitchenware, and reportedly even some live chickens....
>
> With the purchase of WABC, CBS itself was on the air.[13]

No need to worry, however. Paley's determination, hard work and negotiating skills repaid his investments many times over as he created a commercial venture worth hundreds of times what he and others coughed up. His ability to hammer out pacts with affiliates, artists and advertisers turned CBS into a formidable player in the industry, eventually surpassing its most experienced rival (NBC) to finally dislodge it from years of occupying the proverbial catbird seat.

In short order, Paley merged the two webs (UIB-CBS) into one, Columbia Broadcasting System, Inc. He increased the amount of outstanding stock and sold it to acquire badly needed liquid reserves.

Thenceforth for the next two decades, a system cue delivered by network announcers identified the chain as each program left the air with "This is CBS, the Columbia Broadcasting System." In the late 1940s, an edict was handed down from Paley's 35th story office that those announcements would be forevermore altered to "This is the CBS Radio Network." The intent was to clearly demarcate radio from the emerging TV channel.

In March 1929, station contracts were altered to pay the outlets $50 for each hour of network time they carried rather than $500 a week for 10 hours regardless of time. The stations, meanwhile, paid the network for sustaining (unsponsored) programs and were at liberty to sell them to local underwriters. Thus the affiliates and the network lowered their financial sights until the business could operate profitably. In the meantime, Paley kept Judson and White on his staff as program advisers.

Soon CBS was offering its stations 20 hours of programming per week, double the original number. Paley displayed a suave professional manner (temporarily belying his playboy image) in conducting straightforward business transactions. In renegotiated contracts with the affiliates, CBS would pay them only after a fifth sponsored hour was carried. Another new clause: a station's time might be preempted by any sponsored show. Furthermore, Paley personally set out to call on advertising agencies with the intent of deriving and channeling more interest in CBS programming.

The original CBS affiliates' contract, effective in September 1927, enjoined CBS outlets from making their facilities available to any other chain broadcasting company; a similar "exclusivity" provision appeared in succeeding contracts. It wasn't until 1937, nevertheless, that a provision was added enjoining CBS from furnishing programs to other stations in any territory served by an affiliate. The clause, from the standard contract introduced in 1937, read:

> Columbia will continue the station as the exclusive Columbia outlet in the city in which the station is located and will so publicize the station, and will not furnish its exclusive network programs to any other station in that city, except in case of public emergency. The station will operate as the exclusive Columbia outlet in such city and will so publicize itself, and will not join for broadcasting purposes any other formally organized or regularly constituted group of broadcasting stations. The station shall be free to join occasional local, State-wide or regional hookups to broadcast special events of public importance.

During its extensive investigations into the networks' practices in 1937, much of which addressed monopolistic tendencies within broadcasting, the Federal Communications Commission heard CBS's Paley testify that "a new network could not do any better than CBS was doing":

> I cannot see any advantage in organizing something new which I do not think would have any particular advantages or could do a particular job in any better fashion than we can do it. I don't think the public interest is involved just because two people happen to supply a service as against having one person supply an adequate service, especially since by having the one person supply the adequate service we can have greater solidarity and permanence of the very thing he is trying to build up.[14]

But in its assessment, the Federal Communications Commission met Paley's argument with consternation and condemnation:

> This attempted justification of exclusivity, however, fails to take into account the function of competition in our economy. CBS programs may be good; they are not perfect. CBS has not been granted an exclusive franchise to engage in network broadcasting; it has no right to exclude others from the field on the ground that it is already furnishing adequate service to the public, or on any other ground. Competition is in the public interest not because the particular service offered by a new unit is better than the existing service, but because competition is the incentive for both the old and the new to develop better services.[15]

NBC would ultimately receive a kick in the shin when the FCC ordered it to disassociate itself from one of its two webs following the FCC scrutiny. But CBS still felt the sting of a slap in the face from those same investigations.

Across the years contract writing was an ongoing, practically routine matter of business between affiliates and their networks. Provisions attempted to settle disputes and, more frequently, anticipate potential problems and disagreements before they got very far. They covered a wide range of disciplines. A 1937 clause forestalling program rejections by CBS affiliates was representative and read like this:

> The station will broadcast all network sponsored programs furnished to it by Columbia during the time when the station is licensed to operate.... Either the station or Columbia may on special occasions substitute for one or more of such sponsored programs sustaining programs devoted to education, public service or events of public interest without any obligation to make any payment on account thereof, and in the event of such substitution by either party it will notify the other by wire as soon as practicable by deciding to make such programs or the product advertised thereon as not being in the public interest the station may, on 3 weeks' prior notice to Columbia, refuse to broadcast such program, unless during such notice period such reasonable objection of the station shall be satisfied.

From September 1929 until the mid 1960s, CBS occupied the upper 10 floors of a newly constructed edifice at 485 Madison Avenue, New York City. When Paley signed a 10-year lease, it signified CBS's growing resiliency and permanency. Obviously, the upstart chain had been exonerated from the naysayers' earlier claims, by then viewed as "here to stay."

A few months before, when CBS aired 10 hours of continuous reportage of election returns with Herbert Hoover and Al Smith vying for U.S. president, it got a pretty solid indication that listeners loved it: 12,000 congratulatory telegrams arrived following live coverage by announcer Ted Husing speaking from the city room of *The New York World.*

In 1928, the web boasted 17 affiliates or four percent of all stations then in operation. Paley appeared on the air for the first time on January 8, 1929, to announce that CBS had the largest chain of permanent stations in radio history, by then serving 42 cities through 49 outlets. By 1933, the number of affiliates swelled to 91 or 16 percent of all stations, including seven that were owned and operated by CBS: WBT, Charlotte; WBBM, Chicago; WKRC, Cincinnati; WCCO, Minneapolis; WABC, New York; KMOX, St. Louis; and WJSV, Washington. All of those projected 50,000 watts and had no restrictions on operating time, giving them momentous stature in their diverse markets.

Just over a decade later, in 1939, CBS held eight stations, including all of the above except Cincinnati's WKRC, which the network sold that year. It had also added Boston's WEEI under lease arrangement while purchasing Los Angeles' KNX. All were 50,000-watters except WEEI with 5,000 watts. By that time (1939), CBS maintained 113 affiliated stations while its principal rival, NBC, split 167 outlets between dual webs (Red and Blue).

While CBS minimally surpassed NBC in the race for most affiliates in 1931 (76 to 75), those broadcasting giants jockeyed back and forth winning and losing first place for years. The first sign of sustained numerical strength fell NBC's way from 1938 to 1943; 1941 reflected the greatest disparity, with NBC boasting 225 stations for its combined webs to CBS's single web with 118. The figures drew much closer in subsequent years with the two competitors again vying for the leadership. That persisted throughout radio's golden age, with NBC amassing a handful of higher numbers most of those years.

But all that changed after the golden age passed. CBS took off like a rocket in 1964 (CBS, 227; NBC, 202). Of course, NBC had only one chain then. While comparative figures have been widely circulated only through 1982, CBS's lead never wavered and was often quite large. The year 1981 reflected the greatest disparity in which CBS held the upper hand: 400 to 315. You may have read earlier that those were the slumping years for NBC, particularly after the longrunning *Monitor* magazine marathon was disbanded (1975). By contrast, the news and feature vignettes that CBS offered in that period kept a flock of local station owners-managers satisfied.

If you read Chapter 3, you may recall that NBC's Pacific Coast Network was formed on

April 5, 1927, and by 1928, AT&T made available long lines to the West Coast. That allowed NBC to be the first web to stake a permanent transcontinental hookup. But by 1929, CBS still had no tie-ups with the West Coast. The fact that CBS had no such good fortune and NBC did probably festered in Bill Paley's craw. The speculation is based on his spirited aggressive stance so often exhibited in subsequent years.

Not one to be thwarted for long, however, Paley turned to thriving West Coast automobile dealership operator Don Lee. Lee—whom a media pundit dubbed a "mini-mogul"—owned San Francisco's KFRC and Los Angeles' KHJ and was just then putting together a coastal radio chain.[16] He invited Paley to California to spend some time on his yacht chatting. When the two returned to shore, they hammered out terms for a contract that made the Don Lee Network the West Coast unit of the Columbia Broadcasting System.[17] Lee was to be CBS's far Western agent, and from that time forward, CBS had coast-to-coast connections.[18] It was a real coup d'état—another huge feather in Paley's cap, visibly testifying once more to his incisive business knack.

Paley's strengths often rose to the forefront when he was faced with adversity. Owing a bank $125,000 in June 1929, he risked losing control of CBS by trading half ownership in the corporation for shares of stock in Paramount-Famous-Lasky Studios worth $3.8 million. If CBS earned $2 million in profits in 1930–1931, the Studios would buy back the shares in 1932 at a premium. If CBS couldn't deliver on its end of the bargain, nevertheless, it could retain its stock and Paramount-Famous-Lasky would own half of CBS.

Within four months, the stock market crashed. In spite of the devastating economic downturn it fostered, Paley reached his goal and retrieved his appreciating CBS shares. As a dividend, with the studio (by then renamed Paramount-Publix) suffering a stock decline, Paley was credited with saving it by underwriting its debt to CBS. That gave him an unexpected intro into Hollywood.

Recalling this later, at an initial party in his honor—arranged by Lasky—he discovered "just about every glamorous movie star I had ever heard of.... As time went on, I found myself at various dinner parties talking with Marlene Dietrich, Joan Crawford, Norma Shearer, Jean Harlow, Madeleine Carroll, Ginger Rogers, Loretta Young, Paulette Goddard, Norma Talmadge. I met the moguls of motion pictures, too." Of one party, he declared: "It seemed like an unbelievable paradise."[19] To a playboy acquiring the mantle of industry maharaja, it must have been pure ecstasy.

By the end of 1931, the Little Network That Could had in its employ 408 individuals exclusive of talent, which accounted for another 968 personalities. During that year (1931), it supplied its affiliates with 1,437 commercial hours of material and 5,113 hours of sustaining features for a total of 6,550 hours of programming.[20] CBS was definitely a presence to be reckoned with by then, and slowly it was also making inroads—significant inroads—into what had been NBC's private sphere of influence. The rivalry between the upstart and the well-heeled, slightly older web with the backing of a behemoth corporate parent was becoming more pronounced as time elapsed. Was there a chance CBS could overtake NBC? Pick a realm. It was almost certainly bound to happen. While it wouldn't come about overnight, it would still arrive all in good time.

An academic Arthur Judson, still a shareholder, had been principally responsible for CBS's programming fare since the network's earliest days. But desiring a freer hand to maneuver there, Paley transferred him into a new role heading the Columbia Artists, Inc., and Columbia Concerts Corporation, previously noted. Those entities soon processed half the touring artist bookings in America while allowing Paley a free hand in schedule manipulation, a challenge he relished.

According to published figures, Columbia Artists managed 110 radio performers in 1937, took in revenues of $194,757 and earned a profit of $82,671. In the 1938–1939 season Columbia Concerts managed 120 artists plus 17 dancing groups, special attractions and ensembles. Its revenue for the period was $426,413 and it contributed earnings of $94,038. The latter organization also operated Columbia Concerts Service, organizing concerts in communities across America. It served about 375 cities and towns in 1938 with revenues for 1937–1938 of $165,454 and a profit of $20,418.[21]

On December 17, 1938, CBS purchased from Consolidated Film Industries, Inc., the capital stock of the American Record Corporation with its subsidiaries: Brunswick Record Corporation, American Record Corporation of California, Columbia Phonograph Company, and Master Records, Inc. CBS altered the outfit's umbrella nomenclature to Columbia Phonograph Company, a manufacturer of phonograph recordings for home use. Furthermore, in August 1940, CBS also entered the transcription province.[22]

In its first dozen years, CBS net earnings through 1938 totaled $22,522,471. Of this sum shareholders received more than $13.3 million in cash dividends and another $3.5 million in stock dividends with the balance remaining as current assets.

> By 1930 Paley ... continued to feel like a "perpetual underdog" in his competition with NBC, which had fancier offices, larger studios, better equipment, and stronger financing.
>
> A little incident helped Paley to attack his giant opponent. One day in the early 1930s, walking down Broadway, he noticed that a few people were waiting to see a mediocre movie at the luxurious Capitol Theater, while across the street a great many people had lined up to get into a run-down theater showing a very good movie.
>
> "The analogy struck me so forcibly that I never forgot it," Paley reports in his autobiography. "'You know,' I said to myself, 'for radio, it's what goes into a person's house that counts. The radio listener doesn't know what kind of office I have, what kind of studios I have ... I just have to put things on the air that the people like more.... I've got to find things that will be popular.'"[23]

An ambitious Paley wasn't wearing blinders. He was fully aware that in the 1928–1929 epoch, of 60 sponsored shows then on the air in what would later become known as the primetime hours, NBC's dual webs claimed 49 of them, leaving CBS just 11. It wasn't something that a motivated, astute young man on the way up could ignore without giving it his best shot. After all, the thing he had come to invest his life in depended on it. And the business was watching his every move to see just what response he would make.

Amos 'n' Andy had, of course, been lost to NBC prior to Paley's arrival at CBS. Thanks to Columbia Phonograph Broadcasting System president H. C. Cox's ineptness, that jewel slipped through his fingers when Cox miscalculated what Judith Waller was offering on her web-seeking trip to the Big Apple in 1928. But Paley was still able to profess with some degree of accuracy that he "discovered" crooner Bing Crosby (1903–1977) and put him under contract to CBS.[24]

> In June 1931, it happened that CBS owner-chairman William S. Paley was on a voyage aboard the S. S. *Europa* bound for the ship's namesake continent, then crossing the Atlantic. Paley was treated to Crosby's captivating chords in the middle of the ocean, apparently for the very first time. On one of his daily cavorts around the deck, the customarily antsy Paley heard Crosby crooning his new Decca recording *I Surrender, Dear*, piercing the sea breeze from a portable phonograph brought on deck by somebody. Not recognizing the artist, Paley momentarily interrupted the device. On the record label below impresario Gus Arnheim's moniker there appeared, in minuscule lettering, "Chorus—Bing Crosby." It was definitely an auspicious moment, whether anyone realized it or not. Paley wasted little time cabling his office at CBS in New York with orders to deliver Crosby immediately.[25]

On his return, Paley signed Crosby for a quarter-hour beginning September 2, 1931, at 11 o'clock weeknights at an unprecedented rate of $1,500 weekly. Contrast that with the norm for such performances of $100 weekly at the pinnacle of the Great Depression. Crosby quickly became CBS's early darling; that singular act appeared to work in the chain's favor for much of Crosby's show business career. Even after a long stint at NBC (1935–1946) followed by a briefer one at ABC (1946–1949), Crosby returned "home" to CBS to become its property again, enduring as one of its famous final headliners of the golden age (extending to 1962).

Paley and his network turned up other unparalleled performers in the early days of broadcasting that also were destined for iconic status. Among the finds were still more gifted singers like Morton Downey (1901–1985) and Kate Smith (1907–1986), both of whom surfaced in 1930. Smith remained practically steadfast with CBS for the initial 17 years of her radio career.[26] Downey, on the other hand, wavered frequently.[27] His inability to put down permanent roots mirrored a tendency among a number of CBS discoveries in the early years: once they gained fame at CBS, some of those talents were lured to a more prosperous and celebrated NBC.

Plenty of other headliners and noteworthy shows exclusively or predominantly identified with CBS over the same timespan. Included in its versatile stable of stars were impresarios Alfredo Antonini, Archie Bleyer, Percy Faith, Lud Gluskin, Wilbur Hatch and Leith Stevens; the vocal ensembles of The Andrews Sisters, The Chordettes, The McQuire Sisters, The Mariners and The Salt Lake City Tabernacle Choir; singers Gene Autry, Rosemary Clooney, Janette Davis, Vaughn Monroe, Jack Smith and Arthur Tracy; comediennes Eve Arden, Lucille Ball and Hat-

In his peak years (late 1940s to mid–1950s), Arthur Godfrey turned up on more American radio and television sets more times per week than any other performer. With nearly 15 hours of network entertainment to his credit weekly, "the Old Redhead" contributed 12 percent of CBS's annual revenues to his web's coffers. Overprotective of his status, he dumped his headliners and alienated his once-adoring public.

tie McDaniel; instrumentalist E. Power Biggs; sportscasters Phil Rizzuto and Pat Summerall; and entertainers Major Edward Bowes, Arthur Godfrey, Robert Q. Lewis and Art Linkletter.[28]

By 1953, one of those accounted for generating enough advertising revenue to subscribe $27 million (12 percent) of CBS's annual budget. Arthur Godfrey (1903–1983), the original infotainer, appeared on the ether more often than anybody else during his heyday.[29] With a live 90-minute daily morning radio show, *Arthur Godfrey Time*, an hour of that simulcast four days weekly on CBS-TV; a half-hour to an hour of taped highlights of that show replayed on weekends on CBS Radio under the appellation *Arthur Godfrey's Digest*; a live half-hour of *Talent Scouts* simulcast on CBS Radio and TV on Monday nights; and a live Wednesday night variety hour on CBS-TV, *Arthur Godfrey and His Friends*, the Old Redhead was the dominant player in the CBS collect. Occupying nearly 15 hours of network time, he appealed to an aggregate 80 million fans weekly. He could also be heard on Columbia Records. Godfrey was branded "the greatest salesman who ever stood before a microphone" by *Time* magazine and "the greatest communicator of the century" by a biographer.[30] Both may have hit the nail on the head.

Bill Paley and Arthur Godfrey were never intimates and, in fact, seldom hinted they were sharing the same wavelength, much less the same planet. While Paley recognized Godfrey's ability to keep advertisers and audiences satisfied, he wasn't a fan.[31] Godfrey, on the other hand, repeatedly referenced Dr. Frank Stanton on the air—Paley's hand-picked president of CBS—when mentioning officialdom. Yet he derided Paley on several occasions, informing listeners that it was he—Godfrey—who paid the network's expenses for the whole day, even before Paley got out of bed every morning! That galled Paley, although he isn't known to have challenged the Old Redhead with his displeasure.

Unfortunately for CBS, however, Godfrey developed an innate ability, an ostensible addiction, for figuratively shooting himself in the foot. From his lofty broadcasting perch, in late 1953, he began a slow but unmistakable descent from grace after his ego got in the way. One by one he fired the loyal group of professional musicians who surrounded him, and whom legions of Americans admired. As his staff eroded, so did his popularity as well as the audiences he had charmed for nearly a decade, leaving him a lonely, crippled public figure. Eventually he clung to but a half-hour of taped airtime per day. Godfrey persisted nearly two more decades with a rotating singer or two instead of the familiar budding entourage of happier days. He ended his agony by removing himself from the ether on April 30, 1972, at age 68. As CBS's one-time top moneymaker, it was a sad finish to a career that once rode the crest of American amusement.

In another realm, CBS never attempted to match the proliferation of quality musical fare that NBC proffered to its listeners. Included were *The Metropolitan Opera*, *The NBC Symphony Orchestra* and NBC's "Monday Night of Music" that gave them *The Bell Telephone Hour*, *The Cities Service Band of America*, *The Railroad Hour* and *The Voice of Firestone*. All of those appealed directly to refined, urbane, sophisticated tastes, a distinct segment of the radio audience. Yet CBS maintained at least a fraction of NBC's inventory as it bid for a cultured crowd, too.

Paley was particularly proud to have signed the New York Philharmonic Symphony early to perform exclusively on CBS. His opposite number, David Sarnoff, made no secret about loving such music personally; he would have probably filled his chains' schedules with it if he had figured a way to do it. It was a special feather in Paley's cap, therefore, to acquire the Philharmonic in a long-term pact. Reportedly, that entourage's going to CBS gave Sarnoff pause, enough for him to create the NBC Symphony Orchestra with Arturo Toscanini holding the baton. Toscanini had earned a reputation as maestro of both the New York Philharmonic Symphony and the Metropolitan Opera. A few more musical treats for the uppercrust tuning to CBS included *The Longines Symphonette*, *On a Sunday Afternoon*, *World Music Festivals* and some Percy Faith musicales under varied soubriquets.

CBS also performed nobly in the comedy department, tendering a passel of durable sitcoms that surfaced in the latter 1940s through half of the 1950s. You will read about them a little later in this chapter.

One province in which CBS unequivocally excelled was drama. A handful of prestigious, quality anthologies consistently exceeded run-of-the-mill fare produced by CBS's counterparts in classic mainstream outings. Among their number were *The Columbia Workshop* (1936–1947, not continuous, and sometimes under varied monikers), *The Mercury Theater on the Air* (1938, 1946) and *The CBS Radio Workshop* (1956–1957).

Some other wares from this species were typically a cut above average: *Let's Pretend* (1934–1954), *Lux Radio Theater* (1935–1954), *Dr. Christian* (1937–1954), *Suspense* (1942–1962), *The Whistler* (1942–1946, 1947–1955, sometimes airing on a West Coast hookup only), and a few soap operas that exhibited incredibly enhanced writing, direction and acting—*Hilltop House* (1937–1941, 1948–1955), *Ma Perkins* (1938, 1942–1960), *Perry Mason* (1943–1955) and *Wendy Warren and the News* (1947–1958). Still more primetime and weekend narratives were clearly identified with CBS over long running periods: *Grand Central Station* (1938–1940, 1941, 1944–1953), *Armstrong Theater of Today* (1941–1954), *Stars Over Hollywood* (1941–1954), *Mr. Keen, Tracer of Lost Persons* (1942–1951, 1952–1955), *The FBI in Peace & War* (1944–1958), *Mr. and Mrs. North* (1947–1955) and *Yours Truly, Johnny Dollar* (1949–1952).

Perhaps the most famous non-news radio broadcast ever was also a drama airing on CBS. On October 30, 1938, on its regular Sunday night entry *The Mercury Theater on the Air*, director Orson Welles, and a company of radio actors performed a fictional play based on H. G. Wells' fantasy *The War of the Worlds*. While it didn't affect the world, it did thrust a part of this nation into utter pandemonium. Despite repeated announcements that it was "only a play," thousands of dumbstruck Americans panicked, believing what they were hearing to be real, occurring in real time as they tuned in. (Could one's ears really deceive him?) The tale concerned the mythical landing of Martians near the rural hamlet of Grovers Mill, New Jersey. Because the broadcast exhibited such strong qualities of expediency, many people along the Eastern seaboard literally feared for their lives, some of them attempting to get as far from the coastline as they possibly could.

Of course, not everyone was taken in by Welles' Halloween Eve practical joke, but enough were that the broadcast became memorable for its sheer disruption of normal patterns in many people's lives—at least until they were convinced it was all a hoax. Some had a tough time later living their actions down as they faced friends in their local communities, having succumbed to being thoroughly duped.[32] The power of radio to cloud men's minds was never more effectively demonstrated than on that singular night.

As the pressures of eroding audiences and advertisers mounted at mid century, an innovative CBS developed a novel narrative breed. Much as NBC introduced a strain of contemporary police dramas for older listeners starting with *Dragnet* in 1949 (followed by *Broadway Is My Beat, The Lineup, Twenty-First Precinct*, et al. on varied nets), in the early 1950s, CBS came along with a new twist, initiating adult-themed western dramas. The adventures of the plainclothed lawman targeted toward mature audiences (although there was little to excite the censors to be found there) began with *Gunsmoke* on CBS on April 26, 1952. Overnight acclaim netted a nine-year audio run and led to its transfer to CBS-TV, persisting on the tube for two decades (1955–1975). That made *Gunsmoke* the most enduring video western in history, albeit with a different cast from the radio pack.

Familiar characters in a frontier Kansas community came to grips with desperadoes of disparate persuasions whose debauchery, mayhem and murder kept local denizens on edge. One stood tall in the saddle when confronted by it all—Marshal Matt Dillon, played by radio actor William Conrad. While other westerns with mature subject matter followed (*Dr. Sixgun, Fort*

Laramie, Frontier Gentleman, Have Gun— Will Travel, Luke Slaughter of Tombstone, The Six Shooter), none eclipsed the original *Gunsmoke*. It was one of a few bright spots in a decade of generally declining fortunes for network radio.

In the middle of the 20th century, Joseph R. McCarthy, junior senator from Wisconsin, fanned the flames of a witch-hunt in America to ferret out perceived—and often unsubstantiated—subversives. People in government, the professions and performing arts were among the prime targets as "McCarthyism" spread its tentacles far and wide, leaving no stone unturned in a bid to reveal Communist and Nazi sympathizers. Among those who lost jobs, spouses, families, and self-respect—often trading it in for "blacklisting" (meaning no work), disgrace, humiliation, suspicion, innuendo, alcoholism, drugs, welfare, mental and physical disorders, ruined careers and even suicide—were hundreds employed in radio and television.[33]

One of the most astonishing outcomes of that pursuit was to require broadcasting employees to sign statements certifying allegiance to the United States, a flagrant violation of their civil and constitutional rights. Communist Party membership was then legal in America and that level of scrutiny set off alarms. Writing in his autobiography, *As It Happened*, in 1979, Bill Paley admitted: "My own feelings for personal privacy are so strong that I am astonished that I could have tolerated the invasion of privacy that even our mild questionnaire required. Yet, the more I reflect on this, the more I see that CBS, too, was caught in the crosscurrents of fear that swept through the whole country." NBC already had an occupational proviso in place when CBS developed one for its employees and freelancers. CBS was considered the most tolerant of the national chains, and at last capitulated to incessant pressure it received from sponsors. Rightwing journalists loved to tag CBS as "the Red network" and "the Communist Broadcasting System," incidentally.

The CBS "questionnaire"—it wasn't referred to at 485 Madison Avenue as anything like an "oath"—interrogated its coterie on a mere trio of matters:

1. Are you now, or have you ever been, a member of the Communist Party, USA, or any Communist organization?
2. Are you now, or have you ever been, a member of a Fascist group?
3. Are you now, or have you ever been, a member of any organization, association, movement, group or combination of persons which advocates the overthrow of our constitutional form of government, or of any organization, association, movement, group or combination of persons which has adopted a policy of advocating or approving the commission of acts of force or violence to deny other persons their rights under the Constitution of the United States or, of seeking to alter the form of the government of the United States by unconstitutional means?

Any responses in the affirmative resulted in asking for the names of all such organizations, dates of membership and details of activities. Participants could add their personal clarifications. A keen observer of the epoch documented these unparalleled circumstances:

> Most performers signed and went on to their jobs uncaring or oblivious to the fact that a small piece of their guaranteed liberties, the freedom of political belief and discussion, had been chipped away. For others, it set off a wave of fear or righteous indignation or both. Who, they asked, is the Columbia Broadcasting System to question my allegiance to my country? Who is CBS to ask me to protest my innocence about something of which there is no reason to suspect me? ... Particularly disturbing for those who had been or still were members of a listed organization was that CBS made no provision for a hearing or for the right of appeal.[34]

The entire phenomenon was, in effect, McCarthyism in microcosm, and the whole industry took its cue from CBS. If artists appeared on CBS, they had discernibly passed muster. "CBS and the blacklisting became synonymous," noted a source a few years later. "The refusal of Paley and [CBS President Frank] Stanton to take a stand against the vigilantes did no honor to them or CBS," claimed an insightful researcher. "Not only were they unwilling to jeopardize profits, they feared antagonizing the FCC and the Congress, which were controlled by forces sympathetic to blacklisting. Although they knew that the supposed Communists and fellow travelers posed no threat whatsoever to the nation, Paley and Stanton found it expedient to hire only those who were politically neutral. It was easier to go along than to fight."[35]

Four years into all of this, Joseph McCarthy was finally taken to the woodshed for his role in fanning the flames of discontent. It took a CBS Radio newsman to do it, and it occurred on a live telecast of CBS-TV's *See It Now* on March 9, 1954.[36] America's most respected electronic journalist of the epoch, Edward R. Murrow (1908–1965), put the screws to the senator. As the nation sat mesmerized, Murrow challenged McCarthy's lack of hard evidence for many of his undocumented assertions, thereby ruining careers and lives via insinuations he could never prove.

Extolled in American homes for his wartime reporting from the world's hot spots a decade earlier, Murrow threw down the gauntlet and cried "Enough!" to McCarthy's dastardly deeds. His pointed questions of the senator shifted public opinion against him, which had been running strongly in McCarthy's favor. By that year's end, McCarthy was finished. The U.S. Senate publicly humiliated him, censuring him on a 67–22 vote for bringing disgrace upon that body in his efforts to obstruct constitutional process. And after leaning on the bottle too heavily, 21 months later a shamed McCarthy was dead. It had taken a nightly CBS Radio newsman of great principle to overwhelm him and stop the madness, finally bringing the country's long national nightmare to an end.

As the original "Murrow Boy," the electronic journalist who hailed from Pole Cat Creek, North Carolina, Edward Roscoe Murrow set unequivocally high standards on entering broadcast journalism in the 1930s. Today many of his principles are faithfully upheld by successive generations of news reporters and commentators. They practice the skills that turned Murrow into a newscasting legend.

It had been one of broadcasting's darkest hours. When it was over, Paley insisted, "We didn't have a blacklist."[37] In this, as in dealing with television's sudden domination of people's lives at about the same time, the chairman plainly ignored a preponderance of evidence to the contrary.

The McCarthy take-down is one of many examples attesting to the consummate prize that CBS found on its hands when it hired Murrow in 1935 as director of talks. Within two years he provided American radio listeners with eyewitness warm-ups to global conflagration in European zones targeted by Adolf Hitler. One of the best things to come out of those early years with the network was his amassing a cadre of 11 reporters for CBS later dubbed "The Murrow Boys."[38] Those overseas correspondents were the eyes and ears of their countrymen, who regularly tuned in their radios for reliable updates on what was transpiring on the battlefields and in the headquarters where tactical decisions were made.

Murrow masterfully directed the widespread operation from his post in London or wherever he was traveling on the Continent. Americans quickly developed a trust in him and in the lineup he put together, so much so that CBS Radio—while constantly feeling the pressure of other webs in the same chase—grabbed first place in news among audio networks during World War II. With a few exceptions, it held on to it. It began with Edward R. Murrow.[39] It continued with many of his colleagues and successors. It gave Bill Paley many moments to be proud of "his" team.[40]

"When CBS was really riding high in news, it wasn't because of ratings," CBS newsman Robert Pierpoint—and not a member of the elite "Murrow Boys"—allowed. "It was because of the reputation of the Murrow Boys, because of the Murrow legacy."[41] Colleague Daniel Schoenbrun, also a non-member of that early inner circle, affirmed: "For a few brief years, the Murrow team was nonpareil. There was CBS and then the others.... While it lasted it was dazzling."[42]

As time progressed, there were numerous reminders of CBS's solid contributions to an aggressive, comprehensive, accurate radio news product. The web inaugurated the most enduring news presentation in broadcasting history, the *CBS World News Roundup*, on March 13, 1938. Seventy years later, on March 13, 2008, the series was still airing, taking time out that morning for some historical reflection on its journey. On December 7, 1941, CBS newsman John Daly stunned the nation by interrupting network programming, being the first to proclaim that the Japanese had attacked Pearl Harbor, Hawaii. Another CBS Radio reporter, Dan Rather, was the first to deliver the somber dispatch that president John F. Kennedy lay dead in Dallas on November 22, 1963. Rather's radio announcement preceded Walter Cronkite's televised confirmation over CBS by a full 10 minutes, video's initial corroboration on a day that most Americans could hardly leave their radios and televisions. In the following decade—beginning in March 1977—a call-in question-and-answer feature, *Ask President Carter*, debuted, and was carried exclusively over CBS Radio.

Paley beat the competition at its own game—technology—when Columbia launched the first regularly scheduled TV broadcasts in the nation on experimental station W2XAB in New York City on July 21, 1931. Furthermore, the firm developed the long playing phonograph recording as well as color television.

When CBS research scientist, engineer and physicist Peter Carl Goldmark, born at Budapest, Hungary, on December 2, 1906, perfected the LP disc in 1948, the trade dubbed it a breakthrough in sound technology. Goldmark bristled over flipping standard 78-rpm records every five minutes, setting out to devise a better platter. Others had tried and failed; Goldmark and CBS established a new benchmark, a fairly flexible vinyl disc compared to easily breakable 78s.[43] His new 33⅓ rpm discs offered clarity and up to 60 minutes of sound, persisting as the new standard until CDs overtook them in 1990.

After immigrating to the United States in 1933, Goldmark joined CBS in 1936. He was soon developing color television as one of his foremost projects. In the early 1940s, he produced the initial color TV system using a triple-hue rotating disc. While the FCC quickly approved his invention, the design was superseded by an electronic color technique compatible with existing black-and-white sets, approved by the FCC on December 17, 1953. The adopted format was a modification of an RCA-originated schematic.

Not to be outdone, Goldmark continued tinkering, bringing to the market more and more creations. Among them was the first electronic video recording system—forerunner of the contemporary VCR—plus a scanning system used by the Lunar Orbiter spacecraft in 1966 to transmit photographs to Earth from the moon. In 1954, Goldmark became chief engineer and president of CBS's laboratory and CBS was credited for all of his inventions during the epoch. He died in Westchester County, New York, on December 7, 1977, as he turned 71. His contributions kept CBS competitive in the surge toward television during the waning days of radio's golden age.

In an earlier chapter the subject of "Paley's Comet" was introduced, in which the Great Man found a means of attracting to CBS some of the most revered icons performing on other networks. While he was able to win over singer Bing Crosby and comic-quizmaster Groucho Marx from ABC in his late 1940s raids-on-rosters, Paley's biggest quarry—whom he lured with attractive financial incentives—doubtlessly hailed from David Sarnoff's NBC. Although there can be no mistaking that Paley pulled off his escapade to benefit CBS, there is also little doubt that he took fulsome pride in winning such a foremost victory over his archrival. CBS added to its ranks comedians Jack Benny, Edgar Bergen (and his marionette Charlie McCarthy), George Burns and Gracie Allen, Freeman Gosden and Charles Correll (*Amos 'n' Andy*), Ozzie and Harriet Nelson, Harold (*Gildersleeve*) Peary, and Red Skelton. All of them had been unmistakably identified with NBC for many years, and some for nearly two decades.

Paley won the day by dangling before the performers a method of rewarding them far more lucratively than they were accustomed to. CBS found that—if a star formed a corporation with himself as the principal quantity, including being the sole hire and investor—CBS could purchase a show's control from the corporation. It would pay the "enterprise" a lucrative sum for the privilege while the business/star paid taxes on capital gains as opposed to straight income as traditionally was being done. Straight income was taxed many times higher. Thus, the entertainers got to keep more of what they worked for.

In the end it wasn't totally about money, nevertheless. Other factors influenced those talents to make the jump from the network where several had hung their hats for 15 or more years. In Jack Benny's case, he eventually expressed what he may have felt for years: that no matter what he contributed to NBC, he never felt appreciated by upper management.

> Benny chafed under what he came to see as NBC's almost indifferent attitude toward the talent that brought the listeners. NBC, under the leadership of David Sarnoff, seemed at the time to think that listeners were listening to NBC because of NBC itself. To Paley ... that was foolish thinking at best: Paley believed listeners were listening because of the talent, not because of which platform hosted them. When Paley said as much to Benny, the comedian agreed. Because Paley also took a personal interest in the Benny negotiations, as opposed to Sarnoff (who had actually never met his top-rated star), Benny was convinced at last to make the jump—and, in turn, he convinced a number of his fellow NBC performers (notably Burns & Allen and Kate Smith) to join him.[44]

When the dust settled, CBS led the primetime ratings for the first time in two decades. Reversing circumstances in another domain, CBS could then boast of total sponsorship of 29 programs it owned outright. By January 1950, CBS owned 80 percent of radio's top Nielsen-rated shows while NBC could do little but lick wounds. By then NBC had lost $7 million in ad revenue in one year on top of millions of listeners.

In accomplishing its pièce de résistance, CBS had a lot going for it by the fact it could move faster than NBC in raiding an opponent's performing inventory. This is an excellent example of a durable distinction between the two power players: broadcasting was the bedrock of the corporate business at CBS. At NBC, it was a minuscule, though not unimportant, portion of the Radio Corporation of America. Decisions there went through channels and multi-tiered levels of management before being implemented, a hindrance in accomplishing much very cohesively and with dispatch.

The Adventures of Ozzie and Harriet, which left NBC, stayed with CBS for only one season (1948–1949) before moving to a stable berth at ABC, while Groucho Marx's *You Bet Your Life*, which left ABC, stayed with CBS for only one season (1949–1950) before moving to a permanent berth at NBC. All the others stayed put as members of the CBS roster for many years, some for the remainder of their broadcast lives.

There can be no mistaking it: grave damage was inflicted on NBC. Its stature was severely tarnished, so much so that—in obvious respects—it never regained the authority, artists, advertisers or audiences it dominated before the War of 1948.

There are footnotes worth examining which reveal yet other possibilities for the results, while offering valuable insights into radio's status at the middle of the 20th century. Paley and Sarnoff both returned from World War II to pursue opposing obsessions—Paley, to master his chain's fate by controlling radio programming; Sarnoff, after years of imagination, experimentation and planning, to turn TV into reality. Paley's talent raids and program development ultimately culminated in boosting CBS-TV. "He may have thought he was building radio," an incisive biographer allowed, "but his gut—the visceral, even primitive, love for stars and shows that figured in every move he made—was to give his fledgling television network an advantage Sarnoff would never match."[45]

The "legend" of Paley's Comet suggests that it grew out of a misconception. Some within the industry believed the CBS magnate was merely shoring up the web's horde of performers in order to switch them to the rapidly emerging tube. "Paley undertook the talent raids to strengthen radio, not to push into television," his chronicler fathomed. "The raids were deigned to establish him, at last, as the undisputed leader—in radio."[46]

CBS president Frank Stanton confirmed it: "I never heard Bill talk about using the stars for television at all. For him in those days it was all radio. His postwar idea was simply to get control of radio programming. He never talked about television. He didn't see the light until well after the early days ... he didn't pick stars with any idea about leaping into television."[47] A commercial journal went further: "CBS wanted to make sure radio audiences wouldn't go over to television by default. If CBS had the best entertainment and showmanship, it could keep a lot of its circulation *despite* TV."[48]

So intent was Paley on saving radio in the 1940s that, in reality, top aides were asked to support his position at whatever venues they appeared representing CBS. Paley hoped "to slow down the progress of television, trying to indicate the virtues which were uniquely those of radio," according to former publicist William S. Fineshriber, Jr.[49] This factor became clear even to the competition. David Adams, an NBC executive who may have had the ear of Sarnoff, revealed: "When TV was getting started, Bill Paley turned his back on it and thought there was money to be milked out of radio."[50]

Paley understood, inwardly of course, that TV was on its way. In the 1930s he tried to postpone its arrival for as long as possible. In the 1940s and 1950s he was doing it again. For instance, nine semi-commercial television stations were on the air part time in this country when World War II ended, reaching an aggregate of about 7,500 households. Built by electronics manufacturer RCA, one of those outlets was operated by CBS. Each of its telecasts was preceded with a baffling message: "Good evening. We hope you will enjoy our programs. The Columbia Broadcasting System, however, is not engaged in the manufacture of television receiving sets and does not want you to consider these broadcasts as inducements to purchase television sets at this time. Because of a number of conditions which are not within our control, we cannot foresee how long this television broadcasting schedule will continue."[51]

CBS's Stanton understood Paley perhaps better than anyone: "Bill did not want television. He thought it would hurt radio. It was also a question of money.... He didn't see any profit in TV at all. Bill was concerned about the bottom line, that we couldn't afford television, that it was too costly."[52] CBS had made a comprehensive study of TV's potential. It discovered that, whatever its ultimate value, the tube faced "seven lean years"—a desolate spell of enormous capital expense with paltry yields. Paley pondered: "Why starve for seven years when you can continue to feast on radio profits?"[53] While Sarnoff never denied the possibility of some lean years, he was convinced that the potential of the new industry—and Americans' right to enjoy it—justified television's investments and risks. He told *The New York Times* in 1945 that TV would be a billion-dollar industry within a decade. As it turned out, his prediction was eclipsed a few years earlier.

When Stanton was budget planning for television for the first time in 1947, he urged Paley to participate. The chairman shrugged off, feigning an overloaded schedule. He wouldn't be a party to anything that smacked of displacing radio. "Radio was CBS's best hope," he was totally convinced.[54] Fortunately for Radiophiles, it would take the chairman a little more time to overcome that posture.

CBS Radio's advertising revenues continued to prosper until 1950, within a year of TV's initial black ink. A shifting tide is, at last, all it took for Paley to quickly build enthusiasm for the new medium. Embracing TV unconditionally after that, it seemed he was discovering its potential for the first time. Radio's most eloquent defender had been won over to the opposition. The days of the elder broadcast medium were surely numbered now.

One of the impressive byproducts of that epoch, alluded to earlier in this text and pushed hard by Paley, had been in re-taking control of radio programming from the advertising agencies.[55] He returned from World War II totally convinced that it would be in CBS's best interests to call the shots again on what its schedule carried rather than having program packagers supply the content, commercials and, in some instances, even the artists and guests on airwaves furnished by broadcasters. Shouldn't the broadcasters control the ether, too? he pondered. One wag branded it "the single most important business decision that Paley made in his long career."[56] Paley continued: "I would grant NBC its greater reputation, prestige, finances, and facilities. But CBS had and would continue to have the edge in creative programming. *That*, I thought, would be the key to success in post-war broadcasting."[57]

He set about wresting CBS's schedule away from the ad agencies. Initially he created a handful of situation comedies in-house. CBS provided everything but the sponsor's messages—writing, directing, producing, announcing, acting, music, sound effects—the whole bit. Its repertoire of original domestic farces included personality-driven hits like *My Friend Irma* (1947–1954), *Our Miss Brooks* (1948–1957), *Life with Luigi* (1948–1954), *My Favorite Husband* (1948–1951), *Meet Millie* (1951–1954) and *My Little Margie* (1952–1955).

In another realm, on August 16, 1954, CBS announced that the radio and television news operations—which had functioned independently since their formation—were being combined into a single unit. TV news chief Sig Mickelson was given the rank of vice president and named head of the joint maneuver. Only a quadrennial earlier he had overseen 13 individuals in TV news; now he suddenly commanded a staff of 376. If anybody needed a road map to point out the direction the industry was headed at lightning speed, ramping up tube-oriented reporting was a fairly illuminating (and for Radiophiles, ominous) sign.

In post–1955 radio network broadcasting, NBC transmitted *Monitor* and all the webs proffered a minuscule handful of enduring daytime, nighttime and weekend features, most of those series of the unsponsored variety. Of the quartet of transcontinental chains, only CBS demonstrated any real resiliency, however, as it fought to perpetuate its radio programming. Paley was first, foremost and forever a radio man and there is no doubt that his determination to stave off the unmistakable signs of transition during those years benefited the traditionalists who favored the aural media. Despite the erosion of advertisers, artists and audiences, Paley was undaunted by all that transpired about him, blithely plodding along almost as if it wasn't happening. Massive defections to television in the early part of the decade hadn't altered his resolve to persevere with radio. It would take yet a fourth faction beginning with the letter "a" that would finally get his attention.

Since at least the start of the 1950s, CBS Radio affiliates had been asking that network offerings be reduced substantially in order to free more time in the schedule for local advertising selling.[58] A station's own local sales force could sell airtime far more advantageously than it could earn by relying on a fractional percentage of proceeds permitted by the chain for carrying one of its commercial or sustained features. As the decade progressed, however, an occasional disorganized, ineffective voice requesting those reductions eventually swelled into a vociferously united chorus of many. Ultimately, they demanded ample cutbacks, threatening to bolt CBS and go independent or to join another chain. Some of those were prestigious stations with longstanding traditions as market leaders in key places, something CBS could ill-afford to lose. The possibility of their defection would be unthinkable, and finally prevailed on Paley and Stanton.

In December 1958, CBS Radio announced that in January 1959 it would reduce its schedule from 63 to 30 hours weekly. The daytime agenda was significantly pared back. *Arthur Godfrey Time*, which had been programmed earlier in the decade with 90 minutes of variety every weekday, lost an hour of its 90 minutes. Art Linkletter's *House Party* was on for 25 minutes instead of a half-hour. And daytime drama, which had once occupied up to four hours of the weekday log, was diminished to 90 minutes. Only an hour of that was devoted to soap operas with continuing storylines and characters that for decades had been the backbone of the matinee audio landscape: the survivors, for a little while longer, were *Ma Perkins*, *The Right to Happiness*, *The Second Mrs. Burton*, *Young Doctor Malone*. Nearly 300 of their ethereal counterparts had long ago succumbed.

Yet the CBS affiliates were still restless. They wanted more cuts, their protests heated and relentless. Finally, Paley and Stanton ran up the white flag. In mid August 1960, they sent CBS Radio president Arthur Hull Hayes before the news media to make the announcement. Hayes explained that radio must shift from entertainment forms "which can be presented more effectively by other media." A public execution for remnants of CBS's programming was set for the period November 25–27, 1960. It included all weekday dramatic fare along with most of the web's remaining primetime series. Sweeping orders affected *The Amos 'n' Andy Music Hall* and *Have Gun, Will Travel*. Unaffected were Godfrey and Linkletter, a weeknight quarter-hour headlined by singers Bing Crosby and Rosemary Clooney (which debuted only a few months before on February 28, 1960), Lowell Thomas's nightly 10-minute newscast, and a trio of weekend signature dramas: *Gunsmoke*, *Suspense* and *Yours Truly, Johnny Dollar*.[59] CBS's news at the top of many hours wasn't affected (it actually expanded to 10 minutes hourly for a while), and there was a handful of five-minute features offered to stations throughout the day. Most of the rest of the schedule was gone.[60] Paley had fought valiantly to the end and—to his credit—only in the face of insurmountable odds did he finally throw in the towel. Radiophiles had to be in his debt, whether they recognized it or not.

CBS had resided at 485 Madison Avenue, New York, since September 18, 1929. But its headquarters was relocated to 51 West 52nd Street in the mid 1960s. Affectionately dubbed "Black

Rock" by tradespeople, the 36-story glass and ebony granite tower is situated in midtown Manhattan two blocks north of NBC's "30 Rock" (Rockefeller Center). It was officially occupied March 24, 1965, bringing CBS staffers who had been working in at least 15 Big Apple locations together under a single roof.

The actual production and transmission of programs today emanates from other New York facilities. Until the same epoch, CBS Radio aired from the 485 Madison Avenue headquarters. But a dozen years after the network purchased a block-long Sheffield Farms dairy depot in the Hell's Kitchen section of Manhattan, radio programming shifted there. After 36 years on Madison Avenue, the final CBS Radio show aired from there on July 25, 1964; the following day, the first program was beamed from Broadcast Center at 524 West 57th Street.

CBS purchased the site in 1952 but did not begin using it for TV production until 1963, relocating its master control there from Grand Central Terminal in late 1964. CBS News, CBS Sports, WCBS-AM Radio and TV now occupy Broadcast Center with CBS Radio. CBS owns two other major New York TV production facilities: The Ed Sullivan Theater at 1697 Broadway, home of *The Late Show with David Letterman*, and the General Motors Building at Fifth Avenue and 58th Street, home of *The Early Show*. Beyond those, *As the World Turns* is currently taped at a former NBC facility, J. C. Studios, in Brooklyn.

At about the same time these transitions occurred, New York's WINS Radio, a Westinghouse property, became the first local station to adopt an all-news format, on April 19, 1965. Two years later, CBS's flagship outlet, WCBS-AM, switched to a similar blueprint.[61] It was a foretaste of things to come as stations all over the nation marked by diversified mixtures of programming styles began to limit their focus to one field (e.g. pop music, talk, sports, news, nostalgia, oldies, religion). It indicated a sharp break with the past while providing opportunity in which pithy network features sometimes thrived.

In the post-golden era, CBS Radio continued to prosper. Beginning in the 1960s, it aired topical reports throughout the day as did other chains, branding its five-minute segments starting in 1962 under the banner of *Dimension*. Effective December 31, 1963, CBS added advice columnist Abigail Van Buren to its stable of weekday stars. On *Dear Abby*, she meddled in people's personal affairs for 11 years until December 27, 1974. On yet another front, CBS carried former New York Yankees shortstop Phil Rizzuto in a 19-year run of *It's Sports Time*, from 1957 to 1976. In the autumn season of 1965, the web began airing a weekly 25-minute interview series under the nomenclature *Mike Wallace at Large* with the CBS news–public affairs reporter hosting. Early in the 1970s, that entry was overhauled into five-minute segments and broadcast weekdays. It was revamped again in January 1979, offering two five-minute vignettes every Saturday and two every Sunday.

On December 18, 1971, CBS ended one of its last direct connections with radio's golden age by discontinuing a once-popular musical programming service—the remote broadcasts of band concerts. In the 1930s, before recorded music was considered appropriate for radio, the webs and local stations filled much of their schedules with live pickups of bands performing at sundry locations. While most of these webcasts ceased during the 1950s, CBS continued to feed them to a diminishing handful of stations still requesting them. Only 40 outlets were airing the Saturday morning concerts when CBS made the decision to delete them from its agenda.

A wave of nostalgia surfaced on radio in the 1970s. All the major chains as well as multiple transcription distributors reprised a dramatic form that was common to listeners from the 1930s through the 1950s. CBS was swept to the forefront of that movement. It tendered a trio of original 55-minute dramas during the period, proving once again that good material—given the right venue and time to catch on, alongside the support of strong acting and directing—can be very popular with mass audiences in almost any era.

Under the direction of producer Himan Brown, one of the legends in that capacity during the golden age, *The CBS Radio Mystery Theater* bowed on January 6, 1974. With distinguished movie and television actor E. G. Marshall as its original host, this sometimes eerie series of narratives ("tales of the macabre") borrowed the din of a creaking door that Hi Brown had created more than three decades earlier for *Inner Sanctum Mysteries*.[62] The new drama also unapologetically adapted a memorable line attributed to *Sanctum's* resident landlord Raymond. At the close of each episode, as a cheery Raymond did before him, Marshall bid fond adieu to listeners with a crafty gravediggers' grin: "This is E. G. Marshall, inviting you to return for another tale in the macabre. Until next time, pleasant dreams." The creaking door then swung shut tight. *The CBS Radio Mystery Theater* persisted to December 31, 1982, some of it in reruns. It aired seven nights a week through 1979; starting January 1, 1980, the series reverted to weeknights only.

A second innovative CBS drama of the period, also produced by Hi Brown, was the *General Mills Radio Adventure Theater*. A Saturday and Sunday entry, it premiered on February 5, 1977, with actor Tom Bosley as narrator. It was re-titled *The CBS Radio Adventure Theater* on August 6, 1977, and continued to air through January 29, 1978.

On February 5, 1979, CBS launched a weeknight anthology under the banner *Sears Radio Theater*. Produced by Elliott Lewis with music by Nelson Riddle's orchestra, it carried original dramas through August 3 of that year.[63] Each night a different host introduced a specific narrative diversion: there was Lorne Greene on Mondays with westerns, Andy Griffith on Tuesdays with comedies, Vincent Price on Wednesdays with melodramas, Cicely Tyson on Thursdays with tales of romance, and Richard Widmark or Leonard Nimoy on Fridays with adventure stories. Repeats were aired from August 6 through February 1, 1980, after which those reprises shifted to MBS under the moniker *Mutual Radio Theater*. On that chain, it persisted from March 3 to December 19, 1980.

Early in 1981, CBS's *Dan Rather Reporting* replaced *Walter Cronkite Reporting*. Cronkite retired at the same time from a 19-year stint as anchor of the televised *CBS Evening News*, succeeded by Rather in that chair.

Following a precedent established by the other three transcontinental radio webs, CBS at last joined them in diversifying from a unitary programming concept. On April 26, 1982, CBS launched *RadioRadio*, with newscasts aimed at a youth-oriented market, *RadioRadio* airing at 50 minutes past the hour.

Frank Stanton has been cited numerous times already but thus far has not been profiled. During much of Paley's reign, Stanton was his right-hand man. An articulate, steadfast team player who stayed by the stuff while perpetuating CBS's business interests, he was the logical heir to the throne upon Paley's retirement. The fact that it never happened, to be reconciled momentarily, is a discredit not to him but to an egocentric Paley who defied logic at a crucial moment in CBS's existence.

A print journalist assessed Stanton as "the industry's most articulate and persuasive spokesman" across a 27-year career as president and vice chairman of CBS. Under Stanton and Paley, CBS mixed "entertainment programming with high-quality journalism and dashes of high culture" to earn for it the designation as "the Tiffany Network."

Born March 20, 1908, at Muskegon, Michigan, Frank Nicholas Stanton was the son of a woodworking and mechanics teacher. At an early age, the family relocated to Dayton, Ohio, where the youth learned electronics at his dad's workbench. Majoring in zoology and psychology at Ohio Wesleyan University, he intended to pursue pre-med courses upon his graduation in 1930. But med school was out of reach for him in the depths of the Great Depression, so he accepted a scholarship to Ohio State University to study psychology.

Earning a master's in 1932, Stanton subsequently taught psychology while pursuing the doctorate at Ohio State, studying ways to quantify mass radio audiences. During those pursuits he invented a precursor to the Nielsen audimeter-measuring device, installing the apparatus within a radio receiver to tabulate what programs were heard. CBS research director Paul Kesten, then presiding over a department of only two individuals, was so impressed with Stanton's project that he offered him a $55-a-week job. The day after collecting his doctorate in 1935, Stanton and his wife left Ohio for New York, where he ultimately spent his career with CBS.

His novel contributions in research made a hit at CBS. In those days he focused on audience measurement, program ratings and geographical studies of CBS station coverage, and probed into radio's effectiveness in selling goods. In 1938, he was boosted to his first leadership position as director of research, an area soon comprised of more than 100 staffers. In 1941, Stanton was promoted to director of advertising, and by 1944, vice president. In 1945, he was elected general manager and a CBS director. The following year he was appointed president and chief operating officer, succeeding Paley, who was elected chairman of the board. Stanton served in that key role to 1971, when he was named vice chairman and chief operating officer.[64] Across the years, he collected five Peabody awards for excellence in broadcasting along with two Emmys. Upon his retirement in 1973, he pursued myriad opportunities in business, education, government and the arts.

While Stanton played a pivotal role in CBS's rise, it should be understood that he did so notwithstanding a connection with Paley that was often strained and bewildering to onlookers inside the walls at CBS. In her memoir of Paley, *In All His Glory*, Sally Bedell Smith described the relationship between Paley and Stanton.

> Temperamentally, the two men were opposites: Paley, the man of boundless charm, superficially warm but essentially heartless; Stanton, the self-contained Swiss whose business acumen, decency, and understated humor endeared him to his colleagues.
> Paley had a restless, readily satisfied curiosity while Stanton probed more deeply and was interested in a broader range of subjects. Paley acted from the gut; Stanton from the brain. Paley could be disorganized and unpredictable. Stanton was disciplined and systematic. Yet their relationship worked—largely due to Stanton's forbearance and diligence.[65]
> Building on Smith's description, another scribe wrote: "Dr. Stanton did not feel secure in the glamorous social whirl that Mr. Paley dominated. The two men did not socialize. Ms. Smith wrote that Mr. Paley had resented Dr. Stanton's refusal to invite him to his home, calling his associate 'a closed-off, cold man.'" He went on to say that Stanton was admired "as a principled executive with high aspirations," and was viewed by others in the radio and television industry as a leader in the fight against government interference in programming.[66]

One of those battles—Stanton's most public fight for free speech—saw him withstand the feds in a First Amendment watershed crisis. He defied a U.S. House of Representatives subpoena for outtakes of a CBS documentary, a move that affirmed him as the leading proponent of electronic journalism's equivalent status with print under the First Amendment. Likening the outtakes to print reporters' notebooks, as TV cameras rolled, he told the full U.S. House he wouldn't release those outtakes from "CBS Reports: The Selling of the Pentagon." The 1971 investigation exposed a mass push by the Pentagon to buttress the Vietnam War. While the defiance could have put Stanton in jail, following two days of hearings, the House voted 226–181 not to hold CBS and its president in contempt.

Among countless added contributions, Stanton was also responsible for creation of the CBS eye television logo that was unveiled to the public on October 20, 1951.[67] Upon his retirement, top company management extolled him for his "brilliant" career, exclaiming that he brought to CBS and the broadcasting industry "deep intellectual insight, uncompromising integrity and a devotion to excellence."

Stanton, who died at 98 in Boston on December 24, 2006, was "a genuine hero of the fourth estate," said ex-newsman Walter Cronkite. In a puff piece released by CBS following

Stanton's passing, Cronkite lauded his former colleague: "It was William Paley's sagacity and great good fortune to bring along as his chief executive Frank Stanton, who recruited over the years the broadcasters, producers, reporters and writers that constituted an all-star cast, from Ed Murrow on down, that burnished CBS."

Internal strife played a particularly large role at CBS during the waning days of Stanton's career. In violation of his own stated rule, Paley refused to retire. He imposed that compulsory mandate on others, nonetheless, including making the March 30, 1973, retirement of his logical heir, Stanton, obligatory. That was, in many respects, an unwise decision that set the broadcast empire on a course of uncertainty which typified it negatively in many estimates for a couple of decades. Consequently, it well may have played a part in determining CBS's long-range fate, ultimately handing it to outside interests.

By failing to establish the heir apparent in the post for which he had been so carefully groomed for decades—flanked by a resilient management team—Paley ran afoul of common sense. He did so to keep his own hand on the controls a while longer, at the obvious expense of undercutting the institution to which he had devoted his life. With Stanton's departure, Paley installed and quickly forced the resignations of a trio of successive presidents—chief executive officers: Arthur R. Taylor (1972–1976), John David Backe, pronounced *Bock-ee* (1976–1980) and Thomas Hunt Wyman (1980–1986).[68] CBS, Inc. (the nomenclature was officially altered from Columbia Broadcasting System, Inc., on April 17, 1974) was hardly a serene place in those days. It was "agitated," a source declared, over who would eventually follow Paley. Anxiety about the succession began to threaten the web's independence. Declining ratings left CBS vulnerable. The biggest threat came from a takeover bid by cable tycoon Ted Turner.

Determining how many people were listening to a given radio program was Frank N. Stanton's route to a lifetime occupation. After humble beginnings at CBS in 1935 the intrepid contributor who possessed keen insight and exceptional management skills steadily moved up the corporate ladder, only to be thwarted from reaching the top.

Wyman succeeded Paley as chairman, president and CEO in 1983 but was out by 1986 with Paley, then 84, returning as acting chairman. Parenthetically, in his autobiography, Paley ignored novelist Truman Capote's reaction to a young woman's comment about how healthy and energetic Paley had been in his seventies. Capote observed: "Yes, he looks like a man who has just swallowed an entire human being." As the power once again shifted at CBS, a pundit exclaimed: "That was exactly the way Bill Paley looked, I thought, on the night he resumed command of the company he now had dominated for nearly six decades—the night he swallowed Thomas Wyman."[69]

To defend itself against a possible takeover, CBS turned to Loews Corporation president Laurence Alan Tisch, who owned nearly a billion dollars' worth of CBS stock, 24.9 percent, as acting CEO. Tisch was a native of Brooklyn, born March 5, 1923. By January 1987, the CBS board made both Paley's and Tisch's appointments permanent. None of it boded well for a company embroiled in unmitigated turmoil for more than a decade.

That same year (1987) Tisch instituted massive cuts in budget and personnel while selling recording, magazine and publishing interests. Habitually he alienated many within the ranks who should have been his strongest allies. Not long afterward, in 1990, Paley died, leaving a once-proud first-rate broadcast empire in alarming disarray and wide-ranging upheaval. It was a sad finale for a lifelong pursuit that might have experienced a far different transitional outcome had it been handled differently.

Returning briefly to Stanton, the forgotten and dispossessed man in all of the cataclysm that descended upon CBS in the waning decades of the 20th century, perhaps poet John Greenleaf Whittier's "Maud Muller" expressed his personal crisis—and that of a once proud network— best: "For of all sad words of tongue or pen, The saddest are these: 'It might have been!'"

Tisch, then 67, who died at 80 on November 15, 2003, in New York City, was named chairman of the board in December 1990, in addition to his assignments as president and chief executive officer. In less than five years, CBS, Inc., was sold for $5.4 billion to Westinghouse Electric Corporation (November 1995), ending the net's 68-year history as an independent enterprise. A few months hence, on June 20, 1996, Westinghouse and Infinity Broadcasting Corporation announced their intent to combine operations.

On December 1, 1997, Westinghouse Electric Corporation altered its name to CBS Corporation. It should be noted, however, that—as in the case of RCA when it was taken over by GE in 1986—simply because the Westinghouse nomenclature was superseded here by CBS, it didn't altogether go away. A recent search of the Internet, for example, produced two dozen firms that persist in manufacturing consumer goods and business and industrial products with the name Westinghouse affixed to them. This is the result of selling or leasing the appellation to manufacturers relying heavily upon recognition and purchaser confidence in the quality of those commodities based on enduring histories.

Meanwhile, according to its publicists, CBS Corporation became the largest combined television, radio and out-of-home media entity ever. CBS united Westinghouse, CBS, Infinity, TDI and Gaylord Entertainment. Three years later, in 2000, Viacom completed a $39.8 billion merger with CBS Corporation. While known as Viacom, Inc., for the next five years, in 2005, the enterprise was once again identified by the label of CBS Corporation.

In the modern era, CBS RADIO (in all caps) is a division of CBS Corporation. Controlling interest is owned (as this is written, but stay tuned as the sector alters rapidly) by National Amusements, a movie theater and online ticketing enterprise headquartered in Dedham, Massachusetts.[70] Chairman Sumner Redstone and his family maintain voting control of the company through stock holdings. CBS Corporation is also comprised of the CBS Television Network with about 40 TV stations, joint ownership with Warner Bros. (a division of Time-Warner Corporation) of the CW Network, ownership of Showtime pay TV network, Simon and Schuster publishing company, outdoor advertising interests and Infinity Broadcasting.

In mid 2008, CBS RADIO maintained 140 radio stations, all but one of those situated in the nation's top 50 markets. Online streaming, HD Radio, mobile messaging and podcasting augment conventional programming methods. CBS RADIO owns the CBS Radio Network with sales and affiliate relations handled by Westwood One, a New York entity with which CBS has long been identified.

In the mid 1980s, Westwood One began purchasing major U.S. radio chains to enhance its arsenal of programming services pointed toward younger audiences. Its initial buys included MBS in 1985 and NBC in 1987. They were followed by affiliations with CBS Radio News, CBS

MarketWatch.com Radio Network, Fox News and CNNRadio. Thus in the 1990s, three of the four radio webs that had fiercely competed in serving the nation since the networks were formed were fully or partially operating out of the same province. Ironically, only ABC, which began as the NBC Blue network, maintained its absolute independence from the bunch. Westwood One engaged Infinity Broadcasting, now owned by CBS RADIO, to run its radio webs in 1993.

While MBS has since died and NBC's aural version is but a figment of one's imagination (identified as the "one-minute network" in Chapter 3), what of CBS RADIO? Now officially dubbed *CBS Radio News*, the programming entity is by every measure one of Westwood's strongest, most successful, widely acclaimed ventures. As of mid 2008, it offered clients (local affiliated stations) more than two dozen news, news feature, public affairs, forum, and opinion pieces on a continuing basis. Most of those are fed to stations five days a week in bite-sized morsels of one to three minutes' duration.

The most familiar gig to most listeners is, of course, *CBS News on the Hour*, a six-minute newscast anchored by a plethora of CBS News correspondents and provided 24/7. Among the recognizable names there—to those who tune in regularly, at least—are Howard Arenstein, Barry Bagnato, Steve Fudderman, Bob Fuss, John Hartge, Stefan Kaufman, Mark Knoller, Sam Litzinger, Laura Logan, Peter Maer, Cami McCormick, Sharon Middleman, Lou Miliano, Dan Raviv, Dan Scanlan, Frank Settipani and Cynthia Weber. In their day these electronic journalists uphold the traditions that have characterized CBS Radio's superior news force that emanated from the early 1930s.

The World News Roundup, the longest-running news program in broadcast history, meanwhile, remains a hallmark of the CBS schedule. Currently anchored by veteran CBS news correspondent Nick Young, it's fed to stations at 8 o'clock and 10 o'clock Eastern Time weekday mornings. *World News Roundup Late Edition*, its counterpart, is a nine-minute wrap-up of the day's news with Bill Whitney occupying that anchor chair. The segment is fed to stations at 7 o'clock weekday evenings.

Westwood One offers radio outlets simulcasts of the daily *CBS Evening News* with CBS-TV news anchor (as this is written) Katie Couric, the award-winning weekly CBS-TV newsfeature *60 Minutes* and the weekly discussion forum *Face the Nation*. In addition, some of its most popular audio-only features include *The Osgood File* social commentary with Charles Osgood, *Katie Couric's Notebook* with perspectives on world events, *The Dave Ross Show* with opinions on contemporary issues, and *Just a Minute with Harry Smith* providing probing assessments and commentary on world affairs, politics and current events. There are also personality-driven pieces on the day's stock market developments, personal finance, business updates, health, raising kids, entertainment, science, historical events and other general topics of interest to mass audiences.

While it isn't close to being *Suspense, Lux, Johnny Dollar, Gunsmoke*, Godfrey or Crosby, by golly, there's an attempt afoot to satisfy modern ears in an era that is characterized by shorter attention spans and a multiplicity of persuasions. Could this throwback to a kinder, gentler age be about all we have a right to expect as we inhabit the earth in a jet-propulsion society?

5

MUTUAL BROADCASTING SYSTEM
The Network for All America

All of the transcontinental radio networks in the United States developed in uncommon ways when viewed from their origins. Two began as appendages of one of America's largest manufacturing corporations, with tentacles reaching into every corner of a rising telecommunications industry. That duo eventually split, mandated by the feds, and a new chain was formed. Yet another was launched by a handful of well-intended individuals with little idea of what they were doing. Despite everything that went wrong for them, their fledgling enterprise not only survived but ultimately prospered.

And then there was Mutual, "the network for all America," as its announcers were fond of reminding audiences ad nauseam. On finally linking with radio stations in the far West in late 1936, extending all the way to the Pacific, MBS had achieved the unthinkable. Observed *Time*, "Last week, before the year closed, Mutual Broadcasting System accomplished what radiomen have long held improbable: a fourth coast-to-coast network.... Because of the monopolistic nature of chain broadcasting, Federal control of licensing and the scarcity of radio stations not tied up with N. B. C. or C. B. S., successful emergence of a rival network with coast-to-coast outlets depended largely upon co-operation of ... potent ... independents ... and upon securing Pacific Coast facilities."[1] In completing that objective, Mutual had ostensibly realized an impossible dream.

Born out of ostensible "necessity," MBS matured as a method of reining in overhead among a quartet of powerful, strategically situated stations. That four-member faction was accustomed to offering listeners superior programming; the bulk of it was generated by their own individual facilities. If they could combine forces, they reasoned, quality performances might be assured at a fraction of what each was spending to create and deliver imaginative material. As a result, Mutual would be controlled in a strikingly dissimilar model from the organizational blueprints that characterized its larger, already established competitors: the Columbia Broadcasting System (CBS) and the National Broadcasting Company (NBC), the latter possessing double chains, Red and Blue.

That fearless foursome of radio stations and its ownership consisted of:

- WGN, Chicago, officially WGN, Inc., a subsidiary of *The Chicago Tribune*;
- WLW, Cincinnati, owned by Crosley Radio Corporation and its principal, industrialist Powel Crosley, Jr.;
- WXYZ, Detroit, owned by Kunsky-Trendle (King-Trendle in 1936) Broadcasting Corporation; and
- WOR, Newark, owned by Bamberger Broadcasting Service, Inc., a subsidiary of L. Bamberger & Company consumer dry goods mercantile emporium (and an ancillary of R. H. Macy & Company as of 1929).[2]

Three of those were 50 kilowatt clear-channel stations trying to improve on their economic circumstances outside the conventional webs. The fourth, WXYZ, generated an especially compelling audio feature that—since premiering on January 31, 1933—had become a sensation with multigenerational audiences, an epic western-themed narrative, *The Lone Ranger.*

Through some misplaced notion, radio history zealots have mistakenly attempted to chronicle the humble beginnings of this joint network venture with links to that sterling adventure drama, as grandiose as it was. To that reputed masked rider of the plains who, sitting astride the great horse Silver led the fight for law and order in the early West, those modern day folk idol-worshipers have doggedly assigned absolute tribute as the catalyst of MBS's formation. To wit, on April 7, 1999, *The New York Daily News* contended:

> Sixty-five years after it was created expressly to make the Lone Ranger a national hero, the Mutual Broadcasting System is signing off.... The need for Mutual was planted in late 1932, when Detroit's WXYZ decided to launch a Western series with a hero who was "the embodiment of answered prayer."
> On Jan. 31, 1933, the noble, unsmiling Lone Ranger debuted over eight stations called the Michigan Radio Network.... Within a year WGN in Chicago, WLW in Cincinnati and WOR in New York signed on.
> On Sept. 15, 1934, this new alliance became the Mutual Broadcasting System, with WOR as a flagship, "The Lone Ranger" as its cornerstone and expansion as its grand hope.... Hi-yo, Silver, away.

The Lone Ranger, reported another emblematic analyst, "was such an instant success that the program led to the formation of the Mutual Broadcasting System, an outgrowth of the half-dozen stations that originally signed on to air the hit western."[3] Scads of colleagues similarly testified.

As plausible as all of that sounds ... as animated as that vibrant tale depicts ... and acknowledging that George W. "Trendle executives will tell you that Mutual came into existence to give network outlet to the Lone Ranger after unsatisfactory attempts to work out an arrangement with CBS and NBC"[4]—an account passed along from generation to generation by WXYZ vets—it ain't necessarily so.

"The network was formed first and foremost for *economic* reasons, *not* because of the popularity of a particular program," claims 1930s research consultant Elizabeth McLeod. She cites a 1939 document, *Big Business in Radio*, in which historian Gleason L. Archer delved into Mutual's origins. Archer found that in November 1933, an ex-general manager at NBC, George McClelland, was probably among the earliest to circulate the hypothesis that MBS followed only months later: connecting independent stations in a blended enterprise of jointly providing features for the ether, thereby sharing the expenses and profits.[5] But free agent McClelland, prognosticating without benefit of stations or financial backing, was unable to realize the dream all by himself. That may not have prevented his idea from spilling over to others, of course, who possessed the ability and determination to make it happen.

Born October 30, 1894, at Brooklyn, New York, McClelland died October 12, 1934, in New York City, 18 days short of his 40th birthday, the victim of a self-inflicted gunshot, *Time* reported on October 22, 1934. He left behind a wife and two minor daughters. Although he never persuaded others to enlist in his crusade to develop a cooperative radio network, McClelland's ambition was fulfilled under the leadership of others, beginning at just about the time he died.

Less than a year before, an unidentified sponsor approached Chicago's WGN and New York's WOR about the possibility of airing a program concurrently over both outlets. McLeod speculated that the underwriter was the Gordon Baking Company, maker of Silvercup bread, which—just at that instant, November 1933—began airing commercials on *The Lone Ranger*. She conjectured that the Gordon sponsorship may have prompted "The Lone Ranger–formed–Mutual" theory, and may have been the vehicle for ushering WXYZ into the chain's original quartet.

The unknown advertiser proposed paying WGN and WOR their standard rates provided those two outlets assumed the wire connection fee. Executives Wilbert Ernest MacFarlane (1882–1944) of WGN and Alfred Justin McCosker (1886–1959) of WOR mulled this over; most likely both were aware of George McClelland's proposed design for a cooperative enterprise. Whether conscious of it or not, the pair decided to implement an initiative similar to McClelland's, now that at least one show had a guaranteed sponsor. Their stations would form a "mutual" web that could complement the programming, sales and promotional activities of both facilities. McCosker and MacFarlane were to direct the joint effort without any salary adjustments. Archer insists it was this discussion that was the authentic germ of MBS's origination and nothing else. Added McLeod: "The idea for forming a permanent network, and the concept of its cooperative structure originated with McCosker and MacFarlane, with perhaps a bit of inspiration from George McClelland—and it is *they* who deserve the real credit for creating Mutual."[6]

Bert MacFarlane was born at Seneca, Illinois, on August 13, 1882. At 24, he joined *The Chicago Tribune*'s classified advertising department as a stenographer. His tenaciousness in turning a disorganized journalistic function into a model accessory highly profitable to the newspaper and also copied by numerous metropolitan dailies across the U.S. boosted him to greater responsibility. His posts included managing the paper's advertising and business units. Eventually MacFarlane was thrust into supervision of the *Trib*'s radio station, WGN. When the resident of suburban Lake Forest, Illinois, succumbed to death at 62 on October 9, 1944, an editorialist extolled: "He was largely responsible for the organization of the Mutual network and nursed it thru its formative period."[7]

MacFarlane's counterpart in that effort, Al McCosker, who became WOR's managing director in 1926, and later station manager, was born in New York City on September 3, 1886. Popularly dubbed Al "Hollywood" McCosker among promoters of that day, the publicist brought impresario Paul Whiteman, illusionist Harry Houdini and comic actor Charlie Chaplain before microphones for their initial ethereal performances. All of those mics, incidentally, read "WOR." A personal friend of New York Mayor Jimmy Walker (1926–1932), McCosker was credited in 1931 with diffusing an impassioned standoff: WOR news commentator H. V. Kaltenborn had been vocal in criticizing "hizzoner" and the mayor threatened to bar WOR from future municipal events and press conferences. It never happened; observers speculated that McCosker intervened, saving WOR's bacon. Three years later, he was instrumental in launching his station's second network (after CBS in 1927). McCosker died in July 1959 at 72 in Dade County (Miami area), Florida.

During the network's formative discussions, WLW and WXYZ were also operating costly program-creation units at their respective studios. Both indicated strong interest in joining the enclave proposed by MacFarlane and McCosker. While the quad stations officially agreed to the cooperative on September 29, 1934, their initial network program didn't air for a few more days, on October 2, 1934.

The form that the quartet adopted could not be classified as authentic collegiums in nature wherein everything is equally shared. Instead, WGN and WOR were designated principal entities of the faction, underpinning the collective endeavor, accepting the mantle of "ownership" and "control" as well as arranging for the all-important wire transmission connections linking member stations. The latter task would be performed by American Telephone & Telegraph Company (AT&T).

Ten shares of stock were issued to an Illinois-based corporation identified as Mutual Broadcasting System, Inc., on October 29, 1934. Five of those shares were held by WGN, Inc., while five went to Bamberger Broadcasting Service, Inc. Ultimate control of the new chain lay with the Chicago newspaper and the New Jersey department store. It would be their responsibility to guarantee payment for any corporation indebtedness to AT&T, putting a lot of pressure on their shoulders should anything come unglued.

In addition to the wiring arrangements, the corporation entered into the business of selling advertising time for the four-station hookup. For eight months in 1936, following an amendment to MBS's charter, Crosley Radio Corporation held an added five shares of newly-issued stock before returning it to MBS on September 26, 1936.

Crosley's founder, Powel Crosley, Jr., was born in Cincinnati on September 18, 1886. He became a Midwestern manufacturing magnate, producing Crosley cars, Crosley radios, appliances and legions of other goods. He put WLW on the air in March 1922; it became a powerhouse broadcast empire, eventually serving both radio and TV. For a while, starting in May 1934, WLW billed itself "The Nation's Station," projecting a massive 500,000-watt range at night—10 times the clear-channel standard—in an experimental test. WLW maintained a large cast of radio artists who wrote, acted, sang and otherwise performed in copious original productions. Some of the regulars claimed the station's call letters stood for "World's Lowest Wages."

Many moved to more promising opportunities in the big time arenas, but their show-business notoriety officially arrived during stints with WLW, among them sportscaster Red Barber, vocalist Jane Froman, recording ensembles the Ink Spots and the Mills Brothers, America's "beloved mother of the airwaves" and Oxydol's own Ma Perkins, juvenile entertainer Smilin' Ed McConnell, comedian Red Skelton and Singin' Sam "the Barbasol Man." In 1936, Powel Crosley bought his hometown Reds professional baseball franchise and saw its ballpark named Crosley Field. While some considered him an eccentric, Crosley was revered in the region until his death at 74 in his beloved Cincinnati on March 28, 1961.[8]

Some scholars make a weak case for Mutual extending from an earlier quartet of stations that fleetingly attempted to work in tandem in 1929.[9] That failed effort, known as the Quality Network, involved three of the stations that participated more than five years later in MBS—WLW, WOR, WXYZ—plus Chicago's WLS. Within a span of weeks, the Quality Network was history, no longer functioning by September 1929. It, too, had proffered the idea of a radio programming service operated cooperatively wherein its affiliates shared in the costs and profits, an idea believed to have been circulated by multiple factions in the 1920s. "Some writers consider The Quality Network to be the direct predecessor of Mutual, but the two were different companies with only partially similar ownership and should be considered as separate entities. The Quality Network ceased its existence for almost 5 years before Mutual was founded."[10] Nor should it be misunderstood to have been directly related to the separate Texas Quality Network of this period; nothing has surfaced linking the two chains.[11]

McLeod observed: "The formation of Mutual drew comparatively little attention in the popular press. In fact, the very week that the Mutual Broadcasting System was formed, *Radio Guide* devoted more attention to the expansion of George Storer's American Broadcasting System—a more ambitious, more conventional network project that had several stations in the East and Midwest. It wasn't until the spring of 1935 that *Radio Guide* even bothered to give 'MBS' a place in its program listings."

Under a new pact effective January 31, 1935, MBS agreed to pay the four stations their regular card rates for network programs broadcast over their facilities, deducting for itself a commission of five percent and such expenses as agency commissions and line charges. Precisely to the day one year later, the four-station agreement was extended for another year with MBS's commission reduced to 3.5 percent.

At its start Mutual departed from the established style of CBS and NBC by owning no affiliated stations; instead it was owned by a handful of stations. While MBS occupied no central studios then, and maintained no engineering department or artists' bureau as the others did, it didn't produce any programming either with the exception of some European news broadcasts. Its commercial programs were derived from productions at originating stations or by sponsors purchasing time. Sustaining features, meanwhile, were selected from among those aired by stations linked with the network. Thus MBS offered many distinctions when contrasted with existing transcontinental chains—in ownership, programming, affiliations and staffing.

Alfred Justin McCosker, president of WOR, became MBS chairman at the web's inception with Wilbert E. MacFarlane, vice president and business manager of *The Chicago Tribune*, as president. Officers and directors received no pay from MBS, their compensation coming from their own stations. It really was, as MacFarlane told a journalist, a situation in which "the stations run Mutual instead of being run by the chain."[12]

Fred Weber, formerly with both the National Broadcasting Company and the American Broadcasting System, was elected MBS coordinator of traffic and station relations in February 1935. Based in New York, he was soon elevated to general manager of the network. Born June 26, 1906, Weber launched his career as a rate engineer for the long lines division of AT&T. Moving into station relations with radio networks, he landed at Mutual, remaining into the early 1940s. At his death at 67 on August 30, 1973, in Margate, New Jersey, Weber was executive vice president of radio and television of a commercial greeting cards firm.

For a while MBS was comprised of its original quartet of stations while much of eastern and Midwestern America could readily tune in, thanks to powerful transmitters advantageously placed. Even then, however, much of the country wasn't aware of Mutual's existence (the fanzines ignored it for a while). WXYZ, meanwhile, spending money big time, was at one and the same time restless and ambitious. Part owner-manager George Washington Trendle, born July 4, 1884, at Norwalk, Ohio, had more riding on his shoulders than *The Lone Ranger*, and needed more assurance for the future than a solo drama aired on a handful of stations could provide.[13] In essence, MBS seemed like a stopgap measure with little prospect of reaching most of America's more lucrative and most desirable metropolitan markets.

By then Trendle was already dreaming big, imagining an empire built on dramatic adventures appealing to smaller fry that would be generated by a cadre of WXYZ scribes and acted by a corps of Detroit-area thespians. He had brought a second major production, *The Green Hornet*, to the local ether in January 1936 and hoped in due course it would also reach a national audience. It would be followed by *The Challenge of the Yukon* two years later, while several more tales originated there and projected to the pre-teen crowd ultimately never would be as well known as this trio of super-serials.

With all of this in his mind, Trendle led WXYZ out of its newfound federation with MBS in September 1935, only one year after joining it, to form an alliance with the more promising NBC Blue. While contractual obligations prevented him from moving *The Lone Ranger* there until 1942, Trendle's vision of a major radio production center in Detroit proceeded under full steam. He would live to see it exceed his wildest expectations before he finally yielded to death in Detroit at 88 on May 9, 1972.

When WXYZ joined NBC, meanwhile, Windsor, Ontario's CKLW—serving the same geographic territory, including Detroit—replaced it in the MBS quad. CKLW was owned by Western Ontario Broadcasting Company, Ltd.

Powel Crosley, Jr., soon followed Trendle's precedent, becoming the next Mutual founding father to remove his station from that small aggregate. By the end of 1936—just 15 months after its debut—WLW was no longer part of the mix. That withdrawal occurred just as the network evidenced a transition from a slow beginning into something much more hopeful. MBS had become a genuine transcontinental web in 1936. Two things happened to make it so.

In the East, the 13 stations of the New England–based Colonial Network voted to affiliate with MBS. At about the same time, 10 outlets comprising the Don Lee Network on or near the West Coast decided to join MBS, too. Included was a quartet of owned-and-operated stations—

Los Angeles' KHJ, San Francisco's KFRC, San Diego's KGB, Santa Barbara's KDB—plus six California affiliates and, in reality, two bonus outlets in Hawaii connected by shortwave hookup.[14]

On December 29, 1936, MBS became a coast-to-coast web in actual practice.[15] By successively attracting more independents and regional webs—such as the 23-station Texas State Network chain in 1938—within five years, from 1935 to 1940, MBS grew from .7 percent of all U.S. outlets (4) to 19.3 percent (160).[16]

Many of its additions were also simultaneously linked to either NBC or CBS. Of 107 MBS stations at the start of 1939, for instance, 25 were also tied to NBC while another five had a relationship with CBS. Most of those in duplicate categories gave primary allegiance to the bigger webs and aired MBS programming only to fill free time. Furthermore, most of the MBS affiliates were regional and local outlets operating with low power and therefore drew relatively small numbers within their listening ranges. Not surprisingly, MBS lagged NBC and CBS in advertising revenues because of smaller audiences. And because it was a cooperative undertaking, programming was principally derived by a handful of affiliates. MBS maintained a minor central news service in New York City, later in Washington. If that can be overlooked or possibly forgiven, Mutual truly was "the network for all America."

The departure of naissance stations WLW and WXYZ notwithstanding, "Mutual *always* struggled, was always a poor fourth in time sales, and always had to fight to find decent outlets," a Web site expounds. "That the network endured into the early 1950s under its original cooperative structure is a testimony to how strongly WOR and WGN believed in the basic idea—even though it was always an uphill battle."[17]

During this time of surging growth, a governmental inquiry into network practices succinctly summarized the relationship between MBS and ownership, and that of MBS and its rival webs.

> The network corporation itself does not own or operate any stations; however, the stock of the network corporation is owned by various station licensees. This difference has several important practical aspects. To begin with, the licensees which own Mutual are not under common control and, therefore, there is no concentration of ownership or control of radio facilities in any one organization. Likewise, and probably more important, the network cannot control its owners; on the contrary, it is controlled by them. The stations which own Mutual can terminate the ownership relation by disposing of their stock. The choice in the case of Mutual is with the station, rather than with the network as in the case of NBC and CBS.[18]

As the number of stations in the MBS hookup increased, the structure of the operation grew more complex. During the period in which only four stations were associated with MBS, each contributed a fourth of the web's expenses and line charges. As more stations were added, a trio of classifications was instituted: (1) member stations, (2) participating members, and (3) affiliates.

In January 1939, there were just two member stations—WGN and WOR—holding total stock control. Concurrently, there were four participating member organizations: Colonial Network, United Broadcasting Company (licensee of WHKC at Columbus, Ohio, and WCLE and WHK at Cleveland, Ohio), Don Lee Network and Western Ontario Broadcasting Company, Ltd. The remaining MBS tieups were affiliates. Within 12 months, by January 1940, MBS issued more stock to increase its number of member stations. Joining WGN and WOR as joint owners was the four participating members just named plus The Cincinnati Times-Star Company (licensee of Cincinnati's WKRC).[19] Mutual's board of directors was increased and an operating board created to provide representation to the non-shareholding affiliates, by then well over 100 in number.

By autumn of the following year (1941), MBS ownership was realigned yet again.[20] Stock was divided into equal shares held by: WGN, Inc., Chicago; WOR, New York; Don Lee Broadcasting System of California; Baltimore Radio Shows, Inc., owner of WFBR; The Cincinnati Time-Star Company, WKRC; Colonial Network, Inc., of New England; Pennsylvania Broadcasting Company, WIP, Philadelphia; and United Broadcasting Company, WHK and WCLE, Cleveland, plus WHKC, Columbus, Ohio, and WCAE, Pittsburgh.

At the same time this was transpiring, network commercial time was being sold at the card rates of the member stations. Without a network rate card similar to that of NBC and CBS, MBS charged advertisers at the card rates of the stations associated with it. Its stockholding outlets paid MBS a commission of 3.5 percent on all proceeds, after agency commissions, from network shows broadcast over those outlets' facilities. They also shared any network deficit and main line charges. Non-member or non-participating member affiliates, on the other hand, paid a commission of 15 percent. In addition, affiliates paid for line connections from their stations to the MBS main line. All stations associated with MBS received a two percent commission from the web on proceeds of network time sold by them.

In the matter of revenues, MBS's business volume—while increasing dramatically, of course—never rivaled that of its older, bigger brothers in network radio. Following discounts and before commissions, MBS's receipts at the close of 1935 totaled $1.1 million. Within three years that had more than doubled to nearly $2.3 million. By the end of 1940, it reached $3.6 million, a substantial leap in a five-year window.[21]

The intense scrutiny in the late 1930s of local radio stations and the webs with which many of those outlets were affiliated has been reported in previous chapters. There were multidimensional outcomes of those investigations and hearings conducted by the Federal Communications Commission (FCC) at the insistence of Congress. Probably the most reactive was the order in the early 1940s that resulted in the separation of ownership of the NBC Red and Blue chains, ultimately netting the founding of the American Broadcasting Company, born out of the Blue.

The wide-ranging impact of the FCC's edicts won't be reviewed here, with the exception of a specific reference to MBS. Because it is symptomatic of a pervasive environment that encumbered the smallest of the nation's transcontinental radio webs, it has been selected for exhibition, reported directly from the FCC's published summation of its findings. It indicates the stress that the federal panel felt was being foisted upon the American radio consumer by shackles of the dominant opposition forces.

> In the many areas where all stations are under exclusive contract to NBC or CBS, the public is deprived of the opportunity to hear Mutual programs. Restraints having this effect are to be condemned as contrary to the public interest irrespective of whether it be assumed that Mutual programs are of equal, superior, or inferior quality. The important consideration is that station licensees are denied freedom to choose the programs which they believe best suited to their needs; in this manner the duty of a station licensee to operate in the public interest is defeated. The Mutual programs which the stations would broadcast if permitted freedom of choice are, in these areas, withheld from the listening public. In addition, the very fact that Mutual is denied access to important markets immeasurably restricts its ability to grow and to improve program quality.
>
> Not only is regular Mutual program service banned from large areas, but even individual programs of unusual interest are kept off the air. A concrete example of the manner in which exclusivity clauses operate against the public interest may be seen in the broadcasting of the World Series baseball games of October 1939. Mutual obtained exclusive privileges from the baseball authorities for the broadcasting of the series with the Gillette Co. as commercial sponsor. Thereupon it attempted to obtain time from various stations, including stations which were then under exclusive contract to NBC and CBS. CBS and NBC immediately called upon their outlet stations to respect the exclusive provisions of their contracts. Disregard of this reminder would have jeopardized a station's rights under the contracts. This prevented certain licensees from accepting a program for which they believed there was public demand and which they thought would be in the public interest. It also deprived the advertiser of network advertising service in

some areas, and prevented the licensee from receiving income which could have been obtained from acceptance of the program series. As a result, thousands of potential listeners failed to hear the World Series of 1939.

Only strong and compelling reasons would justify contractual arrangements which have the results we have described.[22]

The various networks were given an opportunity to respond to the FCC's observations. While no reaction is included by NBC on this specific issue, CBS contended that "Mutual was the real party at fault, if any existed. Columbia offered to have its stations carry the broadcast [of the World Series], the sole condition being that it not be forced to advertise its competitor, Mutual. The FCC branded that offer 'a mere gesture,' terming compliance with it as 'impractical.'" The FCC jury continued: "Moreover, this CBS argument assumes that the affiliated stations in some way belong to CBS. The position seems to be that when an affiliate broadcasts a Mutual program, CBS is advertising Mutual. This confuses a broadcast by an affiliate of CBS with a CBS network broadcast.... The stations ... should be free to accept or reject programs which are in the public interest, whether or not CBS approves."

Lest the reader think that MBS emerged from this imbroglio unscathed, it also came in for some light chastising by the FCC: "Mutual refused to allow other stations within the territory of Mutual outlets to broadcast the program. This was because of its practice of respecting the territorial exclusivity of its affiliates."

There would come a time when MBS would readily overtake everybody in radio broadcasting as the authentic leader in number of outlets, a fairly widely known fact among Radiophiles. This was a bragging right that it held onto until late in the 1960s when ABC divided its activity into multiple webs, leapfrogging over the rest of the pack to propel itself into first place.

That said, by 1942, MBS with 191 affiliates was already easily outpacing its trio of rivals: NBC Red—136; Blue—116; CBS—115. Within half a dozen years, MBS surpassed 500 stations at 519, a threshold it maintained in consecutive years for the next decade. Its nearest competitor, ABC, had less than half its number with 256 in 1948. MBS hadn't yet come close to a summit, however, even with those lofty figures. Not until 1979, in fact, in the midst of numerous years when the affiliates reached incredible proportions, did MBS hit its zenith of 950 outlets. That year, it favorably compared with ABC's multiple-network of 1,561 stations to 278 for CBS and 268 for NBC.

Beginning in the early 1940s, MBS adopted a blueprint long followed by older rivals CBS and NBC—adding a time option clause to contracts with its affiliates. This gave the web some leverage to guarantee that a prospective sponsor could anticipate clearance for a given show on most or all of the chain's stations and that the show would be presented at the network origination time or another time mutually desirable to both sponsor and stations. While Mutual's pact was limper than those of its counterparts, it reigned in delinquent stations that arbitrarily selected from the smorgasbord of chain-driven features while passing on others. If those stations wore the label of MBS, they were thereafter required to exhibit some loyalty to MBS or provide acceptable reasons for not airing specific programs. MBS controlled only about four and a quarter hours of the Monday-through-Friday schedules of its stations' typical broadcast day. CBS and NBC, on the other hand, ran their programming virtually all day long, likely making their agreements much more contentious to some errant affiliates.

In autumn 1937, a new type of radio commercial practice was instituted over an MBS series with advertising time sold "syndicate style." The Redfield-Johnstone agency signed entertainers George Jessel, Norma Talmadge and the Tommy Tucker Orchestra for *Thirty Minutes in Hollywood* starting October 10, 1937. Then the agency dispatched salesmen to fan out across the country offering the program to local sponsors. Station announcers, often familiar to listeners of a given outlet, delivered the commercials in 30-second slots at the show's opening and closing and 90-second slots in the middle of the program.

In another dimension of selling spot time to advertisers that radio listeners had little reason to consider, MBS was a key innovator. Spot radio is a process allowing purchasers to present commercials to targeted prospects for given commodities and services at sensible rates via programs or announcements on specific stations. Many procedures were implemented to focus a client's "buys" into channels that could be expected to net strong returns on investment. One method, signal-strength maps, depicted results of a device measuring a station's transmitter signal. There were many variations.

In 1948, MBS engineers developed a "listenability" quantifier that calculated listener acceptance instead of electrical output. "Listenability" considered factors like high noise levels in determining coverage, applying "good enough to listen to" as a yardstick. "Signal-strength and listenability maps serve as measurements of the medium itself and eliminate the program factor," one wag explained. "Both are useful because they measure a station's potential coverage, but neither suggests whether people actually listen."[23] That would be up to the more sophisticated audience measuring systems of Elmo Roper, George Gallup, Archibald Crossley, C. E. Hooper, A. C. Nielsen and others, of course.

Earlier we pointed out that some historiographers erroneously claimed that Mutual directly evolved out of the Quality Network which operated briefly in 1929. Some also said that *The Lone Ranger* provided the impetus that finally launched MBS, another theory that was debunked. There is yet another myth that media historians have been fond of perpetuating concerning Mutual. Matter-of-factly for decades countless authorities have allowed: "There was no Mutual Broadcasting System Building."[24] As in the cases of the previous assertions, it ain't necessarily so!

While at its start the network owned no stations or studios and in a real sense did not produce any programming—this was handled by the stations originating each feature, you recall—it wasn't long before MBS needed an origination point for many of its ongoing music, news and dramatic features, as much as those beamed by NBC, CBS and eventually ABC. Mutual *did* have facilities of its own, even though they might have been shared with its local affiliates. Upon joining other stations to form MBS, its course was confirmed by contemporary inquiry: "For WOR it meant becoming a 'flagship' and clearly in a class with WEAF, WJZ, and WABC. Additional studios were built at the New Amsterdam Theatre and the converted Guild and Longacre Theatres in the Times Square theatre district."[25]

Eventually, there were shared studios at 1440 Broadway, a complex that WOR erected in 1926. It consisted of a common master control room on the 25th floor running all audio routing and control for the web as well as for WOR-AM programming and—starting in 1940—FM programming also. In addition, there was a large performance hall on the 25th floor capable of accommodating major broadcasts like the WOR Symphony Orchestra. Originally occupying the 24th floor was the Mutual-WOR news hub along with six studios available to both WOR and MBS. These were replaced in June 1978 (nearly two decades after the MBS ties ended) with a half-dozen state-of-the-art WOR studios on the 23rd floor.

From the beginning of that facility's use, the 18th floor provided music studios and a recording unit consisting of Presto lathes. The lathes could preserve programming from any audio studio in the building, resulting in 16-inch acetate-coated transcription discs. Before magnetic recording tape came into vogue in the late 1940s, network and local shows were transcribed there. Beyond the 18th and 25th floors, a trio of audio studios (14, 15 and 16) was situated at ground level. The three were ultimately reconfigured into a single studio for WOR-TV.

WOR and MBS went their separate ways in 1959. For a while, WOR was Mutual's landlord, renting space to its old web affiliate on the 20th floor at 1440 Broadway. By 1964, however, MBS moved into new owner 3M Company's newly opened facility at 135 West 50th Street between Sixth and Seventh avenues. The structure is situated directly across the street from

NBC's Radio City Music Hall in Rockefeller Center, which would have made it quite convenient for actors, announcers, musicians and others in radio's golden age—by then ended—to hop between those broadcast centers.

In earlier years, with CBS renting space in a nearby office building at 799 Seventh Avenue, there was particularly frenetic activity between Radio City, CBS and MBS at 1440 Broadway during the heyday of daytime drama. "Radio City, Madison Avenue, and Seventh Avenue, together with the Mutual Broadcasting Company studios at Fortieth Street and Broadway (much like those of CBS but smaller), formed a kind of triangular raceway for the busy radio actor," claimed one of their number who supplied an animated eyewitness account of those days. "He [an actor] could make from $10,000 to $30,000 a year on free-lance work alone, but it meant dashing from station to station, hiring stand-ins [substitute actors] for portions of rehearsal periods, tipping starters to hold elevators, and chartering taxicabs."[26] What a joy to watch, if one did nothing more!

The web turned into a news-only operation in its latter days, and its headquarters shifted from New York to 16th and K streets in Washington, D.C., in 1973. Near the end of its long life MBS occupied a northern Virginia address in Crystal City, its final resting place.

While all of the physical transition was occurring, Mutual was generating low budget programming that satisfied millions of listeners, many of them remaining faithful fans until somebody finally pulled the plug. Sustaining and regional features frequently characterized the fare proffered by MBS as corporations with sizeable promotional budgets usually fled elsewhere. They preferred to put their ad dollars into more powerful webs linked with prestigious high-wattage local stations that dominated local landscapes and were potentially able to reach scads of additional consumers.

This translated into fewer comedy-variety-musical shows on MBS. Often those that were there were temporary, showcasing to prospective advertisers, hoping to attract some that would carry those programs to bigger chains. At the same time, Mutual tended to offer steady opportunities in drama, which could be produced for nominal sums, while managing to virtually corner the juvenile adventure market. One intellect affirmed, "Mutual led the way when it came to kiddie action serials—a very inexpensive format that made the network piles of money in the mid-forties." It also fashioned a solid news-and-commentary product that for years attracted a supremely loyal following.

Funny men who spent a portion of their air lives making Mutual audiences laugh included Henry Morgan (*Here's Morgan*), Chester Lauck and Norris Goff (*Lum and Abner*),[27] Bob Elliott and Ray Goulding (*Bob and Ray*).

The Chicago Theater of the Air (1940–1955) was an extraordinary production of Saturday midday matinees that blended music and drama. Relying on famous operettas as their prime vehicle, these live productions were in the vein of *The Railroad Hour* coming along later on ABC/NBC (1948–1954). Occasionally there were condensed renderings of operas like *Carmen*, *Faust*, *La Traviata* and *Rigoletto*, similar to full Met Opera concerts aired later on Saturday afternoons on ABC. Guests on the Windy City cultural series were renowned artists like Igor Gorin, Virginia Haskins, Lauritz Melchior, James Melton, Conrad Thibault and Thomas L. Thomas, who turned up routinely on NBC's "Monday Night of Music" offerings.[28] Henry Weber conducted the Chicago Symphony as choral director Robert Trendler led a 30-voice ensemble. For a lower-rung network, did we mention classy?

Despite the low budgets and repetitive themes of many of the scripts, Mutual could be counted on for some better-than-average narrative series. *The Mysterious Traveler* has stood the test of time, providing a worthy contender to the species for which CBS's *Suspense* has often been heralded. Horror anthology *The Witch's Tale* drew a loyal following for Old Nancy, the "witch of Salem," who claimed to be a "hunner-an'-thirteen-year-old." Weekly she urged listeners to "douse the lights ... draw up to the fire ... gaze into the embers" while spinning a weird yarn. *The Return of Nick Carter*, later renamed *Nick Carter, Master Detective*, and spinoff *Chick Carter, Boy Detective* kept fans of varying ages engrossed in their crime-stopping pursuits. Several more of the same stripe included *Let George Do It*, which originated in 1946 on the West Coast before being beamed for a year (1954–1955) to the nation.

The Lone Ranger, of course, paved the dusty trails of those juvenile adventure serials that dominated the Mutual frontier for so long, although that one may have drawn about as many adults as it did offspring to its legions of steady followers. Beyond it, there was *The Adventures of Superman*, an adolescent feature that held the little tykes like glue, and sold their families many a box of Kellogg's Pep in the process. Mutual also pacified adolescents with audio versions of *Bobby Benson and the B-Bar-B Riders*, *The Cisco Kid*, *Hopalong Cassidy*, *Mark Trail*, *Sky King*, *Tom Mix* and *Wild Bill Hickok*. All those faves of the pampered set were available in one or more extra incarnations like comic books, screen and video adaptations, and proliferating premiums and merchandise.

If asked to name one dramatic feature for which MBS is singularly celebrated, most vintage radio enthusiasts would unhesitatingly acquiesce to *The Shadow* with hypnotic powers "to cloud men's minds." No less a legendary chronicler of the halcyon days than John Dunning cites *The Shadow*, *Fibber McGee & Molly* and *The Lone Ranger* as the aural medium's most defining features (two of those three being Mutual mainstays). *The Shadow* could be "radio's most famous fictitious crime fighter," believes the revered historian, dubbing the program "a synonym for 'oldtime radio.'" Although Lamont Cranston—"wealthy young man about town"—and *The Shadow's* alter ego—was introduced to listeners of sundry CBS series before reaching MBS under his own sobriquet on September 26, 1937, the figure was an overnight sensation. His series became a bastion in a popular block of Sunday afternoon and early evening theater over MBS that included *The Adventures of the Falcon*, *Official Detective*, *The Saint*, *True Detective Mysteries*, *Under Arrest* and more of that ilk.

The Mutual faithful were nevertheless entranced by the intrepid pursuer "who knows what evil lurks in the hearts of men" for 17 years. Upon departing the ether for the final time on December 26, 1954, *The Shadow* was one of radio's most enduring narratives. Eminent thespians played him in the MBS span—Orson Welles, William Johnstone and Bret Morrison; his sidekick, Margot Lane, the only person who knew his real identity (besides, of course, the millions tuning in), was impersonated in memorable runs by Agnes Moorehead, Grace Matthews and Gertrude Warner.

Often into innovative experimentation, to rave reviews in July 1937, MBS offered a seven-part presentation of Victor Hugo's *Les Miserables*. Penned, directed and produced by Orson Welles, the urbane adaptation featured several consummate thespians who would populate Welles' refined *Mercury Theater* on CBS in 1938 and 1946. On a more stable basis, there was the religious-oriented anthology *Family Theater* (1947–1962). When ABC finally canceled the long-running daily fictional anthology *My True Story* (1943–1961), MBS picked it up four times weekly, squeezing another few months of melodrama out for listeners to February 1, 1962. *Family Theater* and *My True Story* were thus extended beyond the prevailing denouement of most golden age fare.

Mutual was, indeed, a vista for numerous auditioning series that subsequently made it big elsewhere in network radio, the result of their humble beginnings at MBS. Soap opera is a genre proving it. Among numerous hits on other chains that laid claim to Mutual inceptions were *David Harum* (1935, on WOR only), *Backstage Wife* (1935–1936), *The Life of Mary Sothern* (1935–1937), *Hilltop House* (1937–1938), *Young Widder Jones* (1938, renamed *Young Widder Brown* on NBC) and *Front Page Farrell* (1941–1942). Similar "discoveries" occurred in other breeds.

Sensing a new trend in the wake of NBC's phenomenal success with its 40-hour weekend production of *Monitor* that debuted in June 1955, MBS and ABC soon answered with similar ventures of their own, albeit on greatly reduced scales. Mutual's version, *Companionate Radio*, followed in July 1955; ABC's *New Sounds* premiered in November 1955. The copies were limited imitations of the big-budgeted *Monitor*, however, and both newcomers paled badly, fading quickly into the night.

As a wave of nostalgia surfaced across America in the 1970s and early 1980s, the national radio chains realized some opportunities to draw new as well as old listeners back to their dials. Mutual offered a suspenseful narrative titled *The Zero Hour* hosted by Rod Serling. It ran in two distinct cycles, from September 10 to December 7, 1973, and from April 29 to July 26, 1974. Each segment contained 13 complete tales in five 30-minute installments.

On March 3, 1980, as the nostalgia craze persisted, *The Mutual Radio Theater* reprised 55-minute transcribed narratives originally presented as *The Sears Radio Theater* (1979–1980) on CBS. The MBS extension continued to December 19, 1980.

One of the species in which Mutual prevailed and at the same time excelled was that of sports broadcasting. Its inaugural event, in fact, on May 24, 1935, was the first ever broadcast of a night baseball game in which the Cincinnati Reds vied against the Philadelphia Phillies. MBS's live *Game of the Day* baseball broadcasts linked with the annual All Star Game, plus the Fall Classic—the World Series, beginning in October 1935—made it the darling web of an athletics-loving audience's heart.[29] By 1939, Mutual signed an exclusive contract to broadcast the Series.

Starting in 1935, MBS aired live football games from the Notre Dame gridiron. Mutual secured exclusive radio network rights to Notre Dame football in 1958, continuing as a web cornerstone for the remainder of its existence four decades hence. It was also the sole radio broadcaster of *Monday Night Football* from 1970 through 1977. Starting in May 1939, MBS carried the annual Indianapolis 500 stock car race competitions.

Mutual is believed to have opened the door to a gaggle of advice series by bringing *The Goodwill Hour* to the network ether in 1936 featuring John J. Anthony, alias of Lester Kroll. The show premiered on New York radio a quadrennial earlier as *Ask Mr. Anthony* and was "dedicated to helping the sufferers from an antiquated and outmoded domestic relations code."

The network established a solid reputation for delivery of a reputable news-and-commentary product, also. With reporter-commentators Cedric Foster, Gabriel Heatter, Fulton Lewis, Jr., Raymond Gram Swing and, later, Westbrook Van Voorhis on its staff, MBS drew a contingent of the informational faithful that tuned in daily for their reports and analysis.

Mutual was constantly a trendsetter. Beginning in 1938, it added rebroadcasts of news reports from the British Broadcasting Company. And lest it be overlooked, in December 1946, MBS gave birth to *Meet the Press*, an institution now in its seventh broadcasting decade. Martha Rountree and Lawrence Spivak guided the venerable public affairs roundtable during its formative era.

As television emerged, there was a brief flirtation among Mutual affiliates with the idea of launching an MBS-TV network. For a while Bamberger's WOR-TV and WOIC, the latter a video outlet in Washington, D.C., maintained letterhead with "Mutual Television" embellishing their identifications. There is no confirmation, however, that a cooperative video service was ever seriously surmounted.

This doesn't mean that MBS didn't influence commercial TV's early development. The web held rights to a number of worthy radio properties that transitioned to the newer medium, including two of the epoch's most popular variants on what would later be labeled the tabloid talk show and reality programming: the crabby gabfest *Leave It to the Girls* (1945–1949) and the sisters' sob-story giveaway *Queen for a Day* (1945–1957). A simulcast of the latter ran from

May 1947 on a local Los Angeles TV outlet; it was later projected to Don Lee TV stations on the West Coast and eventually carried by NBC-TV while a Mutual Radio version persisted concurrently. Lee—the reputed broadcasting industrialist-mogul of the West Coast—was a busy pioneer in TV: throughout the 1930s, his staff diligently experimented with linking pictures and sound, just as NBC's David Sarnoff and—to a lesser extent—CBS's engineers were doing back East.[30]

The first nationwide all-night call-in series, *The Herb Jepko Show*, was initiated over Mutual on November 3, 1975. Jepko was followed as host by Long John Nebel, and then Larry King on January 30, 1978. Before King reached televiewers in the mid 1980s, his series secured many new affiliates for MBS.

> It was not long after the Larry King show first went on the air nationally in 1978 that the competition recognized there were profits to be made through late-night talk programming: the Mutual Broadcasting System had increased its affiliates by close to 200 stations within six months. According to listener surveys, the average caller to Mr. King's program was 30 years old, a college graduate and listened to the show for more than two-and-a-half hours nightly....
> And, most important from an advertising point of view, the latest Arbitron figures show that Mr. King has, on the average, four million listeners each night.[31]

An accomplishment like that couldn't be overlooked by rival webs. In December 1981, NBC launched *Nighttalk*, with financial and relationship experts presiding over its overnight call-in marathon. By April 1982, *Nighttalk* was renamed *Talknet*, its hours extended and its live responses drawing from all over America. ABC began to scratch a similar itch a month later. In May 1982, it introduced its own dialoguing gurus on *Talkradio*. The bug had bitten nearly everybody, starting with MBS, and the innovation seemed ample enough for radio's house to divide it up and have plenty left over!

As the other major chains were doing in the 1970s and 1980s, MBS began experimenting with supplemental audio services, too. On May 1, 1972, it launched two alternative formats aimed at ethnic audiences: Mutual Black Network, with newscasts programmed especially for African-American listeners at 50 minutes past the hour, a service MBS sold in 1979 to the Sheridan Broadcasting Corporation (the Sheridan Network); and Mutual Cadena Hispanica, with newscasts directed at Spanish language listeners at 45 minutes past the hour, a diversion that persisted until 1973 only.[32] When satellite technology consequently became available, on October 17, 1982, MBS launched seven parallel "networks" pointed to specialized audiences.

The Mutual chain was the last of the majors to obtain its own radio stations. In June 1979, its owners bought Chicago's WCFL for $12.5 million from the Chicago Federation of Labor. Six months down the road it added New York's WHN, purchasing it from Storer Broadcasting for $14 million.

From 1934 to 1952, MBS was owned and operated as a collaborative venture (the "Mutual" nomenclature definitely said it all), with participating stations sharing in program origination, transmission, production and promotion expenses as well as advertising revenues (translated: profits). Nevertheless, its business configuration was to experience dramatic upheaval. It was precipitated in the wake of a series of regional and single station acquisitions as the General Tire & Rubber Company of Akron, Ohio, assumed majority ownership of the web in 1952.[33] It would soon adopt the taxonomy General Teleradio as a subsidiary moniker under which its broadcasting interests were consolidated. From that time forward, in fact, the widely-recognized cooperative format that had distinguished MBS since its inception would hardly be applicable over the remaining 47 years of its broadcasting existence. Some observers would even intimate that the shift that took place in 1952 launched a downward spiral from which the chain never recovered. Certainly it wasn't the same pipeline it had been in the previous couple of decades.

General Tire's foray into radio was gradual. It came about in at least three separate and distinct waves. In January 1943, the FCC approved the sale of the Yankee Network—including flagship station WNAC in Boston and three other owned-and-operated outlets, plus contracts with 17 more affiliates, four relay stations, two experimental stations, two high-frequency (FM) stations, along with Yankee's MBS shares, and in addition the jointly-owned Colonial Network—to General Tire.[34]

At the time of General Tire's initial expansion into broadcasting (late 1942), upon agreeing to purchase the Yankee and Colonial networks, General's founder and president William O'Neil shared some insights on the firm's motivation and intents, and most perceptively, the state of America in the years just ahead. "The post-war America is going to be an entirely new America, with increased manufacturing capacity and facilities, entirely changed methods of merchandising and advertising, a tremendous buying power and an even higher standard of living. With this in mind, we are making plans now for our expansion after the war," which, he said, included using the Yankee Network as "a proving ground for our new merchandising plans and our new merchandise."[35]

In General Tire's second sortie into broadcasting, eight years later in late 1950, executors of the estate of Thomas Stewart Lee, who died in 1950, son of Don Lee, who died in 1934, sought to liquidate the assets in broadcasting.[36, 37] The Don Lee Broadcasting System—including radio stations KHJ (Los Angeles), KFRC (San Francisco), KGB (San Diego), Don Lee Hollywood studios assessed at $3 million catering to 53 affiliates, and shares in MBS—were put on the market. General Tire was the purchaser in October 1950 for $12,320,000.[38]

In a third access to broadcasting, General Tire acquired a "substantial majority" of voting stock when the Federal Communications Commission, on January 17, 1952, approved combining its broadcasting interests with those of R. H. Macy & Company.[39] With that transaction, Macy's New York outlets—WOR, WOR-FM and WOR-TV—shifted to the Don Lee Broadcasting System owned by General Tire. Macy's became a part owner of Don Lee. Don Lee paid Macy cash and stock with total value of $3,265,000. The deal included transfer of WOR Program Services, Inc., assessed at $1.2 million from Macy to Don Lee. Macy also agreed to lease its WOR physical operating facilities to Don Lee for 25 years at $315,000 annually.[40]

Most importantly, in regard to prospects for the Mutual Broadcasting System, the transactions gave General Tire principal jurisdiction over MBS: "Control of the Mutual Broadcasting System now rests with the General Tire and Rubber Company, shareholders of the latter learned at their annual meeting" in April 1952.[41] To its dominant position in MBS, General Tire was to strengthen itself by purchasing the interests of Western Ontario Broadcasting in 1956.

T. F. O'Neil, vice president of General Tire and radio and TV properties manager, beamed: "General ... has acquired new television stations in Los Angeles and New York and now owns three television and seven radio stations. This is the limit allowed." Its arrangement brought under one roof the following broadcasting properties: radio stations WOR (New York), WNAC (Boston), WEAN (Providence), WONS (Hartford), KHJ (Los Angeles), KFRC (San Francisco), KGB (San Diego); TV stations WOR-TV (New York), WNAC-TV (Boston), KHJ-TV (Los Angeles); plus the Yankee and Don Lee regional radio networks.[42]

In the meantime, the question that industry analysts were already proffering was: What does this mean to the future of MBS?

Keep in mind that there was another factor complicating this transitory shift: it occurred in a period just as network radio's fortunes were plummeting, while advertisers, artists and audiences were fleeing to television. That resulted in drastic reductions in commercial rates which negatively affected the bottom line. All of it made broadcasting in general, and MBS in particular, of diminishing value, particularly as owners considered upgrading their product.

In theory, General Tire's takeover of MBS appeared to be a repudiation of the basic concept of "mutual" cooperation (and respect) on which the broadcasting enterprise was established — a concept that its founding fathers had wholeheartedly embraced at the web's formation, rejecting the alternative style of the competition. In practice, that repudiation turned out not to be so permanent for this major player in transcontinental broadcasting.

While General's brief ownership may have done little surface damage beyond reversing the schematic that distinguished MBS from the top-down control of affiliates exhibited in the NBC-CBS-ABC paradigm, it furthermore opened a door wide at MBS that had never before been ajar. And in doing so, it let in some varmints that the network had never had to contend with, possibly even threatening its prospects of continuance.

Five years after buying MBS, the General Tire & Rubber Company decided to spin off its holdings in the chain and sell it as a programming service while keeping the stations that had given it control of the web. In July 1957, it traded MBS to a West Coast consortium headed by Dr. Armand Hammer. Discounting the cooperative ownership venture in the line of succession fostered in 1934 by WGN and WOR, owner number two wasn't long in holding the MBS reins: 14 months after acquiring it, in September 1958, the Hammer federation dispensed with its purchase. MBS was next bought for $2 million by an odd couple merged enterprise. The new entity was comprised of Hal Roach Studios, then flush with winning domestic and global telefilm achievements, and Detroit-based industrial representative F. L. Jacobs Company, dealing in auto parts, lace and a whole lot of other unrelated commodities. Hal Roach, Jr., became chairman of the MBS board while Jacobs' leader, Alexander Guterma, was MBS president. Thereby hangs a tale of political intrigue and highly debatable activity not normally found in radio ownership:

> In January 1959, accompanied by Hal Roach, Jr., and other associates — Roach later said he slept most of the time — Guterma flew to Ciudad Trujillo, capital of the Dominican Republic, and negotiated an agreement with representatives of the dictator Rafael Trujillo. For $750,000, paid in advance ... Guterma agreed that for eighteen months MBS would broadcast a "monthly minimum of 425 minutes of news and commentary regarding the Dominican Republic." There would be nothing contrary to Dominican interests....
>
> During negotiations Guterma displayed fancy salesmanship [deriving a fictional story to demonstrate to the Dominicans]. Guterma got in touch with MBS, and next day they heard Walter Winchell proclaim the invented news item over the network.[43]

Shortly after the Dominican deal was struck, Guterma was forced to resign from MBS when he found himself in legal trouble for stock fraud and failure to register as a foreign agent. Eventually, a lawsuit was filed by the Dominicans to recover their money. As a result of these events, the details of the negotiations were revealed:

> It was never clear how far Guterma could have carried his corruption of MBS news. But that a nationwide network could so casually be purchased was thought-provoking.
>
> Participants in the Dominican agreement pointed out, in its defense, that it included the clause: "We shall not carry any news extolling the communist cause but agree that the primary purpose is to exemplify the stability and tranquility of the Dominican Republic and its unequivocal position and stand against communism."
>
> Could anyone object, except perhaps a communist?[44]

"Mutual, by this point, was floundering," a source revealed. "For some years it had been run by owners who were either uninterested (General Tire, Armand Hammer) or now, as a growing amount of evidence would show, criminal."[45]

The Trujillo stratocracy blew the whistle on its arrangement when its expectations weren't met, sued for the return of its capital, and in so doing, allowed the deal to pop out into the open before intense public scrutiny. While Guterma, who was principally responsible for airing the distorted messages, pleaded no contest to the charge, it was never proven that he carried out his commitment. In the aftermath, suspicion settled on some legitimate programmers who might have fallen victim to added publicists just as one network executive had done. At the same time, 130 stations rapidly dropped their MBS affiliations due to those charges of impropriety, temporarily thinning the web's influence still more.

After 23 years as a Mutual affiliate, for instance, in 1959, WOR—one of the corporation's founders—broke away from the network it had helped launch. It had inaugurated CBS before that, you'll recall, becoming that chain's original flagship station in 1927. Breaking new ground in the late 1950s, WOR adopted a talk format while retaining many of its enduring ethereal personalities. It concentrated heavily in personal-advice features that "often sound like soap operas without organ music," an informant suggested.[46]

The merry-go-round on which MBS was spinning, meanwhile, never slowed. By the spring of 1960, yet another owner had jumped aboard, the fourth to take possession of the broadcast network within three years—Minnesota Mining and Manufacturing Company (3M). It provided "much-needed stability to the operation" over the next half-dozen years.

In July 1966, a newly formed private party headed by John P. Fraim became Mutual's fifth owner. Numerous experiments and a few advancements occurred during the Fraim deputation's watch, possible perhaps due to its continuity, something missing under earlier regimes.

Mutual wasn't sold again until September 30, 1977, when Amway Corporation forked over the cash. Still more promising opportunities appeared on its horizon following that transaction. Eight years passed before MBS was transferred a final time, to its seventh owner since departing from its premiering joint-ownership model. In September 1985, Amway sold the network to Westwood One for $30 million.[47] Formed in 1975, Westwood One was a major radio production company and program syndicator, already introduced to readers in chapters 3 and 4. Ironically, in time it would become the corporate umbrella under which old rivals MBS, NBC, CBS, Fox and CNN would spend rainy days—and under which at least one of them, MBS, would utter its final words.

"Mutual ended up simply being a brand name for programming provided by Westwood One. The top-of-the-hour newscasts were written and read by CBS Radio News reporters and anchors in Mutual's final years."[48] Nevertheless, it can be affirmed even now that—in the listening environment of the mid 1980s—Westwood and Mutual together was a good match. The largely adult demographics of Mutual affiliates were complemented by the younger audiences served by the stations purchasing Westwood's programming, much of which was in the pop music field. Added to the mix were Mutual's news operations, which Westwood lacked. With 810 affiliates, Mutual's size also made it a strong second in the Big Four. Norman J. Pattiz, the head of Westwood One, called it "a perfect fit" and "a classic case of two plus two equaling five" in reference to the broad demographic sweep they could offer their advertisers.[49]

In 1987, Westwood acquired NBC, forming a much larger programming service of which Mutual was now only a small part. Mutual's identity was gradually phased out, and when Westwood was taken over by Infinity Broadcasting in 1994,[50] it became little more than a brand name for some news and sports programming as part of the new conglomerate's Westwood One division. Mutual and NBC newscasters shared what had once been the main MBS facility in Crystal City, Virginia.[51]

In April 1999, the end came abruptly for the Mutual brand when it was dropped by Westwood in favor of CNN Radio. A former news team member described it this way: "Official time of Mutual Radio's death was Midnight 4/17/99. No tribute, no mention it was the last newscast ... it just died."[52] In March 2001, Westwood's primary operations were moved to the CBS Broadcast Center in New York City, and the Crystal City facility was closed.

In the blink of an eye, with no fanfare or acknowledgement whatsoever, the first of the four competing transcontinental radio webs in America had been put to rest. Following a colorful history that began as a remarkably innovative endeavor—on one level, more nearly a "private enterprise" than any of its counterparts—it had finally given up the ghost at the age of 65, categorically altering the intended connotation of "retirement at 65."[53]

Ah! But what an astonishing journey that mysterious traveler made on its way to confirm the evil lurking in the hearts of men! There was something incredibly compelling about MBS's forbearance in the face of adversity and insurmountable odds that was surely worth emulating. It was, without question, the little engine that could. While it may have resided only in the shadows of its larger competitors with deeper pockets and far more powerful affiliates, MBS persevered until deemed unworthy by mortals, no longer needed. It had nevertheless run the race with dignity. And by then it had left a legacy that will not soon be forgotten by any who remember those days.

For many of those fans, it had long before—indubitably—become "the network for all America."

6

AMERICAN BROADCASTING COMPANY
A Nobleman's Dream

As a result of its landmark hearings conducted in 1938, the Federal Communications Commission (FCC) reasoned:

> We do not believe ... that any substantial justification can be found for NBC's operation of two stations in New York, Washington, Chicago, or San Francisco. In none of these cities are the better radio facilities so numerous as to make it in the public interest for any one network organization to control two stations; in each case such dual ownership is bound to obstruct the development of rival networks and the establishment of new networks. In Washington (excluding local stations) there are but three regional stations, of which NBC controls two.... In Chicago, the equivalent of two of the four 50,000-watt full-time facilities are owned by NBC.... In San Francisco, the only two stations with better than regional power are NBC's. Competition will be greatly strengthened if the best facilities in important cities are not so tied in the hands of a single network organization. Even in New York, where desirable facilities are more plentiful, NBC's ownership of two clear-channel stations gives it a dominant position which tends to restrict competition on even terms from other networks.
>
> We find, accordingly, that the licensing of two stations in the same area to a single network organization is basically unsound and contrary to the public interest....
>
> In exercising our licensing powers with respect to the renewal of the licenses now held by NBC and CBS ... the Commission will not license to a single network organization more than one station within a given area, nor will it license stations to any network organization in communities where the available outlets are so few or of such unequal desirability as to require that all facilities be open to competition among networks for outlets and among stations for networks.[1]

That opinion, rendered in a crucial arena of network broadcasting, was to have profound effect on the methods practiced by the industry from the early 1940s forward. And for NBC, in particular, it was going to be a deal-breaker. Call it *Divorce, American Style*. There were cracks in the armor, and ultimately they would result in an entirely separate chain to be labeled the American Broadcasting Company.

But first, there was that messy Red and Blue thing to dispose of.

> NBC's witnesses testified that the Red and Blue networks compete vigorously for listening audiences and for the advertising dollar. But the competition between Red and Blue is largely of an intramural character. Even taking into account the changes which NBC has made in its organization since the time of the committee hearings, there is no complete allocation of stations or programs between the Red and Blue networks, nor any clear demarcation between the properties, personnel, income or expenses of the two networks. No claim is made that the two networks compete for affiliates. So far as competition for advertising and listeners is concerned, it is conducted in a friendly manner under the direction of the NBC board of directors and for the financial benefit of NBC.
>
> Although the sales and program personnel allocated to the Red or the Blue network may now engage in friendly rivalry, it is hardly to be supposed that this rivalry will ever reach the point where NBC employees are acting against the best interests of NBC. Under such conditions, there can be no competition as that term is properly used.[2]

If an advertiser was dissatisfied with the power and frequency of a certain station, for instance, many times NBC had the ability to substitute another outlet, something its rivals couldn't do. With dual webs under its control, NBC could make choices between two commercial shows or a commercial and sustaining feature aired at the same hour, again something the opposition couldn't do. By buying time on one of its chains, advertisers could be assured they wouldn't face direct challenges by rival concerns advertising concurrently on NBC's other web. "It seems clear," said the investigative panel, "that the Blue has had the effect of acting as a buffer to protect the profitable Red against competition."

While there are scores of pages of additional testimony and observations of the FCC, the final conclusions are unmistakably clear: in the interest of safeguarding the public trust assigned to it by Congress, and for fairness within the trade, the FCC was convinced that the double-web system controlled by NBC, which in many cases dominated the various markets, wasn't in the best interests of the industry. The bottom-line effect was dissolution of the paired arrangement as NBC officials decided to retain the lucrative Red operation and divest the Blue chain as soon as practicable. The switch wasn't made overnight, of course, but occurred instead in increments.

In his fresh-from-the-inside memoir, announcer George Ansbro paints a tiny glimpse of what life was like for his deputation of human resources situated in "no man's land" between owners.

> Before a buyer could be found ... it became necessary to split NBC down the middle, employee-wise, so to speak. Or more precisely, to split each department. With those of us in the announcing department, it worked like this: Ray Diaz was to become announcing supervisor of the Blue Network Announcing Staff. Ray invited whichever of us NBC guys he wanted, up to a certain number, to switch over with him to form a new Blue Network Announcing Staff. Of course those he invited had the right to decline, with no hard feelings. For instance, of those of us Ray asked to join him, Ben Grauer and Radcliff Hall preferred to stay with NBC.
>
> The split became official in February of 1942. The announcers who comprised the new Blue Network staff were, as best I can remember, myself, Milton Cross, Jack Gordon Fraser, George Hicks, George Hayes, Kelvin Keech, Don Lowe, Jack McCarthy, and Bob Waldrop. No longer did we report to Pat Kelly's space on the fifth floor but to the second floor office of Ray Diaz because, although we were still paid by NBC, we were part of what a potential buyer was going to get when he purchased the Blue Network. On the air we signed off our programs with, "This is the Blue Network of the National Broadcasting Company." Later, when our fledgling company was bought, the sign-off cue became simply "This is the Blue Network."[3]

A contemporary group of journalists shared Ansbro's recollections but offered a slightly different twist on its procedure: "To divide the company into two, NBC and the BLUE appointed managers who would then 'invite' employees to choose a network. Several staff announcers waited to see what decision the great pioneer Milton Cross would make, then followed him to ABC."[4]

An intrepid reporter delving into an oral history repository at New York's Columbia University happened upon illuminating details based on some 1951 verbal recollections of broadcaster Mark Woods. Woods was an NBC vice president for a few years and it fell his lot to sell the Blue Network. His background as an accountant, a post he occupied on joining WEAF in 1922 (WEAF was NBC Red's New York flagship station, you will recall), eventually thrust him into greater financial responsibilities as treasurer and vice president. Despite his presumptive preparedness, nevertheless, one wag decried of Woods: "He was unspectacular, but was always needed because he understood the books."[5]

Equipped with that affinity, as early as 1938, Woods became absolutely convinced that dividing NBC's dual chains could produce a fiscally sound outcome. That was four years before the company was forced to make that happen. Wood's views, of course, weren't widely embraced or circulated; the corporate line stridently argued before the Federal Communications Commission, the District and Supreme courts and anybody else who would listen that separating the Red and Blue webs would be detrimental to the free enterprise system while simultaneously landing a devastating blow against NBC.

After NBC was ordered to separate stations, transmitters, studios, furnishings, equipment and personnel in 1941, on January 9, 1942, it established the Blue Network Company, Inc. In 1943, Mark Woods was appointed president. The Blue was put on the block at an asking price of $8 million, a figure sanctioned by NBC president and CEO David Sarnoff. Woods soon heard rumblings that well connected business tycoon Edward J. Noble, a prominent confectioner who presided over the Life Saver manufacturing enterprise, an ex-bureaucrat and radio station owner, was interested. But the notion faded after Noble signaled that the price was unreasonable. In the end, Noble agreed to the price of $8 million, though he had hoped to purchase the network for $7 million.

> Woods saw a chance to do something for the man who was apparently destined to become his boss. Woods reminded Sarnoff that they had discussed an RCA-sponsored series over the projected independent network. Could they settle that now? Woods had specific figures in mind. For the first year, time costs should be $650,000; talent, $350,000. The total, $1,000,000. With Sarnoff's agreement, Noble was able to recoup a million dollars on the sale.[6]

The $8 million figure was the largest sale in broadcasting history.[7] It topped bids of such formidable contenders as veteran Chicago haberdasher Marshall Field, the storied Pittsburgh Mellon financiers and Paramount Pictures.[8] James H. McGraw of McGraw-Hill Publishing Company soon withdrew as joint owner, leaving Ed Noble as sole Blue network purchaser.[9] Despite his enormous personal wealth, to complete the transaction, Noble put up $4 million of his own money; then he borrowed $1 million from Commercial Bank and Trust Company of New York, and $1.5 million from each of New York's Bankers Trust Company and Central Hanover Bank and Trust Company.[10] RCA, meanwhile, spent $1.1 million on the radio series proffered in the exchange.[11] And Noble did become Woods' boss — Woods was named president of the network while Noble was chairman of the board.[12]

Included in the transaction, furthermore, were three pivotal stations in the Blue's operation: New York's WJZ, the web's flagship outlet; Chicago's WENR; and San Francisco's KGO. Following hearings, the FCC granted approval for the transfer of those stations' licenses. At the same time, Noble's new venture included 143 Blue network affiliates (1943 figure, the year the transition became official, and a figure that would be dwarfed by substantial increases soon afterward).

Radio Corporation of America, parent firm of the National Broadcasting Company, publicly announced the sale of the Blue web on July 30, 1943, to Noble's American Broadcasting System, Inc. It was approved by the FCC on October 12, 1943. The network retained most existing staff and signed leases on two theaters plus equipment and studios at NBC. For the present, principally due to wartime shortages, flagship outlet WJZ continued to air from Radio City on a 10-year lease.[13]

The new net, meanwhile, reported 1944 time sales of $41.3 million — compared to $24.6 million the previous year.[14] Seeking more prestigious nomenclature instead of mere hue, Noble acquired the appellation American Broadcasting Company (ABC) for his enterprise. The changeover involved tricky negotiations with broadcasting czar George B. Storer who owned — and retained — title to a then defunct American Broadcasting System.[15] The Blue chain was officially rebranded on June 15, 1945.

At the separation of the dual webs, the Blue Network was accorded 116 affiliated outlets in the year 1942, the first in which Blue is identified as a true "separate" entity. That compares with 115 CBS stations that year, 236 NBC Red stations and 191 MBS outlets. The Blue/ABC figure would continue spiraling upward until it reached a temporary crest of 360 in 1954 (far below Mutual's 560 that year) before tapering off. ABC recharged that mountain later, nevertheless, surpassing its previous summit recorded in 1966 of 361 stations when it finally got into high gear: two years later, the web diversified into four smaller chains, vastly multiplying its number of affiliates overnight. It catapulted to 500 the first year of the concurrent nets (1968) and continued to proliferate profusely, reaching 2,251 in two decades (1988), having long surpassed in spades every rival in the business. There hadn't been a level playing field in a long, long while.

Edward John Noble, the new network's owner, was suitably well-heeled and politically connected. Born in upstate New York at Gouveneur on August 8, 1882, he was educated at Syracuse and Yale universities. In 1913, he and partner J. Roy Allen purchased the Life Saver mint candy business from a Cleveland manufacturer and turned it into a multimillion-dollar enterprise. Investing heavily in the Life Savers Corporation, Noble became its president while his brother, Robert P. Noble, was vice president. By 1937 their titles and responsibilities were respectively upgraded to chairman of the board and executive vice president. Still chairman in 1949, Edward Noble saw his sibling rise to president of the corporation.

On the way to incredible wealth, he formed the Edward J. Noble Company in 1915 in New York City, shepherding it for eight years, capitalizing on manufacturing and distributing advertising devices and novelties. Having also taken up yachting and flying as sideline interests, on July 9, 1938, Ed Noble was appointed by U.S. President Franklin D. Roosevelt as chairman of the newly created Civil Aeronautics Authority. He resigned April 13, 1939, to become undersecretary of commerce, a post he occupied from June 1939 to August 1940. He left it to support an unsuccessful presidential bid by Wendell L. Willkie.

In 1941 Noble bought New York's WMCA Radio for $850,000. When he bought the Blue web coupled with a trio of influential affiliates in 1943, he allowed that he hoped to make the Blue "a sort of *New York Times* of the industry," adding, "I'd be perfectly happy with meager profits."[16] The Federal Communications Commission rulings prohibited him from continuing to own WMCA while adding WJZ to his portfolio, as both stations served the same market. Thus he, too, looked for a buyer. He found one in Nathan Straus, ex–U.S. housing chief, who purchased WMCA for $1,255,000 in September 1943.

Three months later, Noble sold 12.5 percent of his interest in the Blue Network to Time, Inc., headed by Chairman Henry R. Luce, and 12.5 percent to advertising executive Chester J. LaRoche. He repurchased all of those shares in October 1945. In addition, in late 1943, he sold small percentages of interest in the Blue Network to the web's president, Mark Woods, and Edgar Kobak, executive vice president.[17]

It became obvious to many observers quite early that—coupled with the business acumen that made him prosperous—Noble was eager to share his time and talents to benefit millions who weren't as fortunate. He was deeply involved in numerous nonprofit endeavors; some examples suffice. He gave freely to St. Lawrence University at Canton, New York, from which he received an honorary doctor of laws degree in 1939, and was that institute's trustee chairman. In August 1945, he was appointed chairman of the service division of the New York National War Fund. In October 1946, Noble was named head of the Salvation Army's annual fundraising drive for 1947, a role that was extended to 1948. He was general chairman of the 1953 March for Dimes crusade for Greater New York. For a while Noble was chairman of the board of North Country Hospitals, Inc., operating medical centers in three upstate New York cities.

The American Broadcasting Company's purchase of the King-Trendle Broadcasting Corporation in 1946, including Detroit's WXYZ and Grand Rapids' WOOD (the latter resold a short time afterward), gave Ed Noble an opportunity to diffuse any lingering stability issues in the trade about intentions for his nascent network. Revelations from the Candy Man–turned-broadcaster, while brief, put to rest whatever concerns the industry may have harbored for the short term. His declarations furthermore hinted that Noble accorded his responsibility to a high plateau in influencing the national landscape.

I did not buy the Blue Network as a speculation.... I bought it to acquire an opportunity to build a great radio network. I am not interested in selling the company at any price.... I am not selling and have no intention of selling any of my shares this year or next or any future year so far as one can humanly know. It is my desire and ambition to help develop the still unrealized potentialities of radio as one of our nation's richest assets—bringing entertainment, enlightenment and education to all people.

Taking on this enterprise single-handedly was a challenge, and I expect my personal reward to be in the satisfaction that comes from accomplishment.[18]

Some seven years later Noble relinquished control of ABC as American Broadcasting merged with United Paramount Pictures in 1953, although he remained with the parent firm as a director. He was chairman of the executive committee of the Life Savers Corporation in 1956 when it combined with Beech-Nut Packing Company, a manufacturer of baby foods, chewing gum, peanut butter and coffee. Death overtook him at 76 on December 29, 1958, at his home in Greenwich, Connecticut.

Noble had possessed the necessary physical assets, abilities and zeal to form ABC at the time they were needed. He secured a foundation for a future media empire that was to gradually rival juggernaut chains exhibiting decades of history, experience, affiliates and acclaim. In an arena in which it convincingly challenged its rivals, while it would take time, ABC was to compete fairly and eventually win. Whether those were Noble's objectives or some other, all who labor for ABC today seemingly owe him a deep debt of gratitude. They may be proud of the legacy of Ed Noble, a determined Johnny-Come-Lately who was at the right place at the right time and in so doing secured the fate of legions of workers in the generations that followed.

And what of Mark Woods, ABC's inaugural president? What do we know of him? Just this: Born in Louisville, Kentucky, on December 27, 1901, he was reared and educated in Florida before departing Jacksonville at 18 for a shot at working as an accountant for a boyhood hero, Thomas A. Edison. At 19, he moved on to the American Telephone & Telegraph Company, owner of Manhattan's WEAF, which would be his next stop at age 20. Woods transferred with WEAF to NBC for opening day (1926). In the triple capacity of financial officer, assistant secretary and office manager of the radio subsidiary, Woods "established many of the first policies of network commercial broadcasting," a source affirmed. Progressively, he climbed the proverbial corporate ladder. In 1936, he was elected secretary of Civic Concert Service, Inc., an NBC subsidiary operating annual concert courses in cities across America. He became an NBC vice president at 38 on September 10, 1940.

A few years after his appointment as Blue (ultimately, ABC) network president, *Time* assessed the 47-year-old like this: "Mark is one of the best-liked men in radio, and one of the shrewdest. A near-genius at negotiation, he is often asked to handle the industry's top-level labor relations. Lapped in Mark's sunny smile, even the wintry [James C.] Petrillo has been known to thaw like any spring sap." ... One of the boys [who works for Woods] last week paid his boss a brief but enormous tribute: "Nobody at ABC has an ulcer."[19, 20]

Woods relinquished his post as ABC president on December 30, 1949, becoming vice chairman of the corporation. He resigned from ABC on June 30, 1951, and with partner J. R. Warwick formed Woods & Warwick, Inc., advertising agency on October 19, 1951. In less than six months, Warwick moved on and the business shuttered on April 9, 1952. Woods retired at 50, relocated to the Sunshine State, and died at 82 at Riverview, Florida, on October 7, 1984.

Woods' successor as president of ABC, Robert E. Kintner, was elected in December 1949. Kintner was born September 12, 1909, at Stroudsburg, Pennsylvania, where his dad was school superintendent. Graduating from Swarthmore College with a political science degree in 1931, young Kintner joined *The New York Herald-Tribune* two years later as White House correspondent. Before his service with the U.S. Army Air Force (1941–1944), he collaborated with journalist Joseph W. Alsop, Jr., penning a syndicated newspaper column, *Capitol Parade*, while authoring a couple of volumes, *Men Around the President* and *American White Paper*.

Returning to civilian life following World War II, Kintner was introduced to electronic media by Ed Noble, who hired him as public relations director of his new radio venture. On assuming the reins at ABC in late 1949, he steadily pushed it toward financial respectability by using TV westerns and blood-and-thunder shows as his chief vehicles. He made the decision to televise the Army-McCarthy hearings and was credited with hastening the political downfall of Senator Joseph R. McCarthy. McCarthy's tale of political intrigue through a witch hunt by which perceived subversives at varied levels of American life were exposed is recounted in Chapter 4.

By the early 1950s, according to one informant, "Noble's network was overextended and nearly bankrupt."[21] In a $25 million transaction, ABC merged with Leonard Goldenson's Paramount Theaters in 1953, touching off a power struggle between old and new managers. Three years afterward, when ABC's finances were the best in its history, Kintner left his post. Rejecting an offer from CBS, he joined NBC and within two years was that chain's president. A decade later—having fallen out with RCA/NBC moguls David and Robert Sarnoff—Kintner resigned there. He was soon appointed by President Lyndon B. Johnson as a special assistant and cabinet secretary handling organizational and administrative issues and recruiting high government officials. Failing eyesight forced his resignation only a few months into it in June 1967. Kintner died in Washington at 71 on December 20, 1980.

WJZ, the American Broadcasting Company's flagship station, presents a compelling case study that shouldn't be missed by anyone making a calculated inquiry into the early years and the halcyon days of its web association. WJZ billed itself "New York's First Station" in that embryonic epoch. That really wasn't true, given the proclivities of Frank Bremer, Lee de Forest and others of their ilk who experimented with radio technology in the confines of the Big Apple well before WJZ erected a transmitter in 1921. Also, RCA's WJY was beamed across the ether for a single day some three months prior to Westinghouse's WJZ took to the air. Forgiving that, nonetheless, "It would not be unfair to state that the broadcasting industry in the New York area begins with WJZ."[22]

Its physical addresses all have stories to tell. They included a shack on the roof of the Westinghouse meter factory on Orange and Plane streets in Newark, accessible only by ladder; from there, half the downstairs ladies' restroom of Westinghouse's Newark works; a permanent studio at the Waldorf-Astoria Hotel at Fifth Avenue and 34th Street (site of the Empire State Building today) and linked to Newark by a rowdy Western Union wire; and the sixth floor of the Aeolian Building at 29 West 42nd Street, across from the public library where WJZ was dubbed "the world's first national theater" by RCA president James Harbord. It then occupied NBC studios still under construction at 711 Fifth Avenue in October 1927, with WEAF and the Red chain joining it there a month later; in November 1933, WJZ, WEAF, RCA corporate headquarters, and both webs transferred to Radio City at 30 Rockefeller Plaza. Finally the station and network moved into a home of its own in November 1948 in a renovated edifice that earlier served the New York Riding Club as stables at 7 West 66th Street, a block west of Central Park.

On May 14, 1923, WJZ signed off in Newark forever, transferred to Gotham, and became the property of RCA at the same instant. Perhaps an even more momentous watershed occurred on May 1, 1953, nevertheless. Six and a half years after network flagship WRCA was rebranded WNBC and WABC became WCBS, WJZ's New York nomenclature—oldest in the city—was put out to pasture. On that day, WJZ was re-identified as WABC to more properly reflect its status as a symbol of its network. Four years later, incidentally, Westinghouse regained those infamous call letters, applying them to its Baltimore TV station.

Programming on ABC generally followed a trend that had existed since the history of network broadcasting was inaugurated almost two decades before the chain's formal organization. The steak and potato crowd went elsewhere as upstarts ABC and MBS got the drippings and leftovers. While that certainly wasn't true 100 percent of the time, those webs' shows and personalities stacked against the numerous "name" singers, comedians, masters of ceremonies and venerable sleuths operating on CBS and NBC left a gigantic void between them. The elder Sarnoff and comrades hand-picked the Red network as a keeper when it came time to divide the house at NBC. The decision was primarily based on two quantities: the Red chain had the most popular features and thereby drew the largest audiences and biggest advertisers, and the Red also—and quite possibly for those very reasons—maintained the most powerful and most prestigious affiliates in the markets where NBC controlled two outlets.

From its inception the Blue chain had been viewed within NBC as a feeder web, auditioning shows for the better chain and supplying that fare once it built an appreciable following. It also received many of NBC's sustaining entries (those without sponsorship), including some for educational, nonprofit and public service agencies. Finally, there were shows that simply appealed to smaller fan bases throughout their aural histories. So ABC (and MBS) was viewed by some in the trade as also-ran operations; only through a few rare gems was it afforded an equal place at the broadcasting table during the golden age of radio.

But those gems, nevertheless, as few as they were, stood out like polished stones, shimmering amidst an array of lackluster programming that seldom attained much sparkle. They included personalities like newsmen Martin Agronsky, Elmer Davis, Don Gardiner, Paul Harvey and Walter Winchell; toastmaster Don McNeill; emcee Bert Parks; gossip columnist Louella Parsons; Ozzie Nelson and Harriet Hilliard with their humorous exchanges; juvenile heroes *The Green Hornet, The Lone Ranger* and *Terry and the Pirates*; and the unparalleled soloists and instrumentalists of the Metropolitan Opera Company. Many of them are self explanatory, with headliners that said it all.

Journalist Winchell, for one, became an NBC Blue network property in 1932 who stayed by the stuff far into the ABC era. His bulletin-style Sunday night dispatches of news and gossip revelations were such "musts" in millions of American domiciles that ABC signed him to a lifetime contract in 1950.[23] Winchell was guaranteed $10,000 weekly for as long as he was mentally and physically competent to broadcast his Sunday night quarter-hour. And should he have become incapacitated, he was to receive $1,000 monthly. By 1950s standards, that wasn't a shabby haul. Surprisingly, however, it was a short life; Winchell moved to MBS in 1955.

America's most durable daytime audio feature, *The Breakfast Club*, was commanding entertainment from 1933 to 1968, with all of it on ABC and its predecessor webs. For 35 and a half years, host Don McNeill, a man with sunshine in his voice, was the nation's most ebullient morning greeter. He was flanked by a cadre of singers, instrumentalists, comics, foils and guest artists, many of whom later starred at other venues. All were surrounded by an animated, boisterous theater audience five mornings weekly in downtown Chicago.

McNeill made such a strong showing that for decades he annihilated the competition. His laid-back Midwestern style resonated with listeners far and wide as his homespun philosophy laced with moral bromides lifted the nation during some of its most perilous hours. He was thereby accorded the most enduring performance in daytime radio, Tom Breneman, Arthur Godfrey, Robert Q. Lewis, Art Linkletter, Mary Margaret McBride, Garry Moore, Johnny Olsen, Kate Smith and other august quantities notwithstanding.

One of the most telling signs that radio was in serious jeopardy as television began to encroach on its turf occurred in mid 1949 at the hands of ABC. *The Fred Allen Show*, which had long dominated its time period on NBC Sunday nights and had aired consecutively for 18 seasons, abruptly departed the ether forever. It left at the hands of a highly successful telephone quiz show, *Stop the Music!*, that ABC threw against some of NBC's formidable Sunday night comedies.

The Allen program was irrefutably caught in the shifting fortunes of radio. A couple of radio historiographers went so far as to insist that "Radio actually died when *Stop the Music!* got higher ratings than Fred Allen."[24] Humorist Henry Morgan assured everybody that such an aberration drove "the final nail in radio's coffin."[25]

For all of its short life, ABC had been playing not just second fiddle to NBC's Sunday night laughmasters Allen, Jack Benny, Edgar Bergen and Red Skelton, but third oboe to CBS's counter-programming attempts including private eye *Sam Spade* and a globetrotting troubleshooter, *The Man Called X*, drawing most of the remaining listeners who weren't into comedy. The leftovers, meanwhile, attracted a more sedate, erudite crowd: that handful tuned to ABC which mustered a Sunday night hour of fairly nondescript classical selections by a no-name chamber instrumental staff with occasional guest symphonies. ABC was in bad need of a transfusion at eight o'clock on Sunday night.

It got it when a charming, effervescent emcee, Bert Parks, yelled over a lively orchestra or vocal rendition of a once popular tune: "Stop the music!" And somewhere out there in Radioland, Mr. or Mrs. America, having picked up a telephone at home, was asked to identify the melody just aired for hefty cash and merchandise prizes. The show changed the nation's listening habits—and the routine of millions of denizens on Sunday nights—as the common man and woman sought to become instant winners. Many did, but the biggest was likely ABC, whose entertainment value multiplied overnight, and who persisted at it for a few years until the bloom was off the rose.

The series "created more national excitement than any other game or contest in the country," allowed one wag, and it undoubtedly contributed to the big-winnings craze that led to the television quiz show scandals of the late 1950s.[26] But *Stop the Music!* was an innocent bystander to all of that, a flirtation that set a nation on its ear—with legions of its citizens listening intently for the phone to ring.

Ozzie and Harriet (Hilliard) Nelson brought their brand of lighthearted comedy to ABC in 1949 after introducing it on CBS and NBC. The family-oriented (literally!) human-interest humor of *The Adventures of Ozzie and Harriet* found a permanent berth at ABC, remaining on radio five more years. During that timeframe, the show turned into a pivotal video property for its network, persisting from 1952 to 1966, achieving a record as America's most durable TV sitcom. Many of the Nelsons' fans in the radio era were convinced that the calamities aired were actually occurring before those microphones as presented *right then*—and not submitted in written form by a team of wordsmiths nor even rehearsed. For a series to be that believable—imbuing a nation with lofty ideals and upright values—suggests it carried a great deal of weight in a far more accepting society, taking what it was offered at face value.

Of course, ABC's Saturday afternoon concerts by the stars of the Metropolitan Opera were unparalleled, the pinnacle of classic music broadcasts. Begun under the aegis of the National Broadcasting Company in 1931, the following year those live performances were a staple in the Blue web's weekly agenda. Seamlessly they shifted to ABC, where they remained to 1958 before transferring to CBS and finally a special hookup. With commentary by Milton J. Cross until his death in 1975, those outings exposed the common man and woman who might never afford a trip to New York to prestigious operatic outings. They heard scores of accomplished artists like Placido Domingo, Jerome Hines, Lauritz Melchior, Patrice Munsel, Ezio Pinza, Leontyne Price, Risë Stevens, Brian Sullivan, Gladys Swarthout and many more backed by sterling instrumentalists. While there were other orchestras on the airwaves (the New York Philharmonic Symphony and the NBC Symphony were two), nothing compared to the Met's singular gifts, a feather in ABC's cap back in the day, and still heard now via global connections each winter season.

ABC stepped up to the plate when one of NBC's longstanding advertisers, the Firestone Tire and Rubber Company, arrived at an impasse with that web over its *Voice of Firestone* broadcasts. The program had aired for 25 years on NBC Radio (1928–1953) and was simulcast on NBC-TV four years (1949–1953) when NBC announced it would no longer make available the Monday at 8:30 P.M. Eastern timeslot that Firestone occupied since September 7, 1931. While it would make another less desirable period available, Firestone was dissuaded. It appeared the live quarter-century tradition featuring Met Opera artists singing classical and pop tunes was about to depart the airwaves forever.

At that juncture a hungry ABC—seeking to beef up its faltering Monday night schedule—forged a pact to transfer the series to its radio and television webs. The venerable production left NBC on June 7, 1953, and continued as if nothing happened on ABC on June 14, 1953. Patrons of the arts breathed a collective sigh of relief. The weekly performances persisted on ABC Radio through 1957 and on ABC-TV through 1959, with a video reprise in the 1962–1963 season. Thanks to ABC decision-makers, it was a win-win outcome for everybody.

On the drama sound stage, ABC could claim little to distinguish it, presenting mostly pedestrian fare like *Famous Jury Trials* (1940–1949), *This Is Your FBI* (1945–1953), *The Fat Man* (1946–1951) and *Mr. President* (1947–1953). But it did do something unique with daytime narratives that seemed not only unusual but just as inadvisable. Beyond offering a handful of anthologies with closed-end denouements in one to five chapters weekday mornings—*Modern Romances* (1936–1937, 1949–1951, 1953–1955), *My True Story* (1943–1961), *Whispering Streets* (1952–1959)—the web wiped its slate clean of more continuing sagas while still in the "interim" pre–ABC era.

From its earliest days the Blue Network supported the model of rival webs allowing soap opera to suffice as the vanguard of its daytime programming. In 1929, *The Rise of the Goldbergs*, a long-playing matinee feature that succeeded on other networks, debuted on NBC Blue. Twenty months later, *Clara, Lu 'n' Em*, which premiered at night in 1930 on NBC Blue, switched to the sunshine to be the first network daytime serial. Scores of others followed. The ritual was interrupted when Blue Network officials canceled the chain's seven washboard weepers in 1942.[27]

Just as swiftly as the decision to abandon the form was introduced, new management took pity on disenfranchised audiences all at once. In 1951, after a nine-year absence, the ABC brass altered the daytime slate and reinstituted nine castoff serials, most of them dropped from other webs: *Against the Storm*, *Doctor Paul*, *Joyce Jordan, M.D.*, *Lone Journey*, *Marriage for Two*, *The Story of Mary Marlin*, *The Strange Romance of Evelyn Winters*, *Valiant Lady* and *When a Girl Marries*. Only the last one persisted for more than a few months.

By 1951, housewives were clinging to serials with continuing storylines that hadn't been interrupted by other radio chains; or, they had moved on to debuting TV soap operas (e.g. *Hawkins Falls*, *Love of Life*, *Search for Tomorrow*). Though *When a Girl Marries* was able to squeeze out enough episodes to persist to August 30, 1957, it limped badly on the journey. The glory days of soap opera had gone down the drain at ABC when the plug was pulled 15 years earlier, before the network was formally organized—decisions made, of course, by previous guardians.

An innovation by ABC Radio in 1954 became a watershed in audio broadcasting, though it probably wasn't so recognized at the time of its inception. Seeking to offer listeners programming to satisfy their increasingly mobile lifestyles, the web introduced a five-minute newscast once an hour throughout its weekend programming. ABC's fortuitous experiment was to become a threshold in aural broadcasting that would influence all four major chains in that decade. The "novelty" not only affects surviving network radio today, it is the heart and soul of much of it. For NBC, it's virtually the only remnant remaining of that once diversified leader, for instance.

To gain advantage while distinguishing themselves from competitors, after the hourly newscasts came into vogue across the board, some chains tried to tweak them a little. Instead of programming these bulletins at the top of the hour as others did, ABC tried to gain audience margin by offering many of its headline inserts at five minutes before the hour. Sometimes news flashes appeared on webs at 25 or 30 minutes past the hour, especially on CBS and MBS. NBC incorporated news into its 40-hour *Monitor* weekend program service. CBS finally boosted its emphasis by offering 10 minutes of news on the hour starting November 28, 1960, a schematic that lasted only for a brief spell.

Long before this, ABC-TV premiered on April 19, 1948. Its first affiliate, Philadelphia's WFIL-TV, preceded the chain's initial owned-and-operated video outlet, New York's WJZ-TV, which went on the air in August 1948. For a few years, however, ABC was a TV web primarily in name only. Except in the largest markets, most metropolitan areas had one and possibly two stations, limiting ABC with its late start in broadcasting to tremendous disadvantage. Added to that, the Federal Communications Commission froze applications for new outlets in 1948 while it sorted through thousands of them, simultaneously poring over technical and allocation provisions that had been established a decade earlier. An intended six-month interruption in handing out new licenses continued to 1952.

While ABC could muster little affirmation among affiliates, it did have the advantage of possessing a radio network over its fellow startup chain, DuMont Television. The radio web provided all important revenues and some audience fidelity. ABC also benefited from a full complement of five owned-and-operated video stations in key markets: WJZ-TV, New York; WENR-TV, Chicago; KECA-TV, Los Angeles; WXYZ-TV, Detroit; and KGO-TV, San Francisco.

In due course, the ascendancy of ABC-TV into a competitive venture on a par with CBS-TV and NBC-TV may be largely attributed to the early efforts of Leonard Goldenson and his associates at United Paramount Theaters. It was Goldenson who, in the 1950s, established a secure foundation for ABC that ultimately provided a valuable competitive edge. The rise of the video network is a transfixing tale of ambition, ingenuity and perseverance while achieving the unthinkable against perceptibly insurmountable odds. Because the scope of the present volume is directed to the radio side of the network commercial broadcasting venture, additional exploration into the video network is left to other sources that are capable of satisfying inquiries into the signal accomplishments of American corporate enterprise.

The ABC Radio network found its audience continuing to drift toward television as the 1950s drew to a close. With listenership dwindling and reduced network programming offered, Harold L. Neal, general manager of flagship station WABC, New York, hired Mike Joseph as music consultant to program contemporary "Top 40" music on that station. Also hired was Dan Ingram to be afternoon host and Bruce (Cousin Brucie) Morrow for similar duty in the early evenings. Both attracted huge followings, thrusting Neal to the presidency of the seven ABC owned-and-operated radio stations. Capitalizing on a winning formula, Neal added the same flavor to Chicago's WLS and Pittsburgh's KQV, which experienced similar results.

At about the same time, the web's two O-and-O West Coast outlets, KABC in Los Angeles and KGO in San Francisco, experimented in another direction: their pioneering news-talk formats were met by listener acclaim. Hourly newscasts, commentaries and a few long-running features (*The Breakfast Club, Lawrence Welk* recorded simulcasts, etc.) comprised most of the ABC Radio network schedule by the mid 1960s.

Ralph Beaudin, general manager of Chicago's WLS, was promoted to president of ABC Radio in 1967. He immediately set about attempting to pump new blood into radio by increasing the number of ABC affiliates through a proliferation of concurrent narrowly-focused webs to draw people's attention more pointedly to a given station. In accomplishing this bold move taking effect January 1, 1968, Beaudin split the ABC Radio network into four distinct chains (eventually increased to six), each with format-specific news and features.

Programming was derived for stations that focused on myriad sectors of the audience. Joining the American contemporary (rock outlets), entertainment (middle-of-the-road operators), information (all-news programmers) and FM (classical music stations) webs down the road apiece were direction (adult-oriented music) and rock (album-oriented rock) channels.[28] At the inception of the multidimensional audio undertaking, ABC information aired at the top of the hour; FM programming at 15 minutes past the hour; entertainment services at 30 minutes past the hour; and contemporary features at 55 minutes past the hour.

A Federal Communications Commission restriction forbade a web from providing separate and competing services. To avoid running afoul of this tenet, ABC fed each of its chains with sundry programs from its multiple services, thus technically remaining in compliance because programs from a common supplier couldn't compete with one another. Touting its manifold chains in the trade press, ABC ballyhooed the fact it needed "84 percent to 196 percent less time than any other major network today" to project its schedule.

By the mid 1970s, the seven ABC owned AM and FM stations, and the ABC Radio network, were reportedly the most successful audio operations in America based on audience numbers and profits.[29] By diversifying its operations, ABC, the last American transcontinental chain to debut, had launched a new fad that all the competing national webs would sooner or later embrace.

In the meantime, ABC Radio had been experimenting in other plateaus as it sought to thrive in the years following the medium's golden age. When NBC rolled out *Monitor*, its unstructured magazine marathon that became an instant hit in June 1955, the success wasn't ignored by ABC. In November of that year, ABC attempted to replicate NBC's good fortune with *New Sounds*, a weeknight omnibus. America wasn't listening, however; it had made the decision that *Monitor* was sufficient in that arena, and *New Sounds* was quickly dumped.

On May 4, 1981, a live national call-in show, *Rockline*, originated over ABC's KLOS-FM in Los Angeles and aired over a hookup of 17 stations across the country. Pointed toward teens and twentysomethings, the 90-minute diversion was hosted by veteran disc jockey B. Mitchell Reed.

Noting NBC's successful all-night *Nighttalk* operation inaugurated on November 2, 1981, which evolved into an expanded *Talknet* in April 1982, ABC swung into action again. Beginning May 3, 1982, it aired an all-talk series linking a couple of ABC West Coast stations. A week afterward, they added New York's WABC and — by June 18, 1982 — had 22 stations coast-to-coast carrying *Talkradio* (sometimes appearing in print as *TalkRadio*). Ultimately, its dialoguing format occupied the daily schedule between 10 A.M. and 4 P.M. and again from midnight to 6 A.M., all times Eastern.

In 1986, Capital Cities Communication engineered the first television network takeover since Leonard Goldenson's merger of United Paramount Theaters and ABC. Its $3.5 million buyout of that combo signaled the start of a round of purchases involving all the major networks in the 1980s. Yet the resulting Capital Cities/ABC, Inc., amalgamation became what was "widely considered by investors as one of the best run of media companies."[30] ABC-TV rebounded to reach first place in the ratings after Capital Cities dramatically cut costs while continuing to invest in news and entertainment programming.

In 1995, Walt Disney Company acquired Capital Cities/ABC, Inc., for $19 billion, the second-highest price paid for a U.S. company in the nation's history.[31, 32] It was part of continuing acquisitions of major broadcast empires by other entertainment and manufacturing behemoths.

Throughout the 1980s and 1990s, as radio's music audience drifted to FM, many of ABC's heritage AM outlets—the powerhouse properties upon which the company was founded like New York's WABC and Chicago's WLS—switched from music to talk. ABC Radio Networks presently syndicates conservative talk show hosts like Mark Davis, Larry Elder and Sean Hannity. In addition to its most popular offerings in the modern age, ABC News Radio and to 2009 *Paul Harvey News and Comment*, ABC provides music programming to automated stations with weekly countdown and daily urban and Hispanic morning shows.[33]

While many of ABC's radio stations and network programs remained strong revenue generators, growth in the radio industry began to slow dramatically upon consolidation following the Telecommunications Act of 1996 and the dot-com boom of the early 2000s. In 2005, Disney CEO Robert Iger decided to unload the ABC Radio division, declaring it—this, the network's formation unit, you recall—a "non-core asset." How times had changed! Would Ed Noble and Mark Woods have understood, or might they be singing, "Look what they've done to my network, ma!"?

On February 6, 2006, Disney announced that, with the exception of Radio Disney and ESPN Radio, all other ABC Radio properties would be spun off. They were to merge with Citadel Broadcasting Corporation of Las Vegas, Nevada, an outfit owning hundreds of U.S. radio stations. In March 2007, the FCC approved transferring ABC's 24-unit radio station chain to Citadel; the $2.6 billion deal closed on June 12, 2007. Not long afterward, on September 24, 2007, Citadel removed ABC News & Talk Radio from the satellite services it offered, an acknowledged cost-reduction tactic.[34] It was announced that ABC News, an entity of the ABC Television network, would continue producing ABC News Radio. Citadel agreed to distribute it for a decade, presumably to 2017.

While it goes without saying that this isn't the final chapter to be written in the history of the four transcontinental radio networks in America—there will be subsequent transactions, you may be sure—it puts a modern spin on radio of the 20th century. Occurring as it does in the 21st century, it fittingly brings closure to a tale dating back to 1926. That year General Electric, which begat Radio Corporation of America, saw that offspring begat NBC and its dual webs, one sprouting into ABC.

In one sense, network radio has come full circle. Who could possibly predict what direction it will take next?

7

THE REGIONAL HOOKUPS
Local Radio Gone Wide

The quartet of transcontinental radio networks analyzed in the preceding four chapters was just a portion of the panorama of aural webs serving the American people after the inception of broadcasting in the 1920s. While NBC, CBS, MBS and ABC were the only hookups with their phenomenally extensive reach, there was an added, sometimes overlooked, chain gang that significantly impacted the landscape, too. Usually identified as geographically regional networks, on a continuing basis these ethereal players sometimes fed programming to one or more stations linked by wire or satellite. In other instances, the regional webs offered little or no programming as such. Instead, they were premeditated upon the concept of time-sale packagers for underwriters within a given physical district.[1] Sometimes their entire purpose in existing was the added revenues they generated. Occasionally they were narrowly focused, as on politics, talk, state or territorial news and popular entertainment features.

A number of the regional member stations were also tied to one or more of the transcontinental outfits. Frequently they reflected more of the personality of local denizens than a coast-to-coast broadcaster was able to represent. Their members, often serving in markets with basic similarities, sought to achieve parallel goals and opportunities to provide common services that would offer a competitive advantage to their listening audiences as well as their commercial underwriters—beyond what they could expect to achieve as mere independent outfits. In regard to sponsors, all the webs made time-buying simpler for the advertising agencies by offering blocks of outlets exhibiting extensive coverage with a single order.

By 1941, a total of 20 regional networks existed in the United States. Only six targeted their coverage beyond a single state.[2] Despite the limitations inherent in provincialism, a handful of these territorial webs achieved pervasive recognition well beyond their "borders" due to some potent influence upon the industry. Such was the case of the Don Lee Network, a major Pacific Coast tieup that at one time aligned itself with CBS and subsequently with MBS to feed those nets' features to the far West. At just about the same time, the Colonial Network introduced MBS programming to people living in New England. The Michigan Radio Network provided a conduit for NBC Blue to reach residents of the Wolverine State and adjacent territory. And while the 23-member Texas State Network served Lone Star listeners with MBS programming, there was some diversification at work there: four of its outlets were concurrently NBC affiliates while one was linked with CBS. And so on.

Before continuing, let's distinguish something in the terminology that might be confusing otherwise. The Federal Communications Commission (FCC), charged with overseeing and regulating the radio industry beginning in 1934, classified each broadcast station by one of four designations, defined by its power: clear channel (up to 50kw), high power regional (5kw by day and night), regional (5kw by day and 1kw by night), and local (250 watts by day and 100 watts by night).

Federations of both regional and local outlets were organized—the National Association of Regional Broadcast Stations and National Independent Broadcasters. Neither the stations nor the organizational structures, however, related specifically to the regional networks on which we are focused in this chapter, presented in a format that allows effortless examination of their origins, histories, affiliations, programming and financial returns. The regional webs weren't merely an aberration among the radio listening habits of Americans of the 20th century. Some of those audio fans, in fact, made the geographical outlets their primary choices when they made selections from the smorgasbord of entertaining, informational and educational opportunities available to them.

In surveying the better known regional networks, our procedure will be to present each one in alphabetical order. While considerable material is available about some of these territorial hookups, there are others for which little data has been preserved. No slight is intended toward any. We have purposely endeavored to be as inclusive as possible in conducting the investigations. The fact that one web may produce more substance than another is based solely upon what could be uncovered and verified, pure and simple. Newspaper and magazine clippings, online sources and a wealth of published texts on radio in general have preserved some vibrant anecdotes pertaining to the regional hookups. This one is typical:

In the months leading up to the formation of the Yankee Network in 1930, two of the chain's key stations—WNAC in Boston and WEAN in Providence—offered commercial programming "a bit different from any other group in the country." Engaging a single orchestra to play on both stations, the format allowed advertisers to purchase time in either city. A newspaper account elucidated: "Two announcers are used and each uses a stop-watch. When the music stops the announcers have a minute and a half to make their commercial announcement for their local client over their station. Then the music starts again over both stations."[3] Primitive, yes, but considering the era in which it transpired, probably ingenious. The joint station ownership had found a way to get more bangs for its buck, thereby obtaining twice the programming mileage while operating on merely a shoestring budget.

In a very real sense the outlets cited here comprise a system that can be depicted as embracing the geographical appurtenances of local radio gone wide. Often this turned out to initiate a favorable outcome for the individual stations, their advertisers and listeners. The fact that many times they were able to perform such diversions so creatively speaks well of their recognition of the need to innovate.

Arrowhead Network

Formation: Unspecified.
Originator: Head of the Lakes Broadcasting Company (HLBC).
Original Outlets: WEBC, Duluth; WHLB, Virginia; WMFG, Hibbing (all in northern Minnesota), all owned by HLBC.
History: Arrowhead Network is a trade name adapted from the Arrowhead region of northern Minnesota. The operator interconnected its trio of stations for mutual program service purposes.
Contracts: None required.
Other Webs: Unspecified.
Programming: Unspecified.
Revenues: For 1938, net time sales, after agency commissions, totaled $239,276. All proceeds went to the owner.[4]

California Radio System

Formation: November 21, 1936.
Originators: Joint partnership of McClatchy Broadcasting Company, wholly owned subsidiary of McClatchy Newspapers, and Hearst Radio, Inc., and The Evening Herald Publishing

Company, Los Angeles, ventures controlled by William Randolph Hearst.

Original Outlets: KEHE, Los Angeles; KYA, San Francisco; KFBK, Sacramento; KERN, Bakersfield; KMJ, Fresno; KWG, Stockton.

History: Hearst withdrew from the partnership in November 1937 with McClatchy acquiring sole network control, operating it as one of its departments. Station KYA remained on the chain under an affiliation contract; the other Hearst station, KEHE, was replaced by KFWB, Hollywood. Subsequent additions to the web included KFOX, Long Beach; KTMS, Santa Barbara; and KOH, Reno, Nevada. The latter was owned by The Bee, Inc., a wholly owned subsidiary of McClatchy Newspapers. The California Radio System was disbanded in 1939.

Contracts: A typical affiliation contract stipulated that the web should have free use of an affiliate's facilities for network commercial programs 150 hours per year (and not more than the equivalent of 3.5 nighttime hours weekly). The chain compensated a station at 50 percent of its rate for hours used beyond free time. An outlet placed all its time at the disposal of the network subject to 15 days' notice, except a station could retain three unspecified daytime hours per day. An affiliate could reject any network sustaining program but was required by contract to accept network commercial programs subject only to the optional time provisions. Contracts had no termination date although either party could cancel with six months' notice.

Other Webs: California Radio System wasn't a contract outlet for any other network. In its early years the four McClatchy stations plus KTMS were, nonetheless, individual contract outlets for NBC while KOH was affiliated with CBS.

Programming: Unspecified.

Revenues: After agency commissions, the web's net time sales for 1938 totaled $109,848, of which $88,027 was paid to its four owned stations and $21,821 to the other five outlets comprising the chain.[5]

Colonial Network, Inc.

Note: See related entry—Yankee Network, Inc.

Formation: August 5, 1936, with stock equally divided between siblings John Shepard III, president and general manager of the Yankee Network, and Robert F. Shepard. Familial ties linked the Colonial and Yankee networks, both owned by John Shepard, Jr., through the Winter Street Corporation, a holding company.

Original Outlets: Unspecified.

History: By the end of 1938, 13 stations were affiliates of both the Yankee and Colonial webs. Another outlet was singularly tied to the Colonial chain while four more stations were connected to the Yankee hookup. Colonial was created to make full use of a 16-hour telephone circuit for which the Yankee had contracted but used only partially. Yankee required the circuits about five hours daily leaving up to 11 hours for Colonial access. Colonial wasn't billed for usage except when connections were made with an outlet affiliated with the Colonial but not with the Yankee chain. At the close of 1938, 12 affiliates comprised the Colonial network, with WAAB, Boston, as the web's flagship station. Others: WLBZ, Bangor; WNBH, New Bedford, Massachusetts; WFEA, Manchester, New Hampshire; WLLH, Lowell/Lawrence, Massachusetts; WSAR, Fall River, Massachusetts; WRDO, Augusta, Maine; WLNH, Laconia, New Hampshire; WNLC, New London, Connecticut; WHAI, Greenfield, New Hampshire; WCOU, Lewiston/Auburn, Maine; and WATR, Waterbury, Connecticut.

In its debuting year, 1936, the Colonial Network affiliated with the Mutual Broadcasting System, becoming a shareholder in that chain in autumn 1941. The Colonial and Yankee webs were purchased by Akron, Ohio–based General Tire & Rubber Company in January 1943, then in the throes of developing its own broadcasting subsidiary (named General Teleradio in the early 1950s).

Contracts: Generally, affiliation contracts were three-party agreements between station licensees and Colonial and Yankee tieups. They followed a standardized format that could be customized to particular outlets in regard to time under option to the networks, station compensation, telephone wire charge disbursements and amount of free time given the networks. There was no fixed term on affiliation and contracts could be terminated by any party with 12 months' notice. Colonial and Yankee took options on a substantial number of specified hours of most of their outlets. For example, by the end of 1938, seven stations' options covered the whole broadcast day. Those outlets agreed to air—upon 28 days' notice—all network commercial programs offered during the time included within the option except those which, in the station's opinion, were against public interest, convenience or necessity. Outlets were compensated for broadcasting commercial programs at precise rates, usually 30 percent of the network rate for the station. On occasions, outlets gave the chain specified amounts of free time, varying from one to three hours weekly. Stations were permitted to broadcast all available network sustaining programs without added charge. (To read the exclusivity clause, see the Contracts section under Yankee Network, Inc., later in this chapter.)

Other Webs: Colonial was associated with MBS on a network basis as a participating member. In 1940, Colonial became one of the stockholder owners of MBS.

Programming: Unspecified, although with the Yankee Network maintaining a fairly sophisticated domestic news operation, it's probably reasonable to speculate that Colonial ran a similar bureau in its programming mix.

Revenues: Colonial Network time sales for 1938 reached $190,758, with the web retaining $114,764 (60 percent), compensating a trio of Yankee-owned outlets (WAAB, Boston; WEAN, Providence; WICC, Bridgeport) $53,680 (28 percent) and sending $22,314 (12 percent) to its remaining stations. Of the net time sales, $49,422 (26 percent) was derived from Colonial programming while $141,336 (74 percent) was earned from MBS.[6]

Don Lee Broadcasting System

Formation: December 1928.

Originators: Begun by Don Lee, Inc., a corporation principally engaged in automobile sales that connected its two owned-and-operated radio stations by telephone circuitry to create chain broadcasting.

Original Outlets: KFRC, San Francisco; KHJ, Los Angeles.

History: During Don Lee's premiering month, a trio of stations owned by McClatchy Newspapers—KMJ, Fresno; KWG, Stockton; and KFBK, Sacramento—joined the network. When McClatchy acquired KERN, Bakersfield, on November 14, 1930, that station also affiliated with Don Lee. Yet another McClatchy-owned station, KOH, Reno, Nevada, joined the chain in 1933. In the meantime, in May 1931, Don Lee, Inc., acquired control of KDB, Santa Barbara, plus ownership of KGB, San Diego, with both becoming Don Lee–operated outlets. Four separately owned stations linked with Don Lee in 1932: KOIN, Portland, Oregon; KOL, Seattle; KVI, Tacoma; and KFPY, Spokane. Beginning in June 1932, network operations and ownership of KFRC, KHJ and KGB were vested in the Don Lee Broadcasting System, a wholly owned subsidiary of Don Lee Holding Company, which was wholly owned by the estate of Don Lee (deceased in 1936). The estate also controlled KDB through ownership of its licensee's stock. Don Lee expanded beyond the Golden State into the Pacific Northwest in autumn 1937 via a contract with Pacific Broadcasting Company. (See separate entry under that network heading later in this chapter.) By 1938, there were 28 stations tied to the Don Lee network. Half (14) of those—located in Oregon and Washington—received Don Lee programming through Pacific Broadcasting. Of the remainder, all in California, three stations were owned and operated by Don Lee while 11 were affiliates. KDB, in the latter category, was under common ownership with Don Lee Broadcasting System. Sixteen years following the death of vehicle dealership–broadcasting magnate Don Lee in 1934, his 45-year-old son, Thomas S. Lee, sole heir to a $9 million fortune, leaped to his death from the 12th floor of a Wilshire Boulevard edifice in Los Angeles. He was a "mental disorder sufferer," a newspaper reported, while being "nominal head" of Thomas S. Lee Enterprises, including radio and auto interests and TV station KTSL. His estate sold the video outlet to CBS, while in October 1950 General Tire & Rubber Company purchased three radio stations, access to a radio network that had expanded to 53 affiliates, Hollywood studios valued at $3 million and Don Lee's MBS shares. While for all intents and purposes this brought to an end the Don Lee epoch—although the business didn't officially fold until 1967—it also helped General Tire assume majority ownership of MBS.[7] In early 1952, the firm merged with R. H. Macy & Company's broadcasting interests and General Tire held a strong dominant position.[8]

Contracts: The typical Don Lee pact was for a precise term, with three added terms of one year each, provided both parties gave notice to extend 90 days prior to expiration. Nevertheless, the contract with Pacific Broadcasting Company was for five years although either party could terminate at the end of any year if the net income of Pacific from network business didn't equal the cost of telephone lines. While stations optioned all their time to Don Lee for network commercial programs, they weren't required to take any network shows that could obstruct a local program of sufficient public interest, convenience and necessity. For the most part, Don Lee was entitled to free time over its affiliated stations, not to exceed two hours weekly. For commercial time in excess of free time, Don Lee paid California affiliates specified percentages of network rates. The arrangement with Pacific was different though. Pacific paid telephone circuitry costs north of San Francisco. Pacific received all revenues collected from advertisers by Don Lee for the use of Pacific facilities until such expenses were absorbed. Thereafter, Pacific received 85 percent of such net revenue from Don Lee. Lastly, there was no added charge for sustaining programs supplied to its affiliates by Don Lee.

Other Webs: Don Lee, Inc., became the CBS rep on the Pacific coast in September 1929, supplying CBS programming to its affiliates. The ties between Don Lee and McClatchy and CBS persisted to December 1936. At that juncture the five McClatchy-owned outlets left Don Lee to link with NBC and California Radio System. (See the entry for California Radio System earlier in this chapter.) Furthermore, CBS terminated its affiliation with Don Lee and established its own Pacific coast operations, directly assuming contracts with four Don Lee stations: KOIN, KOL, KVI, KFPY. Don Lee became a "participating member" of MBS then, transmitting MBS programming to its stations. In 1940, Don Lee Broadcasting System became a stockholder owner of MBS, too. The affiliates had no direct contractual relations with MBS, receiving MBS shows only through Don Lee facilities. MBS offered service to Pacific coast stations, in fact, singularly through Don Lee.

Programming: Don Lee Broadcasting System furnished its stations with 16 hours of commercial and sustaining programming daily. Between 16 and 20 percent of the commercial features were provided by MBS with the balance by Don Lee.

Revenues: Net time sales, after agency commissions, of the Don Lee Broadcasting System and its four owned and controlled stations for 1938 were $853,333. Of that amount, $417,324 was derived from Don Lee network time, $129,753 from MBS network time and $306,256 from non-network sales of the four stations. The 28 outlets comprising the network in 1938 received $651,352 from webs. The four Don Lee owned and controlled stations received $547,077 (84 percent) while the 24 independently owned outlets divided the remaining $104,275 (16 percent).[9]

Sidelights: In her Paley biography, *In All His Glory* (Simon and Schuster, 1990, p. 68), Sally Bedell Smith remembers events surrounding Don Lee's tieup with CBS involving its czar, William S. Paley, thusly: "Paley took enormous pride in winning the affiliation of a group of West Coast stations run by a wealthy Cadillac dealer named Don Lee. His accomplishment revealed no particular business savvy, but it did show what he was willing to do to succeed. Lee ordered him to California and forced him to waste nearly a week on his yacht, just so Lee could take the young man's measure. When they finally met in Lee's office, Lee refused to negotiate. 'Mr. Paley,' Lee announced to his secretary, 'is now going to dictate the terms and conditions of this contract that will exist between us.' Paley did so, and admitted later that his terms were probably overly generous to Lee."

Empire State Network, Inc.

Formation: September 23, 1938.
Originators: Unspecified.
Original Outlets: WABY, Albany; WIBX, Utica; WSAY, Rochester; WMBO, Auburn; WBNY, Buffalo; WNBF, Binghamton; WHN, New York (all in New York state).
History: The web was in business 43 days, terminating November 7, 1938.
Contracts: Most of the outlets granted the network two hours of free time weekly. The network compensated them with 30 percent of the revenue from sales over their facilities.
Other Webs: Not applicable.
Programming: During its brief operation the chain sold time largely for political speech-making.
Revenues: The net's total revenue for its 43-day existence was $12,937. If seven stations divided 30 percent equally, each received $554.[10]

Inter-City Broadcasting System

Formation: 1935.
Originators: Separate owners of one New York City station and one Philadelphia station decided to exchange programming via telephone circuitry.
Original Outlets: WMCA, WIP.
History: More stations determined to join the established connection, linked by permanent telephone wire. They included: WPRO, Providence; WMEX, Boston; WLAW, Lawrence, Massachusetts; WDEL, Wilmington, Delaware; WGAL, Lancaster, Pennsylvania; WCBM, Baltimore; WORK, York, Pennsylvania; and WOL, Washington, D.C.
Contracts: WMCA maintained contracts with each affiliate and was the sales agent for the group. The station contacted potential advertisers and processed billing for all stations. Charges to advertisers for network services were the station rates of the individual outlets from which WMCA retained a commission ranging between 10 and 15 percent of billings. All stations except WPRO and WOL were required to clear unsold time for Inter-City commercial features.
Other Webs: WPRO was also a CBS affiliate and beamed only nominal Inter-City programming. WOL was a MBS affiliate, too, and participated similarly.
Programming: Features were offered 16 hours daily and originated in the studios of WMCA.
Revenues: Unspecified.[11]

Liberty Broadcasting System

Formation: 1948.

Originators: Gordon McLendon, who went on the air on a single station with the concept of reaching a vast disenfranchised audience hungry for athletics.

Original Outlets: KLIF, Dallas.

History: In 1950, the alarm went out: "Radio's four major networks were beginning to take serious notice last week of a bustling new rival."[12] Billing itself "America's Great Radio Network," Liberty Broadcasting System grew from one Texas station to 240 airing in 34 states in just three years. It did so by focusing on a single specialty: bringing broadcasts of Major League Baseball (MLB) to an immense audience beyond the clutches of transmitting outlets that served major-league sites. "Sports-minded [Liberty president] Gordon McLendon first got the idea for his network during the [second world] war, when he found that boys from Arkansas argued just as hotly as Brooklynites about big-league baseball, even though the only games they ever heard were the World Series."[13] At 26, McLendon put KLIF on the ether, using teletyped play-by-play dispatches from a Manhattan office to liven up his reportage. On-air talent included baseball commentators Bud Blattner, Jerry Doggett, McLendon and Lindsey Nelson. The resulting stir helped to fill local ballparks, creating buzz in the industry across vast stretches of Texas and Oklahoma. That resulted in more and more outlets linking to those broadcasts. By 1951, the number had risen to 458 affiliates, second only to MBS, which could boast about 100 more stations. With links as distant from Liberty's Texas base as Massachusetts, New York, Oregon, Alaska, Hawaii and Japan, McLendon was optimistic.[14] "By next summer," allowed a wordsmith in August 1951, "brash young Gordon McLendon, 30, confidently expects to have the biggest network in the business."[15] Until 1951, meanwhile, McLendon was paying MLB $1,000 annually for rights to broadcast the games. MLB raised its fee to $225,000 that year and prohibited broadcasts in any city that had a major league franchise, plus the Northeast and Midwest U.S. When the National Football League also banned broadcasts of its games within 75 miles of league cities, it was a knockout punch. It effectively squelched Liberty Broadcasting, with sports being its chief reason for existence. Liberty lost more than 100 outlets overnight while McLendon—having sold half the business in 1951 to Texas oilman Hugh Roy Cullen for $1 million—dropped another $500,000 in the wake of the MLB and NFL rulings. Acquiring only modest profits ($10,000 in 1949, $50,000 in 1950) and faced with mounting debts, the chain ceased operations May 16, 1952. A few days hence a trio of creditors filed bankruptcy against McLendon. A reporter explained that Liberty never turned profitable because "McLendon was so eager to build his empire that he ignored sound programming, often paid more to service his stations than they paid him in affiliation fees."[16]

Contracts: Unspecified.

Other Webs: Not applicable.

Programming: While Liberty's future seemed assured, one journalist wrote: "McLendon still depends on teletyped reports, dressing them up with skillful sound effects and a sense of on-the-spot excitement that has given him bigger audiences in some cities than competing 'live' broadcasts direct from the press box. Explains McLendon: 'I'm not trying to deceive anybody. I'm only trying to give them a colorful broadcast.'"[17] Expanding from a six- to a 16-hour-a-day network in 1950, his chain added sportscaster Ted Husing's broadcasts of Army football games in 1950 to keep an athletic-dominated clientele happy. Furthermore, it inserted music, comedy and drama into its agenda, along with the sports and news staples. There was a popular musical giveaway show along with late-night band remotes. Also added was *Great Days in Sport*, in which founder McLendon recreated stunning occasions of the past from the ring, gridiron, diamond, track, court, pool, course or other venue where notable sports-related events occurred. When the cautious Texas oilman Cullen, who rescued the business by purchasing half of it in 1951, dismantled Liberty's news operation and dismissed its popular staff, the network's attraction to some listeners was instantly tarnished.[18]

Revenues: Unspecified.

Sidelights: As a part of their nostalgia-style branding, two contemporary stations owned by a Washington State outfit—Mutual Broadcasting System (unrelated to the late transcontinental web)—began using Mutual and Liberty nomenclature in the 21st century.[19] KTRW-AM, Spokane, and KTAC-FM, Ephrata, Washington, offered their listeners adult standards, golden oldies and Christian-themed programming under the Liberty and Mutual banners.

In late 2003, Business Wire reported that IDT Media—a division of IDT Corporation, a multinational carrier, telephone and technology processor—announced the creation of Liberty Broadcasting System, a syndicated nationwide talk radio network. "Listeners need a place to go for intelligent talk besides NPR [National Public Radio]," admonished Howard Jonas, IDT's founder-chairman. "That's why IDT is bringing Liberty to radio broadcasting.... Liberty Broadcasting will bring a diversity of opinions to the radio airwaves. Now listeners will have a place to go for insightful talk and reasoning without the bias."[20]

There was no mention in either of the two cited references above that audiences have been reminded of the historic legacy of the adopted appellation; no mention, apparently, that in an earlier life Liberty could be accessed by people hearing 500 stations. While that wasn't a record in affiliate numbers, it was nonetheless staggeringly impressive compared to most broadcast operations of its day—and a powerfully mesmerizing influence on millions of sports addicts who tuned in for a regular fix.

Michigan Radio Network

Formation: January 1, 1933, as a department of Kunsky-Trendle Broadcasting Corporation, whose nomenclature shifted to King-Trendle Broadcasting Corporation in 1936.

Originators: John H. King and George W. Trendle established the firm on April 25, 1930, having earlier engaged in operating motion picture and vaudeville theaters.

Original Outlets: On May 7, 1930, Kunsky-Trendle purchased WXYZ, Detroit; on March 24, 1931, the organization leased WOOD, Grand Rapids; and on December 21, 1931, it leased WASH, Grand Rapids, which shared time with WOOD. After that the Grand Rapids dual outlets were operated as a single station, WOOD-WASH.

History: More contract stations (affiliates) joined the ranks. Between 1933 and 1938, new members of a newly formed Michigan Radio Network included: WIBM, Jackson; WFDF, Flint; WELL, Battle Creek; WKZO, Kalamazoo; WBCM, Bay City; WJIM, Lansing.

Contracts: A standard pact between Michigan Radio Network and its affiliates was for a one-year term. That could be canceled by agreement of a majority of all member stations and the network. With two weeks' notice, the bond provided that an outlet must accept any network commercial program offered at any hour of the broadcast day with this exception: programs not in the public interest, convenience and necessity. A station could reserve for itself not more than one and a half hours from 6 to 10 P.M. for local broadcasting daily if those periods didn't conflict with network commercial programs. Outlets granted the network a daily hour prior to 6 P.M. plus an hour after 6 P.M. that could be sold commercially by the chain and for which affiliates didn't receive recompense. A station was paid a specified rate for network commercial time beyond two free hours daily. Michigan Radio Network paid all telephone circuitry costs and supplied sustaining programs without charge. Contracts stipulated that stations wouldn't allow their facilities to be used by any other broadcasting chain. Stations agreed not to sell time to third persons at rates less than those specified in contracts with the Michigan Network. Commercial program hours normally didn't exceed the number of free hours given the network.

Other Webs: On September 19, 1934, WXYZ became one of the original four member stations of MBS. It withdrew September 29, 1935, joining NBC's basic Blue network. The NBC affiliation provided that Kunsky-Trendle would link the stations of the Michigan network with NBC's commercial programs and most sustaining programs would be sent to WXYZ. Simultaneously, WOOD-WASH joined NBC as an optional outlet.

Programming: Michigan shows originated in the studios of WXYZ. More than half of all web programs were received from NBC Blue. In 1938, King-Trendle entered an agreement with NBC's transcription bureau allowing NBC to transcribe Michigan Radio Network's *The Lone Ranger* feature. Transcriptions were leased to stations "throughout the world" except for particular major trade markets in which Michigan network reserved the right to lease transcriptions.

Revenues: Network time sales for 1938 totaled $133,314. Of that, $83,853 (62.5 percent) was paid to the trio of controlled stations and $49,461 (37.5 percent) was paid to six contract outlets whose total net time sales amounted to $288,238. Net time sales of the three network-operated stations were $651,645 that year, with $113,203 derived from NBC.[21]

Sidelights: *The Lone Ranger*—an epic series that persisted all the way to 1956 and was reincarnated in sundry proliferating formats (movies, comics, books, television, premiums, clothing and myriad merchandising opportunities)—while it was WXYZ's landmark embryonic programming "institution," was purely the precursor of a strain of similar pop-oriented action-packed adventure thrillers to follow. The most notable are *The Green Hornet* and *The Challenge of the Yukon* (the latter often identified as *Sergeant Preston of the Yukon*). These series were distributed far and wide through other networks and by transcription. All derived strong followings and diversified into added formats and marketing sales. As a result, WXYZ and the Michigan Radio Network built a staff of seasoned radio actors, writers, announcers and directors that allowed it to operate a "mini hub," putting original programming on the air nationwide (and globally) several times weekly throughout radio's heyday. In the process, series owners became exceedingly prosperous.

Pacific Broadcasting Company

Note: See related entry—Don Lee Broadcasting System.

Formation: October 1937, after the Don Lee Broadcasting System began carrying MBS programming (December 1936); Pacific's objective was to be a conduit for additional outlets in Oregon and Washington for MBS and Don Lee shows.

Originators: A trio of entrepreneurial shareholders maintained interests in a half-dozen Oregon and Washington stations: Carl E. Haymond, Archie G. Taft and Louis Wasmer.

Original Outlets: Four of the six stations became Pacific network affiliates: KMO, Tacoma, and KIT, Yakima, owned by Haymond; and KOL, Seattle, and KGY, Olympia, with Taft and Wasmer as principal stockholders. Two Spokane stations—KHQ, owned by Wasmer, and KGA, owned by NBC—were NBC affiliates. KGA participated as a Pacific network outlet for certain commercial programs.

History: In 1938, the network maintained nine affiliates in Washington and five in Oregon.

Contracts: With 10 days' notice, a typical agreement required an affiliated station to accept network commercial programs during any period of the broadcast day with this exception: a station wasn't obligated to take any program which interfered with locally-produced shows of significant public interest or public necessity. A contract's term was for one year but Pacific had an option to extend up to four more terms. Pacific contracted for and paid telephone circuitry costs of its main line, including a wire to the Don Lee Broadcasting System at San Francisco. Stations paid telephone connection charges to the Pacific main line. Outlets agreed to give Pacific seven nighttime hours or their equivalent of free time per week for network commercial programs and two more free hours at any time for network promotional programs. For all time used for commercial programs beyond free time, Pacific paid its outlets specified rates. Without additional charge, sustaining programs were available to affiliated stations.

Other Webs: Pacific had the exclusive right to transmit MBS and Don Lee shows in Oregon and Washington. The web agreed not to carry the programs of any other network or to send its series to more than one station in the same city. At the same time, affiliated stations could not permit any other broadcasting company, system or network to use their facilities.

Programming: Pacific had no studio or other production facilities, principally relying on MBS and Don Lee programming, plus—to a lesser extent—its contract outlets. Altogether Pacific supplied its outlets with 16 hours of daily features.

Revenues: For the 14-member hookup in 1938, time sales—after agency commissions—totaled $580,602. Of that sum, $36,468 (six percent) was generated by the Pacific web while the remainder was from non-network net time sales.[22]

Pacific Coast Network

Formation: April 5, 1927.

Originators: Radio Corporation of America on behalf of its subsidiary, the National Broadcasting Company.

Original Outlets: Focused on KGO and KPO, the NBC Red and Blue affiliates in San Francisco, with other unidentified far West stations linked to these.

History: One of the earliest of the regional chains—which likely established a precedent for other hookups that followed—this one is sometimes identified as the Orange web. The Pacific Coast Network stretched from Seattle to Los Angeles prior to the American Telephone & Telegraph Company's ability to extend broadcast wires to connect the West Coast with the Midwest and East. Under-capacity of long lines and prohibitive telephone costs meant generating features in San Francisco over NBC affiliates KGO and KPO. The pair of outlets furnished program wares to a chain of seven West Coast stations. One source indicates this web was largely organized for sales purposes as opposed to programming but to some other historians the latter appears to be of at least equal importance.[23] The chain persisted only until late 1928, when NBC began full time coast-to-coast scheduling on both its Red and Blue nets, thus eliminating a need for isolated West Coast shows.

Contracts: Unspecified.

Other Webs: Only the NBC Red and NBC Blue webs were part of this chain.

Programming: Much of what "originated" in San Francisco had previously aired on the Red or Blue chains in the East and Midwest. Scripts and sheet music dispatched from New York or Chicago made its way by Railway Express to San Francisco. There live productions were recreated by West Coast actors and musicians. That patchwork maneuver lasted only until AT&T made transcontinental broadcast wires available, eliminating the need for many West Coast performers to fill daily schedules.

Revenues: Unspecified.

Pennsylvania Network

Formation: 1938.
Originators: A handful of stations in the Keystone State which banded together during the political campaign season of 1938.
Original Outlets: WCAU, Philadelphia, and others unspecified.
History: This loosely formed coalition proposed to increase revenues by jointly selling time to political parties for one election cycle.
Contracts: WCAU was the group's sales agent but no affiliation contracts as such were written. Sales were subject to acceptance by the stations. The expense of telephone circuitry for temporary periods was shared by the stations on a pro rata basis.
Other Webs: Not applicable.
Programming: Paid political only.
Revenues: As with expenses, revenues were shared pro rata by the stations.[24]

Progressive Broadcasting System

Formation: Publicly announced on September 4, 1950, though broadcasts didn't begin until November 1950.
Originators: Unspecified.
Original Outlets: Unspecified, although the web was Los Angeles–based.
History: The short-lived net intended to affiliate with 1,000 U.S. radio stations which hadn't already linked with NBC, CBS, ABC, MBS or Liberty Broadcasting System. Backers anticipated providing 10-hour broadcast days on at least 350 outlets, acknowledging that 200 stations were needed to "break even." Potential affiliates didn't respond quickly and the chain collapsed in February 1951, having aired for about two months.[25]
Contracts: Unspecified.
Other Webs: Not applicable.
Programming: In its 10 hours of live and recorded shows, Progressive anticipated reviving "many of the 1,000 slowly expiring small unaffiliated stations" in the nation. It promised a common programming blueprint consisting of soap operas, Hollywood gossip, "Cottonseed Clark" (a homespun philosopher) and vocalists on the order of Connie Haines and Mel Torme.[26]
Revenues: Unspecified.

Texas Quality Network

Formation: September 1934.
Originators: This was a cooperative sales group, not a corporation, and had no headquarters or employees.
Original Outlets: WFAA, Dallas; WBAP, Fort Worth; KPRC, Houston; and WOAI, San Antonio.
History: The Lone Star State's largest quartet of radio stations formed a chain connected by telephone lines to provide one another with simultaneous broadcasts. Together they commanded a combined nighttime power of 101,000 watts. The web's programming met with favorable reaction, gradually expanding the scope of the original stations to include affiliates in Arkansas, Louisiana and Oklahoma. The network persisted into the 1950s.[27, 28]
Contracts: Relationships between the member stations were fairly loose. Any outlet could terminate membership with two weeks' notice. Each one was a sales agent for the total group,

soliciting business at a figure equal to the sum of the rates of the stations plus telephone circuitry costs. Sales were subject to acceptance by each station. Contracts were made directly by advertisers with each station but the soliciting outlet billed the advertisers and distributed proceeds pro rata to the other stations after deducting agency commissions, its own commission, time charges and telephone expenses. The network kept no books except a record of telephone wire expenses, maintained at WFAA, initially amounting to $2,690 monthly.

Other Webs: All stations in the originating group were under separate affiliation with NBC. Texas Quality programs were scheduled at hours that didn't conflict with NBC shows.

Programming: A major factor in the web's success was in sharing popular programming such as the *Light Crust Doughboys* series. The chain also featured Kellogg-underwritten *Riding with the Texas Rangers* and Dr. Pepper–sponsored *Pepper-Uppers*, all big hits with listeners.

Revenues: Unspecified.[29]

Texas State Network

Formation: August 1, 1938, "to render program service to stations within the State of Texas" and "to provide a state-wide advertising medium." Operation commenced September 15, 1938. Its chief financial backer was 27-year-old Elliott Roosevelt, son of the sitting U.S. president.

Originators: Unspecified.

Original Outlets: Unspecified, although there were 23 affiliates comprising the web from its earliest days. KPLT, Paris, was operated by the chain under a management contract; the other 22 were contract (affiliate) outlets.

History: A Web site notes that the Texas State Network "was the very first, and is the largest of the more than 30 state networks now operating in the U.S." For that matter, it is one of the few webs of its debuting era to persist longer than a few years, definitely in a minuscule cluster continuing beyond radio's golden age. It has grown from fewer than 25 affiliates to more than 130 AM and FM stations today, all within the Lone Star State's borders. KRLD, Dallas, is the flagship station in the modern age.

Contracts: A standard affiliation contract in the web's earliest days was for one year with an automatic extension for two more years unless the network or outlet gave notice to the contrary. Those early affiliates agreed to carry the chain's commercial features at any time during seven specified hours optioned to the network, with the exception of rejecting any program deemed not in the public interest, convenience and necessity. The seven designated hours were 7:30 to 9:30 A.M., 11:30 A.M. to 1:30 P.M., 5:30 to 7:30 P.M. and 9 to 10 P.M. Arrangements with the Texas State Network were "subordinated" for four affiliates aligned with NBC; their Texas State contracts were modified on the optional-time provision. While no charge was made for sustaining programs, most outlets agreed to pay Texas State $500 monthly for their affiliation, a handful paying less. Each station gave Texas State five free hours weekly for network commercial programs. Texas State maintained network telephone lines at its own expense. The web compensated each outlet according to its station card rate less agency commission of 15 percent plus 15 percent network selling commission. This applied to network commercial shows beyond the free time. A typical contract allowed the network the right to reduce station compensation if a station sold time to advertisers at rates lower than those charged by the chain. It also prohibited outlets from altering network station rates or station card rates without consent of the network and remaining affiliates.

Other Webs: Four of the web's original 23 members were simultaneously NBC outlets while one had a similar relationship with CBS. Texas State Network was affiliated with MBS, supplying some programming to MBS for all America.

Programming: Texas State Network provided its outlets with 17 hours of live talent shows daily. Today the web airs baseball games of the Texas Rangers live plus a variety of discussion features (state politics, lawn and garden, fishing and outdoor, issues of interest, and so forth).

Revenues: Net time sales, less agency commissions, for the network between September 15, 1938, and January 31, 1939, amounted to $79,468. Of that, $47,335 (59 percent) was paid to affiliates. During this period Texas State collected $57,082 from its affiliates under the provision in which the stations reimbursed the network up to $500 monthly or roughly 120 percent of what Texas State paid the stations.[30]

Sidelights: Elliott Roosevelt (1910–1990), founder of the Texas State Network, was born with a silver spoon in his mouth. Aloof and a maverick, he was ambitious, adventurous, dissatisfied and a husband to five women. One source characterized him as having "alienated himself from his parents and siblings both personally and politically for much of his life through widely publicized missteps." He bought a trio of Texas radio stations that led to the Texas State Network's formation. *Time* reported how the shrewd, prominently connected operator managed to get a $200,000 loan to shore up his fledging chain in 1939. Young Roosevelt settled that account for a mere two cents on the dollar. That led to a congressional inquiry after his benefactor asked for (and got) a $196,000 tax deduction. As the maneuvers directly implicated Franklin D. Roosevelt, it was reportedly "one of the most unusual chapters in the history of the 31st President of the U.S."[31] By 1945, the radio chain was prosperous, run by Elliott's ex-wife Ruth Googins Roosevelt Eidson—she and their children got all his stock. The news magazine summarized: "Elliott, an ex-brigadier general without a job, living in a friend's house in Beverly Hills with wife Faye Emerson, was preparing last week for a new venture—probably in radio again. He told a *Variety* reporter: 'If I fathered a flop in the Texas Network I would like to have another one like it right now.'" His next radio venture, as it turned out, was *At Home with Faye and Elliott* in 1946 carried by 42 U.S. radio stations. Subsequently he co-hosted *Eleanor and Elliott Roosevelt* with his mother, the ex–first lady, weekdays on NBC (1950–1951). He left electronic media to focus on print, authoring a score of fictional mysteries based on life at the White House. In one of his latter capacities, he was mayor of Miami Beach, Florida (1965–1969).[32]

Virginia Broadcasting System, Inc.

Formation: February 1, 1936.

Originators: Stock was owned equally by the title-holders of its five participating stations.

Original Outlets: Five stations situated in the Old Dominion State—WRNL, Richmond; WCHV, Charlottesville; WLVA, Lynchburg; WBTM, Danville; and WGH, Newport News.

History: During its initial three months of operation the network was permanently connected by telephone circuitry 16 hours daily. That service was abandoned in May 1936 due to expense. Afterward the web existed only for the purpose of airing special events.

Contracts: There weren't any affiliation contracts. Each station was a sales agent for the whole group, soliciting business at a price equal to the sum of the rates of the applicable stations, with sales subject to acceptance by individual outlets. The soliciting station furnished the program service, billed the advertiser and disbursed proceeds to the other affiliates after deducting its own time charges.

Other Webs: Not applicable.

Programming: Unspecified but sometimes dependent upon an advertiser's wishes.

Revenues: Unspecified.[33]

Yankee Network, Inc.

Note: See related entry—Colonial Network, Inc.
Formation: April 12, 1930, as the Shepard Broadcasting Service, Inc.
Originators: Launched by John Shepard, Jr., through the Winter Street Corporation, a holding company. Nomenclature altered to Yankee Network, Inc., in December 1936.
Original Outlets: WNAC, Boston; WEAN, Providence; WICC, Bridgeport.
History: Familial ties linked the Yankee and Colonial networks, the latter formed in 1936 by John Shepard III, Yankee president and general manager, and his sibling, Robert F. Shepard. By the end of 1938, 13 stations were affiliates of both webs. Four more outlets were tied to the Yankee chain only while one was connected to the Colonial only. Colonial was created to make full use of a 16-hour telephone circuit for which the Yankee had contracted but was used only partially. Yankee required the circuits about five hours daily, leaving up to 11 hours for Colonial access. Colonial wasn't billed for usage except when connections were made with an outlet affiliated with the Colonial but not with the Yankee chain. At the close of 1938, 17 affiliates comprised the Yankee network, the first three named owned by the web itself, the remainder independently: WNAC, Boston; WEAN, Providence; WICC, Bridgeport; WLBZ, Bangor; WNBH, New Bedford, Massachusetts; WFEA, Manchester, New Hampshire; WLLH, Lowell/Lawrence, Massachusetts; WSAR, Fall River, Massachusetts; WRDO, Augusta, Maine; WTIC, Hartford; WTAG, Worcester; WCSH, Portland, Maine; WLNH, Laconia, New Hampshire; WNLC, New London, Connecticut; WHAI, Greenfield, New Hampshire; WCOU, Lewiston/Auburn, Maine; and WATR, Waterbury, Connecticut. By the late 1930s, the Yankee Network affiliated with the Mutual Broadcasting System, becoming a shareholder in that chain in autumn 1941. The Yankee and Colonial webs were purchased by Akron, Ohio–based General Tire & Rubber Company in January 1943, then in the throes of developing its own broadcasting subsidiary (named General Teleradio in the early 1950s).[34] General Tire's acquisitions ultimately included established regional (Yankee, Colonial, Don Lee) and transcontinental (MBS) chains and local services (Bamberger). With affiliates dwindling in 1967, and flagship outlet WNAC preparing to switch to a Top 40 music format (as WRKO), the Yankee Network disbanded that year.[35]

Contracts: Generally, affiliation contracts were three-party agreements between station licensees and Yankee and Colonial tieups. They followed a standardized format that could be customized to particular outlets in regard to time under option to the networks, station compensation, telephone wire charge disbursements and amount of free time given the networks. There was no fixed term on affiliation and contracts could be terminated by any party with 12 months' notice. Yankee and Colonial took options on a substantial number of specified hours of most of their outlets. For example, by the end of 1938, seven stations' options covered the whole broadcast day. Those outlets agreed to air—upon 28 days' notice—all network commercial programs offered during the time included within the option except those which, in the station's opinion, were against public interest, convenience or necessity. Outlets were compensated for broadcasting commercial programs at precise rates, usually 30 percent of the network rate for the station. On occasions, outlets gave the chain specified amounts of free time, varying from one to three hours weekly. Stations were permitted to broadcast all available network sustaining programs without added charge. Most stations were bound by an exclusivity clause that read: "The station agrees not to accept programs directly from any other network other than Yankee or Colonial without permission in writing from Yankee or Colonial, but will accept programs originating with other networks if fed to them by Yankee or Colonial." Nine Yankee outlets were, nevertheless, affiliated with NBC also by late 1938. While Yankee granted territorial exclusivity to its outlets as a matter of practice, it wasn't a matter of contractual right.

Other Webs: Yankee didn't carry programs of any national hookup although nine of its outlets (WNAC, WEAN, WICC, WCSH, WTIC, WTAG, WFEA, WLBZ, WRDO) were individually affiliated with NBC.

Programming: Yankee Network maintained at flagship station WNAC a news service that gathered and edited news, an artists' bureau and a weather service department that forecast climate conditions for New England, New York and Long Island. Newscasts were aired hourly.

Revenues: Yankee Network time sales for 1938 reached $564,225, with the web retaining $428,434 (76 percent) and 13 contract outlets receiving $136,791 (24 percent).[36]

Sidelights: The Yankee Network inaugurated chain FM radio in America in 1939 with an intercity exhibition.[37] WNAC, by way of a 50 kw station at Paxton, Massachusetts, and a relay station at Meriden, Connecticut, was tied to General Teleradio broadcast headquarters in New York City. The Radio Corporation of America (RCA), operating NBC, viewed FM as a major threat to its AM radio enterprise, even though it, too, was running an experimental FM station of its own. "RCA liked to hedge its bets," said a source.[38] RCA was unhappy moreover that Yankee engineers networked across New England by way of cheap off-air FM relays instead of AT&T telephone wires. RCA figured it might create an opportunity for less well-funded groups to compete against RCA's time-honored system. In 1945, RCA successfully pressured the FCC to move the FM radio spectrum from 42–50 MHz to 88–108 MHz, necessitating substantial hardware retooling by FM broadcasters. Some affiliates quit participating in FM, forcing the Yankee Network to lease AT&T wires to fill gaps between stations. The added costs plus obsolescence of present FM radios set FM back at least a decade. As a result, despondent FM inventor Major Edwin H. Armstrong leaped to his death on January 31, 1954.[39]

In another instance, the Yankee Network felt the brunt of the FCC's first major censorship in 1938 by airing anti–Franklin D. Roosevelt editorials.[40] Under the glare of FCC inquiry, the editorials were suddenly history. The FCC ruled that—due to their public interest obligations—radio stations could not editorially support any specific partisan position as a result of that imbroglio. While airing Roosevelt's fireside chats was nonpartisan by that edict, a critique of his proposed legislation was inappropriately prejudiced.

When the Federal Communications Commission endorsed the purchase of the Yankee and Colonial chains by General Tire on December 31, 1942, for $1,240,000 plus some undetermined cash to be added at the actual time of sale, it did so with mixed response.[41] Two commissioners voted against the sale. Paul A. Walker was alarmed that the FCC acted without a hearing on the matter and complained that "broadcasting is of such public concern that every effort should be made to keep it separate from other businesses." The precedent for a transfer having once been set, he admonished, "Where can the line be drawn?" Commissioner Clifford J. Durr, meanwhile, argued that General Tire's control in Ohio presented an opportunity for absentee ownership. "Furthermore," he maintained, "if manufacturing companies could buy radio networks, this might force their competitors to do likewise."

8

WASHINGTON WATCHDOGS
Safeguarding for the Airwaves

Not long after radio broadcasting arrived in the 1920s—and admittedly looking back from an advantaged perspective after decades of implementation—it was inevitable that some type of authoritative intervention must occur to create cohesiveness in the trade. With airwaves' usage quickly turning prolific and sophisticated, it didn't take long for the perception to catch on that the ether belonged to the people and must be judiciously protected for their benefit.

As radio's complexities proliferated, some means of overseeing and regulating it became critical to maintaining an impartial structure. The feds, of course, were the likeliest of keepers; it would ultimately be their lot to preserve radio broadcasting for the nation's denizens, making bureaucrats its overseers as well as its policemen. Governmental intrusion was one of the necessary evils that occur at the birth of new innovations that have sweeping influence over the American people. Radio broadcasting could hardly be any exception.

The initial vestiges in establishing some type of "Big Brother" figure with both eyes trained on the nation's communications practices occurred at least a full decade before Pittsburgh's KDKA went on the air in 1920. KDKA, you may recall, ostensibly is the first recognized commercial station. There were two historic measures enacted by Congress in 1910 and 1912 that failed to satisfy radio broadcasting as we understand the term now when that industry developed a few years later.

The first of those laws, the Wireless Ship Act of 1910, was provoked by a shipping accident the year before. On that occasion a single wireless operator was credited with saving the lives of 1,200 people by using his skills and transmission apparatus to respond to a crisis.[1] The Wireless Ship Act required all U.S. ships with 50 people aboard traveling 200 miles off the coast to be equipped with wireless radio equipment capable of sending signals at least 100 miles. But as one authority observed:

> The Act did not alleviate the problem, existing at the time, of interference between multiple users of the radio spectrum. In fact, by mandating increased use by shipping, it may well have exacerbated the problem. There was already an ongoing conflict between amateur operators and the U.S. Navy and private companies. Amateur radio enthusiasts regarded the new medium as a wide-open new frontier, free from government regulation and corporate influence. They fought against government and corporate encroachment in many ways, including by sending fake distress calls and obscene messages to naval radio stations, and forged naval commands sending navy boats on spurious missions. It was this, in addition to the public outcry after the sinking of the RMS *Titanic* and an international convention agreed in London, that caused Congress to replace the Wireless Ship Act with the Radio Act of 1912.[2]

The 1910 legislation failed to get the job done. The amateur radio operators, Navy and corporations were still bickering. Amateurs forged naval messages and dispatched fake distress calls. The 1910 act was too weak to curtail the difficulties. After considering half a dozen proposals for replacing it, when the RMS *Titanic* sank on its maiden voyage in April 1912, Congress got on the stick: the Radio Act of 1912 called for all U.S. seafaring vessels to maintain 24-hour radio watch and stay in contact with nearby ships and coastal radio stations.

All amateur radio operators had to be licensed thereafter and were prohibited from transmitting via commercial and military wavelengths. The U.S. secretary of commerce and labor was assigned responsibility for implementing the Radio Act of 1912. And the department he represented was empowered to impose fines and revoke radio licenses of those who violated the legislation's provisions. A short time later, in 1913, Commerce and Labor were separated in the government bureaucracy, with wireless concerns remaining with the former.

In the latter part of the 20th century's second decade, meanwhile, there was a growing sentiment of unease in Congress that it had blundered dreadfully 75 years before, and might need to rectify its action. Congress had poured money into the development of the telegraph, then let the end product revert to private ownership. It had authorized $30,000 in expenditures to inventor Samuel F. B. Morse in 1843 to demonstrate his telegraphy system. Morse complied by sending the first dots-and-dashes communiqué (later dubbed *Morse Code*) over a 40-mile span between Baltimore and Washington, D.C., on May 24, 1844. His simple message, "What hath God wrought," satisfied most curious onlookers. Three years afterward Congress sold the exhibition line to Morse interests and the government opted out of further telecommunications pursuits. But by 1919, it was revisiting that decision.

The discussion was fanned by several factors: destructive competition between rival telegraph and telephone enterprises, a monopolistic bent in each discipline of communications tied largely to economies of scale, benefits of governmental control of wireless, experiences of the U.S. Navy during World War I, and the direction that many European nations had taken—all leading to a concerted effort among Congressmen to establish a federally controlled wireless system, including holding full title with authority over it.

Actually, this concept had reached Congress even before America entered the war. A revision of the Radio Act of 1912 was pitched by an interdepartmental radio committee on November 21, 1916. New legislation would permit government stations to compete with commercial interests for the purchase of private stations. Marconi businessmen staunchly opposed that idea, nevertheless, and remained among its fiercest and most vocal opponents. Parenthetically, American Marconi Company, formed in 1902, was an ancillary of Marconi's Wireless Telegraph Company, Ltd. (widely known as "British Marconi") with roots in the Wireless Telegraph and Signal Company begun in 1897 by Italian inventor Guglielmo Marconi (1864–1937).[3]

America's entry into World War I and the Navy's acceptance as operator of all wireless stations on April 7, 1917, isolated the immediate pressure on Congress. But the matter was quickly revived when the war ended. Yet the Navy—suffering from a lack of trained operators and funding following the war—also heard a resounding clamor for the return of some government-operated stations it took over during the war.[4]

The outcry joined by amateurs, the American Telephone & Telegraph Company and American Marconi Company ultimately prevented the feds from controlling the wireless business for the time being. On July 11, 1919, President Woodrow Wilson ordered the seized stations to be returned to their previous owners by March 1, 1920. Amateurs, meanwhile, went back on the air October 1, 1919. Almost eight years were to pass before new legislation would be enacted. By then radio broadcasting was a reality and had to be dealt with directly.

Until 1927, radio had been regulated by the U.S. Department of Commerce. Commerce secretary Herbert Hoover, appointed by President Warren G. Harding in 1921, played a strong role in shaping the fledgling industry. From the start, he was adamant that radio must not depend on paid commercials as a primary method of paying its bills. Hoover considered such ideas frivolous and a waste of listeners' time. Was he then advocating government control of the airwaves, European style? That possibility is scrutinized a little more intensely in Chapter 9.

Hoover advocated that the industry could avoid governmental control through self-regulation.[5] It was a lofty theory but one with little possibility of fruition, given that hundreds of new stations were going on the air to serve a limited number of channels. Outlets were assigned concurrently to a handful of wavelengths, with each station permitted to broadcast only a few designated hours daily to avoid interference with rapidly proliferating newcomers to the airwaves. Unhappiness abounded. Some vociferously argued for more favorable treatment.

A prominent Los Angeles evangelist, Aimee Semple McPherson, who operated her own outlet, experienced so many run-ins over channel-switching that she wired Hoover: "Please order your minions of Satan to leave my station alone. You cannot expect the Almighty to abide by your wave length nonsense."[6] Zenith-owned WJAZ of Chicago, flaunting a deliberate piracy of unoccupied wavelengths, challenged Hoover's authority to allocate them in the first place. In 1926, the U.S. District Court of Northern Illinois found that no law authorized Hoover to assign wavelengths. Rivals were quick to jump on the bandwagon, with the situation deteriorating as mutiny raged among the troops.

> Etheric hell broke loose. Over seven hundred stations, many of which boosted their power, jumped frequencies, and broadcast when they weren't supposed to, battling over ninety-six channels. Forty-one stations pirated the six wavelengths that had been reserved for Canadian use. Over one hundred stations violated the Department of Commerce's directive that there be a 10-kilohertz division between stations, and in some cities there were only 2 kilohertz separating one station from another. Portable stations multiplied. Interference, often in the form of cross talk, overlapping voices and music, or noise, became so bad that in many areas listeners couldn't receive a consistent broadcast signal and [radio receiver] sales began to falter.[7]

As secretary of commerce, Hoover operated under limited powers. He couldn't deny broadcasting licenses to anyone who wanted one. That contributed mightily to the problem at hand, prompting more and more station applications than there were frequencies. A recurring call to Congress from critics to do something about the chaos surrounding broadcasting finally resulted in the Radio Act of 1927.

The watershed legislation was approved by Congress on February 18, 1927, and signed into law by President Calvin Coolidge on February 23, 1927. Its significance in the annals of broadcasting must not be underestimated: for the very first time, it unmistakably spelled out that the government owned the airwaves,[8] and those airwaves were to be licensed in accordance with "the public interest, convenience, or necessity." It was without question a landmark declaration that clearly took control of and responsibility for the conduct of the ether—assigning it to federal forces on behalf of the people's trust. In so doing, the Radio Act of 1927 established a far-reaching precedent never previously defined. It was also a harbinger of things to come.

The legislation was created to "bring order to the chaotic situation that developed as a result of the breakdown of earlier wireless acts," maintained a media scholar, referencing the acts of 1910 and 1912.[9] Congress established a five-member Federal Radio Commission (FRC), with each appointee representing a specified geographical district across the country. Most of radio's responsibilities went to the FRC although a few technical tasks remained with the Department of Commerce's radio division.

Six-year terms of each commissioner were to overlap. The panel was given licensing authority for a year, after which that duty was to be reclaimed by the secretary of commerce and labor. Yet the group's key charge was to "solve the interference problem which developed after the Radio Act of 1912 became unenforceable."[10] The Department of Commerce and Labor hadn't been given authority under the 1912 provisions to assign frequencies, withhold radio licenses, or regulate power or transmission hours.

After the FRC had performed its assignment of frequency allocations—expected to be contained within a year—the agency was scheduled to expire. That didn't happen, of course; its monumental task was far too overwhelming to be completed within a year. And it labored under severe handicaps from the start which impeded its progress. Launching its work on

March 15, 1927, the FRC was created by a Congress that failed to budget money for its operation. As if that wasn't bad enough, two of its five members died only a few months after taking up their tasks while a third left the agency in the same time frame.[11]

Although the new overseers weren't given any official power of censorship, Congress mandated that broadcast programming couldn't include "obscene, indecent, or profane language." Thus, the FRC could consider programming when it set about the task of renewing station licenses; the ability to remove a broadcaster's license enabled the FRC to control content to some real extent.[12]

When uniform broadcast regulation came into vogue and stations were required to obtain a license, a hue and a cry went up in many quarters: some saw it as an infringement on the First Amendment rights guaranteed by the U.S. Constitution. That document stated that government could not stop freedom of speech in the media. Until then anyone could transmit his or her views efficiently and inexpensively. Thereafter, the FRC was not only a governmental watchdog on what was going out over the ether, it was also selective in the type of speech it suppressed. It came down hard on vulgar language in particular, for example.

Furthermore, and almost from its inception, the FRC was accused of being captured by the trade it regulated. Historians and contemporary critics holding that view have cited results of FRC regulation that favored large commercial radio broadcasters advantageously. Frequently this came at the expense of lesser non-commercial types of broadcasters.

The subject of self-regulation of the industry has been mentioned previously. The National Association of Broadcasters (NAB)—formed in 1923 to unify the trade in dealing with the American Society of Composers, Authors, and Publishers (ASCAP)—urged creation of the Federal Radio Commission. The NAB's position was that operating stations had much to lose from unrestrained competition. It augmented the FRC's work throughout that agency's brief lifespan. The NAB soon began to lobby Congress directly on behalf of commercial broadcasting interests, adding the Federal Communications Commission with similar efforts later. The NAB pushed self-regulation of the industry to diffuse growing Washington and public concern. The body also approved a Code of Ethics on March 25, 1929, that sought to prevent fraudulent, deceptive or indecent programming and advertising from being aired.

The chief assignments of the Federal Radio Commission pertained to the broadcasting trade overall and to individual stations specifically. But even during the FRC era, comparatively brief though it was, some of its actions directly impacted the chains that were already playing to listeners in far flung locales. Many more regional webs arrived before the FRC exited the stage in 1934. And of course, a case justifying the inclusion of a chapter on governmental intrusion can be made by this simple fact: had those outlets Washington was regulating not existed in the first place, there would have been no means for the networks of radio's golden age to transmit their programming to the legions of loyal listeners across the land.

In practice, the FRC had little power over the networks per se. The Radio Act of 1927 would have forgotten those geographical and transcontinental webs altogether had it not been for a single obscure sentence added in a last-minute House-Senate compromise in the piece of legislation: "The Commission shall have the authority to make special regulations applicable to stations engaged in chain broadcasting." Is that comprehensive or not? While it may appear to have been cloaked in mystery and was certainly stated in nebulous terms, it left to the FRC's infinite wisdom, collective interpretation and sweeping ability the application of that statement.

The FRC and its successor, the Federal Communications Commission (FCC), were able to regulate the radio networks very well through the affiliates of those webs. Recall what happened to NBC in the early 1940s when more than one station serving the same market and aligned with the same chain was disallowed by the FCC and an appeal by NBC was overruled by the Supreme Court.[13]

> In 1940 the Federal Communications Commission issued the "Report on Chain Broadcasting." The major point in the report was the breakup of NBC, which ultimately led to the creation of ABC, but there were two other important points. One was network option time, the culprit here being CBS. The report limited the amount of time during the day, and what times the networks may broadcast. Previously a network could demand any time it wanted from an affiliate. The second concerned artist bureaus. The networks served as both agents and employees of artists, which was a conflict of interest the report rectified.[14]

Obviously, the networks were operating under the watchful eye of Big Brother, and whatever those corporate entities were doing was hardly going unnoticed. There was more than one way to skin a cat, and sometimes the feds accomplished their purposes by working through the member-stations of the national webs.

Before we undermine the significance of the *Report on Chain Broadcasting*, however, let it be duly noted that the series of investigations conducted by the FCC from 1938 to 1941 that netted those findings were momentous. They had profound effects on the broadcasting industry as a whole and on the transcontinental webs that drove it in particular. One scholar dubbed the resulting edict "the FCC's most dramatic act."[15] It was that all right, and its effects linger unto the present age.[16]

Shortly after he became president, Franklin D. Roosevelt appointed an interdepartmental committee on communications. He directed it to examine the role of nine federal units with intertwining activities in radio involving the public, private and governmental sectors. Reporting in December 1933, that panel urged the creation of an entity to expand the work of the FRC, encompassing the radio functions plus those of the telegraph and telephone industries. Bills were introduced in Congress two months afterward for creating a Federal Communications Commission whose functions pertained to any business relying on "wires, cables, or radio as a means of transmission." The FCC was established July 1, 1934, a result of the Communications Act of 1934.

The FCC merged the administrative responsibilities for regulating broadcasting and wired communications under the rubric of one agency. The new operation was given broad authority to establish "a rapid, efficient, Nation-wide, and world-wide wire and radio communication service." On July 11, 1934, seven commissioners and 233 federal employees began the task of merging rules and procedures from the Federal Radio Commission, the Interstate Commerce Commission and the Postmaster General into one agency subdivided into a trio of sectors: broadcast, telegraph, and telephone. That unit today has expanded duties commanding a workforce of 2,000 individuals with oversight for newer communications technologies like satellite, microwave and private radio transmission.

The seven-member FCC was reduced to five persons in 1983, appointed by the president and approved by the Senate with no more than three representatives of a single political party. The chairman, who sets the agenda, is named by the president. Commissioners serve five-year terms. Today, typical of proliferating Washington bureaucracy, the FCC is comprised of seven bureaus and 10 staff offices.

The 1934 act establishing the agency has been amended frequently, often in response to technical advancements. The entity now shares regulatory powers with other federal, executive and judicial agencies. Still, its most pervasive authority is that of licensing, withholding, fining, revoking and renewing broadcast licenses and construction permits.[17] It's still based on the body's evaluation of whether a station serves the public interest.

Its critics continue to say that the FCC has been too friendly and eager to serve the needs of large broadcast interests. Early FCC proceedings illustrate a pattern favoring business over educational or community interests in license proceedings. Over the years the FCC has often restated public interest requirements in published formats like the 1946 Blue Book, the 1960 Programming Policy Statement and Policy Statement Concerning Comparative Hearing.[18]

While governmental intrusion into radio's affairs has had many benefits, there have been countless occasions when it has been challenged and denigrated by pundits and those with vested interests in the overseers' decisions. A media historiographer suggested that—while today's radio is a mere shell of its former self—"the Federal Communications Commission applauds with apparent satisfaction the idea that radio is serving the public."[19] One senses a dissatisfied customer base. The comments have implications for network satellite radio as well as local stations. Several factors come into play for the perceived absurdities of the Washington bureaucrats who are at least partially responsible for the nation's current breed of station owners (often multidimensional corporations) that may seem to run amok. "Radio today, stuck on a relentless treadmill of news-music-sports, interrupted for warmed-over weather, a commute, and stock updates every ten minutes, has once again shrunk the medium to a single-cell, one-dimensional organism. Hapless stations employ their listeners to entertain themselves with a babble of opinion, most of it mindless and mean-spirited, whipped on by shrill talk-show hosts."[20]

Radio today simply isn't your father's Atwater Kent (or Motorola, Philco, RCA Victor or Zenith, for that matter). Some of the industry's harshest critics assign a measure of present-day realities to government controllers, berating them as part of the problem instead of seeing them as offering solutions to a relentless form of torture (according to some) that blasts forth under the guise of amusement and information. Or, in the words of the Radio Act of 1927: "public interest, convenience, and necessity." To which of those may we attribute this modern jazz?

The forefathers never dealt with today's ethereal environment. Would they be satisfied with what contemporary officialdom is sanctioning now?

9

REMUNERATION
The Hardest Nut to Crack

To succeed in business, commercial enterprises—no matter what sector of the economy they may represent—rely upon a consistent infusion of capital in order to operate. Without financial resources that sufficiently compensate for ideas, services and commodities rendered, most ventures dry up within a short while and fade from the scene.

The same principle applies to the broadcast industry. To assure the intended outcome of providing a montage of high-quality entertainment and informational programming to listeners, turning those efforts into a viable means of communication, radio requires loads of cash to grind its internal gears, which run unremittingly. Maintaining the form's ability to proceed in an uninterrupted mode is a pricey venture. And in its formative period, where to obtain a stream of steady, dependable bucks became of paramount importance to those innovative thinkers on that scene.

A myriad of dynamics spurred the economic considerations. Airing features carried over long distances via telephone wires required great expenditures, a fact that typically went unrealized before the fact. Escalating, and sometimes exorbitant, fees demanded by rising artists contributed to the squeeze. "How will we finance radio?" was proffered as early as 1921, five years before the first transcontinental chain was formed. The answer to that query would pervasively impact network radio. By 1922, one wag admonished, the question had become "a conversational topic."[1] It was posed with arresting urgency in 1923 and 1924. By 1925, it was a topic reaching crisis proportions.

Radio practitioners had engaged in dialogue on the matter almost academically. In its premier edition in May 1922, *Radio Broadcast* magazine rather innocently broached the subject of financing. Those who manufactured radio sets—the initial commercial sector creating a market for radios by way of conventional broadcasting—wouldn't have further motivating coercion to underwrite the expense once the radio-purchase craze subsided, the periodical speculated. "Some different scheme of financing" must be adopted, it maintained, while tendering several potential solutions.

One was "endowment of a station by a public-spirited citizen." Perhaps 10 years before, an affluent Andrew Carnegie devoted himself to dispensing millions of dollars to establish a net increase of more than 2,500 new libraries in America. When *Radio Broadcast* pitched the idea of philanthropists stepping forward to bear the heavy costs of maintaining radio—a noble gesture undoubtedly inspired by Carnegie's unselfish act—with the exception of a few limited donors in a handful of small markets, no one of Carnegie's resource level appeared on the horizon.

A second proposal involved "municipal financing." Even though in some quarters this could be viewed as socialism, the magazine instigating all this pointed out that such a plan had already paid for schools, museums and added public educational and cultural edifices. While this concept ultimately became a reality to a far lesser extent than *Radio Broadcast* had anticipated (such as New York's station WNYC), it never achieved its intended potential on a far grander scale.[2]

Another method advocated by the periodical was "a common fund ... controlled by an elected board." Contributions solicited from the public to pay for operating expenses and talent was kicked around frequently in radio's earliest days. No less powerful an entity than American Telephone & Telegraph Company (AT&T), possessing the wherewithal to do virtually whatever it wished, shamefully participated. It put out the fleece for gifts from listeners to reward artists appearing on sustaining (unsponsored) features airing over its flagship WEAF. While an announced goal of $20,000 was projected, AT&T soon abandoned the idea after collecting just $1,000, supposedly returning those proceeds to the donors.[3]

In another funding scheme, one proffered by Kansas City's WHB, listeners were asked to send cash for fantasy seats in an imaginary radio theater. Ten dollars netted a box seat; five dollars, a loge seat; three dollars, a parquet seat; two dollars, a balcony seat; and one dollar, a gallery seat. While all of it was make-believe, the plan nevertheless generated three thousand very real dollars.[4]

In its initial presentation of potential economic measures for assuring radio's continuity, *Radio Broadcast* surprisingly omitted naming advertising as a means of support. A plan soon adopted by Great Britain and others—a tax levied on receivers to sustain radio broadcasting—was likewise unmentioned at the time in the sweeping panorama summarized by *Radio Broadcast*. But when the publication offered a $500 prize for the best treatise on the subject "Who is to pay for broadcasting—and how?" the winning submission was an essay advocating some rendering of a system already adopted by the Brits.

Each radio set, according to the winning wordsmith, reported in the March 1925 issue, should be taxed at $2 per tube or 50 cents per crystal set. The scribe believed his theory would net $18 million annually that a central broadcasting entity could administer on behalf of the industry.

Those early innovators in Radioland at last did set into motion a system that was to have profound and long lasting effects on a commercial zone whose far-reaching tentacles continue to spread. The design they adopted back then has persisted to the modern era. It has influenced local stations, the networks that supplied so many of them with programming through affiliate relationships, and now cable, broadband and other modern forms of communication as the trade perpetually proliferates. Their conclusions weren't made lightly and were the subject of extensive deliberation.

The methods proposed for financing radio back then—there were many more than we have previously visited—had their proponents as well as their detractors. As we have known for all of our lives, advertising was the system ultimately adopted to pay radio's bills in America. But its arrival as the preferential choice didn't come about readily or overnight.

Among its most outspoken critics was none other than the U.S. commerce secretary, Herbert Hoover. He had been given responsibility for regulating radio in this country up to 1927. For a long while he was inflexible on the matter of subscribing radio's operations by selling commercial time, lobbying hard against it. Hoover considered such ideas frivolous, a total waste of listeners' time.

"It is inconceivable that we should allow so great a possibility for service to be drowned in advertising chatter," the commerce official told participants at a groundbreaking national radio conference in Washington, D.C., in February 1922. "I have never believed that it was possible to advertise through broadcasting without ruining the industry," he persisted. "I don't believe there is anything the people would take more offense at.... The average person does not want his receiving set filled with that sort of material." Hoover's insistence seemed more forceful as time elapsed. By 1924, he minced no words at a subsequent radio conference, informing participants that—in his view—direct advertising was "the quickest way to kill broadcasting."

That same year the U.S. commerce secretary observed: "The hardest nut in the bowl to crack is the solution to the problem of remuneration for broadcasting stations." It was a declaration that could have been expanded two years later to encompass "broadcasting networks." Did Hoover's observation hint that the bureaucrat who had been assigned to oversight for the developing radio business was in any way preparing himself, albeit reluctantly, for a possibility for which he had already expressed grave doubt?

Hoover was by no means a solo voice wailing in the wilderness on this topic. Writing in *Radio News* in 1923, an unidentified editorialist lamented: "If radio fans have to listen to an advertiser exploit his wares, they will very properly resent it, even though the talk may be delivered under the guise of public interest." Another wordsmith sounded the alarm by characterizing commercialization of the ether as "outrageous rubbish" while demanding: "The use of the radio for advertising is wholly undesirable and should be prohibited by legislation if necessary."[5] That criticism was followed by Rep. Sol Bloom (D-N.Y.) championing the need for a new law in 1925 that would ban radio's promulgation of advertising.

"Any attempt to make the radio an advertising medium," the "bible of advertising" trade publication *Printer's Ink* vowed in its issue of February 8, 1923, "would, we think, prove positively offensive to great numbers of people." *The Radio Dealer*, meanwhile, argued in 1922: "The radio industry itself, the makers of sets as well as parts, and the wholesalers as well as retailers, are opposed to the use of the air for advertising purposes.... The one million set owners haven't paid out money for radio for the purpose of listening to reasons why this or that product should be purchased." Still more outspoken sources in positions of high visibility registered among the vocal and print protestors.

One of the counterproposals to advertising that was fleetingly considered by some was the so-called European style practiced in a number of nations, though not in Great Britain. On the Continent the predominant pattern of radio operations was to place it under government sanction or control. In that structure, Big Brother owned virtually everything: the properties, the personalities, the programming, and—to be certain—the potential for propaganda. The environment made it fairly easy—lacking sufficient oversight—for a party line to flourish, leading a constituency unhesitatingly along a course of unbridled socialism.

That method was investigated and soundly rejected by radio's American forefathers. It may have been as much for the potential for lack of programming diversity as for the inherent dangers within the system itself. Nevertheless, the concept hinted at possibilities that Americans had rebuffed ever since the Declaration of Independence was signed. To pursue that line of activity did not, in the judgment of those setting the course of broadcasting in that epoch, attend the nation and its listeners' interests well.

Another process considered by those early thinkers was that of user reimbursement for services rendered. "Perhaps," wrote the trade magazine *Variety* in March 1922, "some way of charging the owners of receiving sets will be worked out." Applying that technique, in order to receive programming, a strategy would be developed by which listeners compensated for the privilege of tuning in, possibly annually, by household or radio receiver. (Multiple variations were proposed, including one extended by the prize winner of the *Radio Broadcast* essay competition in 1925, encountered earlier.) Said one wag, elucidating on the topic in the 1940s:

> For all the discontent with advertising ... it is questionable whether, even today, the average listener would be prepared to pay the modest price required to rid him of advertising altogether—an annual fee of approximately four dollars. For that is the estimated cost of all the programs that we hear. It includes capital outlay and depreciation costs for all the 900 and more stations on the air, their staffs, and program production costs. Jack Benny and Bob Hope, Fred Allen and Kate Smith, and all the rest of those who earn the astronomical fees paid for radio programs, could still be on the air and never a commercial from the beginning to the end, if every listener would subscribe.... But the lure of an illusory something for nothing is too much for most of us.

It didn't gain acceptance in the 1940s any more than it had a decade or two previously. Yet the fundamental idea never went away, becoming a precursor to a concept that would later gain some credence. It re-emerged in the form of pay TV in the contemporary age. That system for subscribing radio's expenses was soundly rejected at the time by those early innovators, nevertheless, seen then as a rather cumbersome, unwieldy, and largely unpopular scheme among the masses.

Yet another initiative was an indirect approach receiving widespread application during network radio's formative years. This semi-advertising model allowed a commercial underwriter's name to be applied to a program title or an orchestra, ensemble, duo or individual performing on its series as a kind of "stand-in" representing its goods or services. In what now seems like a half-hearted, apologetic approach to announcing its existence, this alternative to full-fledged promotion denied the guys who put up the money any opportunity to directly plug their wares (hence, the "indirect" terminology). With that model, "sponsors" (if that classification can be actually applied) really weren't realizing a whole lot of bang for their bucks.

"What is the distinction between announcing an orchestra under the name of a well-known brand of tea or coffee and actually talking about the tea or coffee?" pondered journalist R. D. Heinl in the September 13, 1925, edition of *The New York Times*. To some wizards, he had a point. Even earlier, in November 1922, the periodical *Radio Broadcast* attempted to respond to the provocative query "Should Radio be Used for Advertising?" with this missive: "Concerts are seasoned here and there with a dash of advertising paprika. You can't miss it; every little classic number has a slogan all its own, if it is only the mere mention of the name and the street address *and* the phone number of the music house which arranged the program. More of this sort of thing can be expected. And once the avalanche gets a good start, nothing short of an Act of Congress ... will suffice to stop it."

Despite observations like that one, by the time of the Fourth National Radio Conference, Herbert Hoover was still mellowing. For the very first time, for instance, he openly advocated indirect advertising and apparently did so without any reservation. He was convinced by then that the method could bolster smaller stations without unduly vexing their audiences or engaging the federal government or negatively affecting the giant commercial behemoths already supporting radio.

At the time, "The type of advertising used on radio called for performers who could submerge their own identities to promote a product," explained one critic. The Goodrich Silver Masked Tenor, the Ipana Troubadours, the A&P Gypsies, the Cliquot Club Eskimos, the Gold Dust Twins and others of such nebulous nomenclature were carefully protected, their real names held incognito by their clients. The pundit reminded, "Advertisers in the 1920s and early 1930s wanted the emphasis placed on their brand names and looked to the performers not for prestige (as they would later), but for entertainment that would remind listeners of the product."[6]

But comedy writer Carroll Carroll, who penned many of the lines that fell from the lips of Bing Crosby during that crooner's audio heyday, insisted: "The real gut power of radio surfaced around 1931 when advertisers began to abandon such obvious broadcast nomenclature as the A&P Gypsies, Paul Oliver and Olive Palmer in the Palmolive Hour, the Gold Dust Twins, the Happiness Boys (later the Interwoven Pair—a sock act), the Cliquot Club Eskimos and [replace them] with the use of star talent."

Clients favoring indirect appeals suddenly evaporated into thin air. The anonymous musicians playing nostalgic and semiclassical fare vanished. In their wake, radio's new performing acts became established vaudeville stars (Jack Benny, George Burns and Gracie Allen, Eddie Cantor, Rudy Vallee, Ed Wynn). Those talents sought something new after their stage venues dried up during the years of severe economic depression. That infusion of artists persuaded many listeners that radio was an entertainment pastime instead of an educational pursuit. In that way, it could be commercialized.

After the Federal Radio Commission (FRC) was anointed in 1927 to hold the reins of the business of broadcasting for the American people, the tide of opposition to radio advertising began to moderate. It was not uncommon for the FRC to advocate advertising as the most satisfactory means for underwriting the medium. By 1928, the FRC also simultaneously cautioned "such benefit ... derived by advertisers must be incidental and secondary to the interest of the public." So convinced was the FRC that advertising could be a savior of the system that—following a six-month scrutiny of multiple realms of ethereal practices—it advised Congress: "Any plan ... to eliminate the use of radio facilities for commercial advertising purposes, will if adopted, destroy the present system of broadcasting."

In its June 15, 1932 edition, *Broadcasting*, a trade periodical, proclaimed: "Advertising agencies ... say that any law limiting advertising on the air to announcement of sponsorship would cause most advertisers to cease their use of radio." It was yet another nail in the coffin of indirect advertising that had so widely prevailed during network radio's incubatory years.

Among the most militant foes of commercializing the airwaves were—as well might be expected—a couple of media heavyweights that feared what such shenanigans might mean for their livelihoods: magazines and newspapers. The American Newspaper Publishers Association, in annual session in April 1933, agreed that radio logs were advertising and should be published only when those newsjournals were paid for the space they occupied.

The self-serving opposition of the print media was purportedly out of a fundamental concern for the listening audience. Those who tuned in, claimed the print media moguls, had few alternatives but to hear promotional diatribes with which they were habitually inundated. The inkmens' concern for the public's welfare was far too munificent, of course, and could be dismissed by any perceptive individual. Sponsors themselves wouldn't take long to realize that the major benefit of radio advertising over print was just that: the aural medium could deliver a seemingly endless ensnared audience while at the same time turning their pitches into a more personal persuasive form than mere words on a piece of paper might.

Media scholars Christopher Sterling and John Kittross contended that, by 1928, radio had already become a mass advertising medium.[7] In the span of a few years, broadcast advertising was widely accepted on several fronts, in fact. National audiences were available to hear it, and small businesses—hit hard by the Great Depression—relinquished their advertising activity altogether. The departure from that arena of the lesser quantities saw mega-sized corporations and their ad agencies immediately step into the void. Through several factors that coalesced in that period, American radio broadcasting—including the people on the inside and the folks tuning in at home—gravitated to an acceptance of paid, direct advertising as the single best means of producing the product and underwriting its costs at a profit.

While the anti-advertising case had seemed overwhelming earlier, the American airwaves became the most densely saturated with advertising in the world. What happened? A modern media arbiter offers this insight:

> Like the vapor in Carl Sandburg's poem "Fog," wisp by wisp advertising "crept in on little cat's feet" [sic].
> Americans, more than Europeans, were impatient for more and better programs. They craved entertainment. Entertainers craved money. Businesses craved promotion outlets. Licensees, like lottery winners, craved a chance to profit by "milking," if not selling, spectrum allocations obtained free. Most Americans preferred potential pluralism to perceived centralization—a view broadcasters exploited in lobbying.[8]

Despite some acknowledged irritating side effects that remain linked to it to this day, advertising has consistently withstood the test of time. It became one of the most imposing decisions of those early radio years. Although it took a while after radio's launch until the airwaves were turned into a commercial zone, the outcome was definitely superior to whatever alternatives were devised.

The Radio Act of 1927 took note of the evolution of advertising on the air: "All matter broadcast by any radio station for which service, money, or any other valuable consideration is directly or indirectly paid, or promised to or charged or accepted by, the station so broadcasting, from any person, firm, company, or corporation, shall, at the time the same is so broadcast, be announced as paid for or furnished, as the case may be, by such person, firm, company, or corporation." Such statements also professed implications for stations' corresponding networks. If local broadcasters were required to make such announcements, it stood to reason that coast-to-coast and regional hookups airing paid features in any form via those outlets would violate the spirit of that act if they didn't legitimize their own commercial messages.

In a reference to the Radio Act of 1927, one of most revered media arbiters of that day pontificated: "At this juncture the time-selling stations were still a minority; the climax of a struggle between commercial and noncommercial interests lay ahead. But the balance was rapidly shifting. All this the lawmakers failed to note, or else sidestepped."[9]

The National Association of Broadcasters, formed in 1923, addressed the matter of advertising early in its history, referencing it in its initial Code of Ethics adopted in 1928. About half of that document pertains to sales practices on the ether. Its first concern was given to limiting commercial time. In the evening hours, for instance, when audiences were larger, there were few, if any, straight commercials during network radio's earliest years. According to the inaugural code: "Time before 6 P.M. ... may be devoted in part, at least, to broadcasting programs of a business nature; while time after 6 P.M. is for recreation and relaxation, and commercial programs should be of the good-will type. Commercial announcements, as the term is generally understood, *should not* be broadcast between 7 and 11 P.M." Imagine stipulating something like that today. How far might one get?

As pressures for advertising as the economic support of radio grew, the limits on the number of minutes were clearly identified. Moreover, the distinction between evening hours and daytime hours remained in place. The pattern of maximum time allowed grew as the years rolled along: 1937—daytime, 9 minutes, evening, 6 minutes; 1952—daytime, 12 minutes, evening, 7 minutes; and 1970—18 minutes, daytime or evening.[10]

Today, and for many years under deregulation of the industry, radio—national and local—has squeezed commercial advertising time into every available spot its ownership-management can find, even at the risk of alienating the audience it ostensibly serves. Whereas advertising plugs typically were 60 seconds in duration at the era's launch—with no more than a single commercial aired during any one programming break—that went out the window long ago. Instead, the *bottom line* (translation: *greed*) overtook the *status quo* (translation: *common sense* or, if preferred, *moral integrity*). Broadcasters, especially on the aural ether, began airing 6, 8, 10 or 12 back-to-back plugs for a plethora of products and activities during every commercial break. These are heard in 5-, 10-, 15-, 30- and 60-second snippets that are almost instantly and universally forgettable. They occupy not one minute of time but four- to six-minute blocks often separated before and following programming sectors by nondescript elevator music, although seldom as soothing.

While both local and network programmers were beneficiaries of the direct advertising approach, there can be little question that it became a windfall for the latter contingent. Without it, the possibilities for chain radio's enormous pervasiveness would have been sorely stifled, perhaps never beginning to reach its fullest potential. With it, coast-to-coast broadcasting proliferated, fully assured that it could provide a service that was important not only to audiences but to vendors as well.

There were other quirks besides time limitations applied to advertising in radio's infancy that would be abhorrent to broadcasters of the modern age. In the early 1930s, CBS banned all commercials for laxatives, depilatories and deodorants while censoring features depicting "unpleasant discussions of bodily functions, bodily symptoms or other matters which similarly infringe on good taste." Meanwhile, rival chain NBC circulated a list of 80 taboo terms to its staff that were never to be uttered on the air, among them: *blood, hawk, infection, phlegm, pregnancy, retch* and *stomach.*

Still another eccentricity, finally overcome in the fall of 1932, was that the transcontinental webs wouldn't allow price mentions. Once CBS broke that barrier, however, NBC was quick to follow suit. Until that point, not only could a sponsor not state how much a product cost, it would have been absolute heresy to compare one brand to another over the airwaves! To say it was a different world then surely would be an understatement.

To combat all of this, NBC and CBS opened continuity acceptance departments to enforce their already inscribed commercial policies. Dedicated overseers meticulously scrutinized every piece of commercial copy before accepting it for airing. In 1935, the year after it launched its watchdog unit, NBC observed that 560 prospective commercials had been refused for varied reasons: outlandish or inflated claims (164), "improper" (88), statements disparaging to competitors (87), "unfair competitive references" (42) and myriad explanations (179).

By 1932, the Federal Radio Commission noted paid advertising's mounting presence by observing that the form was underwriting 33.8 percent of NBC's schedule and 21.94 percent of CBS's. "The sponsored programs were getting the best hours and the main attention from radio columns and fan magazines," a source acknowledged. Advertising was depicted as "brief, circumspect, and extremely well-mannered." (With 80 questionable terms that it couldn't air, it certainly *ought* to have been in a dandy spot, don't you think?) A high order of professionalism resulted.

In spite of finding a means of adequately underwriting its expenses, radio continued to face punitive questioning about the course it had adopted. In a resolution introduced by Sen. James Couzens on January 12, 1932, the U.S. Senate acknowledged a "growing dissatisfaction with the present use of radio facilities." It posed several queries of the Federal Radio Commission, among them: Could advertising be limited to an announcement of sponsorship? and Could it be restricted in length? FRC chairman Charles McK. Saltzman replied that these were not practical. "Many products have several uses which must be described to be understood and appreciated," said he.

On the matter of limiting the time devoted to commercials, Saltzman acknowledged that it would "result in a loss of revenue," thereby curtailing program service. The question should be left in the hands of the broadcaster, he felt, who is "in a singularly favorable position to learn what the audience wants to hear." He also noted that a general restriction in this area would "work inequitable results," as not all broadcasters devoted similar amounts of time to advertising. People annoyed by a radio advertiser, Saltzman affirmed, "can promptly eject him."

Observed one media historian: "What seemed to some a woeful deterioration was seen by others in quite different terms. In the face of a cataclysmic economic flood, a new industry [broadcasting] was staying above water. It was even expanding, as many victims of disaster clung to it. For several years following the [stock market] crash, as adjacent businesses crumbled or collapsed, people and activities gravitated toward the broadcasting world."[11] Magazines and newspapers, the recording industry, movie-making, vaudeville and traveling stage shows, orchestras and other performing venues were reduced or disappeared. Their imperiled circumstances led many of those professionals to drift into radio, where they assisted in developing a growing trade.

Once the question was settled pertaining to a method for paying radio's bills, economics became a crucial factor in programming. An hour engaged in 1931 over NBC's cross-country hookup—then embracing 50-plus outlets—netted that chain roughly $10,000 from a program sponsor.[12] An advertising agency took in a 15 percent commission for arranging the sale ($1,500), plus 15 percent more for talent recruitment that might run as high as $6,000 for a primetime series, thereby adding up to another $900 in commissions. All of this was billed to the sponsor that hypothetically could pay out $390,000 to NBC and another $93,600 to the agency for a 39-week season. Thus, a full-season first-rate feature might easily run up a tab approaching a half-million dollars. Considering this was at the height of the Great Depression when consumers had few discretionary dollars to spend, even for the basics, this outlay was little short of incredible. Many corporations were undoubtedly banking on name recognition to serve them well in the post–Depression epoch.

The corporate climate was utterly convinced of radio's effectiveness, however. To wit, in 1948, one such firm—mega household and personal goods manufacturer Procter & Gamble—bought almost 20,000 hours of broadcast time in one year. National and regional firms generated 60 percent of the advertising business attracted by broadcasters that same year, amounting to $239 million. The other 40 percent, $163 million, was derived from local concerns. Six sponsoring firms underwrote about 36 percent of CBS's revenues in 1948, a telling indication that the big chains were absolutely dependent upon a mere handful of sponsors. Just three years before, in 1945, an aggregate of 13 firms paid CBS more than $1 million each for time purchased. Three of those—General Foods Corporation, Lever Brothers, Inc., and Procter & Gamble Company—spent more than $4 million each that year at CBS alone. Seven sponsors and six advertising agencies accounted for half of that network's billings in 1945. CBS's competitors also did well. NBC sold $1 million separately to 11 underwriters while ABC earned $1 million from each of nine sponsors. Much smaller MBS charmed a trio of $1 million buyers.[13]

As the 1930s and 1940s sailed by, radio advertising flourished. Between 1940 and 1945, for example, gross revenues of the transcontinental webs and their owned-and-operated stations increased by 79 percent, from $56.4 million to $100.9 million. Radio outstripped newspapers in 1943 as the country's most profitable ad medium. In 1945, radio revenues earned more than 37 percent of the national advertising dollars spent (not local or regional underwriters), followed by magazines and newspapers in that order. At network radio's advertising zenith in the golden age era, 1948, some 37.5 percent of $561.6 billion that radio collected from all sources, amounting to $210.6 billion, went to the major chains.

No matter how promising all of this might seem to be, some media watchdogs expressed more than casual concern about the stability of radio's livelihood. Peering over the precipice of network radio's long slide toward virtual oblivion at mid–20th century, a prominent exponent of the medium obsessed over radio's inability to control its financial destiny.

> Radio in practice functions mainly as a middleman, subservient to the interests of advertisers; it is almost exclusively dependent on their patronage for its own revenue. Advertisers, in turn, are subservient to economic trends. When business is brisk, advertising expands. When times are hard, there is a tendency to curtail advertising budgets.... Radio's financial rewards derive not ... directly from the quality of its product, but from ... the advertiser's *readiness* to buy time ... and the advertiser's *capacity* to do so....
> There is little that it [radio] can do on its own account to maintain a stable, assured income. In a depression, the finest programs in the world will avail little, if at all, to attract advertisers. Thus radio's capacity to serve the public is limited by economic factors over which it has absolutely no control.[14]

Besides being unable to control its financial fate, radio lost the ability to control its own destiny, too.

Between the late 1920s and 1940s, the big advertising agencies in America became the middlemen of the air. They were go-betweens linking the major chains and their programming underwriters. Their assignments included signing advertising clients while literally generating, producing and staffing the shows those clients sponsored. An eyewitness to all of this procedure noted that the networks could "sit comfortably back at the receipts of custom, conceding slabs of time, and taking in return the increasingly large sums of money proffered by advertisers for time on the air."[15]

The same source eloquently protested: "With the increasing prestige and initiative of radio advertising agencies and the increased demands for time on the air by advertisers, networks have largely abdicated to the interests and point of view of agencies and firms that have become more masters than clients. Yet the networks, not the advertising agencies or their clients—the commercial sponsors of radio programs—are the recipients of a public trust. They, not the advertising agencies or the commercial sponsors, are responsible for the balanced structure of programs, to which the public is entitled."[16]

That all came to a screeching halt in the late 1940s as the networks began to rebel over their plight. Ironically, TV was about to erode the aural medium of audiences, advertisers, artists and agendas just as the webs demanded—and retook—possession of their schedules again. (Until about 1932, some 15 or more years earlier, network radio controlled all of the programming it aired. In the late 1940s, it gradually retreated to that model.) The nets wouldn't have long to enjoy the spoils of battle with the ad agencies, however. Not so when one considers that so much of their dominant position in the amusement and information arenas was about to be successfully challenged and to ultimately evaporate.

A major change that initially appeared in radio in the late 1940s, although not fully realized until the 1950s, one that subsequently encompassed television, too, was the adoption of participating sponsorship in programming. Until that came into vogue, a single underwriter usually purchased a broadcast series exclusively for its commercial messages. Under the participatory arrangement, two, three or more non-competing firms bought into a half-hour or hour-long feature to plug their wares. In radio this may have been done largely to allow megacorporations to maintain a modified presence in the medium while they transferred more and more of their advertising budgets to television. It also gave the "little guy"—medium-sized firms that had been unable to purchase whole shows—an opportunity to buy into broadcasting and thereby compete with larger outfits.

In TV, meanwhile, escalating production costs—far greater than in radio—quickly priced buying the "whole show" out of the rational reach of some of the "big guys." That resulted in a mounting shift toward network radio's new trend to participatory advertising, making it a practical reality in video, too. That new wave has remained standard practice into the present age. It's now in its seventh decade and shows little sign of diminishing any time soon in any electronic broadcast media, in fact.

A radio historiographer was right on the mark in assessing the medium's golden age: "Without advertising, broadcasting, as we know it, would not exist. It is our radio's only source of revenue, accepted and acceptable in preference to any other known method of financing a very costly business."[17] While the portrayal was made more than six decades ago, its veracity is as applicable today as it was when it was originally proffered.

At the other extreme, advertising has had—and obviously always will have—protestors. A singular example may suffice. Lee de Forest, an applicant among several for the prestigious "Father of Radio" sobriquet, expressed dismay in a communiqué to the National Association of Broadcasters meeting in annual session in Chicago in the fall of 1946. Addressing those professionals through a "letters to the editor" submission appearing in the October 28, 1946, edition of *The Chicago Tribune*, de Forest scolded:

What have you gentlemen done with my child? ... You have sent him out in the streets in rags of ragtime, tatters of jive and boogie woogie, to collect money from all and sundry for hubba hubba and audio jitterbug. You have made of him a laughing stock to intelligence, surely a stench in the nostrils of the gods of the ionosphere; you have cut time into tiny segments called spots (more rightly stains) wherewith the occasional fine program is periodically smeared with impudent insistence to buy and try.

The broadcast networks and individual stations would consistently have their advertising. But they would never satisfy a host of detractors of that form of free market technology. Secretary Hoover's counsel that remuneration was the hardest nut in the bowl to crack, even after the question was settled, left us with a quality that is sometimes unsettling, even frustrating. It's a constant reminder that there really is no perfect system. Advertising may simply have been the lesser of the evils available to those who chose it at the time.

10

Czar Wars
The Empire-Builders Fight Back

They were two men with profuse similarities in their compositions that in many ways appeared evenly matched for the offices they held. At times they were linked by credible goals for their industry, bent on accomplishing the same ends. At the very same time they could be ruthless corporate rivals who were unsatisfied short of trouncing each other in the campaigns they waged.

One was Radio Corporation of America's (RCA's) David Sarnoff, the mogul with sweeping authority over an enveloping ancillary unit, the National Broadcasting Company (NBC) with its Red and Blue networks. The other was entrepreneurial tycoon William S. Paley, chairman, CEO and a major stockholder of the Columbia Broadcasting System (CBS).

The pair fought tenaciously, sometimes bitterly, ruthlessly and relentlessly to win everything from small skirmishes to all-out wars. For decades theirs was a game of one-upmanship as each dug his heels in deep, committing himself and the vast resources at his disposal to a never-ending battle of outwitting the other. Did each man merely have increasing the goodwill and commercial interests of the forces he fronted in mind? Or was there something more to their strategically and skillfully applied skullduggery?

Both were brilliant commanders whose drive and determination far outweighed that of many of their contemporaries. The webs they fostered stimulated the lives of legions of American citizens born in manifold generations. As products of the same epoch with comparable yet contrasting goals, the chronicles of their lives are sometimes scrutinized individually. However, in this exposition they will be assessed together, this discourse considering the opportunities that were theirs and what they did with them.

David Sarnoff is the classic rags-to-riches tale of a Russian emigrant Jew who—proclaimed one of his biographers—"probably affected the patterns of the daily lives of more Americans than anyone since Thomas Edison." Sarnoff surfaced during a technological metamorphosis in the early twentieth century. Born February 27, 1891, at Uzlian in the Russian province of Minsk, at nine he migrated with his family to New York City. Arriving on July 2, 1900, the clan resided in squalor on Manhattan's Lower East Side. Yet out of those humble beginnings emerged an inquisitive, imaginative, incredibly bright youth who possessed unbridled ambition.

Telegraphy, wireless communication and transmission of the human voice came into vogue early in his life. Perfecting them grew to be a consuming passion with the adolescent Sarnoff. He possessed a surplus of uninhibited zeal and an insatiable desire for personal recognition. The adolescent accredited himself as the lone individual remaining on the air after president William Howard Taft instructed wireless telegraph operators to go silent as faint distress signals from the sinking *Titanic* wafted across the Atlantic on April 14, 1912. Another bogus claim was that as early as 1915 he forecast the "Radio Music Box" would become a home appliance for entertainment. In reality, his prediction occurred in 1920 as other visionaries offered similar prophecies. The projections proved true a short time afterward.

Throughout this era the American Marconi Company was Sarnoff's employer. When General Electric arranged for the purchase of American Marconi, turning it into RCA, Sarnoff accepted a post as commercial manager of the firm launched on December 1, 1919.[1] Getting in on the ground floor at 28, he stood on the first rung of a ladder that he ascended to the top in an organization he was to mold for the rest of his working life. Impressing superiors and peers, Sarnoff seized every opening that came his way and created some where none existed.

He was bright, sound, energetic, ambitious, at times impatient, and un-intimidated. He knew where he was going and wasted little time in getting there. In May 1921—just 17 months after the firm's founding—Sarnoff was named RCA's $15,000-a-year general manager. Two years later *American Magazine* affirmed, "David Sarnoff is conceded to have a greater all around knowledge of radio development and management than any other living man." On January 3, 1930, at age 39, he was installed as RCA's president. His star had reached celestial heights in record speed while he was still at a very young age.

Sarnoff became something of an icon upon the formation of the National Broadcasting Company in September 1926. The watershed occasion was marked by a four-hour NBC inaugural broadcast from the Waldorf-Astoria Hotel on Monday, November 15. A reviewer allowed: "Everyone in the great hall, everyone in the radio field, knew that the National Broadcasting Company was largely the product of his [Sarnoff's] foresight, his planning, his obstinate advocacy of the idea.... David Sarnoff recognized the inevitability years earlier than anyone else and years before it was technically possible.... He had staked his reputation and the capital of his corporation to make nationwide broadcasting a reality."[2]

The characteristics shared by Sarnoff and his formidable archrival, William S. Paley, were uncanny. While the latter wasn't born in Russia as was Sarnoff, Paley's Jewish parents were. Both were from the Ukraine. In the late 1880s, while still in their teens, they immigrated to the United States with their natural families. Both clans selected Chicago for permanent settlement; the city was yet another mega metropolis producing impressive future leaders. The two kids wed and to their union was born Bill, their first child, on September 28, 1901. By then, incidentally, Sarnoff was already 10. While the Paleys appeared to be better off financially than the Sarnoffs, it would be a stretch to say they enjoyed very many of the world's goods at the time.

Recalling those days in a personal memoir more than three-quarters of a century later, Paley—who often embellished his own circumstances—was loath to disclose his early brush with hardships. His dad, at 21, was "probably a millionaire" when he opened the cigar-manufacturing firm Samuel Paley & Company in 1896, Bill reported. The hovel they lived in on Chicago's Ogden Avenue also doubled as his father's workplace. Thus, in their childhoods, both Sarnoff and Paley knew the sting of impoverishment. Although the Samuel Paleys would join the middle class and eventually become authentic millionaires, it would be some years before fortune smiled on those blue-collar Windy City denizens.

Beginning in 1922, while earning notoriety as a playboy—quite early in his career and most eager to please his dad—a flashy Bill Paley was a salesman for his father's expanding cigar concern. By then the firm was lucratively operating in Philadelphia. Before long the younger man was named vice-president of advertising. His future was assured, promising. But he was restless, determined to secure another commercial line of work that was prosperous, glamorous and, possibly most of all, respectable. Well heeled by then, his father came to his son's rescue.

In 1928 the senior Paley bought into the Columbia Phonograph Broadcasting System. It was a shaky enterprise competing—without being much of a threat—with NBC's dual chains. A year earlier the Columbia Phonograph Company had bought a fledgling United Independent network when a major rival, the Victor Company, merged with RCA, appreciably boosting Columbia's panic level. Columbia Phonograph lost $100,000 in its first month in radio and immediately looked for a buyer.[3] Sam Paley and a few more investors bought Columbia out. Bill Paley was designated to run the operation. In one indiscriminate motion he was literally set for life, at 27 presiding over a corporation that was destined to become a major player in network broadcasting. The chain's name stuck; the upstart was soon known as the Columbia network and eventually as CBS.

While there were many traits that Paley shared with Sarnoff, there were several that became identifying symbols. Among them: (a) Paley exuded flamboyancy, put on airs and took delight in displaying his wealth and his women. He had a voracious appetite for both. While Sarnoff was a philanderer, too, his womanizing affairs were private by contrast and he remained wedded to one mate throughout his life. Paley married twice, divorcing the first wife after originally breaking up her home with Jack Hearst, an heir to journalist-entrepreneur William Randolph Hearst's billion-dollar fortune. Paley had numerous liaisons throughout their years together. (b) Unlike Sarnoff, who was prepared in Russian boyhood to become a rabbi, Paley usually hid his Jewishness under a bushel except on some rare occasions when he viewed its acknowledgement as potentially advancing his own purposes. (c) Paley was outwardly coarse and could be vulgar among associates and confidantes, unlike his competitor, who habitually exhibited an air of refinement, or at least did so publicly.

Both men, however, could be evenly matched with ill tempers, heartlessness and despotism. While Sarnoff's fiery manner could be observed for sustained periods, Paley held his in check much of the time, cunningly awaiting a precipitous moment to strike an unsuspecting prey. Although he could be as volatile as Sarnoff, he tended to give his quarry plenty of room as he awaited fateful encounters. Afterward, he usually lapsed into reticent solitude again.

Thus in the mid to late 1920s, two fairly young men were suddenly thrust into the role of broadcasting giant. They were the original powerbrokers in a trade that had not long existed, a field relying on cutting edge technology. Taking the helm of opposing ethereal empires, those individuals' decisions would pervasively impact American life and thought from that time forward. It was an auspicious and heady prospect. And it was soon obvious that both relished the chance to occupy the catbird seat in their respective domains.

"In the beginning there were few in the NBC offices who took his [Paley's] Columbia Broadcasting System seriously—proof that they had not yet taken the measure of the youthful millionaire's business talents," noted an observer. Yet, by the close of the Second World War, organized opposition was mounting, for example, to RCA's intent to be at the forefront of television engineering and production.

The same source affirmed: "The assault was spearheaded by the Columbia Broadcasting System, with Zenith covering the flanks; which spelled command respectively by William S. Paley and Commander Eugene McDonald, two of the shrewdest and boldest strategists in the radio business. Sarnoff had a healthy respect for their abilities." In the span of a few years NBC considered CBS a worthy opponent, highly competitive and potentially threatening to the possibilities it saw for itself as the dominant player in a budding mass medium.

For a couple of decades it had been clear to the professionals in the trade that one of the most markedly distinguishing factors separating the two mavericks rested in Sarnoff's zealous plans from NBC's inception to enter television. He was convinced as early as 1923 that video would be the next great step in mass communication. By 1928, he established a trial TV station and—after 11 years of experiments—displayed the embryonic medium to curious onlookers during the 1939 New York World's Fair. Two years beyond he was on the air in Gotham with WNBT, one of the nation's first commercial TV stations. The Second World War temporarily halted expansion but gave him some time to work out the kinks and refine RCA's business plan.

For his contributions, including commitment of substantial sums of RCA money without any recompense since 1928, Sarnoff was cited by the Television Broadcasters Association in 1944 as the "Father of American Television." It was a title he wore proudly. He had earned another during the war that he liked even more. He was a communications consultant to general Dwight

D. Eisenhower then. Ike bestowed Sarnoff with the status of brigadier general. Henceforth staffers in the RCA building resolutely greeted Sarnoff with the salutation "General." He ate it up.

One of Paley's many coincidences with Sarnoff was that he, too, was on Eisenhower's staff during the war. He was deputy chief of the psychological warfare branch, a rather difficult-to-define task. But there was no mistaking one defining attribute: of the two broadcasting giants, Paley was unequivocally considered the radio man. He wasn't demonstrably anxious to exploit the wealth of a healthy aural web to finance the costly prospects of newer technology, clinging unapologetically to his passion past mid century. Both men returned from World War II to pursue opposing obsessions, in fact. Paley aimed to master his chain's fate by controlling radio programming; after years of imagination and experimentation, Sarnoff expected to turn TV into widespread reality. Each man would achieve plenty of triumphs in his personal quest.

CBS president Frank Stanton proclaimed: "I never heard Bill [Paley] talk about using the stars for television at all. For him in those days it was all radio. His postwar idea was simply to get control of radio programming. He never talked about television.... He didn't pick stars with any idea about leaping into television." Paley's intents notwithstanding, an incisive biographer exclaimed: "He may have thought he was building radio, but his gut—the visceral, even primitive, love for stars and shows that figured in every move he made—was to give his fledgling television network an advantage Sarnoff would never match." A Web site labels Paley "the best-known executive in network television," a fascinating prospect considering that for much of his career his interests and expertise were unmistakably focused elsewhere.

One of Paley's primary methods in achieving his unintended feat was witnessed in the infamous talent raids he conducted in 1948 and 1949. Swooping in on personalities at other chains over which the listeners had long fawned, his exercise was dubbed "Paley's Comet" for the lightning speed with which it was completed. A handful of star legends were offered extraordinarily profitable long-term tax-savings incentives for signing with CBS, putting considerably more bills into their pockets than they were accustomed to having before.

When the dust settled, Paley had attracted Bing Crosby and Groucho Marx from ABC. Beyond those notable gains, however, he scored his most triumphant coup d'état against NBC and his old nemesis. From Sarnoff's compound he absconded with top-draw legends Jack Benny, Edgar Bergen and Charlie McCarthy, Freeman Gosden and Charles Correll (*Amos 'n' Andy*), Red Skelton, and George Burns and Gracie Allen. Along with them went Ozzie and Harriet Nelson plus Harold Peary (*The Great Gildersleeve*), who headlined a new CBS sitcom. It was "the biggest upheaval in broadcasting since Paley bought CBS in 1928," one wag pontificated.

Without question, the biggest prize in the lot was NBC's most colossal moneymaker, Benny.

> While Benny was top of the proverbial heap on NBC, CBS czar William S. Paley cast a hungry eye upon the comedian. Paley apparently had good reason to believe Benny could be had: he learned that NBC refused to deal with Benny in terms of buying Benny's holding company package (a tax break major entertainers enjoyed in those years).... Paley reached out to Benny and offered him a deal that would allow that package-buy—a tremendous capital gains tax break for Benny at a time when World War II had meant taxes as high as 90 percent at certain high income levels.[4]

Paley recognized that talent like Benny, not the station's reputation, was what drew listeners. He also offered Benny the personal attention Sarnoff withheld.

"How could you do this to me?" was the first question out of Sarnoff's mouth when he encountered his archrival after "Paley's Comet" blazed across the ether with such incredible velocity. It hurt Sarnoff dreadfully, wrecking his network's primetime schedule and—nearly as badly—crushing his now-deflated spirit in its wake. Until the innovation of *Monitor* in 1955, in fact, NBC remained both humbled and hobbled, never to regain the status it brandished in its glory years.

For the first time in two decades, CBS singularly occupied the pinnacle of the ratings heap. Moreover, the web boasted full sponsorship of 29 programs that it owned outright, a complete reversal of its enduring underdog status. By the start of 1950, CBS owned 80 percent of radio's top 20 Nielsen-rated shows while NBC could do little but lick its wounds. Not the least among the atrocities it suffered was a $7 million loss in ad revenue in one year, to say nothing about the millions of listeners who defected to CBS while continuing to follow their favorite icons.

When NBC countered with a weekly 90-minute glitzy Sunday night star-studded production headlined by Tallulah Bankhead labeled *The Big Show*—throwing it in multiple time periods against some of the performers Paley had swiped from under its nose—Sarnoff was once again thwarted. *The Big Show* fizzled big time, persisting just one and a half seasons (1950–1952), while costing an astronomical bundle to produce. Sarnoff had surely had better days.

A Paley biographer offered readers a number of comparisons between the two magnates running CBS and NBC. "Although Sarnoff had the superior intellect, he was deliberate and methodical and in his eyes, everything Paley achieved came too easily. To Sarnoff, Paley was a child of privilege," added the chronicler. "Sarnoff never appreciated that Paley was a creative and shrewd entrepreneur who leaned on and learned from his top administrators.... Paley was not in charge all the time as Sarnoff was."

Identifying Sarnoff as "a starched shirt who remained aloof from NBC executives," the author maintained further: "Sarnoff surrounded himself with a tight circle of loyal RCA yes-men. He was a visionary, and did not absorb ideas from others as Paley did." At the same time, "Paley shared some of Sarnoff's traits—an enormous ego, a hunger for publicity, a growing contempt for underlings. Yet Paley's strivings were nearly invisible, his actions always veiled in gentility. Sarnoff was harshly despotic, and fairly bristled with cockiness and authority."

Sarnoff also lacked Paley's feel for popular culture. The RCA executive enjoyed nothing better than listening to classical music, maintaining scorn for comics such as *Amos 'n' Andy*, Benny, Fred Allen, Bergen, Skelton and Bob Hope, all of whom had made his radio empire prestigious and him an utterly prosperous man. "His idea of relaxation was to sneak down to Studio 8-H in Rockefeller Center and listen to the rehearsals of the NBC Symphony," said a biographer. "When his wife tuned into *Amos 'n' Andy*, Sarnoff left the room. He had nothing but contempt for comedians. 'If comedy is the center of NBC's activities, then maybe I had better quit,' he ... confided.... Given a preference, he would have aired only symphonies and classical dramas on NBC."

An ex-aide revealed that Sarnoff saw broadcasting as "a means of bridging cultural differences, bringing people together in greater understanding of one another." Another source insisted: "His outlook on life was simply too serious to accommodate to popular taste.... He did not understand the hunger for easy entertainment."

To an unmistakable degree Sarnoff's mission—in his mind, at least—could be equated with an awesome sensitivity for polish, without acknowledging any personal bias. That could translate into appealing to a scholarly, sophisticated audience, of course. "His quest for quality was explained as a search for prestige," a biography conceded. "In truth it derived from his natural preferences. No matter how logically he justified superior programs, he was in fact responding to his own hungers for beauty, music, culture, the education he had missed."

Paley, on the other hand, had a genius for mass programming, primarily because it reflected *his* personal tastes. It was also the route to serious revenue, a fact that was never lost on him. He appreciated entertainers that the public adored, and typically pursued them with demonstrable energy. When Alice Faye came to New York, he filled her hotel room with flowers.

Sarnoff, meanwhile, didn't send her a single posy. "Paley had a good ear for musical talent," a wordsmith confirmed. "He knew enough about dramatic structure to criticize a program intelligently. To Paley, Sarnoff was a hardware man in a software business."

Sarnoff, the broadcasting pioneer and idealist, was nevertheless perceptibly vexed that his opposite number was lauded publicly as "radio's restless conscience." In his view Paley was an opportunist devoid of any long-range vision for the business. "Paley needed to see how something worked before he could embrace it," a journalist suggested. "Paley reaped where Sarnoff sowed—which rankled Sarnoff no end."

Although Paley won the biggest battle that the two men fought in their radio sparring when he carried out his blitzkrieg talent raids, he didn't win every time. Some of his and Sarnoff's most inglorious moments were spent contending over prestigious musical plunder. At least one of those occasions is worth closer examination.

Paley struggled doggedly to acquire the aircasting rights to the Metropolitan Opera when that distinguished performing group was entering the ether in 1931.[5] Shrewdly presenting his case, he invited Met chairman Otto Kahn to a sound quality exhibition. The broadcasting tycoon noted that Kahn was greatly moved by the meticulously prepared presentation. Exclaimed Kahn: "Just imagine hearing that wonderful music and we don't have to look at those ugly faces!"

Paley was sure that such glowing affirmation concluded the matter—that CBS had the Met in its pocket. But the thing that had provoked the opera officials to consider radio broadcasting in the first place—a compelling urgency for an infusion of cash following the collapse of the stock market and patrons' reluctance to spend many funds on such venues in a tight environment—ultimately became the deciding factor. With it came Paley's undoing.

When word that CBS was about to sign the Met leaked to NBC president Merlin H. Aylesworth, acting on behalf of his superior Sarnoff, Aylesworth determined to make an offer the Met officials simply couldn't refuse. Having already tendered $60,000 to broadcast the opera company's initial season on the air, Aylesworth reached into the air and pulled out the number $122,000. His gambit paid off. Paley had anted-up $120,000 for the prize. A beaming Sarnoff got what he wanted for his network and himself and overwhelmed his strongest rival in the fray. While Sarnoff would lose some major wars in the years ahead, he had won a stunning conquest that day.

Having already scored a coup with the New York Philharmonic in 1930, a prize Sarnoff no doubt had wished for, Paley in the same year attempted to lure the Met to CBS for a series of Sunday afternoon concerts. When Sarnoff decisively won that fight, however, Paley was seething. "It was a bitter blow and one that I resented for a long time," the CBS chairman admitted. He consoled himself, nonetheless, with the knowledge that he was paying only $35,000 annually for the Philharmonic. NBC, conversely, was soon shelling out $191,000 to retain the Met, a tab some $156,000 beyond what it was costing CBS for the Philharmonic, and an extremely comforting thought to Paley.

Another instance in which music for the sophisticates became the spoil of battle involved Sarnoff's resolve to engage the services of globally renowned impresario Arturo Toscanini. Toscanini was the ex-conductor of both the Metropolitan Opera and the New York Philharmonic Symphony. While this particular pursuit didn't directly implicate Paley, its outcome obviously created another display of one-upmanship.

At least in Sarnoff's mind, it also solidified NBC even more as the network that catered to an upscale, erudite, uppercrust audience. At the same time, it pacified Sarnoff's personal conviction that one of radio's imperative functions was that of imbuing listeners with healthy cultural infusions, and especially fine musical programming. It should come as little surprise, then, that the RCA chairman didn't rest on his laurels long, only temporarily satisfied by the plum he won by signing the Metropolitan Opera broadcasts and the appurtenances accompanying it. Sarnoff's reach invariably extended his grasp.

By 1936, he envisioned a pre-eminent symphony orchestra that would play the world's most beautiful classical compositions over NBC. While NBC Blue offered its listeners the Met and CBS presented the New York Philharmonic Symphony to its patronage, NBC Red—the original chain and, in widely held opinions, the most alluring—had very little that could play to the crowd Sarnoff wanted his pivotal network to project. The creation of a recognized entourage of eminent instrumentalists would fix that and at the same time trounce CBS. With that accomplishment, for the first time NBC's dual webs could boast of broadcasting more prestigious musical features than its leading rival. For Sarnoff, it would be a win-win-win achievement, meeting corporate, listener and personal goals. Losing this was out of the question.

NBC programming vice president John F. Royal is believed to have proffered the name to Toscanini as the leader of the planned aggregate. Sarnoff was quick to endorse it. There was but one man on earth, the chairman convinced himself, qualified to direct such an elite body of accomplished artisans. There was just one problem: Toscanini had reached an impasse with the Philharmonic in 1936 and stormed out, returning to his native Italy and vowing never to conduct an American orchestra again.

Toscanini's intimates advised Sarnoff that it was futile to attempt to alter the mind of the cantankerous maestro once he had put his foot down. But Sarnoff could put his foot down too, as evidenced by his determination to win the Metropolitan Opera. Thereby hangs a prolonged cat-and-mouse game of stalking, coddling and soothing a savage beast until—with concession after concession made by NBC—Sarnoff got what he was after.[6] Details of the pursuit, capture and controversial aftermath with a highly temperamental, ultra-demanding impresario may be found in *Music Radio* by this author (McFarland, 2005).

The upshot of the chase was that Sarnoff accomplished his win-win-win pursuit, and the NBC Symphony Orchestra—created with nearly 100 superlative instrumentalists—persisted from 1937 to 1954. The outcome demonstrated once again the power commanded by men like David Sarnoff and William Paley. It also underscored the resolve and fervor with which they worked when they saw something they wanted.

Neither man genuinely respected the other; both saw qualities in their adversary that they despised. Yet they could become friendly in public if a situation called for it, and certainly did so when they appeared together in Washington to lobby for common purposes that supported collective advancement of mass communications. Yet neither was the kind of individual who could call the other indiscriminately and invite him to dinner or a party for the social elite. It wasn't in their natures to desire spending very much time with their antagonists.

Sarnoff retired in 1970 and the following year, at age 80, he died in his sleep of cardiac arrest on December 12, 1971. His contributions to radio were passed over in a eulogy at his funeral, which praised his visionary work leading to television. Paley was among the mourners at his memorial service.

Paley was president of CBS from 1928 to 1946 and chairman of the board from 1946 to 1986, acting chairman a year thereafter and chairman again from 1987 to 1990. He found it almost impossible to relinquish the reins and anoint a successor who pleased him. Death overtook him at last; he succumbed to kidney failure on October 26, 1990, at 89. He had remained active for two decades following the retirement of his old adversary.

Paley and Sarnoff offer an interesting contrast in the beginnings of broadcasting. While they were frequently at odds with one another—hidden at times behind clenched teeth, no less—at the same time they accomplished great purposes that paved avenues we travel now in modern communications. Despite the intense methods of those magnates, the legacies of their momentous accomplishments will not likely be abandoned any time soon.

11

Halcyon Days
A Showtime Sampler

This chapter begins with a disclaimer: people who love old time radio may very likely think of it as the most unjust segment of the book. It attempts to please all of the readers all of the time, an irrefutable impossibility.

The author apologizes profusely here and now to those who experienced radio in its heyday and who may be still wedded to programs and personalities that lured them to their receivers daily, weekly or whenever their faves aired. All who fit in that category—whether you heard the shows live or in the years since via the magic of recording tape, discs, MP3s or what have you—have preferences. It's only natural. The author's personal regret is that you will not find all of them here. Hopefully some of your favorites appear in these synoptic vignettes. And if you never had the opportunity to hear the shows in the first place, these snippets will introduce you to what entertained and informed America so many decades ago via the transcontinental audio chains.

The format selected is to focus on nine genres that aired in the peak of chain radio from 1935 to 1955. It begins following a winnowing process when the kinds of mainstay series were determined (prior to 1935) and it persists until TV finally dealt radio-listening an overpowering blow (beyond 1955). For each of the nine genres, five representative programs have been selected for delineation. Effort has been made to cite some of the most popular entries under each classification.

Be aware, too, that there are no admissions for categories like advice, disc jockey, gossip, news, politics, public affairs, religion, sports, teen comedy, variety and similar subgenres covering territory that is too often similar, undistinguished, unappealing, controversial or difficult to separate from another breed.

Here are 45 programs that symbolize what radio network listeners heard when they tuned into their receivers during the halcyon days of broadcasting.

Audience Participation

Art Linkletter's House Party

It took producer John Guedel and his business partner and soon-to-be series host Art Linkletter (whose moniker was eventually added to that of the show's) one long night to dream up the motif for *House Party*. Learning that an ad agency was seeking a new audio exhibition in 1944, Guedel and Linkletter cordoned themselves off to scratch out a few ideas. The following morning their hypothesis for a matinee human interest series sold; for a very long while their night's work compensated them handsomely. From January 15, 1945, virtually without interruption to October 13, 1967, the feature was a network daytime radio staple on CBS (except 1949, on ABC). So great was its draw, largely with housewives, students and night-shift workers, a simulcast entry persisted on CBS-TV from September 1, 1952, through September 5, 1969, re-branded in later years as *The Art Linkletter Show*.

Moonlighting as master of ceremonies of the Guedel-Linkletter stunt feature *People Are Funny* (1942–1960, NBC), Linkletter was a gregarious host whose warm disposition resonated with audiences. The daytime fare was characterized by beauty and fashion tips, contests with studio and home audiences, health hints, recurring guests with sage advice—and all of it a frothy mixture of pervasive interplay between host, guests and fans. In one of its most popular games, "What's in the House?," contestants pursuing clues were normally awarded home appliances on winning. In another segment, Linkletter figuratively brought down the house by "peeking in some lady's purse." Invariably he rummaged through a woman's handbag, retrieved an item and displayed it for all to see (such as a rum flask or a roll of toilet tissue), nonchalantly inquiring: "Why on *earth* would you have *that* in there?" By then the crowd of onlookers had dissolved into total bedlam.

But the hit of the show, without any question, was the daily visits of a quartet of precocious youngsters from a Los Angeles–area school. Summoned to respond to Linkletter's leading statements, invariably they added further pandemonium. When the emcee attempted to comfort a small lad who had lost a pet, telling him "I have a feeling God has carried your dog to Heaven to be with Him," the dimpled darling shot back: "Mister, what on earth would God want with a dead dog?" Over the years 23,000 tykes were interrogated by an inquisitive Linkletter; it netted multiple books titled *Kids Say the Darndest Things* and a 1990s TV series hosted by comic actor Bill Cosby. Only a minuscule handful of network daytime series successfully challenged the dominance of the radio serials in the 1940s and 1950s. *House Party*, exuding fun in multifaceted forms, was one of them.

Arthur Godfrey's Talent Scouts

By the early 1950s, Arthur Godfrey subjugated every entertainer on radio and television. Projecting him to the forefront of daytime celebs, his meteoric rise to fame via a 90-minute weekday morning variety series, *Arthur Godfrey Time*, was simulcast on TV for an hour. Backed by a staff of vocalists and instrumentalists well liked by radio listeners, the entry propelled him into the limelight. By July 2, 1946, Godfrey acquired his own weekly primetime half-hour to audition budding artists (never neophytes, as elsewhere on the air) for their next rung up the ladder of success. *Talent Scouts*, frequently preceded by its host's name, ran on CBS through October 1, 1956. It was so popular that a simulcast on CBS-TV aired from December 6, 1948, beyond the radiocast's end, to July 21, 1958. Concurrently its star presided over *Arthur Godfrey and His Ukulele* and the *Arthur Godfrey Digest* on CBS Radio and—with his morning troupe—on a mid-week variety hour, *Arthur Godfrey and His Friends*, on CBS-TV. By then he was generating 12 percent of his web's annual revenues, underscoring the entertainer's status in the industry.

All these shows demonstrated Godfrey's ability to banter in a genteel, gregarious manner. On *Talent Scouts* he chatted amiably with guests who introduced him to not-widely-known performing discoveries. Aspirants sang, played an instrument, joked or did whatever distinguished them in competition with several other candidates in a weekly half-hour. At the show's end, an applause meter, a common apparatus in radio, measured the studio audience's vociferous responses to determine which talent was the week's winner. That individual's prize was a string of appearances on Godfrey's daily morning show for the remainder of the week, gaining more exposure which often led to still bigger opportunities (personal appearances, record contracts, radio, TV, film, etc.). Over the years the winners included up-and-coming celebrities Tony Bennett, Pat Boone, the Chordettes, Roy Clark, Van Cliburn, Rosemary Clooney, Wally Cox, Vic Damone, Connie Francis, Robert Goulet, Steve Lawrence, Al Martino, the McGuire Sisters, Carmel Quinn, Lu Ann Simms, Leslie Uggams and more. It was hardly an amateur hour.

Behind the scenes Godfrey's ferocious ego got him into trouble. He was lord and master of all his shows, a fact most people weren't aware of until, in late 1953, he began firing some of his heralded daytime minions. Legions of adoring fans instantly turned on him, beginning a long slow decline from which his career never recovered. While *Talent Scouts* persisted a few years, many took a jaundiced view of the paramount entertainer and found him wanting. The daily radio series continued to 1972, though it was little more than a figment of its former self. Godfrey's stars dispersed, leaving behind images of Camelot while spawning contemplations of what might have been.

Stop the Music!

Here was a show that helped make an also-ran network competitive while tolling the death bell for a longstanding comic's career—one that perceptibly *owned* a Sunday night time period for 17 seasons. *Stop the Music!* was ABC's solution to languishing in the ratings cellar after captivating funnymen at NBC gained the spoils of primetime. Providing a satisfying alternative for anybody not heavily into laughter or ABC's little appreciated chamber music orchestras, CBS offered a diet of second-string crime dramas that garnered most of the crowd beyond NBC's mirthful mania. But when ABC cast the string-players and horn-blowers aside in favor of *Stop the Music!* on March 21, 1948, salvation was assured. For a quadrennial, until August 10, 1952, that show solidified ABC as a genuine contender among the webs.

The series followed a simple strategy: before a live studio audience, an orchestra played unnamed tunes and vocalists warbled unidentified solos (mumbling over the actual words in titles). An ebullient master of ceremonies, Bert Parks—the same man who later crooned for a quarter-century "There She Is, Miss America!" at the infamous beauty pageant—yelled in the midst of those anonymous songs: "Stop the music!" A denizen in Radioland picked from the white pages of a telephone directory had been telephoned by ABC and at that very moment was on the line awaiting a chance to name the tune currently being performed. If he or she could do it, valuable cash, merchandise and gift awards awaited.

So enamored did prize-hungry Americans become that they tuned out NBC comic Fred Allen, thereby bringing a quick end to Allen's long reign on Sunday nights. "Radio actually died when *Stop the Music!* got higher ratings than Fred Allen," affirmed one source. Another claimed the stir drove "the final nail in radio's coffin." While those assessments were far too generous in estimating its influence, *Stop the Music!* nevertheless had a profound effect on Sunday night listeners, on a long-playing comedian and on ABC. Few audience participation entries created that kind of hysteria. For a brief while its acclaim outstripped some of the legendary icons of radio. And while it may have been but a flash in the pan, it was clearly a phenomenon that nobody had ever previously witnessed.

Truth or Consequences

One of the foremost masters of ceremonies, Ralph Edwards, was initially familiar to listeners of matinee misery introducing *Against the Storm* and *Life Can Be Beautiful*. Addicts *of Coast to Coast on a Bus, Major Bowes' Original Amateur Hour, The Phil Baker Show, Town Hall Tonight* and *Vic and Sade* turned the announcer's name into household words in the 1930s. With as many as 45 shows to his credit that were beamed across the country weekly, Edwards still wasn't happy. More than anything else he wanted a level of security that could be satisfied by producing and starring in his own primetime series. He derived a concept based on an old parlor game (Forfeit) that his family played during his youth in Colorado. Edwards sketched a proposal for an innovative half-hour that he labeled *Truth or Consequences*, centered on funny stunts involving studio contestants. Subsequently he gathered a small group of friends, made an audition tape of a sample show, and sold it promptly—with him as producer and emcee. He was literally fixed for life.

Truth or Consequences premiered on CBS March 23, 1940, but most of its years to its last audio gasp on September 12, 1956, were spent as an NBC citadel. At various times from 1950 to 1965, there was a separate "televersion" that shifted into and out of day and nighttime slots at CBS and NBC. The show's premise involved silly stuff like having a blindfolded couple carry on a normal conversation while feeding each other blueberry pie; having a contestant sing "Donkey Serenade" with a chorus of live donkeys accompanying; and having a soldier telephone his steady sweetheart at home as he attempted to talk evenly, not revealing that a curvaceous, well-stacked model was sitting on his lap and tousling his hair. Sometimes a gag went on longer as a contestant was dispatched across America to retrieve an unusual object or information or maybe to convince someone of something perhaps difficult to believe. It might take two weeks or a few months to complete some feats. Weekly, those contestants checked in during the broadcast.

The most famous tryst was a series of hidden voices in the late 1940s in which celebrities (comedian Jack Benny, prizefighter Jack Dempsey, silent screen star Clara Bow and others) helped the show raise sums for charities by dropping clues to their identifications. In 1950, the little burg of Hot Springs, New Mexico, legally altered its nomenclature to Truth or Consequences, New Mexico. Edwards and company aired live from that venue several times. While Edwards was the show's only audio host, the video effort went to Jack Bailey (*Queen for a Day*) and others. By then Edwards was fully immersed in emceeing a human interest spin-off of the original, *This Is Your Life*, which launched on radio (1948–1950) and became a fan favorite of nighttime TV (1950–1965, not continuously, with syndicated reruns as late as 1988).

You Bet Your Life

A John Guedel production (*House Party, People Are Funny*) called *You Bet Your Life* was a vehicle exclusively designed for the zany, at times irascible, silent and talkies film star Groucho Marx. Marx's one-line comebacks to almost anything a contestant said kept an approving studio audience—as well as those at home—in stitches. It aired between October 27, 1947, and September 19, 1956, and was at different times on ABC, CBS and NBC Radio. A telecast variation played on NBC from October 5, 1950, to September 21, 1961, ending under the banner *The Groucho Show*.

Marx was never at a loss for words; what most didn't realize was that he was aided and abetted by cue cards hanging out of view above the contestants' heads. The contestants appeared in pairs. Marx's interviews with contrasting guests were often literal riots, sometimes squeezing the time for a simple question-and-answer quiz to follow based on their knowledge. If a player echoed a "secret word" which had been revealed already to the home and studio audience, there was an added cash prize. Players were carefully picked to allow the host plenty of material to play off. One of the funniest bits involved a man of Mexican descent living in San Antonio whose sobriquet included a double surname: Ramiro Gonzalez Gonzalez. On being introduced, Marx allowed: "What does your wife call you—Ramiro or Gonzalez?" To which the guest replied: "She call me Pedro." Seeing his chance, Marx inquired: "And where are you from, Mr. Gonzalez Gonzalez ... Walla Walla?" The studio crowd dissolved into unreserved pandemonium.

You Bet Your Life was the first broadcast series to embrace the rerun. The entrepreneurial producer John Guedel, ever an enterprising fellow who smelled money, adopted a fictitious number (3.4) during the show's original season. He informed ABC Radio officials that—since the typical listener heard just 3.4 shows per season—the chain could profit by repeating 13 of the better *You Bet Your Life* shows (all were prerecorded on audiotape) during Marx's upcoming 13-week summer hiatus. The brass bought it and the rerun was born. If you want to know whom to throw brickbats at now, Guedel's the guy.

Personality-Driven Comedy

Bob and Ray

Bob Elliott and Ray Goulding were hired separately in non-comedic roles by Boston's WHDH Radio in the mid 1940s. Their association there led to the discovery that each man possessed a capacity for offbeat material that sometimes bordered on the outrageous. Together they cultivated a modified form of comedy that allowed them to turn ordinary situations into exaggerated foot-stomping merriment. The duo was given a half-hour weekdays (*Matinee with Bob and Ray*) to test the limits of their creative abilities. There they would introduce a range of comedic vignettes embracing parodies of network soap operas, stars, mysteries and quiz shows while welcoming drop-in visits by recurring guests that the audience soon came to readily recognize.

With Elliott and Goulding taking all the roles, there was Mary McGoon, Wally Ballou, Biff Burns, Arthur Sturdley, Webley Webster, Dean Archer Armstead, Steve Bosco, Charles the Poet, Lawrence Fechtenberger and many more characterizations. All were amusing and some of those exchanges were stretched beyond belief. Although Bob and Ray persistently played it for real, the idea that "something like this couldn't happen in real life" continually shocked the fans back to reality.

The two men's fame couldn't be contained in Beantown forever. News of their foolishness spread like wildfire, soon reaching NBC in New York. By July 2, 1951, they were projected to a national audience of appreciative listeners via NBC Radio. While the pair shifted frequently between webs under various appellations—airing between 1951 and 1984 over MBS, CBS and PBS, plus added series on various local New York stations—*Bob and Ray* was a hit whenever and wherever it appeared. Its pithy exchanges never went out of style, as popular at the end as it had been four decades earlier. Spawning showbiz careers for its headliners, the program thrust them onto the nightclub circuit and more personal appearance venues, to advertising, video (1951–1953, NBC-TV), recordings, books and varied other merchandising opportunities. In the end, their attempts to be funny had actually turned into some pretty serious business.

The Edgar Bergen and Charlie McCarthy Show

Radio's Edgar Bergen set the stage for the later success of *Howdy Doody* on TV, even though his mythical figures appealed to widely separated age groups. Bergen's marionettes—Charlie McCarthy, Mortimer Snerd, Effie Klinker, Podine Puffington and Lars Lindquist—made an instant hit with radio audiences when he began introducing them on NBC May 9, 1937. Their series ran all the way to July 1, 1956, in its latter seasons appearing on CBS.

Despite the proliferating puppetry, there was never any doubt that it was the monocle-wearing McCarthy's show. The best parts of each week's script included verbal exchanges between the namesake stars. Bergen was an inspired ventriloquist who took paternal responsibility for his opposite number by meting out good-natured advice to his little friend. McCarthy, on the other hand, speaking in a whiny, nasal-toned voice, invariably found something to disagree over. He chuckled frequently and took delight in calling attention to any perceived flaws he found in his "maker." He'd dish out animated jibes in rapid succession and usually received more placid ripostes from Bergen. The studio audience reveled in McCarthy's accusations as the pair tangled, even though it was generally lighthearted jesting.

McCarthy saved his most caustic comments, nevertheless, for frequent show guest W. C. Fields, who became his most celebrated adversary. The duo sparred relentlessly, each one lapsing into name-calling and shameless physical descriptions that perpetually kept the studio audience howling. But when the show's guests included bombshell film actresses like Betty Grable, Dorothy Lamour or Jane Powell, McCarthy put away childish pranks and simply went bonkers. Over that kind of quarry he fawned incessantly, drooling at the mouth, sometimes virtually speechless as those beauties graced the stage. For a dummy (whose antics the folks at home could only imagine), he did well, remaining an object of listener adulation for 19 years.

The George Burns and Gracie Allen Show

Although they had equal billing, this married couple headlined a show that was wholly dependent on the skewed behavior of one of its stars, Gracie Allen. It took a big man, George Burns, to recognize that his wife was *the* laugh-getter, and to yield to her as the quintessential straight-man. He fed her many of the lines that brought the guffaws, allowed her enough rope to involve them in a variety of zany situations, and—in 1941—extended the life of a floundering show for another 17 years. Allen played a showbiz spouse whose elevator didn't reach the penthouse: a total wacko. What made sense to her didn't to anybody else and vice versa. The expressions that fell from her lips were carefully crafted by a staff of wordsmiths under the hovering oversight of her husband, designed for maximum audience response.

"Gracie, those are beautiful flowers. Where did they come from?" George asked one day. "Don't you remember, George?" she replied. "You said if I went to visit Clara Bagley in the hospital I should be sure to take her flowers. So, when she wasn't looking, I did." It was typical fare for this scatterbrain, and the whole half-hour was a continuous romp in which a familiar cast (neighbors, mailman, announcer, Gracie's friends, George's business associates)—interacting with a dimwit—constantly was as confused as she, although in different ways. Mistaken identities, expressions that could be misinterpreted and common sense got twisted to the delight of home and studio observers.

The pair persisted on radio from February 22, 1932, to May 17, 1950, shifting erratically between CBS and NBC. They achieved greater exposure in a TV incarnation on CBS between October 12, 1950, and September 22, 1958, when health forced Gracie's retirement. While Burns carried on another season with the same cast—sans Gracie—on NBC-TV, it wasn't the same. The bloom was off the rose without Gracie to throw lines to and his show vanished. After she died he attempted a comeback on ABC-TV in 1964–1965, with Connie Stevens playing a daft dame in *Wendy and Me*. That fizzled, too. There was but one Gracie and nobody duplicated the success she had had with a few cards short of a deck.

The Jack Benny Program

Neither newspaper columnist Ed Sullivan nor stand-up comedian Jack Benny could have imagined where Benny's career was headed when Sullivan persuaded the nightclub entertainer to appear gratis on his debuting CBS Radio interview forum on January 12, 1932. As the pair chatted amiably, an ad agency official tuning in—then seeking a format and star for a client (Canada Dry)—was impressed by Benny's sharp wit in delivering comebacks to whatever Sullivan instigated. By May 2, less than four months afterward, Benny was on the air regularly, and literally became an overnight hit. Over the next 26 years (to June 22, 1958), his show was an audio institution, shifting to NBC October 1, 1933, and returning to CBS January 2, 1949, for the duration of its aural life. The last change was a result of the famous radio talent raids.

While reluctant at first, the star transferred *The Jack Benny Program* into a video incarnation on October 28, 1950. It appeared until September 10, 1965, though not continuously. All but the final season (on NBC) was on CBS. By then he had been a broadcasting legend for 23 years. Playing the role of an ethereal entertainer, on the air Benny and a company of regulars was frequently in "preparation" for an upcoming show. Singer Dennis Day rehearsed his number "for this week's show" and Mary Livingstone (Benny's real-life wife), announcer Don Wilson, bandleader Phil Harris and valet Rochester Van Jones (Eddie Anderson) interacted with the star by helping him get ready for the occasion—or some other fictional event. Along the way there were laughs galore, often at Benny's expense.

In character he was cheap to a fault, kept his wealth locked in a vault several floors beneath his house, was a lousy violinist while insisting he was a virtuoso, maintained that he was 39 and carried on a long-running feud with fellow NBC comic Fred Allen, increasing the audience numbers for both shows. Benny was also believed to be the most beloved radio comedian, in the day he lived and today, especially among adherents of that genre's shows. He was, one critic insisted, "The most popular and best loved comedian of radio's Golden Age." No one immediately comes to mind that can refute it.

The Red Skelton Show

Best known for a plethora of imaginative characterizations, Red Skelton is recalled as the man who introduced the airwaves to George Appleby, Freddie the Freeloader, Gertrude and Heathcliffe, Junior the Mean Widdle Kid, Clem Kadiddlehopper, Willie Lump-Lump, Cauliflower McPugg, San Fernando Red and Bolivar Shagnasty. From a career that began at 10 in roadshow burlesque, medicine and minstrel shows, on showboats and vaudeville stages, Skelton went on to become the consummate pantomimist on video renditions of his durable series. *The Red Skelton Show* lasted from October 7, 1941, to May 26, 1953, variously on NBC and CBS Radio. The televersion on those webs persisted from September 30, 1951, through August 29, 1971.

Studio and home audiences were never in any doubt that this was total put-on, intentionally trying to make the fans laugh. Unlike most other shows where there might have been an attempt to cover up a fluff or ignore a part of a set that fell down or someone backstage who accidentally kicked over a waste can, unplanned interruptions only made it funnier. If the unseen waste can calamity could be heard by the audience, Skelton might stop in mid-sentence, pause, grin at the camera (in the TV embodiment) and say: "I told the crew if they could add a little bedlam here, it would liven up a pretty dead script." The audience would dissolve into unabashed hysteria, an added bonus, and just what he wanted. Skelton sometimes rattled off a line intended to be funny that didn't generate much response. On such occasions he'd turn to the microphone while panning to the camera: "I don't write 'em ... I just read 'em!" It never failed to unleash the hearty guffaws he had just missed.

With a supporting cast, his series was a composite of monologue, two or three comedic sketches, possibly a pantomime vignette for TV and one or more stars from stage, screen and broadcasting. If the guests were vocalists or instrumentalists, they usually performed their talent. Many were corralled into taking a part in one of those sketches, too—often being Skelton's foil, or temporary partner in crime, perhaps skipping a line unintentionally and hearing one of his good-natured ripostes. Here was a show that, while rehearsed, never took the script—

or the rehearsal—seriously. In failing to do so, it kept America laughing for three consecutive decades.

Situation Comedy

The Amos 'n' Andy Show

No one could have anticipated how far in time and territory they would go in entertaining America when Charles Correll hooked up with Freeman Gosden in 1919. Their paths crossed as traveling talent agents for a Midwestern stage show. They became fast friends and eventual business partners, landing the duo in radio in 1925 over Chicago's WGN. On the side they recorded musical numbers for the Victor Talking Machine Company. Ultimately the pair worked out a couple of black characterizations, named them Sam and Henry, and went on the air nightly under their new aliases over WGN beginning January 12, 1926. In a scripted comedic narrative they played pals from Birmingham, Alabama, who arrived in the Windy City in search of work. Both white, Correll and Gosden applied a wide range of dialects to impersonate numerous figures in their sketch, never attempting to denigrate anybody but to provide loads of mirth based on believable depictions. Most people of multiple ethnic origins saw it that way; incredibly drawn to them, their listeners created quite a stir. The originators quickly sensed opportunity knocking beyond the shores of Lake Michigan.

When they attempted to reproduce the show by transcription for other markets, WGN wouldn't allow it. The boys picked up their marbles, transferred to Chicago's WMAQ, and fulfilled their intent. Since WGN owned the *Sam 'n' Henry* nomenclature, Gosden and Correll carried on as *Amos 'n' Andy* over WMAQ. There they were blacks from Atlanta who arrived in Harlem, New York, seeking their fortunes. By August 19, 1929, NBC Blue was beaming the duo coast-to-coast. In a short while their infamy led cinemas to briefly interrupt films when *Amos 'n' Andy* was on the air to pipe the show into theaters, thereby preventing their patrons from missing episodes. President Calvin Coolidge left word that he wasn't to be disturbed when those favored comedians broadcast. For a brief while, the country could hardly go about its business in their quarter-hour.

The duo continued to May 22, 1955, the last dozen years as a true sitcom with a strong cast of support players taking most of the peripheral roles Gosden and Correll had earlier voiced. The show alternated over NBC Blue, NBC and CBS. A TV experiment in the early 1950s with other actors in the leads ran into racial trouble and was soon withdrawn. In a move that allowed a few more years of exposure for the best-recalled funnymen of the ether, CBS put them in an unfamiliar role as disc jockeys. From September 13, 1954, to November 25, 1960, they presided over *The Amos 'n' Andy Music Hall.* By their swan song, Correll and Gosden had been broadcasting those characterizations more than three decades, a remarkable distinction afforded very few of their contemporaries.

Baby Snooks

While there never was a sitcom about a truly vile parent or a really gloomy child, *Baby Snooks* was, according to one scholar, "the closest to a family comedy about a bad seed." Another pundit called her "the most notorious brat of the air." It seemed ludicrous that a preschool tyke could so dominate her parents, and especially her father—with whom she spent so much time—frequently earning little more than a reprimand. When her dad could take no more of her tricks, nonetheless, she suffered the consequences. The devilment that she could think up was sure to provoke unbridled laughter. She even dressed to impress the studio audience, so closely identifying with the role that it was difficult to separate Snooks from the woman who portrayed her.

It was actress Fanny Brice's second career. Following an illustrious run on stage, including 13 years with the Ziegfeld Follies, plus a futile attempt in flicks, she reverted to a younger age, trotting out a figure she had exhibited before private groups. Now refined and ready for mass consumption, the part rejuvenated her faltering career: the misbehaving imp transformed a falling star into one of entertainment's brightest. Many of the traits Snooks demonstrated reflected on Brice's turn-of-the-century beginnings when she fended for herself in Gotham. Out of it grew a little girl who brought giggles to millions for her audacity in standing up to her elders. Her mischievousness was an affront to parental supervision while it provoked unabashed hilarity among fans.

The Snooks character formally emerged out of *Maxwell House Presents Good News* over NBC beginning November 4, 1937. After it was showcased there and on subsequent General Foods–backed series, *Baby Snooks* materialized under its own sobriquet in the 1944–1945 radio season. The part of Lancelot (Daddy) Higgins, absolutely crucial to the plots, was played at varying times by Frank Morgan, Alan Reed and Hanley Stafford, the latter the best remembered. Vera (Mommy) Higgins was portrayed by Lalive Brownell, Lois Corbet and Arlene Harris, the latter again supplying the long-haul voice. Robespierre Higgins, Snooks' infant brother, was interpreted by child impersonator Leone Ledoux. But it was Brice who made the show. When she died unexpectedly May 29, 1951, her series ground to an abrupt halt. There was no attempt to replace her. She was one of a kind, and when she passed so did her alter-ego.

Fibber McGee & Molly

Jim and Marian Jordan tried radio comedy sketches earlier to little avail. But when writer Don Quinn plunged them into the figures of Fibber McGee & Molly, the couple found they had hit the mother lode. For 15 consecutive seasons (1938–1953), they provided the pillars of NBC's Tuesday night foundation. Their performances persisted in manifold timeslots on that chain from April 16, 1935, to September 6, 1959, ending as part of the *Monitor* magazine entourage on weekends. At their peak the pair played to 40 million fans weekly.

The premise of the show was simple: take a bumbling husband with grandiose dreams in a small burg (mythical Wistful Vista), add a devoted wife who overlooked his idiosyncrasies, toss in a handful of local denizens who could play off whatever situation prevailed—one often prompted by McGee—and have them all stop by the McGee domicile on Tuesday nights. That was the recurring framework. Included was a litany of running gags that audiences anticipated, and the most famous being an overstuffed closet. Weekly the closet door was opened to the thunderous commotion of everything in it crashing to the floor in a prolonged sequence of commotion. Knowing what was coming, the studio audience reveled beforehand in uncontrollable laughter, dissolving into unrestrained chaos once it occurred. "No picture could have been funnier than what the listener was seeing," affirmed comedian George Burns of McGee's closet.

The characters were not only familiar, they were exaggerated, off-center and side-splitting to a fault. Among the regulars were Abigail Uppington, Mr. Old-Timer, Wallace Wimple, Throckmorton P. Gildersleeve, Beulah, Charles LaTrivia, Foggy Williams, Teenie, Doc Gamble and Harlow (Waxy) Wilcox. McGee sparred with them all, dishing out invectives to some and limiting his missives to passing observations for the others. Most of them got off one-line zingers that kept the studio audience in a perpetual state of uproar. When an installment ended, whatever project McGee had set his mind to that week had usually sputtered and flamed out, sometimes leaving him with egg on his face. Yet in spite of his eccentricities, Molly stood by him. Could a man ask for more?

The Great Gildersleeve

If you caught the name of Throckmorton P. Gildersleeve in the *Fibber McGee & Molly* entry, it wasn't a mistake. Gildy was a disenchanted neighbor of the McGees that the audience took such a fancy to he became one of two figures to be spun off into separate series. (The other was *Beulah*.) In his NBC sitcom between August 31, 1941, and March 27, 1958, *The Great Gildersleeve* was most prominently the water commissioner of Summerfield, not far distant from the McGees' hamlet of Wistful Vista. He moved there to assume the duties of raising teenage niece Marjorie Forrester and adolescent nephew Leroy Forrester, who were now orphaned. They lived in a home left by his late sister and her husband, the children's parents. Also there was a live-in black housekeeper and cook, Birdie Lee Coggins, whose emblematic characterization endeared her to listeners.

Along the way Gildersleeve became pals with a handful of local men who formed the Jolly Boys Club, an often rowdy, audacious lot that spent more time cutting one another down than building up harmony among them. Included in that cluster were Judge Horace Hooker, druggist J. W. Peavey, barber Floyd Munson and police "Chief" Gates. All were given to extremes and idiosyncrasies, with Gildy playing off all of them. At the same time, Gildy fancied himself as a ladies' man, picking up a string of girlfriends—most often one at a time, some with whom he nearly made it to the altar. Among their number were Leila Ransom, Adeline Fairchild, Kathryn Milford and Eve Goodwin.

Listening together to *The Great Gildersleeve* was a warmhearted tradition in many American homes in the 1940s. Although the part originated by Harold Peary and transferred to Willard Waterman in 1950 went to a 1955 syndicated videocast version, it died quickly there. By then, most real families appeared to have moved beyond the homespun tales of life in small town America. It would take an Andy Griffith to rekindle similar interest during the following decade.

Our Miss Brooks

Could a schoolmarm be a consistently funny lady? Eve Arden proved it every week from July 19, 1948, to June 30, 1957. In CBS Radio's *Our Miss Brooks*, which also landed on CBS-TV from October 3, 1952, to September 21, 1956, the wisecracking Connie Brooks charmed a nation with outrageous antics. As an English teacher at fictitious Madison High School, her focus on learning incorporated a series of complex predicaments that inevitably tossed her from the frying pan into the fire. She and her nemesis, principal Osgood Conklin, played by enormously talented character thespian Gale Gordon, were seldom on the same wavelength. They routinely spent those half-hours practicing one-upmanship (or one-upwomanship, as the case might be).

Aiding and abetting Miss Brooks was a cast of regulars who landed her into trouble leading to her weekly downfall. There was the bashful biology bachelor teacher, Philip Boynton, who made Miss Brooks swoon—although he had eyes only for his pet frog, McDougall; Walter Denton, her perennial student, who was predestined to instigate campus riots on his way to graduation; Harriet Conklin, Denton's sweetheart and the principal's daughter, a bystander who seldom took sides on the issues between her father and her favorite teacher, although she had an innate ability to complicate them; Stretch Snodgrass, proficient in basketball and deficient in English, a Denton co-conspirator who innocently, but frequently, stirred the pot that brewed between Miss Brooks and Mr. Conklin; and Maggie Davis, the landlady of the home in which Miss Brooks boarded, chewing the fat with her over low teaching wages, Brooks' incessantly out-of-commission car and the dire consequences to befall her "if Mr. Conklin finds out" about the prank she and her cohorts had hatched that week.

The thing is, there was never any doubt in the audience's mind that Conklin *would* find out before the show left the ether. And once again, after promising her how she would suffer for her participation in whatever conspiracy had occurred, he would raise the volume next, throw a vehement tantrum and erupt into rage that shook the very foundations of Madison High. When he had finished, normalized relations returned—for a little while. They lasted until Miss Brooks and her co-conspirators launched another clandestine maneuver the following week as the routine started anew. In its overall thesis, the show exhibited a one-joke theme. But the joy was in the details as a house of onlookers and listeners predictably dissolved into unrestrained hysteria with every new revelation.

Drama Anthology

The Cavalcade of America

Unique among the more prestigious aural anthologies, *The Cavalcade of America* focused upon historical narratives as a source of material. At its start over CBS on October 9, 1935, one of the most durable dramatic series offered brief historical sketches under multiple topics. It was less than desirable, however, with the brevity of those vignettes and a lack of continuity proving to be among its greatest weaknesses. Truth be told, there just wasn't much to hold on to in that initial season. The producers learned something from their mistakes, however, and made a few determined alterations in the second season. At that juncture the show became an enduring run of biographical introspectives into the lives of accomplished stalwarts like telegraph inventor Samuel F. B. Morse, rubber baron Charles Goodyear and early feminine physician Elizabeth Blackwell. Yet those stories were "sanitized," a critic noted, carefully crafted in order to avoid offending the affluent, while purposely not including people of color, to prevent a largely Caucasian audience from getting upset.

But in 1940, with a substantial increase in the show's budget and hiring a Yale history professor to oversee its authenticity, things lightened up. Writing improved, Hollywood and Broadway stars were imported and an emphasis on "what really happened"—allowing chips to fall where they really did—typified the storylines more and more. The show moved to NBC's Blue network at the start of 1940, then transferred to the Red chain that summer and remained securely entrenched until it ended March 31, 1953, as an award-winning feature. Under a trilogy of sobriquets, a similarly-themed *Cavalcade of America* appeared on NBC-TV (one season) and ABC-TV (three seasons) between October 1, 1952, and October 23, 1956.

Sponsored by E. I. du Pont de Nemours Company, one *Cavalcade of America*'s earliest objectives—beyond selling the United States via favorable historical reportage—was to stem the tide of harsh criticism against du Pont. "Merchant of Death" was a badge the outfit wore following World War I which the public applied to its colossal profit-making from gunpowder manufacture. The firm's directors were quite sensitive about charges of wartime profiteering. The radio series was widely respected, nonetheless, winning back friends through an ethereal public relations maneuver, a concept that was successfully copied by a few other commercial enterprises.

Dimension X and X-Minus One

In the final decade of the golden age of radio, several new forms of airwaves amusement surfaced, among them science fiction theater. Introduced on NBC on April 8, 1950, "*Dimension X* was ahead of its time," claimed one historian. "The science-fiction boom did not pick up for another couple of years, and serious science fiction was not yet on radio until *Dimension X* premiered." The noble venture—which drew mature fans in a period in which TV was siphoning off many of audio's faithful—presented adaptations of writers of sci-fi literature ranging from Isaac Asimov to Ray Bradbury. Fifty broadcasts aired before the series ended on September 29, 1951.

Later in that decade there was a subsequent feature on NBC, *X-Minus One*, which gained substantially greater acclaim than the premiering one. Some scholars consider it an extension of *Dimension X*, as about 30 of the original entry's scripts were rebroadcast. A handful of practiced scribes penned mostly fresh material that comprised those narratives, however. The program persisted through 125 dramas, ending January 9, 1958. Typical episodic titles for the double series consisted of "The Man in the Moon," "And the Moon Be Still and Bright," "The Martian Death March," "The Last Martian," "Tunnel Under the World," "The Merchants of Venus," "Dr. Grimshaw's Sanitarium" and "Mars Is Heaven."

In the early 1970s, during a then-sweeping nostalgia resurgence in America, NBC returned some previously aired transcribed tales of *X-Minus One* to the ether. If the web had assigned the show to a permanent timeslot on a given day it might have attracted both old and new listeners. As it was, NBC programmed the reprise monthly, sometimes on Saturdays, sometimes on Sundays, often as filler material preceding or following athletic competitions. That inconsistency invariably left the fans wondering when and where it would air. In so doing NBC doomed the idea, which virtually lost its ability to appeal to an ongoing audience. Within a couple of years it bombed completely and was withdrawn. In its day, however, it had been an incredible drawing card for NBC. With hodgepodge scheduling, it simply did little to save a faltering network that could have used a little life support just then.

Grand Central Station

Grand Central Station was a misnomer for this Saturday matinee feature, for there is no such animal. The celebrated New York train depot on which it was based is Grand Central Terminal. Perhaps "Station" sounded more imposing to the producers when the series was put together for its debut over NBC Blue on September 28, 1937. It would spend time with CBS, NBC and ABC before the final train left the station on April 2, 1954, then in a five-day-a-week strip over ABC. While it hadn't been a continuous ride, it ran for much of that period.

For most of its life the choo-choo business was merely a ruse to transfer listeners into the provocative tales that *Grand Central Station* proffered. Most concerned an individual or individuals who were deposited in that hallowed hall by an inbound diesel-pulled entourage (despite the sound of a steam engine, which never went to Grand Central in the first place). It was a literal "vehicle" for launching the yarn and moving on from there—usually with little obligation to refer to transportation again. Sometimes the arrivals were met by familiar faces and occasionally by unfamiliar ones. And in a few cases, greeters unexpectedly failed to show at all, creating a clever twist. There was a lot more plotting to make the play captivating, of course. The railroad had done its part; now the characterizations became the meat as the narrative's storyline kicked in.

Grand Central Station burst onto the airwaves with one of the most compelling and memorable epigraphs in Radioland: "As a bullet seeks its target, shining rails in every part of our great country are aimed at Grand Central Station, heart of the nation's greatest city. Drawn by the magnetic force of the fantastic metropolis, day and night great trains rush toward the Hudson River, sweep down its eastern bank for 140 miles, flash briefly by the long red row of tenement houses south of 125th Street, dive with a roar into the two-and-one-half-mile tunnel which burrows beneath the glitter and swank of Park Avenue, and then ... [bell clangs, train hisses, echo chamber for] ... Grand Central Station! Crossroads of a million private lives! Gigantic stage on which are played a thousand dramas daily!" It was the stuff of which buoyant comedy and frothy romantic narrative was predicated.

Lux Radio Theater

Of all the dramas in Radioland, none was more plush, more persuasive or powerful than the *Lux Radio Theater*. Glamorous Hollywood film stars fell all over themselves when invited to be a part of one of its elaborately produced aural duplications. These recreations were captured in glitzy style on a Monday evening hour witnessed by studio audiences often clad in fancy duds. More importantly, legions of added fans were tuning in at their residences coast to coast.

For most of its run the pattern was simple: take a blockbuster movie that already had won rave reviews with audiences and critics alike, reduce its script to about 48 minutes of dialogue for primarily unseeing observers, and air it with its top two, three or four key actors reprising their parts in an audio-only rendition. The luminaries were supported by a cast of seasoned thespians who filled the supplementary roles. It was grandiose in every way. Sponsoring Lever Brothers Company made sure of it, budgeting huge cash outlays to showcase its Lux beauty complexion bar while attracting some of the country's most ardent movie aficionados. Presiding at varying times over the swanky marathon were Tinseltown producers Cecil B. DeMille, William Keighley and Irving Cummings.

The 927 cinematic recreations included memorable films like *Our Town, Wuthering Heights, The Philadelphia Story, Mrs. Miniver, For Whom the Bell Tolls, It's a Wonderful Life, Miracle on 34th Street, Sorry—Wrong Number, The Man Who Came to Dinner, Cheaper by the Dozen, I'd Climb the Highest Mountain, Showboat, I Can Get It for You Wholesale, The African Queen, Angels in the Outfield, The Day the Earth Stood Still, The Glass Menagerie, How Green Was My Valley, David and Bathsheba,* and *Come Fill the Cup*. While *Lux Radio Theater* began on NBC October 14, 1934, airing mostly Broadway plays in New York, the series transferred to CBS the following year. And when the series shifted to Hollywood on June 1, 1936, it really kicked into high gear, exhibiting all those celluloid epics from then on. In its final season the show returned to NBC, ending its long audio reign on June 7, 1954. (There was a dramatic anthology titled *Lux Video Theater*, first on CBS-TV, then NBC-TV, between October 2, 1950, and September 12, 1957.) Back in the day, however, there was absolutely nothing to compare with *Lux Radio Theater*'s eloquence and devotion to the motion picture as a form of mass entertainment.

The Mercury Theater on the Air

Without any doubt in the minds of most people who remember "back when"—or who have a working knowledge of what transpired during much of radio's golden age—the single most famous broadcast of the epoch transpired with an innocently-planned episode of *The Mercury Theater on the Air*. It was provoked by director-star Orson Welles' adaptation of H. G. Wells' science-fiction novel *The War of the Worlds*. An intended Halloween spoof aired on the eve of that holiday, October 30, 1938, it pitched some of East Coast and Midwest America into panic, setting off alarms that the planet—and indeed, the country—had been compromised with the arrival of the first aliens.

Despite the fact that several disclaimers were provided throughout the hour-long broadcast to the effect that the story was only a play, in their determination to be ruled by their ears and not what was between them, many listeners either chose not to hear it or to disregard it. In the bedlam that followed, thousands made irrational, quick-thinking, sometimes desperate-sounding attempts to get as far away from Grovers Mill, New Jersey—where the Martians had purportedly landed in a space capsule—as rapidly as they could. Many awoke the following day with some explaining to do, having realized their mistake and sheepishly having to account for their wild reactions to friends, relatives, neighbors and cohorts. Never was a single mythical radio play from the golden age known to have had that much effect upon the nation's denizens.

The Mercury Theater on the Air was an otherwise satisfying testament to strong writing, producing, directing and casting. Although it was brief, appearing on CBS with only 22 dramas between July 11, 1938, and December 4, 1938, it included adaptations of some trendy novels, plays and other fiction. They included *A Tale of Two Cities, The Affairs of Anatole, The Count of Monte Cristo, Julius Caesar, Seventeen, Around the World in Eighty Days, The Pickwick Papers,* and *The Bridge of San Luis Rey*. But it was *The War of the Worlds* that undoubtedly made the pithy entry famous forever, a show that is still broadcast on tape and performed on stage during the Halloween season by the current generation.

Juvenile Adventure

The Green Hornet

There was a buzz about this feature that was as literal as it was figurative. It was ushered onto the airwaves to the unmistakable, albeit exaggerated, din of a hornet, with the appropriate accompaniment of a signature theme—Nicolai Rimsky-Korsakov's "Flight of the Bumblebee." Debuting over MBS on April 12, 1938, *The Green Hornet* had been running more than two years over Detroit's WXYZ. It was the second phenomenally successful adolescent adventure in a trilogy generated by a company of thespians at WXYZ (the forerunner was *The Lone Ranger*; the finale was *The Challenge of the Yukon*). *Hornet* shifted to the NBC Blue web on November 16, 1939, eventually dovetailing into ABC, and remained airborne to December 5, 1952. It appeared variously one or two half-hours per week. It was obviously better on radio than video, playing on ABC-TV just one season, September 9, 1966 to July 14, 1967.

The masked protagonist was a first-rate crimefighter named Britt Reid. He happened to be the offspring of Dan Reid, nephew of the Lone Ranger (making the Ranger the younger Reid's great-uncle). It was one of manifold similarities between the epic *Ranger* series and this one. (Catching crooks was both men's aims—the apple didn't fall far from the tree.) Britt Reid was normally accompanied by a Filipino valet, Kato, "the only living man to know him as the Green Hornet." Don't you see the "only living man" motif and ethnic qualities that existed between Kato and the Ranger's Native American sidekick Tonto? Even their names have an analogous ring.

The Hornet pursued "the biggest of all game—public enemies that even the G-men cannot reach!" But when G-man J. Edgar Hoover bristled over that, the epigraph was softened to "public enemies who try to destroy our America!" Reid was a crusading journalist committed to exposing underworld figures dedicated to destroying life as we know it. Having risen to editor and publisher of *The Daily Sentinel* (do you also catch the likenesses with Superman and his crusading journalistic pursuits?), Reid and Kato set out in their high-speed super-dooper Black Beauty automobile (think Kitt of TV's *Knight Rider*, although Beauty paled by comparison) to track down marauders and other forms of hooligans and put them away. If this show seemed like a composite of a number of others, it was, although—arriving as early as it did— it was honing a formula for some of those to follow.

Jack Armstrong, the All-American Boy

When General Mills stumbled upon *Jack Armstrong, the All-American Boy*, it not only unleashed a narrative that would perpetually bind a generation of Wheaties cereal consumers to their radios, the food processor mined gold for itself at the same time. It had the good fortune of cultivating one of the most enduring iron-clad relationships between product and listeners in Radioland. Wheaties' links to sportscasting in the golden age of radio are, of course, storied, with many professional athletic players' likenesses appearing on its product boxes. But the *Jack Armstrong* era gave General Mills about 18 consecutive years to recurringly plug its "Breakfast of Champions": from July 31, 1933, to June 1, 1950, alternately on all four transcontinental chains, followed by the spinoff tale *Armstrong of the SBI* (Scientific Bureau of Investigation) on ABC from September 5, 1950, to June 28, 1951. Can you think of another cereal with that much concentrated broadcasting exposure?

In the storyline Armstrong waved the flag for Hudson High, being its star athlete (no surprise there) as well as an honor student (a lofty aim for real folks). Together with a troupe of likeminded adolescents, siblings Billy and Betty Fairfield, along with their Uncle Jim Fairfield— who happened to pilot his own aircraft—young Armstrong directed them in aerial adventures that routinely whisked the quartet to far-flung locales across the nation as well as the globe. They snuffed out crime ranging from espionage agents, fascists, communists and similar ruffians as well as more conventional louts like counterfeiters, burglars and gangsters of myriad common stripes. It must have been difficult to keep one's mind on algebraic expressions, the War of 1812 and English lit with such exciting alternatives lurking around the bend. And besides, how did those kids have time for formal classroom studies anyway? (No mention of home schooling—or airways schooling—then.)

It took a half-dozen actors to play the lead over the 17 years *Jack Armstrong* aired, plus five more thespians to play Billy, five actresses to play Betty and one man to appear as Uncle Jim. When the latter gave out, a criminal investigator, Vic Hardy, was supplied; he was also impersonated by a solo actor. To maintain just the fearless foursome across the years it took an awful lot of talent (18 players) to pull it off. Although the series never made it to TV, extensions abounded: a theatrical serial, comic books, a syndicated newspaper comic strip and Big Little Books. On the side General Mills relied upon young Armstrong as something much more valuable than a mere heroic crimefighter. They turned him into a cash cow as well.

Let's Pretend

Nila Mack gets much of the credit for this show. The innovative CBS creator paid meticulous attention to every detail in writing, casting and directing the children's fairy tales that were turned into unparalleled fantasy dramas on *Let's Pretend*. Beginning March 24, 1934, and continuing to the final broadcast on October 23, 1954, it offered superlative adaptations of familiar—and sometimes not-so-familiar—nursery rhymes and other works especially for juveniles. The narration, music and storyline was a blend of sterling talent, prepared on a child's level and enunciated so clearly that its meaning was understood by even the show's youngest fans. Yet it appealed to adolescents of all ages, including many younger teens.

The carefully crafted renditions embraced childhood favorites like *Beauty and the Beast*, *Cinderella*, *The Frog Prince*, *Goldilocks and the Three Bears*, *Hansel and Gretel*, *Jack and the Beanstalk*, *Jorinda and Joringel*, *The Little Mermaid*, *Little Red Riding Hood*, *The Princess and the Pea*, *Rumpelstiltskin*, *Sleeping Beauty*, *Snow White and the Seven Dwarfs*, *The Three Little Pigs*, and *Tom Thumb*. There were dozens more.

A permanent company of seasoned children's voices, auditioned and trained by Nila Mack, performed those re-creations of popular childhood literature. As the young actors and actresses matured, many went on to play imposing roles elsewhere on radio as well as on stage, screen and television. Among their number: Albert Aley, Arthur Anderson, Jack Ayers, Charita Bauer, Donald Buka, Gwen Davies, Michael Dreyfuss, Michael Grimes, Florence Halop, Jackie Kelk, Joan Lazer, Bill Lipton, Jimmy Lydon, Bobby Readick, Walter Tetley, Sybil Trent, Dick Van Patten and Miriam Wolfe. "Uncle" Bill Adams shilled for longtime sponsor Cream of Wheat, frequently involving a live studio audience predominantly made up of raucous youngsters who were rehearsed in advance. They spoke or screamed on cue, particularly when Adams needed their interactive input in completing his commercials for the hot breakfast cereal.

The Lone Ranger

An epic, according to Webster, is "a long narrative in elevated style recounting the deeds of a legendary or historical hero." If ever a youthful adventure qualified for epic status, it was this one. It premiered January 31, 1933, from Detroit's WXYZ, initially beamed to a handful of Michigan outlets. The definitive western thriller, *The Lone Ranger* was the catalyst that established a major radio production empire outside the usual origination points for the transcontinental webs. The series was picked up by MBS on November 21, 1933, moved to ABC May 4, 1942, and ended first-run programming September 3, 1954. Reruns were carried by NBC from September 6, 1954, to May 25, 1956. A televised incarnation, complete with separate cast, appeared on ABC from September 15, 1949, to September 12, 1957, giving the program almost a quarter-century on the ether. It is still seen today in reruns in limited markets and sporadically on cable.

The Lone Ranger had been a Texas Ranger when the men in his detail were ambushed and massacred by outlaws. The outlaws left, thinking they had killed them all, but an Indian named Tonto came upon the scene, found one still alive, and helped him recover. The two formed a partnership to fight crime, riding the trails of the Old West together seeking to avenge the rights of those who had been harshly and unjustly dealt with. Theirs was a constant pursuit that encountered murderers, swindlers, robbers — despots of virtually every stripe, most of whom had greed on their minds. Tonto was the only individual to know the Ranger's real identity and he kept that secret.

The actions of the protagonist on behalf of justice, goodness and mercy were responsible for positively affecting millions of youngsters tuning in the thrice-weekly narrative adventures. By setting an example of moral and ethical values during such a long period of broadcast history, the character touched the lives of more than one generation with his uplifting examples — without preaching the ideals. The heroic figure preferred using his fists to shooting a culprit, and all of the bad guys (and a few bad girls) were ultimately rounded up. Created by writer Fran Striker, *The Lone Ranger* was responsible for an extensive cornucopia of merchandise in addition to comics, a newspaper strip, movies and other forms of amusement. The show appealed to as many adults as it did kids, extending its life to multiple age cohorts, a claim unfamiliar to the majority of prevailing juvenile fare.

Sky King

"America's favorite flying cowboy," Sky (Schuyler J.) King was the captain of both the *Songbird* and the *Flying Arrow* while owning the large spread known as the Flying Crown Ranch near imaginary Grover, Arizona. With a trio of escorts, the ex–FBI agent and Navy pilot went to incredible lengths to track and apprehend evildoers in the modern West. A menacing Dr. Shade became a particular nemesis to King, prowling his castle on the Arizona plains (listeners must have pondered why anybody would want to erect a castle on an Arizona desert). Shade incessantly provoked ill will for Sky and his buddies. With aviation as a vehicle aiding his expeditions, meanwhile, King never refused a chance to bring down cattle rustlers, espionage agents and other ruffians of diverse persuasions.

King's sidekicks included his teenage niece and nephew, Penny and Clipper King, and his ranch foreman, "Uncle" Jim Bell. The show was often episodic in format with cliffhanger chapters. But it occasionally switched to storylines completed in single installments, too. The Songbird, which appeared (on television, at least) to be little more than a crop duster holding four occupants, sans any storage space or rest rooms, ferried that intrepid little quartet far beyond their native turf—to destinations like Africa, Asia, Europe and Latin America. King and his compatriots weren't averse to pursuing big game around the globe to make planet Earth a safer place for you and me. The tykes tuning in accepted it with wide-eyed abandon, to say nothing of all that schoolwork Penny and Clipper were fortunate enough to habitually miss! There was never a concern about makeup work, which would have only detracted from their prioritized crusades.

The aural *Sky King* debuted over ABC on October 28, 1946, and—moving to MBS in 1950—persisted on airwaves and airways to June 3, 1954. Meanwhile, the video manifestation premiered on NBC-TV on September 16, 1951, shifted to ABC-TV the following year, and ended September 12, 1954. But it wasn't quite finished yet: CBS-TV offered it in reruns from 1959 to 1966, thereby getting all four transcontinental webs involved in the tale's transmission. In addition, a single entry comic book, *Sky King and the Runaway Train*, surfaced in 1964.

Music

The Bing Crosby Show

From the 1930s to the 1960s, according to radio historiographers, Bing Crosby drew the largest and most sustained following of any vocalist on radio. Almost assuredly that was true among male singers but it seems likely to have applied to all harmonizing artists. Not long after his debut over CBS on September 2, 1931, Crosby's name became a household word in millions of American domiciles. He was one performer for whom there was instant recognition by almost everybody. And while he devoted significant portions of his career to NBC (*Kraft Music Hall*, 1935–1946) and ABC (*Philco Radio Time*, 1946–1949), the predominance of his aural broadcasting years were spent as a CBS property. When Crosby returned to CBS in 1948 (while aircasting a series on ABC), he "stayed by the stuff" there for the remainder of his radio run. It carried him beyond the generally accepted end of the golden age, to September 28, 1962, as he shared a microphone with vocalist Rosemary Clooney in a final showcase.

Unlike a number of other performers of his vintage, Crosby didn't get bent out of shape over television. In fact, with the exception of guest appearances on others' shows and hosting a few hour-long variety specials, he had done little video when *The Bing Crosby Show*, an ABC-TV sitcom, launched on September 14, 1964. That feature lasted one season, to June 14, 1965.

Performing on TV simply wasn't his cup of tea. Crosby starred in scads of movies instead while making legions of recordings, owned his own TV production company and made personal appearances beyond his radio series.

In the mid 1940s, he got into trouble with longtime sponsor Kraft Foods Company by refusing to fulfill his contract obligations because the cheese manufacturer and NBC refused to let him prerecord his shows on audiotape. That was a sacrosanct network rule at NBC and CBS and Crosby wanted to break it. A deal to terminate his contract was ultimately approved by Crosby and Kraft and he moved to ABC. As a new network hungry for leverage, ABC would do anything to attract a star of Crosby's magnitude. He broke the transcription barrier there and scores of other shows at NBC and CBS were soon prerecording, too. Crosby may have been a maverick but he knew how to sing and to negotiate.

The Kate Smith Show

Under a glut of broadcast titles and formats, Kate Smith became an American icon, a pop diva who not only enthralled audiences with her vocal range but attracted a loyal following for her deeply held values communicated through chatty monologues. She became a symbol of American patriotism, too, raising buckets of money for wartime humanitarian efforts while proliferating in multiple entertainment venues—radio, television, stage, screen, recordings and writing. Smith is best remembered for an enduring association with composer Irving Berlin's "God Bless America," which she introduced to listeners on Veterans Day 1938. Radio made her familiar to most Americans. In a career that encompassed five decades, she captured the hearts of incalculable numbers of her fellow countrymen. During her epoch on the ether she was unquestionably one of the nation's most respected and prestigious performing figures.

Labeled "The Songbird of the South," Smith was born in Washington, D.C., a city figuratively astride the Mason-Dixon Line. Many performers of her era were branded with identifying labels to make them stand out from their competition and this was a badge she wore proudly. Her first network performances, arranged by record promoter Ted Collins—who became her lifelong friend, producer and announcer—occurred in 1930 over CBS. While Smith gained her own show on NBC on March 17, 1931, in due course she resided at all four transcontinental webs. Her show aired for its final time on MBS January 2, 1959. Between those parameters she hardly left the airwaves—and certainly not for any extended period—being in constant demand by an adoring public. She appeared on more than 15,000 broadcasts altogether.

While playing in only a handful of motion pictures, Smith recorded an incredible 3,000 melodies, large numbers of those discs selling like hotcakes. She also readily made a transition to television, presiding over her own NBC series under multiple sobriquets from September 25, 1950, to June 18, 1954, in concurrent daily matinee and weekly primetime outings. That was followed by a run on CBS-TV from January 25, 1960, to July 18, 1960. Her signature song, "When the Moon Comes Over the Mountain," was her familiar theme as her musical performances arrived and departed the ether. One wag commended her as "the most influential woman in the history of radio." Whether she was that or not, she had a powerful impact upon the medium, just as she did with U.S. citizens who admired her for a plethora of patriotic and charitable causes in which she invested her life.

The Metropolitan Opera

In the early years of broadcasting, management of the esteemed Metropolitan Opera Company vehemently opposed any notion that its concerts be aired beyond the confines of the

Opera House itself. Attempts to do that would not only debase those venerated performances, they claimed, but furthermore would diminish some of the Met's income-earning potential. "Why give patrons something for free when they will gladly pay for it?" they reasoned. The Met changed its tune (a figure of speech) after the stock market crash of 1929, however, after few people had discretionary dollars for entertainment. With whole sections of seats suddenly empty and CBS and NBC still clamoring for the Met for handsome fees, economic realities altered its stance. Desperately needing fortifications to stave off the wolf threatening them with closure, Met directors gave their approval. In a dogfight (reported in Chapter 10), NBC outsmarted CBS and began airing those live concerts weekly. It was the launch of a proud tradition that lingers to this day (although not on NBC).

The ethereal Met debuted December 25, 1931, and continued on NBC's Red or Blue chains (eventually Blue became ABC) through the 1958 season. (Seasons were about five months long, usually lasting from fall to early spring.) At that juncture the Met shifted to CBS. In 1960, it was fed to a hookup of global stations under auspices of the Texas Company, which continued underwriting it on behalf of Texaco oil-based commodities. After Chevron acquired Texaco in 2001, the new combo announced that—beginning in 2004—it would no longer sponsor the sophisticated musical series. Despite that pullout the Met has continually found resources to air the broadcasts and, as of the 2008–2009 season, what began almost eight decades ago continues every Saturday afternoon.

From the first broadcast in 1931 until his death on January 3, 1975, opera critic Milton J. Cross, an accomplished musician as well as commentator, hosted the Met series. "His resonant voice was an instrument in itself, one that produced a burnished announcer-profundo sound," proclaimed one historian. In the half-century from 1940 to 1990, a survey revealed, the Met performed 133 operas. The five most often heard, and presumably most often requested, were Puccini's *La Boheme* (36 performances), Verdi's *Aida* (33), Bizet's *Carmen* (31), Puccini's *Tosca* (29) and Verdi's *Il Trovatore* (25). From 1935 to 1958, Met broadcasts were supplemented by a companion feature, *The Metropolitan Opera Auditions on the Air*. Met general manager Edward Johnson hosted the talent tryouts until 1947, when Milton Cross added them to his duties. The opera outfit extended contracts to those artists satisfying its demanding expectations.

The Voice of Firestone

The Voice of Firestone was a broadcasting institution, supplying a faithful audience of adherents with engaging forms of music every week for three decades, including pop standards, classical, semiclassical, folk, Broadway show and other tunes. Those live performances from New York with full orchestra accompaniment, dancers, chorus and guest artists featured some of the most celebrated voices available. The long-running series relied heavily on the Metropolitan Opera Company for most of its stars but also drew from stage, screen and broadcasting productions.

In the 22 years between 1941 and 1963, Firestone's 10 most frequent soloists were Richard Crooks (115 performances), Eleanor Steber (107), Christopher Lynch (69), Risë Stevens (58), Thomas L. Thomas (43), Margaret Speaks (40), Jerome Hines (37), Gladys Swarthout (34), Igor Gorin (33) and Eugene Conley (28). Typical numbers featured in the half hours ranged from "Strike Up the Band," "June Is Busting Out All Over," "Stars and Stripes Forever" and "Blue Skies" to "Smilin' Thru," "Thine Alone," "Song of the Open Road" and "On the Street Where You Live." Howard Barlow, early veteran CBS staff impresario, conducted the Firestone Orchestra and Chorus in the halcyon days from 1943 to 1957.

The program emerged on NBC December 3, 1928. On September 7, 1931, it shifted to the 8:30 P.M. Eastern Time period on Mondays and settled in for the long haul. A simulcast on NBC-TV was added September 5, 1949. After 25 years on the air, when the NBC brass asked Firestone to move elsewhere on its agenda, the firm balked. Convinced listeners and viewers preferred its long established slot, Firestone expected to withdraw the long-standing feature. Just then ABC stepped up to the plate, offered to simulcast the show at 8:30 Mondays on its web and a deal was struck. On June 14, 1953, the program transferred to ABC Radio-TV without missing a week—or a beat. It persisted on radio to June 10, 1957, with two more years on the tube. It returned for another year on ABC-TV in 1962–1963, ending at last on June 16, 1963. *The Voice of Firestone*'s greatest achievement may have been that it offered millions the opportunity to hear (and see) good music in live performances. In so doing it educated some to a style they weren't familiar with while winning many converts in the process.

Your Hit Parade

Until the 1950s, when a pervading ascendancy of the disc jockey—with play-lists of top-40 tunes—was ushered in, people looked to *Your Hit Parade* as their only established source of America's tastes in pop music. And as the nation's exclusively widespread oracle of the genre's fads, the radio feature reigned complete as a form of Grammy Awards every week. Its insuperable influence continues to be felt: "Practically all of the music programming on radio today, particularly 'hits' radio, owes a debt to this concept," claimed NBC historian Marc Robinson in 2002. "In 1942," another source explained, "everyone in the country was singing, listening, and dancing to the *same* tunes, which were played on *all* radio stations *and* on juke boxes, and selling both sheet music and single records." It was a far cry from today's tailored Ipod tunes, customized to individual audiences of one. While it wouldn't work now, in that day, *Your Hit Parade* not only flourished but prospered.

The series essentially measured what people preferred in current tunes every week. For 52 weeks a year, in fact, the American Tobacco Company bankrolled the enterprise. It did so by enlisting hundreds of "song scouts" who were dispatched weekly, calling on the nation's disc jockeys, bandleaders and record and sheet music sales clerks. From these "authoritative sources" they gathered critical data on the songs most requested and what recorded tunes were purchased most often. The music industry itself also fed off the frenzy that erupted; songs surfacing on *Your Hit Parade* became self-perpetuating, improving jukebox and phonograph record sales. More than 33 million discs were purchased in 1938 alone, up 27 million over 1932. Record-player sales soared, too. Those were peripheral effects of the data-gathering, which was dispatched to the advertising agency behind *Your Hit Parade*. That information was tabulated and remained tightly under lock and key until its revelation to the world on live broadcasts. *Radio Guide* pointed out that this made the series "an endless popularity poll on a nationwide scale."

Your Hit Parade originated April 20, 1935, on NBC, and transcended the chasm between that net and CBS before winding down to its final radio exhibition on NBC January 16, 1953. A televersion embracing those webs ran at separate times from October 7, 1950, to April 24, 1959. A summer reprise on CBS-TV in August 1974 lasted five weeks. Over the years legions of vocalists graced *Your Hit Parade*'s stage as regulars, including some who hit the big time. Among their number: Buddy Clark, Georgia Gibbs, Lanny Ross, Bea Wain, "Wee" Bonnie Baker, Frank Sinatra, Lawrence Tibbett, Johnny Mercer, Dinah Shore, Ginny Simms, Martha Tilton, Dick Haymes, Doris Day, Eileen Wilson, Snooky Lanson, Dorothy Collins, Russell Arms, June Valli, Gisele MacKenzie, Johnny Desmond and Margaret Whiting.

Mystery Anthology

Dragnet

By the time he created *Dragnet*, actor-director-producer Jack Webb was no stranger to detective crime drama. He had cut his teeth acting in several earlier series. While appearing in *The Adventures of Philip Marlowe*, *The Whistler* and like pursuits, Webb was notably playing namesake leads in *Pat Novak for Hire* (1946–1947), *Johnny Madero, Pier 23* (1947) and *Jeff Regan, Investigator* (1948). Following Dragnet's debut, he also starred in *Pete Kelly's Blues* (1951). But it was as Los Angeles police sergeant Joe Friday that his name is forever embedded in the hearts and minds of vintage radio and television buffs.

Dragnet was a departure from everything that had preceded it. For the first time a mature-themed series appeared, ushering in an array of similarly-patterned police dramas (think *Broadway Is My Beat*, *The Lineup*, *Twenty-First Precinct*, et al.). These nitty-gritty entries dispensed with the glamorous side of lawman's work. Instead they maintained a spotlight on the day-to-day activities that went on behind the scenes in pursuing, capturing and disposing of criminal elements. Thus, when Webb and his focus on out-of-the-ordinary investigative tactics came on the scene on June 3, 1949, audiences took notice that "here is something new." *Dragnet's* loyal band of early followers mushroomed, allowing it to persist on radio to February 26, 1957. In the meantime, Webb and company transferred into TV regulars, too, appearing on the small screen from December 16, 1951, to September 6, 1959. A second tube series—*Dragnet '67*, followed by *Dragnet '68*, *Dragnet '69* and *Dragnet '70*—ran from January 12, 1967, to September 10, 1970. *Dragnet* was exclusively an NBC property on radio and TV. The video versions were repeated endlessly for years in syndicated reruns on various stations.

Webb's radio sidekicks were played by actors Barton Yarborough, Barney Phillips, Martin Milner, Harry Bartell, Vic Perrin, Herb Ellis and Ben Alexander. The latter, in the sustained part of officer Frank Smith (1952–1957), was featured in the same role on television in that era. "Smith's character gave the show a touch of comic relief, offering counterpoint to Friday's matter-of-fact character," observed one wag.

The FBI in Peace & War

Frederick L. Collins' copyrighted book *The FBI in Peace and War* was the inspiration for this hard-hitting series of federal law enforcers. Under that hypothesis, the show took off making up tales that gave Federal Bureau of Investigation head lawman (in real life) J. Edgar Hoover a nervous stomach. (But then, Hoover similarly bristled over *Gangbusters*, *The Green Hornet* and other crimestopping radio fare, so why make an exception?) Hoover was reportedly so agitated that he and his agency subsequently sanctioned a similarly themed ABC entry, *This Is Your FBI* (1945–1953). In fact, that series was privy to official bureau files while a largely fictionalized *Peace & War* "sounded authentic" but wasn't, according to an informed scholar.

"Both were sold as completely 'authentic'; both original authors visited the FBI academy; both shows were packaged to rousing march music," noted historian John Dunning. Meanwhile, *Peace & War* exhibited one of the most memorable signature openings in radio. It featured Sergei Prokofiev's classical "Love for Three Oranges" accompanied by bass drum and a deep male voice in an echo chamber repeating the brand name of Procter & Gamble's grimy-hands soap: "L-A-V-A! L-A-V-A!" If that didn't sell a billion bars all by itself, it's a genuine surprise.

The dramas themselves were hot pursuits following racketeers, swindlers, dope ring masterminds, counterfeiters, burglars, forgers, auto thieves, impersonators for evil intents and the like. In action snippets the audience heard the culprits plotting their next moves. Then fans were enthralled with agent Adam Sheppard (actor Martin Blaine) and his team of investigative sleuths as they picked up the hooligans' trails and approached their prey for the capture. The show had a long run, always on CBS, from November 25, 1944, to late in the day for audio drama, expiring September 28, 1958. For much of its life the series was produced by Betty Mandeville, one of the medium's few female program executives.

Gunsmoke

Another of those innovative mature-themed dramatic sectors that appeared in golden age radio in its final decade (in addition to police and sci-fi consortiums) was that of the adult western. While not written and produced exclusively for grown-up listeners, *Gunsmoke*—the first of a profusion of like-minded narratives on the western prairie (think *Dr. Sixgun, Have Gun—Will Travel, Luke Slaughter of Tombstone, The Six Shooter*, et al.)—set the tone and standard of all that followed. Emanating from 1870s Dodge City, Kansas, *Gunsmoke* was the epic tale of sheriff Matt Dillon: "the first man they look for and the last they want to meet."

Interacting with the protagonist was a strong cast of recurring players including faithful whiny-voiced townsman Chester Proudfoot, crusty country physician Charles (Doc) Adams and saloon gal Kitty Russell, who evolved into Dillon's quietly subdued romantic interest. For his part Dillon exuded integrity, courage and strength, frequently exhibited in the face of odds that would have withered a lesser man. At six-foot-seven, he was an imposing figure with an indomitable will and possessing nerves of steel. The stories delved into human experience on the frontier, often incorporating a test of an individual's character.

Always a CBS property, the series debuted on April 26, 1952, and remained through June 18, 1961, more than a half-year beyond the phase-out of most of its web's entertainment fare. The fact that it appeared at a time when Americans were, by and large, turning off their radios and turning on their TVs categorically blunted its potential. When the radio series ended with the 480th broadcast, it had already completed the sixth season of a 20-year run on the tube (September 10, 1955 to September 1, 1975) during which it increased from a 30-minute feature to an hour-long drama. Five made-for-TV movies appeared in 1987, 1990, 1992, 1993 and 1994. William Conrad impersonated the radio hero. While he auditioned for the part on television, he was passed over for James Arness. In that incarnation an altogether new cast appeared, with the exception of announcer George Walsh, whose immortal deliveries opened the show in dual mediums.

Suspense

Suspense was a whole lot more than actress Agnes Moorehead's portrayal of the invalid Mrs. Elbert Stevenson in Lucille Fletcher's play, *Sorry, Wrong Number*. But if anybody who listened to that series over long periods of time was asked to name its most memorable performance—that would be the response of most of its loyal fans. So popular was the adaptation, in fact, that CBS repeated it after it was first aired on May 25, 1943, some seven times. Thespian Orson Welles termed the *Sorry, Wrong Number* outing "the greatest show of all time" while a radio historiographer proclaimed it "the most effective radio show ever." A frustrated Mrs. Stevenson, in case you missed it, overheard a murder plotted, not realizing that she was to be its victim that very night. Unable to communicate her fears to anyone who would adequately investigate, she was killed, striking terror in the hearts of millions of eavesdroppers.

Suspense—which had gone on the air July 22, 1940—ended as CBS swept its final few dramas out, on September 30, 1962, having been allowed to continue to the virtual end of that sound stage. The series drew Hollywood stars of screen and airwaves through its portals on a regular basis. All the announcer had to do was to mention that Jack Benny, Jim and Marian Jordan (*Fibber McGee & Molly*), Cary Grant, Lucille Ball, Peter Lorre, Judy Garland, Ozzie and Harriet Nelson, Dinah Shore, Henry Fonda, Frederic March, Humphrey Bogart or more of their ilk would appear "next week" and a huge turnout was guaranteed. The show resonated with big names that seldom performed on the aural airwaves. "If I ever do any more radio work, I want to do it on *Suspense*, where I get a good chance to act," declared film legend Cary Grant.

The reason for his enthusiasm reportedly was attributed to producer William Spier (serving 1943–1948). He personally oversaw everything that transpired, molding the storyline, voices, sound effects and music "into audio masterpieces," observed one source. Composer Lucien Moraweck acknowledged that Spier's musical knowledge was so expansive, "Sometimes he even knows more than the musicians." Meanwhile, George Walsh, the announcer who introduced both radio and television manifestations of *Gunsmoke*, turned up here with his deep bass voice to introduce those chilling plots each week, imploring: "And nowwwwww ... another tale ... well-calculated ... to keep you in ... *Suspense!*"

The Whistler

While there was no recurring investigator in the gripping tales aired on *The Whistler*, there was a narrator whose voice exuded a decided edge that gave fans the heebie-jeebies: "*I ... am the Whistler ... and I know many things, for I walk by night. I know many strange tales hidden in the hearts of men and women who have stepped into the shadows. Yes ... I know the nameless terrors of which they dare not speak!*" Spooky. Creepy. A breezy announcer then fawned over *The Whistler*, "rated tops in popularity for a longer period of time than any other West Coast program." (Longer in popularity than *Jack Benny* and *Fibber McGee & Molly* and *Lux Radio Theater*? Wow.)

The tales themselves were sometimes docile, sometimes frightening. They were "mystery presentations that depict the plight of people who were suddenly caught in a destructive web of their own misdeeds," read one assessment. Invariably it was the denouement of each show, following the final commercial that those *Whistler* devotees awaited. "The strange ending to tonight's story" revealed some twist of fortune that nailed a killer just when he thought he had gotten away with his transgression. As *The Whistler* summarized what happened next, "The voice was an unforgettable tenor," wrote historian John Dunning, "the message dripping with grim irony. *It all worked out so perfectly, didn't it, Roger*, he would coo, while listeners waited for the shoe to drop.... When the finger of fate struck, some fatal flaw of character or deficiency in the master plan that was so obvious that everyone had overlooked it" unraveled totally. The killer, so it was revealed, had become his own worst enemy, and the fans distinguished a genial smirk as the Whistler bid adieu.

The show premiered over CBS's West Coast hookup on May 16, 1942. It didn't reach the nation, however, until July 3, 1946, affording only a summer run that year. It returned to CBS nationwide in spring 1947 and continued through September 29, 1948, after which it lapsed back into a CBS West Coast venture to July 31, 1955. A half-dozen seasoned actors played the mysterious Whistler "who knew many things" over the series' long haul: Everett Clarke, Bill Forman, Gale Gordon, Bill Johnstone, Joseph Kearns and Marvin Miller. A large company of West Coast thespians supplied the voices of the many figures that turned up in those narratives. A half-hour syndicated TV anthology, with Bill Forman's voice as the Whistler, appeared briefly in 1954. In addition, there were six motion pictures based on the character released between 1944 and 1948, plus a seventh in 1994.

Vocational/Avocational Sleuths

Casey, Crime Photographer

Casey, Crime Photographer—which at different times went under the appellations *Flash-gun Casey*; *Casey, Press Photographer*; and *Crime Photographer*—was a kind of laid-back mystery drama without the startling revelations and intense action inherent in many of its contemporaries. Between assignments Jack Casey, a photojournalist for the fictitious *Morning Express*, hung around the Blue Note Café with reporter Annie Williams, his romantic distraction. "When not solving murders," a radio pundit noted, "he was mostly concerned with negotiating small loans to tide him over to payday and trying to keep his stomach calm with soothing liquids." The locale's ambiance was enhanced by Casey's exchanges with barkeep-crony Ethelbert (no last name) and the Blue Note piano. The continually soothing melodies from tickled ivories added to the drama's rest-easy style.

Originated in the novels of George Harmon Coxe, the figure Casey, and his cohort Williams, were regularly involved in the pursuits of their newspaper, most of them pertaining to homicides. The hero could turn into an amateur detective by merely studying a photo he had shot at a crime scene. Predictably he derived clues that the police had missed and thereby caught killers who might have gotten away. The pair from the fourth estate often crossed with law enforcement officials and in particular police captain Bill Logan.

Matt Crowley and Jim Backus played Casey in the first few months on the air, but Staats Cotsworth is more memorably recalled for that role (1943–1955). Five actresses shared the part of Williams. CBS was unkind to the series in that it shipped it into and out of 14 different time slots, causing loyalists to be constantly frustrated over attempts to find where it was airing in any given week. The series premiered July 7, 1943, and departed for the last time April 22, 1955. *Crime Photographer* was introduced on CBS-TV April 19, 1951. Never as popular on the small screen as on radio, however, it lasted to June 5, 1952.

Mr. and Mrs. North

The New York yuppies that passed themselves off as a publisher and his homemaker-spouse possessed an innate ability to deliver lighthearted wisecracks as they stepped over bodies in dark alleys. At the same time they were often rendered unconscious by unknown assailants dispensing blows to the head. No explanation was offered why a couple of misfits could be so successful in reading clues that trained professional lawmen missed as they tracked down miscreants (many of them murderers). Nevertheless, Jerry and Pamela North were adept at doing so. Even their friend Bill Wigand, a homicide lieutenant, was surprised by their inordinate knack in the sleuthing arena.

Mr. and Mrs. North is rooted in a series of fictional tales penned by Richard Lockridge that appeared in 1930s issues of *The New Yorker*. In 1940, the scribe and his spouse Frances collaborated, turning the focus of a mythical young affluent couple into—according to one pundit—"the most successful amateur husband-wife crime fighting team of the time." First the Lockridges produced a book (*The Norths Meet Murder*) followed by stage, film, radio and television adaptations of their engaging characters.

The radio series debuted on NBC December 30, 1942. The program resumed on CBS July 1, 1947, following a six-month absence on NBC, and persisted through April 18, 1955. Joseph Curtain and Alice Frost are best remembered in the roles of Jerry and Pam (1942–1954). A CBS Television incarnation of the amateur detectives with Richard Denning and Barbara Hale as the Norths aired from October 3, 1952, to September 25, 1953, and on NBC Television from January 26, 1954, to July 20, 1954.

Mr. Keen, Tracer of Lost Persons

Mr. Keen, Tracer of Lost Persons holds the distinguished record as the most durable detective in the history of broadcasting, including radio, television and every other conveyance. With 1,690 broadcasts between its NBC Blue launch on October 12, 1937, and its final denouement over CBS September 26, 1955, "the kindly old investigator" easily surpasses his closest rivals: *Nick Carter, Master Detective*, with 726 performances; *The Adventures of Sherlock Holmes*, with 657; and *The Adventures of the Falcon*, with 473. *Keen* simply aired more hours and caught more cold-blooded killers than anybody in the trade in any medium.

Actually, over its long run the *Keen* feature was two very different series. Inspired by novelist Robert William Chambers' tome *The Tracer of Lost Persons* published in 1906, prolific radio producers Frank and Anne Hummert borrowed Chambers' hypothesis involving a romantic matchmaker. They altered that author's concept to focus on missing persons exclusively. Thus was born their original premise in which Keen, operating a small private detective agency in New York, searched for people who had disappeared. Sometimes they vanished of their own free will for diverse reasons. Other times they turned up missing under coercion and not of their own doing. By late 1943, however, the Hummerts decided to dispense with the missing persons theme and instead gave their hero a more purposeful existence. Transferring *Keen* into a new realm, they set the tone that the feature pursued for the remainder of its life.

Keen had always been flanked by partner Mike Clancy, a rather befuddled Irish sidekick. Clancy seemed destined to ask the dumb questions in order to make Keen look brilliant, to utter stupidly obvious lines for the benefit of the radio audience and certainly not for Keen, who wasn't blind ("Saints preserve us, boss! He's got a gun!"), and to provide the muscle at the close of the drama when a killer was fingered and got out of line, threatening Keen with bodily harm. Keen and Clancy followed clues to reveal a slayer and to "send him to the electric chair." Keen seemed to know the mind of a judge or jury long before a culprit got to the courtroom—or even to jail before that. While Keen and company have been parodied and ridiculed through the years by comedians and vintage radio aficionados alike, the duo provided captivating entertainment as the kindly old investigator worked his way through the clues. Many listeners attempted to outguess him, eliminating some suspects as an episode evolved. In the end, a show that could persist for 18 consecutive years, 12 months a year, without repeats—and at times air weekly half-hours while a separate nightly quarter-hour tale-by-installment was concurrently broadcasting—had to have a lot going for it.

The Shadow

"Who knows what evil lurks in the hearts of men? The Shadow knows ... heh, heh, heh." That instantly recognizable opener dispatched through a filter at the start of *The Shadow* crime detective adventure each week foretold of drama. It culminated with the creepy Shadow hidden from view by his extraordinary ability "to cloud men's minds," challenging the iniquitous malefactors he was instrumental in bringing to justice. Under the tutelage of an Indian yogi priest—while spending time in the Orient as a bon vivant—he had mastered the knowledge of making himself invisible. He decided to use that ability to track down evildoers and put them away, devoting "his life to righting wrongs, protecting the innocent and punishing the guilty."

As in *The Lone Ranger*, *The Green Hornet* and a few more crimestopping narratives, only one person knew that the Shadow was really Lamont Cranston, well-heeled playboy with a social conscience. He had long ago revealed his true identity to "the lovely Margo Lane," his "constant companion." For all of Miss Lane's fidelity, she was usually granted no more than some peril from which the Shadow could liberate her. Of scads of resources that document the series, only one surfaces questioning the propriety of Cranston's and Lane's relationship, perhaps intimating that the pair might fare well in today's environment. With Miss Lane, countered one wag, Cranston "confronted the maddest assortment of lunatics, sadists, ghosts and werewolves ever heard on the air."

After stalking, cornering and exposing his prey for the despotic deeds they committed, *The Shadow* left the air with a chilling reminder followed by a mockingly eerie laugh: "The weed of crime bears bitter fruit.... Crime does not pay.... The Shadow knows...." The character appeared initially shrouded in ambiguity on CBS's *Detective Story Hour* on July 31, 1930. He turned up on a handful of added features before the Shadow headlined a separate crime drama series debuting on MBS September 26, 1937. He continued on that chain through December 26, 1954, although not consecutively. It took nine actors to play Lamont Cranston over the lengthy run, but one stands out for durability and delivery—Bret Morrison, in the role twice, 1943–1944, and 1945–1954. Eight actresses portrayed Margot Lane after she was introduced in 1937 to the end of the run. Gertrude Warner prevailed the longest, 1949–1954.

Yours Truly, Johnny Dollar

Johnny Dollar was the famous "private insurance investigator with the action-packed expense account." As a mythical figure in radio mystery, the thinly veiled playboy was authoritative, dynamic and charming; in the decades since, he has become a symbol to hero-worshipers among vintage Radiophiles. They have put him on a pedestal among celebrated audio sleuths and become rabid in their devotion. Without doubt *Dollar* was a radio watershed: it held the dubious distinction of featuring the last aural-only detective on the ether, a 13-year veteran who swam upstream against an ebbing tide, pressing for nearly two years beyond the popularly accepted "day radio drama died," November 25, 1960.

Yours Truly, Johnny Dollar surfaced February 11, 1949, and persisted through September 30, 1962. Always a CBS property, it took eight actors to complete the title role in 886 total performances: Dick Powell (audition only), Charles Russell, Edmond O'Brien, John Lund, Gerald Mohr, Bob Bailey, Bob Readick and Mandel Kramer. Bailey appeared in the most shows—194 half-hours, 72 half-hour repeats, one audition and 281 quarter-hours, or 548 broadcasts. A very loyal fan base still exists, with some of those adherents stridently partial to one or the other actors, who—on request—will obligingly enumerate reasons for their favoritism. Dollar reported the details of his escapades in the first person, the radio listener "overhearing" his expense summaries, a motif embraced by several on-air investigators. At the end of every episode he'd total up his costs for submission to the insurance company paying his fee, then add his signature: "Yours truly, Johnny Dollar."

The central figure "had an analytical mind, a nose for trouble, and the brawn to take care of himself when the going got dirty," a critic pontificated. Frequently impatient, Dollar was just as likely to pad his expense account. Although a confirmed bachelor, he kept a love interest, Betty Lewis, on the string for years. Unlike some of his contemporaries, he respected professional law enforcement officers and often called on stoolies and tipsters for information he needed in tracking down people and merchandise. Sometimes he was partially repaid in repossessed commodities he encountered in dealing with their often onerous temporary owners.

Soap Opera

Backstage Wife

One of the hardiest perennials emanating from the Air Features production factory owned by prolific programming wizards Frank and Anne Hummert, *Backstage Wife* proffered a consistent theme the Hummerts dipped many a dishpan drama in. In fostering matinee misery upon a quite suspecting audience, they often took a damsel from Podunk and wedded her well above her social stratum (think *Amanda of Honeymoon Hill, Lora Lawton, Our Gal Sunday, Stella Dallas*, et al.). The soapy serial's daily epigraph said it all: "Now we present once again *Backstage Wife*, the story of Mary Noble, a little Iowa girl who married one of America's most handsome actors, Larry Noble, matinee idol of a million other women—the story of what it means to be the wife of a famous star." That opened the door to a bevy of unprincipled vixens determined to get their claws into Larry Noble, yet another identifying Hummert motif practiced repeatedly in their dramas (*Lora Lawton, Our Gal Sunday, Young Widder Brown*).

Larry, the infamous Broadway thespian, was the object of affection of just about every wily female—married, engaged, single—on the planet. Young starlets, with stars in their eyes, were particularly drawn to this handsome fellow. Though he consistently played into their hands, he seemed blinded by their intents. At the same time he was possessive at home, an extremely jealous man who went into a rage any time another male peered in Mary's direction. She, on the other hand, was one of the kindest, most gentle, gracious, considerate, trusting and forgiving women on the planet. The truth was, she deserved far better and he didn't deserve her. As in most Hummert dramas, a group of mischief-making malefactors would cycle through the plots, spending a few weeks or months (and in some cases, a year) making trouble between the Nobles in an attempt to win one or the other for themselves. When they departed, another entourage was ushered in to cause new consternation for the central figures. The overarching hypothesis was predicable; as the daily episodes played out, listeners were fascinated by how Mary and Larry dealt with the crises instituted by the opportunists who came their way.

This drama-by-installment first appeared on MBS August 5, 1935. It transferred to NBC the following spring and for 17 years (1938–1955) was entrenched in the web's 4 o'clock Eastern Time quarter hour. When NBC abandoned most of its daytime serials, CBS picked up the popular feature and squeezed out a little more doom and gloom, to January 2, 1959. Two actresses played Mary—Vivian Fridell (1935–1945) and Claire Niesen (1945–1959)—while the part of Larry went to Ken Griffin (1935–1945), James Meighan (1945–1951) and Guy Sorel (1951–1959).

Ma Perkins

She was "the mother of the airwaves," possibly more beloved than anybody else in all of radio Serialdom. With 7,065 chapters over a 27-year span to her credit—and surpassed in endurance by only one drainboard drama—in millions of American homes *Ma Perkins* was like a visit with friends every day. At her peak she and the familiar denizens of mythical Rushville Center somewhere in the Midwest appealed to listeners on two networks (NBC and CBS) at different hours in the same quarter-hour storyline, all of it performed live. Only a handful of soap operas could make that claim. Widowed Ma and her daughters Evey and Fay and son John (who died on a European battlefield during World War II), family friend and lumberyard business partner Shuffle Shober, Evey's hubby Willie Fitz and their son Junior, and Fay's husbands (she had the innate ability of picking men who died young) were as familiar as old shoes. Writer Orin Tovrov, who may have been better at what he did than anybody else, made sure of it: staying by the stuff for more than two decades (ca. 1939–1960), he had plenty of time to gently develop those characterizations in warm, recognizable human beings who interacted in predictable ways with each other. It was a tale of small town America growing up in its epoch, and so real that many people with rural roots readily identified with it.

The narrative first aired on August 14, 1933, in Cincinnati. By December 4, 1933, it was on NBC in Chicago. It wound down to a final installment on "the day radio drama died," November 25, 1960, one of a quartet of remaining open-ended dramas departing CBS that day. Virginia Payne played the namesake role from beginning to end, never missing a performance over those years. Several others in the cast had long runs, too.

For most of the drama's life—to late 1956—the Procter & Gamble Company underwrote it on behalf of its Oxydol detergent. Some people thought its title was actually "Oxydol's Own Ma Perkins" because that opening introduced it for 23 years. Even after P&G withdrew its participation, the tie had been so indelibly imbedded that many were reminded of the former sponsor's brand when they thought of the soapy saga. Perhaps P&G could have saved a fortune by quitting earlier.

Perry Mason

He was one of only a minuscule handful of males who headlined daytime dramas at the height of radio's golden age. Perry Mason was a dapper, dashing, handsome, brilliant young professional whose daily quarter-hour was filled to the brim with intrigue and spine-tingling thrills guaranteed to keep addicts securely fastened to their radios for succeeding action-packed installments. Unlike the popular televersion in which cold-blooded killers were revealed on the witness stand, there was little mystery about the identity of the perpetrators here: Mason knew, and so did his listeners, virtually from the start of every case, which might run for hundreds of chapters. Finding out whodunit wasn't the point at all. Instead Mason's aural pursuits frequently involved finding—and protecting—innocent collateral victims destined to become future prey of those culprits if the bad guys could locate the quarry first (and the good guys were often missing for a while, even from Mason, who was similarly in hot pursuit).

Anyone who stood in harm's way was the impetus of the crusades of this "defender of human rights ... champion of all those who seek justice." In getting there, *Mason* offered a chilling tale of mayhem in the midst of milady's matinee menagerie. Stuck in the middle of an afternoon of domestic divas and beleaguered heroines, *Perry Mason* was welcome relief in the mire of otherwise uninterrupted melodramatic misfortune. The series launched on October 18, 1943, and continued to December 30, 1955, always on CBS. While four actors filled the role of the persistent attorney, including Donald Briggs, Santos Ortega and Bartlett Robinson in the early years, beginning in 1947 the part belonged to John Larkin. He is best recalled as the quick-thinking authoritative figure that breathed life into the relentless hard-driving Mason and thereby kept the cat-and-mouse game on high intensity. He was flanked by ever-efficient secretary Della Street, played at different times by Joan Alexander, Jan Miner and Gertrude Warner.

Mason on radio was preceded by lawyer-novelist Erle Stanley Gardner's popular 1930s hero classic pulp fiction which found a soft spot in the hearts of prolific fiction readers. That acclaim led to the radio adaptation, masterfully achieved by the superior scripting of Irving Vendig, who—together with Larkin in the role—turned the series into one of the most mesmerizing crime dramas on the air. It would have gone into a TV fabrication at the time had Gardner—who inspired the character—not balked. When he failed to back down (for a while), Vendig, Larkin and company put the same idea to work in a daytime television soap opera classic with foreboding themes—under a new appellation. They called it *The Edge of Night*; it lasted from 1956 to 1975.

The Romance of Helen Trent

Two daytime serials were among the more than three score assembled largely for women listeners by Air Features, Inc., the mass-production factory of Frank and Anne Hummert, with identical themes: each saga prevented a virtuous heroine (although married once and widowed) from slipping down the aisle a second time; instead those protagonists were treated to endless years of unvarnished agony, tortured over the men they loved, yet unable to make a lifetime commitment. One was *Young Widder Brown*, occupying a late-afternoon quarter-hour on NBC from 1938 to 1956. The other, *The Romance of Helen Trent*—with 7,222 chapters, certified as the longest-playing narrative of hundreds of dishpan dramas—maintained a lock on CBS's 12:30 P.M. Eastern Time quarter-hour for the final 24 years of its 27-year run (complete from October 30, 1933 to June 24, 1960).

In Helen's tale of torment she was a dress designer for a Hollywood movie studio, qualifying her for circumstances that the typical housewife tuning in could never reach but could lollygag over. One of her "sisters" had risen above the drudgery of common life sans modern conveniences (i.e., using wringer-washers, few dryers, doing endless mending and ironing, having no dishwashers or microwaves or disposals or icemakers, making beds and creatively fixing meals with little money, all the while tending to children). Without all that, Helen Trent should have been blessed. As it was, hers was a shabby existence over silly stuff preventing her from saying "yes" to dashing young attorney Gil Whitney, who loved her deeply. She thwarted his every proposal—and when she didn't, he found reasons to delay marrying her "until just the right time."

If listeners thought about it very much they realized there would never be a "right time" for those two. Just as tearoom proprietor Ellen Brown could never marry *her* longtime beau Dr. Anthony Loring, neither could Helen wed Gil—or anybody, for that matter. It would have blown the Hummerts' simplistic formula for the pair of dramas; if the young widowed woman with a Prince Charming on the string got to the altar, what then? A story about two eligible people who sought desperately to tie the knot but were kept from doing so would be out the window—with years of plotting going down the drain. To avoid it the Hummerts saddled Helen (and Ellen—notice the similarity in names?) with rotten men of every persuasion, some quite dangerous, who intervened to stop any weddings from occurring. What a despicable way to treat a lady! When the show left the air the final time, the duo was still unhitched. Ever the pragmatists, the Hummerts made sure that—if the network changed its mind and wanted Helen to pay a return visit—that hallowed premise still would be undisturbed.

Wendy Warren and the News

If there was a serialized yarn in radio's glory days that came close to reality, it might have been this one. A well-educated young woman became a dedicated journalist who navigated the chasm between print and electronic media to fill capacities as a spirited professional in dual provinces. *Wendy Warren and the News* began with a three-minute capsule of each weekday's headlines delivered by respected CBS newsman Douglas Edwards. That was followed by a one-minute dispatch of "news from the women's world" from the fictitious radio journalist (played by actress Florence Freeman). After a commercial, Wendy went off into more conventional dramatic fare, playing out her life's story as a crusading reporter for a mythical newspaper, *The Manhattan Gazette*. Connected with the daily news program for CBS, however, Wendy's life advanced by one day as each episode typified a new "broadcast day." On other soap operas, accomplishing that might take weeks of domestic suffering.

This drama, appearing as it did at high noon on the East Coast over CBS (from June 23, 1947, to January 3, 1958), possessed an inordinate ability to draw men into its audience as well as women. Aside from airing at lunchtime and containing hard news attracting many men, there was surely another reason that males listened—the imaginary storyline. Rather than totally wallow in self-pity and domesticated misery as did some counterpart serialized queens, *War-*

ren spent a great deal of time pursuing and exposing foreign terrorists who were determined to bring down our system of government, thwarting the liberties of Americans. In that day, for a protracted portion of its life, this drama-by-installment was a tale of identifying, tracking and ridding the nation of outside infiltrators bent on doing harm. In hindsight it appears that wordsmiths John Picard and Frank Provo could have been penning their series in a contemporary age—and not six decades earlier.

Wendy was the daughter of a retired widowed newspaperman, Sam Warren, who shared a home with his matronly sister, Dorrie ("Aunt Dorrie" to Wendy) in Elmdale, Connecticut. To their residence Wendy took refuge from the labors and unrest that dazed her in the Big Apple. On occasional weekend visits to nearby Elmdale she found solace from the harried demands of big-city life. But she primarily invested herself in the pressures of New York City and in so doing her competence as a professional rose like cream to the surface. It would be a very long while before another supremely capable young lady, Mary Richards—who tossed her hat into the air on TV's *The Mary Tyler Moore Show*—exhibited similar proficiencies in yet another fictionalized series of broadcast journalism. While Wendy was applying her skills and proving her remarkable abilities, that descendant of the fourth estate was merely in diapers.

12

SIGHT RADIO
No Renaissance for Imagination

One of the labels that brigadier general David Sarnoff wore with pride—besides that title—was the "Father of American Television," previously encountered. It was bestowed on him in 1944 by the Television Broadcasters Association and signified his sizeable involvement in that industry from its infancy. It was Sarnoff, the chairman of the board of the Radio Corporation of America (RCA), who maintained a searing vision for television long before practically anybody else. Since 1928, he committed tens of millions of RCA dollars along with corresponding manpower to foster video's development. If he were right (which he was), RCA would recoup all of its outlay down the line while creating a windfall in profits through sales of RCA-manufactured receivers, parts and the commensurate technology necessary to operate the system.

Sarnoff brought it to the forefront of public awareness, introducing a primitive organism that he exhibited during the 1939 New York World's Fair. Subsequently he patiently awaited its burst onto the global stage, temporarily delayed by the intervention of the Second World War. Had it not been for fate stepping in at that precise moment, TV would have stridently challenged radio in the early 1940s. Some scholars assertively insisted their conviction that—without the war—the possibility existed that radio's golden age could have ended with the close of the 1940s instead of the 1950s. The potential for TV was never dismissed. As the global conflagration concluded, manufacturers and the radio chains were anxious to market the tube to American consumers.

During the wartime time-out Sarnoff forces tinkered, modified, regrouped and prepared early models for hundreds of dealers' showrooms (in what was to be a brand new industry). By the postwar epoch, with America's economy moving into high gear once more, sets were being mass-produced for public utilization, coupled with accompanying technology that delivered a persuasive entertainment product seemingly worthy of the wait—at least, to the curious, and that was almost everybody.

Two decades before, a visionary writing in *The New York Times* on September 13, 1925, had confidently predicted that within five years every home in the nation would offer visuals of the programming that people were then hearing. An illogically tall order! While it didn't happen as that rabid journalist stipulated, in less time than the source projected, there was movement afoot to bring it to fruition "some day." By April 16, 1930, the entertainment trade newsjournal *Variety* was enthusiastically reassuring subscribers with a banner headline: "Television Near Ready."

Truth be told, the first working TV demonstrations occurred in 1925, instigated by Charles Francis Jenkins, an American, and John Baird, a Scotsman, the latter experimenting in Great Britain.[1] While General Electric launched the first regularly operating TV station in Schenectady, New York, in 1928, and a few others followed, the stock market debacle in October 1929 that resulted in the Great Depression curtailed those tests. Radio, operating far less expensively, took off while TV stalled.

RCA/NBC opened a New York City TV station in 1930 and CBS followed suit in 1931.[2] It took Columbia (CBS) to launch the first regularly scheduled telecasts in the nation. That occurred on July 21, 1931, on experimental station W2XAB in Gotham. Sets were being marketed in 1938, the same year *Variety* published in a May issue its initial review of a visual program. Another entertainment industry periodical, *Billboard*, added TV reviews to its table of contents in 1939. With its August 1939 edition, the fanzine *Radio Mirror* optimistically renamed itself *Radio and Television Mirror*. It looked as if TV was here to stay.

Following the infamous Sarnoff-backed public TV exploitation during the 1939 World's Fair, electronics manufacturer Allen B. DuMont opened a TV station in the Big Apple in 1940.[3] He also simultaneously announced plans for a hookup of TV stations that would bear his own surname (DuMont Network). NBC rallied in 1941 by linking New York City, Philadelphia and Schenectady together in a chain. Each member of the trio possessed the capability of relaying shows it originated to the other two stations, though no regular series was yet scheduled.

CBS and NBC obtained licenses for commercial programming on their New York stations beginning July 1, 1941. But by the end of the year the outbreak of the Second World War stunted growth and hindered innovative programming. The requirements for manufacturing sets and for advancing new technology were harnessed for the war effort. It was a stunning setback for those with enduring screen dreams that had to be put on hold yet once more.

When the war ended in 1945, people within the broadcasting industry who were pushing TV—which most of the country had yet to experience—moved heaven and earth to secure a permanent foothold for it. As more stations went on the air, not much programming aired before 6 P.M. local time, when a small pack of viewers might be available in a few large metropolitan districts to see it.

During this time frame CBS brought out the first color television receiver ahead of its perceptually more sophisticated high-tech rival RCA. While the Federal Communications Commission (FCC) quickly approved CBS's invention, its design was eventually outdated by an electronic color technique compatible with existing black-and-white sets. The latter replica was finally approved by the FCC on December 17, 1953. The preferred system was a modification of an RCA-originated schematic. The decision was a major hindrance to CBS and especially to web chief William S. Paley.

In spite of such disappointments, Paley struggled mightily—as noted elsewhere—to thwart the inevitable takeover of broadcasting by television, thereby circumventing radio and assigning it purely to stepchild status. If radio had a stubbornly stalwart guardian in the late 1940s and early 1950s, it was Paley, seemingly a solo voice crying in the wilderness. "When TV was getting started, Bill Paley turned his back on it and thought there was money to be milked out of radio," recalled an NBC official.[4] A commercial journal went further by declaring that Paley "wanted to make sure radio audiences wouldn't go over to television by default. If CBS had the best entertainment and showmanship, it could keep a lot of its circulation *despite* TV."[5]

So focused on saving radio was Bill Paley in the 1940s that, in practice, his chief subordinates were requested to defend his stance at any venue where they represented CBS. Paley hoped "to slow down the progress of television, trying to indicate the virtues which were uniquely those of radio," a CBS publicist established.[6] Several more citations by and about Paley on the topic are included in Chapter 4.

The bottom line is that the CBS executive stood in the path of television for as long as it seemed feasible to do so. To him, old time radio aficionados of today and the listening public of that era, all persons who enjoyed those shows, likely owe the man a mammoth debt of gratitude. Long after rival chains had thrown in the towel and essentially canceled their schedules wholesale, CBS's enduring presentation of its programming traditions—uninterrupted and often sustained (without sponsorship)—throughout the 1950s and into the early 1960s was probably due to the extraordinary forbearance of one man. To Paley, more than anybody else, goes the allegiance of legions of grateful fans.

By the early 1950s, it was clear that radio was about to be displaced by Americans' avaricious and unending drive for something new. "The problem was a horde of loud, vulgar, squat, ugly, one-eyed monsters that invaded America's homes and mesmerized the inhabitants therein for hours at a time. To make matters worse, the public willingly invited these monsters into their living rooms, and they multiplied like rabbits. Far-seeing science fiction writers had been predicting their arrival for years, and now here they were—television receivers."[7] "Radio's Frankenstein?" blared a headline in a 1946 issue of *Variety*. In that publication's September 29, 1948, issue, the topic of TV as a monster was explored in depth, it having continued to proliferate. Not long afterward, meanwhile, NBC president Niles Trammell assured the broadcasting industry that "within three years, the broadcast of sound or ear radio over giant networks will be wiped out."[8]

Most chain officials saw it differently, however. TV's escalating costs were a major determinant. "They felt that television would grow slowly enough to make a gradual radio-television transition during the 1950s," media observers pontificated.[9] A 1949 investigative report noted: "We seriously doubt that television will ever become a truly nationwide medium (as compared with present radio patterns and service) if it has to depend on the economics of advertising alone."[10] But the public wasn't buying it—instead, they were buying television receivers by the droves. That voracious appetite, plus advertisers' fascination with the new medium and the impatience of radio executives to make a mark in it, left network radio "a dying operation" by 1950.[11]

More people watched TV that year than listened to radio in a handful of Northeastern cities and Los Angeles. Research predicted that when more video stations and sets were available, radio would crumble. Doomsayers envisaged that when urban areas became inundated with television, radio could hope for no more than 15 percent of the primetime audience.

While most of the country was still not yet served by video in the late 1940s, the medium was already swelling with lightning speed. The networks stretched their grasp from New York to Washington, D.C., in 1946, to Boston in 1947, and the Midwest in 1949. Almost half the TV sets in the country were operating in New York City in 1949. Boston, Chicago, Detroit, Los Angeles, Philadelphia and Washington accounted for nearly all of the remainder. While 108 stations were on the air by 1947, two or more of them were situated in just two dozen cities.

Temporary networks were patched together for major sporting events like heavyweight fights and World Series games. Still, at best, the nation's TV map was spotty. As sales of receivers soared, station license applications swamped the Federal Communications Commission. That body promptly perceived that it would get more TV applications than available channels. Acting in accord with the Truman administration in 1948, the FCC ordered a six- to nine-month moratorium before processing further requests. So intricate were the issues, however, that the restriction was permitted to continue for 42 months, until July 1, 1952, when the processing resumed.

Significant expansion of television in America resulted when the coaxial cable was extended to the West Coast, completed September 10, 1951.[12] That year coast-to-coast television became a reality. That year, also, more Americans watched television between the peak three hours of 9 P.M. to midnight than listened to radio—for the very first time. "Television was already conducting itself provocatively, trying to get radio to pucker up for the kiss of death," lamented comedian Fred Allen.[13]

By December 31, 1954, two and a half years since the FCC's ban on applications for new stations was lifted, 308 new TV outlets had gone on the air. In seven years (1948–1955), operating TV sets in the U.S. jumped from 190,000 to 32.5 million, an increase exceeding 6,000 percent. Telecasters pocketed $41 million in profits in 1952 while network billings skyrocketed 12,250 percent from 1947 to 1955—from $2.5 million to $308.9 million.

> Americans had already begun to adapt their habits to accommodate their favorite programs. Studies showed that when a popular program was on, toilets flushed all over certain cities, as if on cue, during commercials or the moment the program was over. Radio listenership was significantly down. People went to restaurants earlier. Products advertised on television soared in public acceptance. Book sales were said to be down. Libraries complained of diminished activity. Above all, television threatened the movie business. By 1951, cities with only one television station reported drops in movie attendance of 20 to 40 percent.[14]

Academician Charles Siepmann was much more optimistic when citing television's effect on radio at the midpoint of the 20th century, an assessment that now appears to have been misguided.

> It seems almost certain that, of all the media, radio will be the hardest hit. There are prophets of disaster who foresee its total displacement by television. There will be a temporary disequilibrium but, once the present craze is over, subsequent adjustment to a more normal pattern of behavior seems possible.... Radio will continue to hold a number of trump cards. As we probe the distinctive attributes of radio and television and their relation to the needs and circumstances of the consumer, we discover grounds for the belief that radio's days are far from numbered....
> Both self-interest and public interest now seem to require that radio study how to win back the audiences it has lost through default of service, and to build audiences it has hitherto considered not worth courting. Lesser majorities of taste and interest than that for entertainment are still capable of providing advertisers with a rich reward for their investment.[15]

Of course, Siepmann could only speculate what would take place. As it turned out, the usually perceptive media scholar missed this call by many miles. While his confidence in radio and the public was certainly well intended, he was surely operating on the wrong wavelength. Possibly he could not foresee all of the factors that worked against a renaissance of the audio medium.[16] Perhaps he couldn't fathom the incredibly colossal welcome that TV was about to receive. At any rate, given the benefit of hindsight, it appears that Siepmann's optimistic opinion of radio as the comeback kid was a tad too generous.

As their young families grew, Americans' horizons for home entertainment expanded. Television had already made significant strides into their lives. An increased birthrate in the postwar epoch meant more and more individuals gathered around large black-and-white sets with rectangular 13-inch screens. Those oblong boxes dominated living rooms throughout the land, much as radios had done in the prior generation. A middle class society perpetually growing used to material wealth—something it had been denied during wartime and the depression years of the previous decade—provided a fertile atmosphere in which TV would prosper.

In the meantime radio shows that, for years, had held listeners in rapt attention were fading by carload lots. Loyalties were swept aside in favor of the newfangled system that allowed people to witness live pictures with sound. While the aural medium's last epitaph hadn't been written quite yet, it seemed inevitable. Radio time sales slipped to $453,385,000 in 1954, a five percent decline from the previous year, and the first dip in time sales since 1938.

On August 16, 1954, CBS announced that its radio and television news operations, steadfastly preserved separately, were merging into a single corporate division. TV news chief Sig Mickelson was to head it; he was given the rank of vice president. Only a quadrennial earlier, Mickelson had supervised 13 people. Now he was to command 376. If anyone needed a telling sign of which way the wind was blowing, that was a pretty ominous one.

The earliest example of the extraordinary influence of television on America was the spectacular rise of comedian Milton Berle. Berle was an archetypical vaudeville slapstick comic. Some pundits maintained that he flopped in radio. Whether he did or not, he successfully burst onto

TV screens in 1948. "The early history of television and the story of Berle's show were close to being one and the same thing," an eyewitness submitted. "The very success of Berle's show accelerated the sale of television sets; those Americans who did not yet own sets would return home after watching him at their neighbors' houses and decide that, yes, it was finally time to take the plunge."[17]

A textbook wordsmith affirmed: "By 1948, radio had enjoyed the privileged status of an only child for 28 years. But in that year, a smarty pants kid, television, began to emerge as the dominant national medium."[18] A CBS vice president, Hubbell Robinson, Jr., minced no words as he compared the changing state of affairs to Custer's last stand: "Television is about to do to radio what the Sioux did to Custer. There is going to be a massacre," he presaged.[19]

An important byproduct of Berle's overnight rise in the public's consciousness was that his phenomenal popularity stirred other comedians into considering the new medium, too—including stars who had held back from making the jump from their comfortable radio digs. Berle proved to be as much a catalyst in attracting peers as he was adept in gaining fans and selling TV sets. As several of his contemporaries witnessed his meteoric rise to fame, they aspired to a greater share of public acclaim for themselves. One by one, many of audio's most revered, legendary stars—including some who had been skeptical and reluctant to test the waters until they could see evidence of the tube's significance—began making the transition to the small screen. George Burns and Gracie Allen, Jack Benny, Red Skelton and a plethora of other funny people were among those soon leaping onto the bandwagon.

It can be reasonably argued that TV began to develop a large following only after several of the bigger names in radio began appearing there. Coupled with it was some of the largest advertisers in broadcasting reallocating their capital. By 1950, some of TV's top-rated shows had arrived from the aural medium. One radio chronicler aptly surmised: "With such programming, what had begun as 'sight radio' began now to destroy its 'hearing-only' competition."[20]

In mid 1949, one of the most telltale signs that radio was in serious jeopardy occurred. *The Fred Allen Show*, which had long dominated its Sunday night time period over a very long run, hurriedly left the ether forever. It

One of network radio's most durable comedians, Fred Allen, saw his air castle crumble at the hands of an upstart quiz on a rival chain. The ex-vaudevillian began starring on radio on October 23, 1932, cultivating a style that assured him of a dominant position with listeners. Yet when ABC's *Stop the Music!* drew more patrons than he, the long-entrenched NBC Sunday night powerhouse faded quickly.

departed at the hands of a prospering telephone quiz show—*Stop the Music!*—that competitor ABC Radio had thrown against some of NBC's formidable Sunday night comedies. The Allen program was irrefutably caught in the shifting fortunes of radio.

A couple of media historiographers went so far as to project that "Radio actually died when *Stop the Music!* got higher ratings than Fred Allen."[21] Humorist Henry Morgan assured everybody that an aberration like Allen's departure drove "the final nail in radio's coffin."[22] While Allen would no longer headline his own show, that wasn't the end of his professional career by any stretch of the imagination, and it certainly wasn't radio's end. There was a whole lot more worthwhile stuff yet to be introduced and that would eventually come down the pike with some regularity.[23]

Allen, meanwhile, wasn't sure whom to tag with his misfortune, but TV was one of his prime targets and had been since it first arrived. The acerbic-tongued comedian had long ago mounted a campaign to expunge it forever. "Television is a triumph of equipment over people," said he, "and the minds that control it are so small that you could put them in the navel of a flea and still have enough room beside them for a network vice-president's heart."[24] (The humorist had been cut off the air for more than a half-minute in April 1947 when he violated a sacrosanct NBC policy by poking fun at network vice presidents, incidentally.) TV, Allen allowed, was "a device that permits people who haven't anything to do to watch people who can't do anything."[25] The comic at last offered this appraisal of the new medium: "When television belatedly found its way into the home after stopping off too long at the tavern, the advertisers knew they had a more potent force available for their selling purposes. Radio was abandoned like the bones at a barbecue."[26]

Well, not quite. And not yet.

Allen's exodus from radio was only a start, and far from the "final nail" in the coffin. Radio's golden age would take another decade to fully expire, succumbing to a slow and painful passing experienced by a dwindling corps of faithful listeners. Surprisingly, even Allen later admitted that shows like his had simply run on too long. "Even without the coming of television, [there was] a gradual shrinking in the mass audience. The audience and the medium were both getting tired. The same programs, the same comedians, the same commercials—even the sameness was starting to look the same."[27]

The dedicated devotees of radio, however, maintained that there was something in an aural transmission that could never be successfully duplicated by a visual means. The all-important ingredient, which was instantly displaced in TV, was *imagination*. In the theater of the mind, images were precisely etched on a listener's brain as perceived, never as a common representation affixed on a small screen. For all of its creditable enhancements, video could never impart that attribute. Whether the fans realized it or not, that had to be a contributing factor in their reluctance to utter "farewell" to enduringly beloved programs and entertainers. Little by little, the insidious one-eyed monster enveloped more and more living rooms across America, tearing away the remnants of people's long established habits. Radio, as they had always known it, would never pass this way again.

One of the countermeasures network radio applied for holding the line against the encroaching invader on its turf was to develop new audio series that would maintain present listeners while potentially attracting new ones. The webs found a few niches to highlight, largely by exploiting some heretofore ignored dramatic forms. Then they saturated the aural ether with them. Ironically, the best of the lot soon found their way into tube replications. A trio of the most successful newly minted genres, which debuted about midpoint in the 20th century, focused specifically on the adult listener. They included police, western and sci-fi narratives, all bearing mature themes. Prime examples of the sophisticated threesome include *Dragnet*, *Gunsmoke* and *Dimension X*.

Television, of course, had a major bearing on all that was happening in entertainment at the time. Now more than ever TV was becoming widely understood to be radio's greatest foe. Serious radio defenders within broadcasting's ranks continually sought alternatives to add impetus to the industry's first medium and dampen video's ability to ravage radio's audiences. Instituting certain new styles of programming, ... was an attempt to cope with the erosion of both fans and sponsors caused by TV. Such developments would not have been necessary much earlier, of course, nor might their listeners have been as receptive to such striking changes as they were at mid-century.[28]

Even some of those who seemed destined to populate those small black-and-white video screens were, at first, reluctant to do so. Jack Benny, for one—long one of radio's most esteemed entertainers—hung back for a good while. On one occasion, in 1959, while waiting for his own videotaped series to air, he switched channels a half-hour before his show, was consumed by an hour-long *Bonanza* adventure, and forgot his own show. "If *I* won't even watch me, what chance do I have?" he roared.

He was reluctant to jump aboard the television bandwagon for more than one reason. Benny was fearful that the public might not embrace his style of comedy once they saw it. They adored it, of course, and his characteristic mannerisms were an instant hit after they became viewable. But Benny hesitated all the same. He made no bones about radio being his "first love." In 1946, after appearing on a TV special, he exclaimed: "Hold off television! Science be damned! Long live radio!"[29] For years America's potentially most beloved comic was guarded about the visual medium. Pundits recounted his fondness for radio and often suggested that he wasn't comfortable under television's glaring lights. He plainly comprehended a one-eyed fiend for what it was:

> By my second year in television I saw the camera was a man-eating monster. It gave a performer a close-up exposure that week after week threatened his existence as an interesting entertainer. I don't care who you are. Finally, you'll get on people's nerves if they get too much of you. I don't care how wonderful or handsome or brilliant or charming you are—if the public gets too much of you, they'll be bored. Given that kind of magnification combined with intimacy that's characteristic of television, the essence of a comedian's art becomes inevitably stale. The audience gets to know you inside and outside. Your tone of voice, your gestures, your little tricks, the rhythm of your delivery, your way of reacting to another performers' moves, your facial mannerisms— all of these things, so exciting to an audience when you are a novelty, soon become tedious and flat.[30]

Benny wasn't alone in his unwillingness to wholeheartedly join his friends in the land of TV. Plenty of his contemporaries were literally terrified. Many radio actors, for example, both daytime and prime time, faded from the airwaves once there was no longer any paramount call for their services as aural broadcasters.

There was also, in essence, a total sector of broadcasters that was not only reluctant to embrace television but which disdained it for quite some time. Eventually, albeit perhaps grudgingly, its members joined the "enemy" to become some of its most notable achievers while deriving a principal source of their livelihoods from video. They were authoritative audio journalists who dispatched news and commentaries about current events.

At the forefront of their number was none other than the most respected mentor of many, Edward R. Murrow. For some years he cast a jaundiced view at any who might seek to dignify televised reportage. "I wish television had never been invented," Murrow exclaimed.[31] On his inaugural telecast of the CBS public affairs series *See It Now* on November 18, 1951, he apologized: "This is an old team trying to learn a new trade."

The formidable fraternity known as "the Murrow Boys"—colleagues whom Murrow had hired to report from European theaters in the Second World War—were universally hostile to TV in its infancy. To them TV had absolutely nothing to commend it: at the time, they earned far more from sponsored radio newscasts than they ever could hope to gain from the tube. They despised the lights, cameras, makeup and other show business trappings required. CBS newsman Daniel Schoenbrun summarized: "In radio, you threw a switch and you spoke."[32] TV needed a whole staff working together. One of the "Boys," Howard K. Smith, admitted: "We felt it was kind of unmanly to go on TV and perform, just as it was in an earlier era somehow unmanly for newspapermen to go on radio."[33] Even Don Hewitt, the venerable executive producer of CBS-TV's *60 Minutes*, confessed: "Radio was for adults and television was for children.... I sort of think they may have been right."[34]

There were still others outside the industry proper who remained skeptical about the new medium. One of them was no less than the scholarly president of Boston University, Daniel Marsh, who disparaged: "If the television craze continues, we are destined to have a nation of morons."[35]

TV shows that added radio incarnations are one of the incongruities in broadcasting that occurred in the decade of the 1950s, network radio's last hurrah. While their number wasn't large, the fact that they occurred at all seems to contradict what was happening widespread. Normally, if the dual mediums were working in tandem, radio almost always took the lead in this period. Popular features aired there frequently lent themselves to televersions, thereby assisting in solidifying the newer medium. Radio favorites became TV favorites, carrying their audiences along as they jumped from audio to video. This was particularly true in the late 1940s and early 1950s.

Yet there actually were a number of programs surfacing on the tube throughout the latter decade that eventually produced either identical or entirely separate audio-only adaptations. A few of the more notable include *The Original Amateur Hour* (which had been on radio from 1935 to 1945, went on TV in 1948 and returned to radio eight months later), *Hopalong Cassidy*, *What's My Line?*, *Tom Corbett—Space Cadet*, *My Little Margie*, *The $64,000 Question* and *Have Gun—Will Travel*.

The quiz show scandals of the late 1950s will not ever be forgotten so it seems. There are occasional reminders of it in the modern age. It occurred as several TV game shows with stupendous giveaway prizes were rigged to juice up the ratings. Unsuspecting Americans, meanwhile, awaited the next shoe to drop, failing to realize that some contestants had been supplied with correct answers to questions in advance to heighten series' dramatic effect. The reality only came to light when a few of the players began talking publicly. The careers of a dozen or more individuals who carried out those backroom deals were ruined. Ten who lied to a grand jury pleaded guilty to perjury. As a direct consequence, the huge cash giveaway programs instantly left the air—including those tainted and those that weren't—giving duped viewers time to catch their breath and get well past it before any quiz shows with megabuck payouts returned to the small screen.

The most outspoken skeptics within Radioland were at last persuaded to come around. By the end of 1953, even members of "the Murrow Boys," who had held the strongest disdain for TV, began to acknowledge that it had totally eclipsed radio as the dominant broadcast news system. Bill Downs, Richard C. Hottelet, Daniel Schoenbrun and Howard K. Smith along with Robert Pierpoint all came to the conclusion that radio, for their purposes, was dead and the future belonged to television.

One of the most compelling and persuasive forces in all of this reallocation of opinion and shifting assets was, of course, the imperative of revenues. Growing numbers of influential advertisers in radio for a very long while were increasingly pulling out of the medium, leaving titanic gaps between shows on the air and a satisfactory method of paying for them. For a while the big chains continued to present some of their most popular audience favorites without interruption. They did so either by sustaining the shows (offering them without sponsorship) or recouping some of their very real financial losses through multiple participation advertising (brief time periods sold to underwriters within programs).

In an effort to retain longstanding advertisers while attracting newcomers to network broadcasting, in early 1951, CBS—followed by NBC, ABC and MBS—slashed their commercial radio rates across the board as much as 15 percent. Despite the acute reductions, nevertheless, mainstay sponsors like Kellogg's, Pillsbury and Standard Brands withdrew from radio almost totally. Eight years earlier one of their major rivals, General Mills, had allocated half its 1946 advertising budget of $10 million to radio. Radio depended on that kind of commitment. Underwriters, however, wanted substantial audiences and when the fans began to vacate the premises in search of something new, so did the bill-payers. As more and more sponsors withdrew or drastically curtailed their audio involvement, the webs could hardly turn a blind eye endlessly to the financial challenges that resulted. If they did so, they would eventually find themselves out of business.

Even CBS's Bill Paley was finally starting to budge. Although CBS Radio's advertising revenues continued to prosper until 1950, within a year of TV's initial black ink Paley unconditionally embraced the newer medium, to some extent as if he was realizing its potential for the very first time. Radio's most eloquent guardian had been won over to the opposition. The days of the elder medium were surely numbered then when Paley fell away from his long heralded stance.

There were copious qualifiers beyond television for radio's diminishing influence. Yet TV was almost single-handedly awarded the blame for chain radio's "demise" as it had been exhibited since the 1920s. Some leading issues will be addressed in the succeeding chapter (13). The economic factors, in the meantime, simply could not be ignored by those charged with operating the aural webs. When major corporations moved the bulk of their advertising allocations out of radio into television, radio management was in a tough spot.

The radio networks had created television, applying astronomical sums they earned to finance its development. Before TV became a thriving commodity, CBS president Frank Stanton recalled, "We had to keep radio strong because we had to pay for television out of radio."[36] RCA's David Sarnoff announced in 1946 that NBC-TV's projected $8 million startup cost would be financed from radio profits.[37] A time-bomb was ticking beneath network radio as its executives attempted to successfully remain astride dual horses.

With the passage of time, a by-then spirited, well-entrenched television—well on its way to the future—discovered radio was a drag. The picture was now quite clear: network radio, in its familiar trappings, had outlived its usefulness to the descendant it had conceived.

13

THE SPINMEISTERS
Rancor Among the Ranks

The name of Frank Conrad is familiar to most old time radio buffs that are into preserving the history of the medium. His connections with what is generally perceived as America's "pioneer station" make him one of the forefathers of modern radio.

Conrad, who earned his livelihood as a Westinghouse engineer, initially operated experimental station 8XK in Pittsburgh, a minute detail that looms large in the annals of evolving radio development. His early test model was converted to KDKA in 1920. Not long afterward, that outlet became the infamous originator of the fabled Harding-Cox election returns that aired on the evening of November 2, 1920. That extraordinary feat resulted in nearly all radio historiographers branding KDKA as the nation's foremost outlet. The occasion authentically signified "the beginning of radio" in many scholars' minds.

For all of the hoopla associated with that eventful and uncontested premier, nevertheless, Conrad set yet another precedent—one practically lost to history—more than a year prior to the momentous Harding-Cox exhibition. On October 17, 1919, while running KDKA's precursor, 8XK, Conrad entertained whoever was hearing him by offering recorded musical selections. By placing a microphone in front of a gramophone, he spun discs between chatter. In so doing—while not verified beyond a shadow of doubt—he appears to possibly have been the world's first disc jockey (DJ).

What a heritage! What a legacy! This could be the start of something grand![1]

Conrad's attempt made him something of a celebrity within the territory where he could be picked up. Responses he got by mail indicated widespread affirmation for his efforts. Many called for certain songs (recordings) to be aired. Unable to cope with escalating demands commensurate with his unexpected rise to fame, Conrad demurred. Instead of answering explicit musical requests, he determined to "broadcast" (his word) the records he had on hand for a couple of hours every Wednesday and Saturday night.

Yet after awhile he exhausted his supply. But the owner of nearby Wilkinsburg's Hamilton Music Store, who was among his most ardent listeners, made a deal with the upstart DJ. For mentioning their availability from his shop while on the air, all the vinyl discs he could possibly use would be furnished to Conrad by the enterprising vendor. In that instant the engineer-turned-showman launched what appears to be the first sponsor-broadcaster liaison in ethereal history. The records Conrad played on his gramophone became the most popular sellers among Hamilton's clientele. This not only established a pattern to be repeated infinite numbers of times, it was moreover an early verification of the power that radio possessed to attract prospective buyers and to move merchandise.

Back to the point: Conrad, as far as we have been able to ascertain, was the first DJ. Among several precedents he set, platters and patter—playing recordings interspersed with DJ chatter between tunes—was to become a model that would gradually extend to the majority of commercial radio stations in the USA. And during the golden age of radio, it would become a network staple as well.

While music was invariably a good "fill" for unused airtime, or to establish mood, or to distinguish between scenes of a comedy, mystery or drama production, aural series focused primarily on music became a prominent genre in 20th century radio—one that persists in the 21st century. The varieties were many broaching country, gospel, classical, jazz, popular, rock 'n' roll (in many instances now identified as oldies), waltz, dance, opera, novelty and more. All of these were placed on records by sundry artists and eventually became the nucleus of legions of successful record-spinning diversions.

As time elapsed, particularly in the 1950s, when TV made serious inroads into radio's turf, it became easier and easier for the aural networks and local stations to abandon time-honored formats. Instead, many relegated more and more airtime to turntables, an engineer and someone to blab to an unseen audience. It was cost-effective and a strong indicator of the direction radio management would be heading in the future. Much of the time between record selections was designated for commercials and the networks and stations simply raked in increased profits with little financial outlay.

As local stations got a taste of this arrangement, they cultivated an unquenchable thirst for more. When those outlets sold advertising time themselves instead of receiving trickle-down residuals from their affiliated webs, they kept all of the proceeds at home. They began asking the chains to relinquish added hours of the network schedule so they might sell more of the 24-hour day themselves. DJ shows were most often likely to get the nod when station management negotiated the release of time for more local programming.

Sometimes the network honchos listened to the cries of their partners in Radioland and responded affirmatively. More often, they didn't, however. But the local owners were a hardy bunch, persistent and not easily intimidated nor thwarted. They believed their quest to be justifiable and never backed down. Eventually they raised a voice of unified protest, demanding the release of more and more time. MBS, ABC and NBC—perhaps in that order—gradually responded affirmatively, although it took NBC almost until the end of the 1950s to give back very much of its time-honored schedule. By then NBC was programming the all-weekend magazine *Monitor* that ran several hours during the week, too. NBC didn't give back substantially there until the 1960s. That web may have been staving off a shutdown of most of its enduring shows to avoid reducing the aural ether to an almost total presence of CBS.

CBS was the singular holdout throughout all of this. Chairman William S. Paley had long ago made it perfectly clear he loved radio. Just as passionate was that body of local CBS station owners who were determined Paley and his tribe would relinquish more of their sacrosanct schedule. They cajoled and wailed and urged and threatened. Little by little CBS officials cut back but never in enough quantity to satisfy the hound dogs nipping at their heels. CBS continued to throw an occasional bone their way until the pressure became almost overwhelming. In December 1958, CBS announced that effective early in 1959, it would slice its then 63-hour-per-week broadcast schedule to 30 hours weekly. Gone were some of the listeners' longtime favorite soap operas; *Arthur Godfrey Time* was reduced to 30 minutes weekdays; most of the primetime private eyes were dumped; and several more durable series were either partly or wholly trimmed.

Did that satisfy the troops? Briefly. In reality, it seemed the more time they gained for local sales, the greater their appetites grew, and their complaints turned more pointed and vociferous. It didn't take long to determine that they were obviously still an unhappy lot, so much so that their protests turned to uncompromising demands. By then the station owners were calling for mutiny among the ranks. Several of their number represented some pretty prestigious outlets in a few strategic markets, either by locally perceived dominance or wattage power or history or some other mitigating factor or combination thereof. This time, without the concessions they sought, they agreed to walk out on CBS, defecting from their long-established ties. They intended to join another network if available or go the independent route. In so doing,

CBS could be left without a commanding presence in their lucrative markets. Either way, a CBS station could face a formidable competitor in those markets. Not until then did they gain the full attention of the CBS brass. That's all it took to win what until then had been an unwinnable war.

In mid August 1960, CBS Radio president Arthur Hull Hayes appeared before journalists, proclaiming that radio must shift from entertainment forms "which can be presented more effectively by other media." He announced a public execution for remnants of CBS's programming during the time frame November 25–27, 1960. Missing thereafter would be all weekday dramatic fare (seven programs deleted) along with most of the web's few primetime series. CBS's news at the top of the hour would expand to 10 minutes and a handful of five-minute daytime features were being added. Except for a limited few series, nearly everything would scatter.

It was the best of times for the station owners that had fought a hard and prolonged fight. Yet it was the worst of times for listeners who gave up enduring favorites (including, for some, mythical friends like *Ma Perkins* who had been daily visitors in their homes for 27 years). It was a decisive loss, too, for CBS, having relentlessly fought its affiliates in an effort to remain solvent as a full-service radio network, its long-favored schedule now compromised. From that age forward, for sure chain radio would never be the same.

> Radio on the network level was now a supplementary, secondary entertainment source. To survive, it had to do better those things which television could not do....
> What was passing away was an era in American cultural history. What had begun in the 1920s as an experimental toy and a popular fad, had emerged in the next decade as the most compelling medium in communications.... Radio became an entertainment, informational, and artistic utility.... Radio from 1920 to 1960 mirrored the American civilization ... it served.
> Despite ... creditable achievements, radio as heard since the early 1930s was dead.[2]

It had filled "an opportune time ... a right time for everything."[3] And when that era ended, radio was transformed into some uncommon designs that were as varied as the disparate society in which it played.

Radio was no longer in demand as a comprehensive entertainment source. Television supplied that. The aural medium turned the bulk of its time back to local stations to concentrate on substance that TV couldn't provide faster, more conveniently or more efficiently. As the golden age wound down, an NBC Radio vice president, Matthew J. Culligan, addressing a brigade of ad agency executives, declared as much:

> Radio didn't die. It wasn't even sick. It just had to be psychoanalyzed.... The public didn't stop loving radio despite TV. It just started liking it in a different way—and radio went to the beach, to the park, the patio and the automobile.... Radio has become a companion to the individual instead of remaining a focal point of all family entertainment. An intimacy has developed between radio and the individual. It has become as personal as a pack of cigarets [sic].[4]

More than any other symbol of that period, the disc jockey became the new linchpin of the aural ether. It was he—in a few cases, she—who inherited the bulk of the time the local stations won back from the major chains. And DJs proliferated everywhere. Unquestionably more than anybody else, for a few years the platter-spinners dominated what America was listening to on a profusion of transportable radios then in vogue, carried everywhere by many who were buying into radio's sudden portability.

From the late 1950s and until talk radio became the dominant viable alternative, the platter-and-patter syndrome flourished across the United States. Some of those DJs were inspired by the legacy of Martin Block, whose local New York shows under the banner *Make Believe Ballroom* became an institution. They fostered such a draw that they landed him in a spot on ABC Radio between 1954 and 1961.

Many others aspired to his feat, though few attained his iconic standing. Among the network radio DJ giants were Amos 'n' Andy impersonated by Freeman Gosden and Charles Correll (*The Amos 'n' Andy Music Hall*, CBS), Leonard Feather (*Platterbrains*, ABC), Eddie Gallaher (*On a Sunday Afternoon*, CBS), Robert Q. Lewis (*Waxworks*, CBS), Howard Miller (*The Howard Miller Show*, CBS), Bob Poole (*Poole's Paradise*, MBS) and Peter Potter (*Juke Box Jury*, CBS). Of course we mustn't overlook NBC's and CBS's durable *Your Hit Parade* with host Andre Baruch in timely live renditions of what purportedly were the most popular tunes played on jukeboxes and sold in record stores every week.

Beyond the career-oriented DJ broadcast personalities, there was a handful of maestros who eventually laid their batons aside to slip into air chairs and man the turntables on their own local or national turntable series: Del Courtney, Tommy Dorsey, Benny Goodman, Joe Reichman, Jack Teagarden, Ted Weems and Paul Whiteman come to mind. Whiteman's *The Human Side of the Record* was an ABC weekday matinee feature in the waning days of the 1940s.

There were many others with familiar names in local radio, some of whom applied their platter-spinning to supplement more lucrative incomes principally derived elsewhere—or to project their careers elsewhere, among them: Steve Allen, Dick Clark, Bill Cullen, Arthur Godfrey, Durward Kirby, Jack Lescoulie, Jim Lowe, Gene Rayburn, Robert "Wolfman Jack" Smith and Jack Sterling.

The profession of the radio DJs was regrettably stained by the actions of a segment who sold their souls by greasing their palms. Suspicions began to surface when a few trade journals hinted that some spinmeisters were being romanced with all sorts of perks to curry their favor. At first there was intimation that the

One of the disc jockeys who moved from solo markets to the big time of network radio was Bob Poole. He had a talent for mixing requisite duties of identifying artists and titles on record labels with a decidedly humorous bent, letting him intersperse some very droll material between tunes. On MBS's *Poole's Paradise*—with the DJ at his turntables twice weekdays plus Saturdays at his peak—listeners grinned over his amusing asides, while he addressed his fans as "my little chickadees." To the melee he added telephone quizzes, separating him still further from his contemporaries.

practice originated with the producers of "rhythm and blues" recordings, an ancestor of the mid 1950s "rock 'n' roll" craze.

Some disturbing issues came to light about 1954 as an industry insider—one of the nation's premier DJs—proclaimed in print that "the public did not determine its own preference in music, but instead was almost completely influenced to accept the music played for them by the nation's disc jockeys."[5] That disclosure, coupled with rising indications that the DJs were being heavily wined and dined by record producers, netted arched eyebrows. Obviously, the unprincipled efforts to manipulate individuals in key spots had profound effects on determining what was aired. That appreciably figured into what was purchased in phonograph record shops all over America, influencing millions of dollars changing hands every week. It was a lucrative prospect with mind-boggling possibilities. The results could literally make or break an artist's career, a recording's sales and a publisher's future. The potential was intoxicating.

A music historiographer summarized the outcome:

> The subject got much additional publicity as time went along, with the climax coming in 1959. Investigation of the quiz shows on television gathered radio and the disc jockeys up in its momentum, and shook them around, too. "Payola," a word with far-reaching connotations, but actually coined many years earlier, was now in standard usage by the public in general. Yet the same public sat back and looked on with only lukewarm interest as attempts were made to prove that many of the nation's top disc jockeys had a good thing going for themselves with an under-the-table arrangement to see that the right discs were programmed....
> Not a great deal came of the "payola" investigation except to cast a reflection on the innocent along with those who may have been guilty.[6]

With all due respect, some of the nation's better-known DJs were caught in the quagmire and their services promptly terminated. A pundit noted, "In the end, no deejays were packed off to prison, but the broad brush wielded by the investigators ruined the careers of dozens and dozens of radio disc jockeys." While a pall of gloom was shed over the innocent victims of the debacle, the loss of job and reputation was undoubtedly deeply demoralizing to those actually experiencing it.[7]

Toward the end of the 1950s, a dramatic shift occurred in the traditional composition of disc jockey formats that radio listeners long had been accustomed to. The Storz-owned radio chain introduced "top-40 radio" which revolutionized the industry. Owner Todd Storz devised the model after observing that discriminating patrons frequently repeated their plays of a handful of tunes in a beer joint jukebox. That bit of humanity's behavior made a valued impression.

Storz pondered: wouldn't the results be similar if radio listeners had a choice? If everything else was equal except the playlists, he theorized, audiences would most likely pick the station that repetitively offered the songs they most wanted to hear over—say—one that just played records. Consequently, the limited top-40 hit list was born. It spread like wildfire from the Storz-owned stations to hundreds of other outlets.

There were some tradeoffs once the new design was implemented. "Indicating to deejays what they could play, the top-forty format cut off the power source for the personality disc jockeys and, many believe, led to the dilution of the power of rock-'n'-roll," an informed source declared.[8]

The DJ-oriented phase would prevail in radio for a decade or so before losing ground to mounting competitors hankering for equal opportunity on the ether. The next chapter exploits the successors. In the meantime, let it be noted that—when the golden age of radio passed—the DJs were waiting in the wings to occupy the time the multiplicity of shows had vacated. The DJs generally weren't the instigators causing network radio to pass from the scene. Rather, they were the beneficiaries, the professionals who inherited the "space," filling it with their style of entertainment. They can't be accused of killing old time radio, only of filling the void it had occupied.

Those record shows—originated nationally and locally—would be superseded down the road a spell. Depending upon one's point of view, many Americans might not have realized just how well off they were under the spinmeisters—until the next wave arrived and carried radio to places no one had dreamed it would go.

In the meantime, in recent decades listeners have experienced a very different type of disc jockey programming that departs significantly from that which they heard through the 1960s. After the personality-oriented series went out of vogue, segueing into talk-dominated radio, the celebrated platter-and-chatter hosts were diminished and many faded away entirely.

But when some enterprising entrepreneurs discovered a renaissance mode for the genre that encouraged greedy station owners to make even greater profits by going into automated programming, the local DJ in many places was banished forever. In his place was a single distant voice speaking simultaneously in hundreds of markets as he championed the "one size fits all" model. The DJ frittered away time with idle chatter between discs, serving up that all-encompassing brand of "amusement" to millions of listeners. The inane patter linked the tunes and endless commercial segments, another "worst of times" scenario for listeners. "Gradually, the DJs began to intrude on the discs, until the songs sounded more like backup music for the host's banter. This eventually gave way to robot DJs, who were just plugged into the Top 40 charts, which in turn led to today's characterless DJs and syndicated formats—the worst of all possible musical worlds."[9]

Today, pontificates a radio historiographer, radio is "stuck on a relentless treadmill of news-music-sports, interrupted for warmed-over weather, commute, and stock updates every ten minutes."[10] Not so in the halcyon days of the DJ. While that epoch was never as extraordinary as the golden age that preceded it, the phase was indubitably far better than the "babble of opinion, most of it mindless and mean-spirited, whipped on by shrill talk-show hosts" available to radio audiences today.[11]

The interval of the local DJ appears to be history in many quarters. Americans may not have realized just how well off they were until the spinmeisters disappeared from the scene—and those syndicated hookup, often vitriolic, never-at-a-loss-for-an-opinion talk show hosts arrived. Surely radio's forefathers never had anything like this in mind when they began connecting dots across the ether.

14

RACONTEURIAL RESURGENCE
The Spielers Have Their Say

While disc jockeys (DJs) continued to predominate with what Americans heard blaring from their radios in the 1960s, toward the end of that decade the spinmeisters' influence had been substantially reduced.[1] A new wave of radio programming had entered the arena by then and was vying for the listeners' attention. In a growing number of metropolitan markets, in particular, key stations simply stopped playing music one day and adopted a news-and-information format the next.

Telephone call-in series, interviews, news and public affairs were all hallmarks of radio without music. With network radio already having been reduced primarily to strictly verbal communication—banishing audience participation, comedy, drama and variety earlier that decade or in the 1950s to the Valhalla of radio entertainment—the switch in agendas appeared to hold promise for the webs' affiliates. Sponsors, so it seemed, were signing up in droves.

New York's WINS Radio, a Westinghouse property, is a good example. WINS became the first Gotham station to adopt an all-news format, on April 19, 1965. Two years later, CBS's flagship outlet, WCBS-AM, switched to a similar motif.[2] It was a foretaste of things to come as local stations all over the nation marked by diversified mixtures of programming styles began to limit their focus to single fields (e.g. pop music, talk, sports, news, nostalgia, oldies, religion, and so forth). While the all-news format required a heavy investment in capital and personnel, a few prestigious outlets in major metropolitan districts were able to pull it off quite well. The same thing happened in a handful of key markets in which all-sports programming, including a whole lot of interviews and listener comments between games, appeared.

As time went on the talkathon syndrome gained an upper hand in copious markets, disseminating across the country. Talk was usually one of the easiest and least expensive forms to produce while roughly guaranteeing enormous listener turnouts. Especially was this true with the right combination of host, time period, subject matter and slant. In this manner it was a remarkably appealing vehicle to potential advertisers.

Not that talk was new, mind you. But it did come cheap.

It had been around long before the late 1960s and 1970s. In radio's halcyon days and even into the 1960s people listened intently to the observations and counsel of sundry spokespersons on the major webs offering a variety of topics. Among their number were John J. Anthony, Joyce Brothers, Betty Crocker, Galen Drake, Jimmy Fidler, Arlene Francis, Joe Garagiola, Hedda Hopper, Mike Jensen, Dorothy Kilgallen, Ted Malone, Mary Margaret McBride, Charles Osgood, Louella Parsons, Phil Rizzuto, Gene Shalit, Bill Stern, Pat Summerall, Mary Lee Taylor, Abigail Van Buren, Sidney Walton and Walter Winchell. All of them satisfactorily proved that—given a motivating premise and a compelling format with an insightful entertaining host or hostess—people would tune in regularly, and even become faithful adherents. These radio speakers set a quality standard that their medium would attempt to replicate down the road.

There were whole conversational series, too, back then—shows without headliners that were predominantly talk-oriented, including: *The American School of the Air, America's Town Meeting of the Air, The Baptist Hour, The Catholic Hour, The Hour of Decision, Information*

Please, Meet the Press, The National Farm and Home Hour, National Vespers and *The University of Chicago Roundtable.* Each was acclaimed within segments of the national audience. All of them permitted Americans to "listen in" to great scholars, authorities in myriad fields, orators, clergymen, public figures and other well-versed personalities who shared their expertise with their fellow countrymen.

What was happening in local radio from the 1960s forward was the precursor of today's satellite network all-talk programming blueprint to which many of today's outlets unswervingly subscribe. (Their number seems to multiply by the week.) Over much of the dial recorded music—which had ruled the roost when the golden age of radio faded—took a back seat to the spielers. The shifting sands were fine-tuned in the 1970s. By the 1980s, hundreds of stations in large cities and tiny villages offered individual viewpoints on every topic imaginable—including some that would have been forbidden in polite conversation during earlier epochs.

The talkathon style that became the hardiest, flourishing wherever it was planted, was doubtlessly the telephone call-in show. That breed seemingly proliferated so easily, and cost a station so little to put it on, that it became a scheduling mainstay in the 1980s, 1990s and 2000s. Hosts of the oral exchanges could well be local market celebrities. Just as often, however, they might live as geographically distant from the stations airing their voices as the DJs that might have preceded their inception on the ether. Sometimes the raconteurs then and now are well-informed figures dispensing helpful, how-to advice to the enhancement of devoted fans. These talk show hosts' themes may range from finances to health, religion, education, sports, self-help, hobbies, current events, relationships, government, law, politics, jobs, safety, autos, agriculture, home economics, travel, do-it-yourself, gossip—infinite numbers of arenas.

Some narrow-minded bigots also populate another extreme. These individuals, a close observation confirms to almost anybody with an open mind, frequently conduct little more than rants and harangues, often exhibiting bully pulpit tactics. Such ventures on the air are often characterized by intolerance and the host's particular brand of biased, strictly focused interpretation on issues pertaining to a variety of current events. This isn't to say that they don't have huge followings that buy into their invective completely; it recognizes the fact that they are a motivating force within the talkathon mold, one that is genuinely appreciated by legions of enamored cohorts.

Anybody who thought that the conversational exchanges of the airwaves might run their course in a brief while, possibly even hoping that they would—just as the disc jockey epoch did—has been in for a rude awakening. In some markets talk radio is now well into its fifth decade of broadcasting. The fact that you can pick up talk shows on dozens of AM and FM channels at any time of the day or night in thousands of American communities, as well as over the Internet and through constantly increasing horizons of technology, is a testament to the form's allure, resiliency and profitability. It's a modus operandi that, quite frankly, shows no sign of abating whatsoever.

As talk radio became firmly entrenched on the ether, one network, NBC, recognized an opportunity to capitalize on the growing phenomenon. All the major chains were expanding into multiple focuses, strategies and supplementary webs following ABC's move into diversification of its basic services in 1968. Under that arrangement ABC was able to concentrate programming into specific designs for theme-oriented affiliates, thereby picking up hundreds of new stations.

One of the most popular theses that had prospered among affiliate and independent outlets all over the place, of course, was conversational radio. By the late 1970s, it was well established almost everywhere. This hadn't escaped the notice of NBC executives, who decided in the early 1980s to wade out into those promising waters with their own sidelight venture.

Nighttalk, launched on November 2, 1981, gave NBC a laboratory model to test its plan.

For two hours on weeknights beginning at 10 o'clock Eastern Time, financial guru Bruce Williams addressed the money concerns of callers to his live show. Therapist Sally Jessy Raphael followed with three hours of answering questions about listeners' psychological concerns. When the nation's insomniacs and after-dark workforce were quick to embrace *Nighttalk* enthusiastically, NBC's intents were confirmed. Arriving when *Nighttalk* did—two full decades following the traditionally accepted outer limits of radio's golden age—must have seemed like a transfusion to a chain that had been on life support, as some critics intimated, for more than a decade. NBC responded quickly. In April 1982, it introduced an expanded undertaking appointed under the appellation *Talknet*.

From darkness until dawn, beginning as early at 7 P.M. in the East, the nocturnal venture featured Williams and Raphael at earlier hours. Along with them, health specialists Bernard Meltzer and Harvey Ruben aired multi-hour features via satellite distribution. From time to time there were yet other personalities with compelling interests added to the blend. The success of *Talknet* could be confirmed in its durability: it persisted into the mid 1990s, well after NBC Radio was twice sold in the 1980s. The all-night talkathon continued practically until the chain—in the previously mentioned shuffle of webs in the late 1990s—lost its ability to remain viable and to compete for a substantial national radio audience, given shifting trends in audio broadcasting's direction.

MBS had been the first network to attempt overnight programming, putting celebrity interviewer Larry King on the air in 1978. His success there had opened doors for him to move into television with a primetime talk show, chatting with public figures from many quarters. In the meantime, ABC Radio officials—eager to replicate both MBS's and NBC's good fortune with after-dark features—diversified yet again. On May 3, 1982, the month following NBC's debut of *Talknet*, ABC premiered *Talkradio*. Six hours of telephone chit-chat on its AM stations was ABC's original scheme, beginning at 1 A.M. Eastern Time weeknights. Originating in Los Angeles, the endeavor introduced Ira Fistell in a three-hour "anything is up for discussion" call-in format followed by three hours with Ray Briem interviewing people then currently in the news, coupled with listeners' calls. *Talkradio* eventually led to *ABC News & Talk Radio*, a subsequent venture that persisted to 2007.

In the modern era, a couple of intrepid suppliers of public radio programming in the United States project similar ambitions. These might be seen by some at times as a throwback to the heady days when NBC and CBS duked it out for ethereal supremacy on the nation's aural airwaves.

American Public Media (APM), headquartered in Minneapolis–St. Paul, Minnesota, is the second largest producer and distributor of such audio wares. The unit is also honored as the chief purveyor of classical music in the country. Dating to 1967, APM now boasts an average listenership of 15.5 million weekly. APM operates 40 public radio stations and 29 translators in the upper Midwest, California and Florida, with links to nearly 800 outlets in those territories. APM's more than 20 current regular features include the award-winning series *A Prairie Home Companion*, *Performance Today*, *Marketplace*, *Marketplace Money*, *The Splendid Table* and *Speaking of Faith*. Nearly half of its offerings are daily or weekly shows of an all-talk genus, indicating heavy involvement in a field in which contemporary radio hookups are prominently residing.

From another producer, one of the most universally admired web-oriented talk projects today is the inspired *All Things Considered*.[3] Offered daily by National Public Radio (NPR), this enduring multifaceted series has been airing since 1971.

Parenthetically, NPR, organized in 1970—about which we have said little until now—is a global producer and distributor of noncommercial news, talk and entertainment programming. Like APM, NPR is a privately supported, not-for-profit membership organization. It appeals to 26 million Americans weekly in partnership with upwards of 900 independently operated public radio stations. Each NPR member outlet supplies local listeners with a fusion of national and local programming. With original online content and audio streaming, meanwhile, NPR.org offers hourly newscasts, special features and a decade of archived audio and information. NPR may be picked up via AM/FM, digital and satellite radios, the Internet, podcasts and other methods. It generates more than 130 hours of original programming weekly. While NPR is headquartered in Washington, D.C., it isn't a government agency. It staffs 36 news bureaus and offices around the world, half of them in the United States.

Back to *All Things Considered*.

For a couple of hours every afternoon, issues of import to Americans of various persuasions are discussed by knowledgeable talking heads. Sharing their unique take on myriad matters, the spokespersons frequently fill in the gaps of missing information that have been circulating in listeners' minds. There are news headlines and fascinating features in abundance that lend sparkle to the mix.

While it's a far cry from Jimmy Fidler, Mary Margaret McBride and Abigail Van Buren in the days of yore, this captivating program maintains a tradition that those early spielers and their contemporaries flung onto the ether in their day. *All Things Considered* with its smorgasbord of absorbing topics can be undeniably confirmed as a living link with network radio of yesterday.

And for those who hearken back to what used to be, it's a reverie that—all things considered—can't be considered all bad.

Epilogue
When You Wish Upon a Star

In 1957, the Soviets launched Sputnik 1, the inaugural satellite containing an on-board radio transmitter operating on dual frequencies. From that time onward, the age of telecommunications was upon us. In 1958, Americans responded with Project SCORE, among other things applying a tape recorder to maintain and transmit voice messages. Several more breakthroughs occurred before the American Telephone & Telegraph Company—acting in tandem with several communications parties, including some controlled by the Brits and the French—put the first active direct relay communications satellite in orbit. The blast-off of Telstar on July 10, 1962, the first private enterprise venture of that type, foretold the future: radio technology had moved into an even more advanced state and satellite would become a fixed means for diffusing broadcasts in the years ahead. With advancing technology, it was a matter of time until those humble origins would be radically expanded, reaching horizons that probably no one could possibly envision in satellite's embryonic days.

Satellite is but one instrument in developing the expertise that seems to know no cessation. Combined, that technology has allowed global exchange to proliferate radically. Who could possibly envision where the next generation of communications technology may take us? Sometimes new announcements arrive so quickly we've hardly had time to adjust to the previous plateau.

Focus for a moment, if you will, on the satellite as a symbol of all of the newer models of linking people together for faster, more efficient interaction. Think of the satellite as a twinkling little star ... up above the world so high ... like a diamond in the sky.[1] And imagine all the voice signals it simultaneously radiates from here to there and back to earth again.

Some of those voices are still broadcast by network radio and are being heard by millions of people simultaneously. It may not be as in the days of old (depending upon your personal connotation of old), but there are still remnants of a form that was popular five, six, seven, eight or more decades ago. Could what we were once accustomed to ever return?

In 1959, The Kingston Trio folk-singing group recalled a passenger interminably trapped on the Boston subway. He was unable to cough up five cents extra when the fare increased while he was in transit. Unable to disembark because of it, the fate of the mythical traveler was never learned. In 1940, shortly after his death, novelist Thomas Wolfe's newly-published tome proclaimed: "You can't go home again."

The dire circumstances on which these suppositions are predicated occurred before satellites were destined to reach their zenith. With those billion-dollar babies zipping around the sky, can anything within the creative mind of man be considered impossible? Did we not put men on the moon? Have we not created modern marvels like vehicles to convey us on land and sea and sky? And bridges and dams and tunnels—and telecommunications? Could network radio of the past never pay us a return visit?

Perhaps someday we'll find a way to tap into Allen's Alley and McGee's closet and the Inner Sanctum and who knows what else, and be able to revisit them all again (besides hearing playbacks of old recordings)—even if it's with contemporary characters in modern settings. A little audience participation, comedy, drama, music and variety just might be welcome relief to a transcontinental audience saturated with talk, talk and more talk.

> *Star light, star bright,*
> *The first star I see tonight!*
> *I wish I may, I wish I might,*
> *Have the wish I wish tonight!*[2]

From the far horizons of the unknown come transcribed tales of new dimensions in time and space—these are stories of the future, adventures in which you'll live in a million could-be years on a thousand may-be worlds.[3]

Tune in again ... tomorrow!

APPENDIX

Ex Chains
Webs of Extinction

Following is a directory of United States radio networks that operated in the past. While this compendium doesn't purport to be inclusive, more than three dozen leading chains have been assembled for these introductions. An overriding purpose in their presentation is to exhibit their striking diversity. What isn't to be missed is a panorama of network types that have existed, often in narrowly focused dimensions appealing to limited sectors of the national radio patronage. Transmission methods have also been modified to encompass newer technologies, a significant disconnect from their original telephone- and telegraph-wire roots.

ABC News & Talk Radio

A news, talk, and entertainment channel originally programmed and distributed by ABC Radio Networks as a satellite service until June 12, 2007. At that point it was transferred to Citadel Broadcasting Corporation of Las Vegas, Nevada, along with a 24-unit chain of ABC stations. While Citadel pledged to distribute ABC News Radio—produced by ABC News of the ABC Television Network—at least until 2017, it removed ABC News & Talk Radio from the air on September 24, 2007, in a budget-trimming ploy. (*See following entry.*)

ABC *Talkradio* (sometimes appears as *TalkRadio*)

Beginning May 3, 1982, ABC *Talkradio* was that networks' reply to MBS's nighttime success with talk-show personality Larry King that began in 1978. There was also some new competition—NBC *Nighttalk*—from November 1981, renamed *Talknet* in April 1982. *Talkradio*, meanwhile, initially programmed six hours of phoned-in conversations on ABC AM stations beginning weeknights at 1 A.M. Eastern Time. Originating in Los Angeles, ABC's effort introduced Ira Fistell in a three-hour "anything is up for discussion" call-in format followed by three hours with Ray Briem interviewing people currently in the news, coupled with listeners' calls. *Talkradio* established underpinnings of ABC News & Talk Radio. (*See previous entry.*)

Amalgamated Broadcasting System

A network that premiered September 25, 1933, backed by comedian Israel Edwin Leopold (Ed Wynn) and Hungarian-born violinist Ota Gygi, which lasted five weeks, to October 28, 1933. It was Wynn's intent that the projected 100-station chain would offer an alternative to CBS and NBC. Concomitantly Wynn worried that he might personally lapse into penury, but would rely on the chain to safeguard him, shoring up the uncertain footing of his professional career. Allowing Gygi to run the show at the web's inception while Wynn was absent making a movie, however, proved "the biggest mistake of his career, if not his life," a media historian conjectured. Gygi promptly alienated the print press and potential advertisers, two groups the project needed desperately. Tales of fraud and graft surfaced. The budding web went down in flames—netting a loss to investors above $300,000. *Time* claimed Wynn resigned from it on realizing "he was a showman, not a businessman." Despite the trouncing, in 1934, others created a winning proxy, Mutual Broadcasting System, inspired by some of Wynn's fundamental concepts. (*Mutual is the subject of Chapter 5.*)

Blue Network

The Blue was a crucial segment of the National Broadcasting System (NBC) from the Blue's establishment January 1, 1927, until its divestiture October 12, 1943, a result of a 1941 ruling by the Federal Communications Commission (FCC). The panel's edict resulted in NBC selling one of its double chains, retaining the Red web that transported its most popular programs and personalities. NBC dispensed with the Blue, which was often branded by secondary features and showbiz types along with educational and sustained fare. On January 9, 1942, NBC created the Blue Network Company, Inc. Blue was put on the block in 1943 and attracted buyer Edward J. Noble, a multimillionaire candy-maker. Until then the purchase price of $8 million was the largest sale in broadcast history. On June 15, 1945, the Blue nomenclature passed from existence; Noble had fruitfully negotiated use of the appellation American Broadcasting Company (ABC) with industry magnate George B. Storer, who owned a similar sobriquet. While today's ABC's roots lie in NBC's Blue chain, Noble and successors expanded and developed it far beyond its heritage as a mere "also ran" web. (*More detail on NBC Blue/Blue/ABC appears in Chapters 3 and 6.*)

Business Radio Network

A 1980s 24-hour audio service providing local stations with business, financial and investment updates and talk programming.

Catholic Radio Network

Catholic Radio Network, which soon altered its moniker to Catholic Family Radio, went on the air in December 1998. It was a conservative-oriented talk-based broadcaster purportedly offering "accurate and correct teachings of the church, that artificial birth control is wrong, abortion is wrong and euthanasia is wrong," allowed investor John Neal, a Denver businessman. Backers were able to buy seven radio stations formerly run by the defunct Children's Broadcasting Corporation (Radio AAHS) for $37 million. "Its key players were quick to wave off and set themselves apart from existing Catholic media," wrote one journalist. "They didn't get into this business to preach to niche markets of little old ladies in the choir.... They were taking to the airwaves to engage in 'stealth evangelization,' said CEO John Lynch, a former Pittsburgh Steelers linebacker and broadcast executive who came out of early retirement to run the network.... Lynch and company sketched a bold game plan—a line-up of hard-hitting talk shows that would win over fallen away Catholics, make converts out of Protestant scoffers and unbelievers, and gain a hearing for conservative Catholic political ideas." Its leaders promised to be selling stock and to serve the nation's top 50 markets within a year. It didn't happen. Unable to attract listeners, ratings or advertisers, the venture collapsed. In spite of seven-figure gifts from a handful of well-heeled Catholic businessmen, plus contributions of many of lesser means, it was an uphill financial battle from start to a quick finish in May 2000. Stations were put up for sale and disposed of piecemeal. Some programming, meanwhile, was absorbed into the Eternal Word Television Network.

CBN Northeast

This was a five-station FM chain (one of the country's first) with origins in the Rural Radio Network. Launched in 1948 in upstate New York, that web was signified as the world's first all-radio, no-wireless hookup. (*See entry for Rural Radio Network.*) From 1969 to 1982, its successor, CBN Northeast, simulcast TV programs of the Christian Broadcasting Network (CBN). The radio net—acquired by CBN through a corporate bequest—was dismantled when CBN sold its licenses to separate interests. CBN was established by evangelist Pat Robertson in 1961 at Virginia Beach, Virginia. That web later cycled through a succession of names and owners: The Family Channel, Fox Family Channel and ABC Family. CBN is presently a production house for *The 700 Club* and other religious-themed shows. Since the dissolution of CBN Northeast, a replacement religious web sprang up in the territory it occupied: Family Life Network, airing on different stations, covers much of the Empire State's upstate area.

Colonial Network

With fewer than 20 stations comprising the Colonial Network at its debut on August 5, 1936, the web was created to make full use of a 16-hour telephone circuit. The jointly owned sister Yankee Network, established in 1930, had contracted for the line but used it only some of the time. These dual chains mostly shared the same affiliates. From its start, however, Colonial provided the Mutual Broadcasting System with New England outlets for MBS programming. In 1940, Colonial and Yankee became a joint MBS stockholder. In January 1943, the Colonial and Yankee networks were absorbed by the General Tire & Rubber Company of Akron, Ohio. The acquisitions were part of progressive steps by General to control an influential segment of American broadcasting. General divested its radio properties in July 1957. (*More details in Chapter 5.*)

Don Lee Network

Don Lee was a far West chain launched in December 1928 by the multimillionaire proprietor of manifold California automobile dealerships. Having purchased a station in San Francisco and another in Los Angeles, Lee grafted a trio of added stations to his fledgling web in December 1928. Gradually acquiring more and more outlets, by the time the network was sold to General Tire & Rubber Company of Akron, Ohio, in October 1950—16 years after its founder's death—the Don Lee empire reached 53 affiliates. Significantly, Don Lee gave two transcontinental chains their first coast-to-coast exposure: CBS, with which it was linked from September 1929 to December 1936; and MBS, from December 1936 to 1967. Up to one-fifth of a typical 16-hour Don Lee programming day was provided to the chain's stations by MBS while Don Lee created the remainder in its $3 million Hollywood studios. The 1950 sale to General Tire for $12.3 million included three radio stations, access to the Don Lee Network, the broadcast studios and shares in MBS owned by Don Lee. A Los Angeles television station, KTSL, was sold separately by Don Lee to CBS on January 1, 1951. (*More detail appears in Chapters 4, 5, 7.*)

Enterprise Radio Network

This was an all-sports web founded by Scott Rasmussen, son of ESPN's initiator Bill Rasmussen, which aired from January 1981 to September 21, 1981. It proffered sportscasts twice hourly and live phone-in sports dialogue from 6 P.M. to 8 A.M. Eastern Time nightly, seven days per week. At its crest the web boasted 74 stations from Florida to Washington state and from California to Maine. Lack of advertising revenue prevented Rasmussen from keeping the operation afloat; he hired more than 100 announcers, producers and reporters to staff his web, and they worked gratis for the final six weeks that Enterprise was airborne.

I. E. America Radio Network

This was a left-leaning aural syndication service evolving out of a storied legacy of earlier broadcasting efforts that began in Tampa, Florida, in 1987 (including the Sun Radio, Peoples Radio and United Broadcasting networks). The I. E. (information entertainment) America Radio Network was largely underwritten by United Auto Workers (UAW). While the union pumped $5 million into the project when it acquired the United chain in 1996, with substantial cash infusions as time progressed, the outfit faltered nevertheless. Despite the fact it proffered several attractive on-air personalities, it encountered programming troubles and most especially budgetary difficulties, losing a reported $900,000 annually. Operating from a $2 million facility near Detroit's Michigan state fairgrounds, the web finally got the heave-ho when the UAW—tired of throwing good money after bad—pulled the plug on February 27, 2004. Most of the net's on-air talk-show stars (Peter B. Collins, Thom Hartmann, Jim Hightower, Mike Malloy, Doug Stephan, Peter Werbe, et al.) were able to peddle their wares elsewhere, largely via others' syndicated or local station ventures.

Independent Broadcasters Network

In a complete reversal of the traditional method of money changing hands in radio, the 1990s Independent Broadcasters Network (IBN) of Tampa, Florida, hired talk-show hosts that paid the web to carry their shows instead of the chain paying them. Personalities sold their own commercials to support the enterprise. "What we are really doing is allowing the talent to be owners of the product and to share in its success," said IBN chairman Doug Stephan. IBN was a 24-hour-a-day operation fostered by investors and talk-show hosts Stephan, Irwin H. (Sonny) Bloch and Steve Weigner and syndicated columnist Jack Anderson. On February 3, 1995, Reuters announced that IBN would merge with Spartan Funding Company, and Bloch would become Spartan's president and CEO. On July 3, 1995, *Broadcasting & Cable* reported: "Sonny Bloch's Independent Broadcasters Network, which distributed his now-defunct financial talk show to more than 200 radio affiliates, has gone dark.... According to court-appointed receiver Michael Eskridge, 'The network never made money, and that includes when Bloch's show was on the air.' Bloch was arrested and indicted last month by the Securities and Exchange Commission on 35 counts of fraud." Convicted of tax evasion for persuading hundreds of mostly elderly listeners to invest in worthless securities, bilking them of $21 million and leaving many penniless, Bloch was sentenced to 21 months in a federal prison. He was released five months early, then in the final stages of cancer. He died at 61 on March 20, 1998, before he could be sentenced on the $21 million telemarketing scheme.

Keystone Broadcasting System

Launched in 1941 with headquarters in New York and relocated to Chicago in 1948, Keystone Broadcasting System (KBS) remains an obscure entity from the annals of radio history. Its details have been preserved and acknowledged only casually by media historiographers. On October 18, 1942, KBS president Michael Sillerman told a newspaper reporter: "Due to the fact that over 200 smaller communities in the country, representing principal trading centers, cannot hear network programs there has been established a special transcription network known as the Keystone Broadcasting System composed of 202 radio stations from coast to coast. These stations rebroadcast on transcriptions well-known network programs in most of those areas of the country which are either not reached by the major wired networks at all ... or not serviced by one or more of the major networks." Not to be confused with a Keystone Broadcasting Company that operated broadcast stations in Pennsylvania, Ohio and New York (1924–1940), Keystone Broadcasting System—"which includes radio stations in many parts of the country" in a 1973 account—can be sketchily traced through a newspaper trail. KBS remained active at least until 1989 and possibly beyond, although its year of departure is still elusive.

Liberty Broadcasting System

At its inception in 1948, Liberty Broadcasting System (LBS) had a one-track mind and that was baseball. It was formed by Dallas station owner Gordon McLendon, who successfully pitched re-creations of Major League Baseball (MLB) games to disenfranchised athletics-starved audiences in the hinterlands. In so doing LBS capitalized on a niche market that widened to 458 outlets by 1951, duplicating games through wire reports backed with superimposed sound effects and other devices until the games could be aired live. Not only that, LBS broadcast National Football League (NFL) contests in the fall season, plus myriad entertainment and sports-talk features. Plagued by financial difficulties, however—McLendon proved a smart entrepreneur but a rather deficient businessman—it all came apart at the seams when MLB and NFL boosted their fees to exorbitant sums for airing their scrimmages. Liberty collapsed—ending McLendon's dreams of owning the world's largest network (intending to surpass MBS) in number of affiliates—on May 16, 1952.

Metromedia Radio

Arising from the wiped out DuMont Television Network, Metromedia Radio, an aural news service begun in the 1960s, developed from earlier organizational monikers: DuMont Broadcasting Corporation (1946), Metropolitan Broadcasting Corporation (1957), Metromedia (1961). Industrialist-financier John Kluge, successor to Allen B. DuMont, began buying TV and AM-FM radio properties to link to his WNEW-AM-FM operations in New York after becoming owner-chairman in 1958. The TV stations were sold in 1985 to form the nucleus of Fox Broadcasting Company, effective March 6, 1986. Nine major-market radio stations were sold in a separate pact in late 1986 and then resold by the early 1990s. A 1986 newspaper article summarized, "Metromedia is in the process of liquidating itself."

Mutual Black Network

Like its counterpart transcontinental webs were doing in the same epoch, Mutual Broadcasting System (MBS) inaugurated a couple of alternate formats on May 1, 1972, aimed at ethnic audiences—the first of a handful of parallel chains designed for specific groups of listeners (although the other diversions wouldn't appear until 1982 when satellite technology assured feasibility). The Mutual Black Network (MBN), one of the original choices, programmed 100 news and sports capsules weekly at 50 minutes past the hour, slanted toward African Americans. Additionally, the hookup offered feature programming and—from spring 1974 to spring

1975—a quarter-hour weekday soap opera, *Sounds of the City*. By 1974, MBN was beamed to 98 U.S. affiliates. MBN was sold by MBS to minority stockholder Sheridan Broadcasting Corporation (as the Sheridan Network) in 1979.

Mutual Broadcasting System

The first (and—as this is written—thus far, only) one of the original quartet of transcontinental chains to shut down, the Mutual Broadcasting System (MBS) persisted from September 29, 1934 (with programming beginning three days later) to April 17, 1999. Formed by an association of four powerful Midwestern and Eastern stations, MBS differed at its start from competitor hookups: instead of being run by hierarchy at a broadcast headquarters, it was directed instead by member stations. Indeed, MBS's outlets supplied the programming, sharing their local efforts, including a news bureau and limited studio facilities at its New York City affiliate. Although the stations were often less desirable and less exalted than those of rival networks—frequently less powerful in wattage—MBS nevertheless proliferated. By 1979, it boasted 950 affiliates, unsurpassed by all other hookups in radio history to date except ABC, which subdivided its web in 1968 to a quartet of feeds to focused-model outlets. (National Public Radio is currently within 100 stations of surpassing Mutual's pinnacle also.) It was the only national radio network from the early era that did not develop a video counterpart. MBS's original replica began to dissolve in 1952 when it was bought by General Tire & Rubber Company. For decades it proceeded through a succession of owners, finally ending in the hands of Westwood One in 1985, which pulled the plug on it a dozen years later. It had brought legions of Americans millions of hours of information and entertainment in between the parameters of time that it filled. (*Mutual is the focus of Chapter 5.*)

Mutual Cadena Hispanica Network

Like its counterpart transcontinental webs were doing in the same epoch, Mutual Broadcasting System (MBS) inaugurated a couple of alternate formats on May 1, 1972, aimed at ethnic audiences—the first of a handful of parallel chains designed for specific groups of listeners. The Mutual Cadena Hispanica Network or Mutual Spanish Network (MSN), one of the original choices, programmed 100 news and sports capsules weekly at 45 minutes past the hour, slanted toward Spanish-speaking Americans. This alternative chain failed to meet its backers' expectations, nonetheless, and was discontinued in 1973.

Mutual Lifestyle Radio

As one of its myriad branding diversifications in the 1970s and 1980s, Mutual Broadcasting System dispatched *Mutual Lifestyle Reports* as nucleus of its Mutual Lifestyle Radio. Affiliates received newscasts at 55 minutes past the hour offering offbeat "feel-good" items tailored to contemporary and album-oriented rock radio station listeners.

National Black Network

Eugene D. Jackson and Sidney L. Small were some of the first African Americans to introduce a transcontinental aural web in the United States. Debuting in 1973 from New York City, their National Black Network (NBN) proffered five-minute newscasts on the hour mixed with sportscasts of similar duration on the half-hour multiple times daily. In addition, NBN broadcast a live overnight show, *Night Talk*, with host Bob Law along with assorted public affairs features. NBN instituted a second in-depth news service—American Urban Information Radio—in the early 1980s, offering hourly news at 50 minutes past the hour. In 1992, NBN and its chief rival, Sheridan Broadcasting Network, combined to form the American Urban Radio Networks. That company operates a handful of African American themed audio webs beamed to hundreds of stations across America in the current age.

National Negro Network

Founded by Chicago–New York adman W. Leonard Evans, Jr., on January 20, 1954, the National Negro Network (NNN) was truly the first black-owned radio chain in the United States. With only 40 stations carrying its programming at the start, the web constantly swam upstream against the better-heeled, long-established chains proffering tenured histories with advertising clients. Lacking that, NNN soon failed, despite the fact a handful of underwriters (Pet Milk Company and Philip Morris Company among them) signed to co-sponsor a daily quarter-hour serial starring singer Juanita Hall, *The Story of Ruby Valentine*. The chain announced plans for full web coverage of Negro sports, news and public affairs later in 1954. "We're starting small, but we're going to wind up big," Evans told a news magazine scribe, himself a magazine publisher later. Although the number of U.S. radio stations aiming their wares at Negro audiences had grown from four in 1943 to 270 a decade later, that was small potatoes considering there was in excess of 2,500 stations in America then. That fact, and a shortage of advertising revenue, squelched what appeared to be a brilliant concept for a presumably receptive niche market.

NBC News and Information Service

Following the demise of its spectacular two-decades-old programming concept known as *Monitor* in January 1975, a new National Broadcasting Company (NBC) president instituted the News and Information Service (NIS) over 33 stations on June 18, 1975. NBC furnished subscribing outlets with 55 minutes of news and features every hour 24–7 with the exception of a few Sunday hours. The remaining five minutes of each hour were filled with *NBC News on the Hour*. Some stations carrying NIS were assessed monthly fees of $10,000. The chain didn't particularly mind if the outlets airing it were NBC affiliates or not. It needed 150 stations to make it financially viable. But NIS was airing in just 62 markets when it reached dismal ends, scrubbed in less than two years on May 29, 1977, as NBC sought new alternatives to regain lost credibility and viability.

NBC *Talknet*

The National Broadcasting Company's NBC *Talknet* succeeded the web's *Nighttalk* feature which began November 2, 1981. In that era the national chains were witnessing a widespread interest in programming during the overnight hours that could potentially boost advertising revenues while reaching millions of awakened Americans. By April 1982, with success written all over *Nighttalk's* experimenting trial, *Talknet* was beamed to stations all over the nation. Advice-oriented in focus, the service featured specialists (Bruce Williams, Sally Jessy Raphael, Bernard Meltzer, Harvey Ruben) who accepted listeners' telephone calls and dispensed help on issues pertaining to finance, relationships, health, etc. After NBC and its parent firm, the Radio Corporation of America, was sold to the General Electric Corporation in 1986, and NBC Radio was again sold the following year to Westwood One, *Talknet* persisted several more years. Gradually Westwood One began to diminish and dismantle NBC as a major radio presence. *Talknet* was abandoned in the mid 1990s although some of its leading on-air personalities continued appearing elsewhere.

Progressive Broadcasting System

A fleeting operation that became airborne in November 1950, Progressive Broadcasting System sought to attract no fewer than 1,000 independent radio stations across America. It needed 200 outlets to sustain it financially and targeted 350 as its initial goal. Programming, backers announced, would be offered 10 hours daily, including soap operas, Hollywood gossip, a homespun philosopher labeled Cottonseed Clark and name recognition vocalists of the caliber of Connie Haines and Mel Torme. Its unidentified instigators' dreams were little more than that, as it turned out. By February 1951 their new entry was off the ether, a victim of the medium's declining fortunes while several upstarts were desperately attempting to compete against transcontinental chains that had been lauded by loyal listeners for decades.

Radio AAHS

Operating from flagship station WWTC-AM in Minneapolis and run by the Children's Broadcasting Corporation, Radio AAHS (pronounced Oz) took to the airwaves in 1990. It was the first American network with programming pointed toward a crowd below age 12. At its peak, 1996, AAHS counted 29 member stations. The outfit changed its name to Intelefilm Corporation along the way, expanding its original premise to embrace printed works plus goods and services to digitize and manipulate video and audio files. The firm found advertisers a tough sell for its radio venture. "From Day One," wrote *Business Week* in 1998, AAHS "struggled to impress national ad buyers, who represent a huge chunk of the estimated $220 billion in purchases made and influenced by children." The news magazine also cited ratings: "Arbitron, the company whose listener logs are the lingua franca of radio ad-buying, does not track listeners under 12. Without hard numbers, AAHS sales reps had to resort to anecdotes and indirect audience measures, which weren't always persuasive in an industry obsessed with familiar, quantifiable measurements." Eventually the enterprise fell victim to Walt Disney Company's ABC Radio Networks, and especially its startup kids' chain, Radio Disney, which it battled for a long while. While admired by kids and parents alike, in 2002, AAHS filed for Chapter 11 bankruptcy and became a footnote in broadcast history.

RKO Radio Network

Established as a subsidiary of RKO General in the 1970s, the RKO Radio Network reportedly was the first aural chain beamed by satellite. Newscasts were fed on the hour and at 50 minutes past the hour to stations subscribing to the service. RKO provided sports, music and public affairs programming to its member clients, too. "RKO was very popular from the start, signing up hundreds of affiliates coast to coast," the Wikipedia Web site affirmed. It acknowledged that an advertising billing scandal involving RKO's TV outlets eventually led to the radio web's sale in 1985. A succession of owners operating under diverse monikers ran the radio business: United Stations (later known as Unistar), Infinity Broadcasting, Viacom, and Westwood One. In the years RKO owned it, one of its most imposing features was *America Overnight*.

Three hours of interviews with financial-advice authorities by Dallas radio personality Ed Busch was backed by three hours of celebrity interviews conducted by Los Angeles figure Bob Dearborn. Their extraordinarily popular effort debuted on September 1, 1981, three years after Mutual had turned nighttime coast-to-coast talk programming into a viable audio panorama with Larry King, just months before NBC and ABC did the same with their own personality-driven features.

Rural Radio Network

With headquarters in Ithaca, New York, the Rural Radio Network (RRN) was purportedly "the first all-radio, no-wireline network in the world." Going on the air June 6, 1948, and remaining through January 31, 1960, the chain consisted of six interconnected commercial FM stations in New York state. It was launched as an innovative broadcast service focused on the regional agricultural community. RRN grew out of an informal hookup in the 1940s of maybe 10 AM outlets that were fed a weekly five-minute program over leased telephone lines under auspices of the Ithaca-based Cooperative Grange League Federation Exchange. Competition from TV and a lack of affordable, well-performing FM receivers caused its original business plan to falter. The member-stations were acquired by new owners that altered the format in vain attempts to achieve profitability. When purchased by the Ivy Broadcast Company in 1960, it was renamed Ivy Broadcasting Network. In 1966, Chenango and Unadilla Communications bought it, the parent company then bought by Continental Telephone Company two years later. Through a corporate donation, the network was acquired by televangelist Pat Robertson's Christian Broadcasting Network in 1961. (*See entry for CBN Northeast.*) One of the nation's earliest FM webs was dissolved more than a decade later when Robertson sold the stations piecemeal to new owners.

Satellite Music Network

Satellite Music Network (SMN) was launched in 1981 at Mokena, Illinois, slightly southwest of Chicago. Operating under assorted music formats, SMN is believed to have been the first satellite-dispatched web providing five 24-hour days weekly focused on that genre. Offering affiliated stations major market artists that they might never have afforded, most of those outlets—frequently situated in small- to medium-sized markets—could operate almost unmanned, requiring little more than a computer and satellite hookup. Two-, three- or five-minute newscasts were slotted at the top of each hour with "holes" left open for local spots at other times. The programming was live and carefully avoided references to weather or anything of a provincial nature. When an 800 telephone number was added, disc jockeys took requests from listeners across America. As the 1980s progressed, SMN served 600-plus radio stations in the United States and the Caribbean. The network was absorbed by ABC Radio in late 1989, with its operations shifting to Dallas several years earlier.

Sheridan Broadcasting Network

Founded at Pittsburgh in 1972, the Sheridan Broadcasting Corporation, parent of the Sheridan Broadcasting Network (SBN), grew out of four radio stations owned by businessman-attorney-academician Ronald R. Davenport, Sr., and his wife, Judith. Programming and advertising was specifically designed to appeal to African American listeners. By 1976, the firm owned half the Mutual Black Network, buying the remainder in 1979. On March 1, 1992, a business journal announced the merger of dual black-oriented radio webs, NBN Broadcasting, Inc., and

SBN, to form American Urban Radio Networks. Davenport was named co-chairman in a venture that included a trio of added chains (STRZ Entertainment Network, SBN Sports Network, SPM Radio Network). *Black Enterprise* reported that "the new company could be the nation's largest media vehicle targeted to black consumers." Davenport stated that the joint venture "could reach approximately 90% of all African-Americans.... Clearly, we are stronger together than we are separately." The joint venture continues to prosper in the modern age, boasting several hundred affiliated stations with a diversity of formats.

Sports Fan Radio Network

The Sports Fan Radio Network (SFRN), the Internet's initial sports talk chain, premiered August 27, 1996. From its operations base at Fort Lauderdale, Florida, the web dispatched 70 hours of programming monthly. *The Drive*, its first and possibly foremost show, hosted by ex-collegiate kicker Scott Kaplan, focused on outrageous situations on and off the field, mixing athletics and amusement. Joining Kaplan were Tom Alexander, Sid Rosenberg and Allyson Turner. Other personalities in SFRN's purview were Nanci Donellan, Scott Ferrall, J. T. the Brick, Bill Lekas, Keith Olbermann, Chris Russo and Tim Ryan. The web ran into trouble against upstart Fox Sports Radio with the fat wallet of Clear Channel Communications behind it. Unable to contend profitably against ESPN, Fox and One on One Sports, SFRN unraveled. It folded in May 2001 and Fox absorbed most of its affiliates.

The Source Radio Network

Excelsior Radio Networks and *Source* magazine launched The Source Radio Network (TSRN) on July 1, 2002. Produced in New York, the syndicated service supplied fare to U.S. hip-hop radio stations. Among its offerings was a Sunday three-hour music-and-interview feature, *The Source Street Beat*. Principals included disc jockey Jeff 2X, David Mays and Ray Scott. On a weekday hip-hop prep show, *The Daily Dose*, listeners were treated with "up-to-the-minute text and audio content along with special event coverage, hip-hop radio satellite tours and a wide variety of daily features, interviews and reports from the world of hip hop." Founded in 1988, Excelsior produced and distributed music programming in a variety of formats to more than 2,000 American radio outlets, and diversified into print, video and Internet services.

Transtar Radio Network

Begun by C. Terry Robinson in 1981, Transtar Radio Network (TRN) was reportedly "the first radio network to provide 24-hour music programming to local affiliates." Its history was subsequently entwined with United Stations Radio Network (USRN) with origins also dating to 1981. The latter purchased the RKO Radio Network in 1985, and two years afterward USRN entered an advertising sales and marketing agreement with Transtar. "This alliance worked so well," claimed one wag, "that in 1989 the two companies merged." The successor firm was branded Unistar Communications with USRN's chief operating officer Nick Verbitsky staying on as CEO. Unistar was absorbed into Westwood One in 1993.

Unforgettable Favorites

Taking the "radio network" concept to another dimension, ABC Radio Networks introduced a satellite-distributed format to subscribing stations in 1998 that was branded both as

Unforgettable Favorites (UF) and Memories. Many stations received the feeds with a musical playlist comprised of soft oldies and adult contemporary standards. Artists like The Beach Boys, The Beatles, The Bee Gees, The Carpenters, Neil Diamond, Linda Ronstadt, Carly Simon and James Taylor were regularly featured. When some outlets replaced that targeted audience with others as the 2000s wore on, some of UF's luster tarnished. Feeling the pinch, ABC decided to discontinue that model. In summer 2006, UF was folded into an adult standards layout, Timeless Classics (which originated as Stardust in 1981). The new effort was identified on-air as Timeless Favorites but was reduced to Timeless in 2007 as Citadel Broadcasting acquired the ABC Radio operations. A diversionary satellite web in the meantime, The Christmas Channel, operating seasonally, included Christmas tunes under the branding Unforgettable Favorites following these changes.

United Independent Broadcasters, Inc.

The forerunner of the Columbia Broadcasting System, United Independent Broadcasters, Inc., was established January 21, 1927, although no programming aired until September 18, 1927. The web was launched by George A. Coats, Betty Fleischmann Holmes, Arthur Judson and James Andrew White. With 16 stations plagued by persistent financial crises, the fledgling operation was rescued by the Columbia Phonograph Company on April 5, 1927, thereby altering the moniker to Columbia Phonograph Broadcasting System, Inc. The net was renamed Columbia Broadcasting System on November 19, 1927. Control shifted to the new majority shareholding Paley family on September 25, 1928.

United Press International Network

The first wire service to initiate its own radio news web, Washington, D.C.–based United Press International (UPI)—formed when United Press and International News Service merged May 24, 1958—is dated from later that same year. By the early 1960s, UPI began offering a four and a half minute newscast at the top of the hour. Instead of paying local affiliates to air its programming as most commercial chains were doing, it charged the outlets that put its features on the ether. In doing so, UPI allowed them to sell up to 90 seconds of local, spot and national commercial time within its newscasts. Associated Press, which launched its own radio network in the 1970s, follows that model today. Among UPI's familiar voices were Eric Sevareid, David Brinkley and Walter Cronkite. UPI's competitive audio venture lasted from 1958 to 1999.

United Stations Radio Network

In 1981, American pop icon Dick Clark and businessman Nick Verbitsky pooled their resources to inaugurate the United Stations Radio Network (USRN) with Verbitsky as chief operations officer. Their first series, *Dick Clark's Rock, Roll & Remember*, still on the air in many markets today, became a quick sensation that helped boost subsequent efforts. In 1985, the chain bought the RKO Radio Network. In 1987, it entered an advertising sales and marketing pact with Transtar Radio Network. That arrangement worked productively for both companies and—in 1989—the two merged, taking the appellation Unistar Communications. Nick Verbitsky continued as CEO until Unistar was absorbed into Westwood One Radio Network in 1993. After the demise of the original web, Clark and Verbitsky decided to do it all over again. In 1994, they formed United Stations Radio Networks and bought a radio comedy services firm with five on-air entities, DB Communications. They were back in business later that year and today offer dozens of programming services reaching more than 5,000 radio stations.

Washington News Desk

Washington News Desk offered a five-minute newscast at the top of the hour to stations subscribing to its service. Appearing in the 1990s, the startup was short-lived.

Yankee Network

Launched April 12, 1930, and serving mostly New England markets, the Yankee Network was linked with a sister chain, the Colonial Network, which debuted August 5, 1936, and served the same territory and ownership. The dual chains mostly shared the same affiliates. Colonial was created to make full use of a 16-hour telephone circuit. The Yankee Network had contracted for the line but needed it only part of the time. As Colonial began, the two webs became the New England conduit for programs of the Mutual Broadcasting System in addition to those of their own webs. Yankee and Colonial became a joint MBS stockholder in 1940. In January 1943, the Colonial and Yankee networks were absorbed by the General Tire & Rubber Company of Akron, Ohio. The acquisitions were part of progressive steps by General to control an influential segment of American broadcasting. General divested its radio properties in July 1957, although the Yankee Network persisted under that name, operated by a succession of owners, until 1967. (*Related entry appears under Colonial Network.*)

Z-Rock Radio Network

Continuing a diversification binge begun in 1968 that had proven enormously profitable, ABC Radio introduced a nationally syndicated 24-hour network based in Dallas, Texas, on September 1, 1986, known as Z-Rock (Z-R). The web was selected by *Billboard* magazine for its annual awards in March 1990, "the only fulltime hard rock/metal programming ever nominated." After a decade of embracing this music, ABC discontinued the chain on December 31, 1996. Bits and pieces of Z-R remain, however. A handful of former affiliates continued to apply the identifying terminology, while there are still connections to it at this writing via the Internet.

Chapter Notes

Chapter 1

1. U.S. Communications Act of 1934, sec. 3(p).
2. *Report on Chain Broadcasting*, Federal Communications Commission, May 1941, Introduction C.
3. Francis Chase, Jr., *Sound and Fury: An Informal History of Broadcasting.* New York: Harper and Brothers, 1942, p. 38.
4. Federal Communications Commission, *Report on Social and Economic Data Pursuant to the Informal Hearing on Broadcasting*, October 5, 1936, Sec. IV (A) (b) (1).
5. Ibid.
6. WEAF, WJZ and WABC bore new designations down the road, some of them encountering successive branding or call letters. This will be detailed in subsequent chapters.
7. Chase, p. 28.
8. Hadley Cantril and Gordon W. Allport, *The Psychology of Radio*. New York: Harper and Brothers, 1935, p. 99.
9. Gerald Nachman, *Raised on Radio: In Quest of The Lone Ranger, Jack Benny, Amos 'n' Andy, The Shadow, Mary Noble, The Great Gildersleeve, Fibber McGee and Molly, Bill Stern, Our Miss Brooks, Henry Aldrich, The Quiz Kids, Mr. First Nighter, Fred Allen, Vic and Sade, The Cisco Kid, Jack Armstrong, Arthur Godfrey, Bob and Ray, The Barbour Family, Henry Morgan, Joe Friday, and Other Lost Heroes from Radio's Heyday.* New York: Pantheon Books, 1998, p. 18; Charles A. Siepmann, *Radio's Second Chance.* Boston: Little, Brown and Co., 1946, pp. 82–83.
10. *Supplementary Report as to Social and Economic Aspects of Allocation Hearings to the Federal Communications Commission*, Sec. II (A), Table II, July 1, 1937.
11. Ibid., Sec. II (C), Table VII.
12. Ibid., Sec. II (C), Table VIII.
13. Adapted from Ibid., Sec. II (C).
14. Chase, p. 40.
15. *Supplementary Report as to Social and Economic Aspects of Allocation Hearings to the Federal Communications Commission*, Sec. II (C), Table IV, July 1, 1937.
16. J. Fred MacDonald, *Don't Touch That Dial! Radio Programming in American Life, 1920–1960.* Chicago: Nelson-Hall, 1991, pp. 37–38.

Chapter 2

1. Francis Chase, Jr., *Sound and Fury: An Informal History of Broadcasting.* New York: Harper, 1942, p. 27.
2. General Electric Company formally organized in 1892 when two earlier competitors combined. In 1919, GE purchased U.S. citizens' stock in the American Marconi Company, giving GE control of most of the country's ship-to-shore and international radio stations, plus rights under existing Marconi pacts with ship operators. GE launched the Radio Corporation of America in October 1919 to run its stations, preferring to concentrate GE energies on manufacturing.
3. Among the early subscribers of independent stations, several of which eventually joined hookups, were metropolitan dailies like *The Atlanta Journal, The Chicago Daily News, The Chicago Tribune, The Dallas News, The Kansas City Star* and *The Louisville Courier-Journal*, along with a handful of major retail emporiums like L. Bamberger and Company, Gimbel Brothers, Shepard Stores and Wanamaker's.
4. Chase, p. 24.
5. Prior to RCA's involvement with WJZ, that was the second station underwritten by Westinghouse following three months of successfully operating KDKA in Pittsburgh. WJZ and WHN in New York shared time on one wavelength frequency, each broadcasting at different hours.
6. The call letters for WEAF originally assigned were WDAM but Western Electric objected, suggesting WECO. At the time the U.S. Department of Commerce wouldn't allow customized call signs and leased the next call letters then available in alphabetical sequence. They turned out to be WEAF, which wasn't identified with its sponsors until it became synonymous to local listeners.
7. This author explores a handful of precursors to WEAF's radio commercial in *Sold on Radio: Advertisers in the Golden Age of Broadcasting.* Jefferson, N.C.: McFarland, 2008, pp. 19–20.
8. Portions combined from dual sources: Gleason L. Archer, *History of Radio to 1926.* New York: American Historical Society, 1938, pp. 397–398; Bob Schulberg, *Radio Advertising: The Authoritative Handbook.* Lincolnwood, Ill.: NTC Business Books, 1989, p. 16.
9. The precise fee is in question; at least one respected source intimates that the commercial time was sold for $100 but doesn't specify if that covered a single or multiple broadcasts. The figures used are provided by Erik Barnouw, widely considered to be one of the media's most knowledgeable, meticulous and reputable investigators.
10. An "indirect" approach to early radio advertising often consisted of applying no more than a firm's name or one of its products' brand names to identify a series and its performers without more pointed commercial pitches. Thus, in that era, listeners were accustomed to hearing the A&P Gypsies, the Armour Star Jesters, the Crazy Water Crystals, the Interwoven Pair, the Lucky Strike Dance Orchestra, etc., without accompanying commercial messages.
11. For a comprehensive diagram of the patents and a detailed description of what they involved and who participated, see Christopher H. Sterling and John M. Kittross, *Stay Tuned: A Concise History of American Broadcasting.* Second Ed. Belmont, Calif.: Wadsworth, 1990, pp. 53–58.
12. Chase, p. 37.
13. Adapted from Sterling and Kittross, p. 67.

14. Ibid.

15. While that occasion signaled what is broadly touted as "the birth of radio," there were numerous antecedent test models, principally cited as experimental stations, often of shortwave genus.

16. The call letters for WCAP were derived from the Chesapeake and Potomac Telephone Company division of AT&T.

17. One source projects the radio audience for the inauguration at 15 million. While there were no reliable measurement systems in place to substantiate the numbers, bearing in mind that two experimental webs aired the occasion carried on 25 to 30 stations, higher figures appear plausible.

18. U.S. population figure from *Information Please* for 1925.

19. Costly expense of line usage to the West Coast limited permanent service past Kansas City at that time.

20. Gleason Leonard Archer, *History of Radio to 1926*. New York: American Historical Society, 1938, p. 361. The 13-station hookup included: WEAF, New York; WCAP, Washington; WWJ, Detroit; WJAR, Providence; WEEI, Boston; WCAE, Pittsburgh; WSAI, Cincinnati; WOC, Davenport; WCCO, Minneapolis; WGR, Buffalo; WOO, Philadelphia; KSD, St. Louis; and WTAC, Worcester.

21. Gleason Leonard Archer, *Big Business and Radio*. New York: American Historical Company, 1939, p. 246.

22. Jim Cox, *Sold on Radio: Advertising in the Golden Age of Broadcasting*. Jefferson, N.C.: McFarland, 2008, p. 25.

23. A third process considered was to establish a handful of "superpower" outlets (a series of "mini webs") operating with 50,000-watt transmitters, beaming their programming to more distant listeners. While this plan would have helped some, it didn't exceed the reliability and flexibility of local stations coupled with insulated telephone wiring. The latter offered unequaled quality that was suitable for transporting the human voice through the ether as well as other essential sounds.

24. Sterling and Kittross, p. 68.

25. Adapted from Sterling and Kittross, p. 68.

26. AT&T's Washington, D.C., outlet, WCAP, was removed from the air. WCAP and WRC (the latter owned by RCA) had shared a wavelength band. With the dissolution of WCAP, its time and programming shifted to WRC.

27. GE and Westinghouse would sell their shares in the enterprise to RCA in 1930. In a rather bizarre turn of events, GE would buy ex-partner RCA in 1986 (founded by GE in 1919). With that latter transaction also came the National Broadcasting Company, an outgrowth of their mutual dealings six decades earlier.

28. *The Oakland Tribune*, September 13, 1926.

29. Alfred Balk, *The Rise of Radio: From Marconi Through the Golden Age*. Jefferson, N.C.: McFarland, 2006, p. 74. Balk observes that RCA agreed to compensate AT&T for the use of its wires during the following decade at a rate in excess of $1 million annually.

30. Chase, pp. 35–36.

31. Erik Barnouw, *A Tower in Babel: A History of Broadcasting in the United States; Volume I, to 1933*. New York: Oxford University Press, 1966, p. 204.

32. "Four Years of Network Broadcasting," a report by a National Advisory Council on Radio in Education and the American Political Science Association panel, in *Radio and Education*, 1936.

Chapter 3

1. In 1984, acting on a federal order, AT&T divided into eight companies and until 1996 majored in integrated telecommunications equipment and services. It has since concentrated on global networking, IP solutions for business and government clients, and traditional service alternatives for consumers and small enterprises.

2. On January 1, 1984, newly named AT&T Technologies, Inc., assumed Western Electric's corporate charter and assigned its work into multiple sectors. WE as an identifying soubriquet ended in 1995 when AT&T Technologies changed its name to Lucent Technologies; that firm then spun off to a handful of competitive enterprises the following year.

3. WEAF became the flagship station of the NBC Red chain. After the NBC Blue chain was cut from the web in the early 1940s, WEAF (then identified as WNBC) was the flagship outlet of the National Broadcasting Company.

4. Some might say that was NBC's sole intent, yet both chains were formidable—and at times, contentious—opponents.

5. Erik Barnouw, *A Tower in Babel: A History of Broadcasting in the United States; Volume I, to 1933*. New York: Oxford University Press, 1966, p. 189.

6. Christopher H. Sterling and John M. Kittross, *Stay Tuned: A Concise History of American Broadcasting*. 2nd ed. Belmont, Calif.: Wadsworth Publishing, 1990, p. 105. According to these authors, AT&T launched the Broadcasting Company of America to (a) hassle the Radio Group into conceding more to AT&T on non-broadcast issues and (b) pave the way for the anticipated buyout by RCA of AT&T stations.

7. American Marconi, formed in 1902, was an ancillary of Marconi's Wireless Telegraph Company, Ltd. (widely known as "British Marconi") with roots in the Wireless Telegraph and Signal Company begun in 1897 by Italian inventor Guglielmo Marconi (1864–1937). His successful 1895 tests sending dot-and-dash signals through the ether led to a 1900 patent for "tuned or syntonic telegraphy" and the first wireless transatlantic communications in 1901. By 1914, American Marconi controlled 90 percent of U.S. ship-to-shore commercial dispatches. Marconi's lab experiments had awesome effects in proving later theories about transmissions over long distances while his telegraph system played a role among pioneer hookups that preceded the founding of NBC. After World War I, Owen D. Young persuaded GE directors to buy controlling interest in American Marconi. On the day of RCA's creation in October 1919, GE and RCA signed a cross-licensing pact permitting reciprocal use of each other's radio patents. The next month GE shifted American Marconi's corporate resources to RCA, and the U.S. Navy turned over to RCA the American Marconi stations it held.

8. Ben Gross, "Men, Mikes, and Money." *Collier's*, April 17, 1948.

9. Virtually every network feature was aired live until crooner Bing Crosby broke the sound barrier, finding a sponsor (Philco Radio Corporation) and a chain (ABC) that let him prerecord his weekly show. When he did that starting October 16, 1946, many other stars jumped on the bandwagon, obliterating one of web radio's policies heretofore set in stone.

10. For information on when *The Jack Benny Show*, *The Bob Hope Show*, and *Information, Please!* originated on NBC Blue, consult Jerry Haendiges, "Vintage Radio Logs," http://otrsite.com/radiolog/index.html. Informa-

tion confirming this, and adding *Fibber McGee and Molly*: Ron Lackmann, *Same Time, Same Station: An A–Z Guide to Radio from Jack Benny to Howard Stern* (New York: Facts on File, 1996).

11. NBC History Files, Folder 998, Library of Congress. http://lcweb2.loc.gov/cgi-bin/faidfrquery/F?faidfr: 2:./temp/~faid_wzkO::.

12. Ibid., Folder 784.

13. Ibid., Folder 299.

14. Ibid., Folder 431.

15. *Report on Chain Broadcasting*, Federal Communications Commission, May 1941, Sec. VI C.

16. Ibid.

17. Bill Jaker, Frank Sulek, and Peter Kanze. *The Airwaves of New York: Illustrated Histories of 156 AM Stations in the Metropolitan Area, 1921–1996*. Jefferson, N.C.: McFarland, 1998, p. 10.

18. Obviously then the G-E-C notes could not possibly have stood for General Electric Company (which currently owns NBC-TV), as some observers have erroneously reported.

19. A variant sequence, G-E-C-G, known as "the fourth chime," was applied during World War II and in disasters to note the special significance of related announcements.

20. The Red and Blue chains maintained affiliations with numerous independently owned stations, some signing with one of the two networks and some joining either web for individual broadcasts based on the specific requirements of advertisers, network or station.

21. Increasing control that CBS and NBC exerted over affiliates led to scrutiny by the Federal Communications Commission (FCC) in the late 1930s. It was discovered that broadcasting was centrally dominated by the webs, resulting in government intervention. Under Congressional pressure, in March 1938 the FCC began to look into "all phases of chain broadcasting" as well as "the broadcasting industry generally" to determine if rules were needed to control the chains' overbearing style. Out of these findings, released in May 1941, new policies clamped down on the monopolistic tendencies of the two major webs.

22. The exceptions were Chicago's WGN and New York's WOR, which together owned the MBS.

23. *Report on Chain Broadcasting*, Federal Communications Commission, May 1941, Sec. VI A 1.

24. Ibid., Sec. VI, A 3.

25. CBS offered a similar plan to its outlets also in 1936, while MBS continued to write pacts that bound stations and network for one year only.

26. Ibid., Sec. II B 4.

27. *Report on Chain Broadcasting*, Federal Communications Commission, May 1941, Sec. II B 3.

28. *Report of Federal Trade Commission on the Radio Industry*, 67th Congress, 4th session, 1923, p. 37.

29. RCA Annual Report, 1924, p. 14.

30. *Radio Broadcast*, June 1929, p. 78.

31. RCA Victor Company, Inc., was designated to assume the assets and business of the Victor Talking Machine Company with respect to phonographs and records and manufacturing and sales rights of RCA's radio apparatus. On January 1, 1932, RCA transferred its RCA Photophone, Inc., to RCA Victor Company, Inc. In January 1935, RCA Radiotron Company, Inc., and RCA Victor Company, Inc., merged into RCA Manufacturing Company, Inc. By the 1940s, that subsidiary not only made radio receivers, transmitters, tubes, phonographs and records but also transcriptions, sound equipment for motion picture studios and theaters, public address systems, motion picture and radio equipment for amateurs, electron microscopes, electronic pianos, TV transmitters and receiving sets, radio compasses, communications equipment and copious other commodities, underscoring its powerful influence in multifarious commerce.

32. Erik Barnouw, *A Tower in Babel: A History of Broadcasting in the United States; Volume I, to 1933*. New York: Oxford University Press, 1966, p. 208.

33. John Dunning, *On the Air: The Encyclopedia of Old-Time Radio*. New York: Oxford University Press, 1998, p. 32.

34. Erik Barnouw observed in *The Golden Web: A History of Broadcasting in the United States; Volume II, 1933 to 1953*. New York: Oxford University Press, 1968, p. 187: "During 1942–43 NBC-red and NBC-blue divided up stations, transmitters, studios, control equipment, microphones, sound effects, desks, chairs, wastebaskets, filing cabinets, and staff members."

35. This chronicle continues in greater depth in Chapter 6.

36. Noble wanted a more commanding name for his network than *Blue* and acquired rights to *American Broadcasting Company* from broadcaster George Storer in 1944.

37. Alfred Balk, *The Rise of Radio: From Marconi through the Golden Age*. Jefferson, N.C.: McFarland, 2006, p. 258.

38. Barnouw, *The Golden Web*, p. 70.

39. Paley's considerable efforts in this field are explored in Chapter 4.

40. *The Washington Post*, March 18, 2002.

41. *The New York Times*, March 18, 2002.

42. *The Washington Post*, March 18, 2002.

43. While at NBC, Weaver collected two Emmy medals and a Peabody Award, was inducted into the Television Academy of Arts and Sciences' Hall of Fame, and earned many other distinguished honors.

44. Adapted from Erik Barnouw, *The Image Empire: A History of Broadcasting in the United States from 1953*. New York: Oxford University Press, 1970, p. 61.

45. *The New York Times*, December 9, 1955, p. 55.

46. *Variety*, December 19, 1948; *Time*, February 21, 1949.

47. Sally Bedell Smith, *In All His Glory: The Life of William S. Paley, the Legendary Tycoon and His Brilliant Circle*. New York: Simon and Schuster, 1990, p. 266.

48. Jim Cox, *Say Goodnight, Gracie: The Last Years of Network Radio*. Jefferson, N.C.: McFarland, 2002, p. 24.

49. Ibid.

50. Ibid.

51. Dunning, *On the Air*, p. 86.

52. *Variety*, February 12, 1958, p. 49.

53. www.oldradio.com/archives/prog/nbc.htm.

54. On December 5, 1982, Bruce Williams attempted to land an aircraft at Princeton, New Jersey and crashed. He was critically injured and rendered almost clinically dead by the time he arrived at Princeton's Medical Center. A week later he was on the air from his hospital room, broadcasting his show for a week from there before his release. Afterwards, for three months his program originated from his home.

55. Kevin L. Goldman, "Radio's Latest Boom: Late-Night Talk Shows." *The New York Times*, May 2, 1982.

56. Ibid.

57. Sterling and Kittross, p. 474.

58. www.solarnavigator.net/music/RCA.htm.

59. RCA suffered further indignity when a French firm

purchased its consumer electronics division. Only Zenith among large American competitors continued making TV receivers in the U.S. then.

60. As TV developed around the country, financing for television often came from the income of radio, confirmed Jaker, Sulek and Kanze in *The Airwaves of New York*, p. 15.

61. Some historians place the sale of MBS as high as $39 million. The $30 million figure was reported by *The New York Times* on July 21, 1987.

62. The flagship station changed call letters from WEAF to WNBC in 1946, became WRCA in 1954 and returned to WNBC in 1960.

63. *The New York Times* of October 8, 1988, reported that the closing tribute airing at noon the previous day was 90 minutes in duration, not 66. The 66 may have been a misplaced reference to WNBC's 660 spot on the radio dial.

64. Jaker, Sulek and Kanze, pp. 133–134.

65. *The New York Times*, October 8, 1988, p. 32.

66. www.oldradio.com/archives/prog/nbc.htm.

Chapter 4

1. Erik Barnouw, *A History of Broadcasting in the United States; Volume I, to 1933*. New York: Oxford University Press, 1966, p. 193.

2. WOR opened studios and offices near Times Square at 1440 Broadway in 1926 although it persisted in identifying itself as emanating from Newark, New Jersey, where it originated. It eventually maintained a recording device that repetitiously acknowledged "WOR, Newark."

3. In spelling out more about the formation of United Independent Broadcasters Association, on June 23, 1927, *The New York Times* reported: "A figure of $5,000 an hour has been mentioned as the rate for advertising. The rate for the Red Network of the National Broadcasting Company, which includes about twenty-five stations, is $5,000. The rate for WEAF, when used with the associated stations, is $480 an hour, otherwise $600 an hour, according to a representative of the National Broadcasting Company." While this might have been big news in that embryonic period, nothing like it would appear in a major daily journal now except under rare circumstances. Of course, there would be many more contingencies in setting current rates, too.

4. Be aware that, in early 1929, RCA and Victor did fuse their respective efforts in much the same way that CBS's predecessor and Columbia blazed a trail. Getting enough cash to remain in business was CBS's principal objective, while RCA was acquiring a unit to grow more business.

5. Jim Cox, *This Day in Network Radio: A Daily Calendar of Births, Deaths, Debuts, Cancellations and Other Events in Broadcasting History*. Jefferson, N.C.: McFarland, 2009.

6. Barnouw, 1966, p. 224.

7. Jim Cox, *The Great Radio Sitcoms*. Jefferson, N.C.: McFarland, 2007, p. 39; adapted from Judith C. Waller, *Radio: The Fifth Estate*. New York: Houghton Mifflin, 1946, pp. 18–19.

8. Gleason L. Archer, *Big Business and Radio*. New York: American Historical Company, 1939, pp. 314–315.

9. On January 3, 1929, the sales company (Columbia Phonograph Broadcasting System, Inc.) was dissolved and United absorbed its activities.

10. Alfred Balk, *The Rise of Radio: From Marconi through the Golden Age*. Jefferson, N.C.: McFarland, 2006, p. 82.

11. In 1927, while his father Samuel Paley and uncle Jay Paley were in Europe, Bill Paley bought a one-hour program to advertise La Palina cigars on Philadelphia's WCAU. At $50 per broadcast, on his return and discovery of what his nephew had done, Jay Paley put a stop to that "foolishness." A few weeks later, Samuel Paley realized that the market was sending him a message: "Hundreds of thousands of dollars we've been spending on newspapers and magazines and no one has ever said anything ... but now people are asking me, 'What happened to the *La Palina Hour*?'"

12. The WABC call letters were originally applied to an Asheville, North Carolina, station owned by Asheville Battery Company. In the meantime, broadcaster A. H. Grebe of New York City had been operating WAHG in the Big Apple, the call letters for his Atlantic Broadcasting Company. He was able to negotiate a deal with the Asheville firm to acquire WABC for his enterprise and opened studios in a 17th floor penthouse apartment in Steinway Hall at 113 West 57th Street. Grebe went on the air as WABC on December 17, 1926.

13. Bill Jaker, Frank Sulek, and Peter Kanze. *The Airwaves of New York: Illustrated Histories of 156 AM Stations in the Metropolitan Area, 1921–1996*. Jefferson, N.C.: McFarland, 1998, p. 27.

14. *Report on Chain Broadcasting*, Federal Communications Commission, May 1941, VII A 1.

15. Ibid.

16. Leonard Maltin, *The Great American Broadcast: A Celebration of Radio's Golden Age*. New York: Penguin Putnam, 1997, p. 20.

17. The arrangement with Don Lee extended through December 1936. At that time, five stations then owned by McClatchy newspaper interests left Don Lee to join NBC and California Radio. CBS terminated its affiliation with Don Lee and established its own operations on the Pacific coast, directly taking over contracts with four stations previously linked with Don Lee (KOIN, KOL, KVI, KFPY). Don Lee became a "participating member" of MBS and transmitted MBS programs to its outlets at that juncture.

18. Balk, pp. 83–84.

19. Balk, pp. 85–86.

20. *Report of the Federal Radio Commission in Reply to Senate Resolution 129*, January 7, 1932.

21. *Report on Chain Broadcasting*, Federal Communications Commission, May 1941, III C.

22. Ibid., III D.

23. Peter Baida, "A Legendary Chairman." *American Heritage Magazine*, July–August 1987.

24. Harry Lillis (Bing) Crosby was born May 3, 1903, at Tacoma, Washington. He died at 74 in Madrid, Spain, on October 14, 1977.

25. Jim Cox, *Music Radio: The Great Performers and Programs of the 1920s through Early 1960s*. Jefferson, N.C.: McFarland, 2005, p. 56.

26. "The Songbird of the South," Kate Smith, was introduced to British monarchs in 1939 by U.S. President Franklin D. Roosevelt as "*This* is Kate Smith—*This* is America!" Her rendition of Irving Berlin's epic "God Bless America" premiering on her CBS *Kate Smith Hour* November 10, 1938, painted her as a kind of patriotic national symbol. As she sang it across subsequent decades, it caused hair to rise, spines to tingle, and standing ovations to occur. While she would make more than 3,000

recordings, that one became her signature oeuvre. Born in Washington, D.C., on May 1, 1907, Kathryn Elizabeth Smith was noticed by an enterprising Columbia Phonograph Company agent, Joseph Martin (Ted) Collins, when he caught her 1930 show at New York's Apollo Theater. Gaining her trust, he became her lifelong business partner (a multimillion-dollar pledge made by a simple handshake). His collegial liaison with CBS led Collins to book her there in the 1930–1931 radio season as featured artist on a weekly quarter-hour, *Freddy Rich's Rhythm Kings*. It was Kate Smith's initial continuing transcontinental gig. While she sang on NBC briefly in 1931 and an array of aural webs from 1947 to 1959, CBS Radio had a virtual lock on her services from 1930 to 1947. It was a period in which Smith was almost never off the air, often appearing concurrently on weekday matinee and weekly primetime shows. Smith performed regularly on lots of television, too, before her death at 79 on June 17, 1986 in Raleigh, North Carolina. (Data adapted from this author's *Music Radio*, pp. 245–260.)

27. Born at Wallingford, Connecticut, on November 14, 1901, Downey sang Irish ballads at amusement parks, Elks Club gatherings and church socials during adolescence before performing while crossing the Atlantic more than 20 times. Singing on board cruise ships in the 1920s, he was backed by impresario Paul Whiteman's entourage, possibly becoming the first vocalist to collect comparable billing with a band. Premiering on radio over WEAF in 1927 followed by stints on London's BBC in 1928, Downey became an American legend thanks to CBS. He headlined his own quarter-hour show four times weekly from New York's Delmonico Club in 1930–1931, generating 10,000 fan letters per week. That catapulted him into featured vocalist on CBS's *The Camel Quarter-Hour* the next season. With recognition as "Radio Singer of the Year" in 1932, Downey left CBS for NBC, returning a year later. A checkered schedule carried him back and forth between the two predominant webs, adding MBS in the late 1940s, finishing his radio career as star of *The Coke Club* on CBS (1950–1951). Paid $4,500 per show by then, Downey was also a director of the firm sponsoring him. Popularly dubbed "The Irish Troubadour" and "The Irish Nightingale," he died at 83 at Palm Beach, Florida, on October 25, 1985. (Data adapted from this author's *Music Radio*, pp. 283–284.)

28. While Art Linkletter devoted most of his air time to the daily *Art Linkletter's House Party* on CBS Radio in 1945–1948 and 1950–1957 and on CBS-TV in 1952–1968, the weekly *People Are Funny* he hosted ran on NBC Radio from 1943 to 1951 and 1954 to 1960, and on NBC-TV from 1954 to 1961.

29. Godfrey was born in New York City on August 31, 1903, and died there on March 16, 1983. A comprehensive overview of his life is in this author's *The Great Radio Audience Participation Shows* (McFarland, 2001), pp. 19–32.

30. Arthur J. Singer, *Arthur Godfrey: The Adventures of an American Broadcaster*. Jefferson, N.C.: McFarland, 2000, p. 3.

31. Sally Bedell Smith, pp. 260, 270.

32. One of the most genuinely amusing, yet presumably authentic, accounts of that night that subsequently appeared in print is reported in comic Steve Allen's *Bigger Than a Breadbox* (New York: Doubleday, 1967), pp. 20–32. Allen describes what happened in *his* family that night which might be typical of the kinds of reactions playing out in thousands of other American domiciles.

33. There is a fuller account in this author's *Say Good-night, Gracie: The Last Year of Network Radio* (Jefferson, N.C.: McFarland, 2002), pp. 6–9.

34. Rita Morley Harvey, *Those Wonderful, Terrible Years: George Heller and the American Federation of Television and Radio Artists*. Carbondale, Ill.: Southern Illinois University Press, 1996, p. 98.

35. Sally Bedell Smith, p. 306.

36. That series had originated as *Hear It Now* on CBS Radio on December 15, 1950. Its acclaim there made it a natural for transfer to video as that medium overtook radio.

37. Ibid., p. 307.

38. The 11 members of that esteemed aggregate were Mary Marvin Breckinridge (the only woman), Cecil Brown, Winston Burdett, Charles Collingwood, William Downs, Thomas Grandin, Richard C. Hottelet, Larry LeSueur, Eric Sevareid, William L. Shirer and Howard K. Smith.

39. To be accurate, CBS news editor Paul White organized the Columbia News Service in 1933, the first of the national webs to maintain a news operation. With bureaus in New York, Washington, Chicago and Los Angeles, it also relied on reporters of many of the country's metropolitan dailies as stringers. But the "personality" in electronic news didn't exist until Murrow came aboard. He was born April 25, 1908, at Pole Cat Creek, North Carolina, and died April 27, 1965, at Pawling, New York. A sweeping assessment of his extensive professional contributions appears in this author's text *Radio Speakers: Narrators, News Junkies, Sports Jockeys, Tattletales, Tipsters, Toastmasters and Coffee Klatch Couples Who Verbalized the Jargon of the Aural Ether from the 1920s to the 1980s—A Biographical Dictionary* (Jefferson, N.C.: McFarland, 2007), pp. 202–206.

40. Despite the good years, Paley and Murrow would eventually separate—Murrow disenchanted with his beloved CBS and its executive leader. It was a pattern reproduced many times as Paley turned on seemingly loyal associates in management capacities and booted them out, including a succession of presidents, plus his most enduring confidante-strategist Frank Stanton. More on Stanton and that scenario appears elsewhere. In 1961, Murrow was invited by president-elect John F. Kennedy to run the U.S. Information Agency in Washington, D.C., and accepted. It was a colossal failure for CBS, where he had staked his career and worn the unmitigated leadership mantle in broadcast news.

41. Stanley Cloud and Lynne Olson, *The Murrow Boys: Pioneers on the Front Lines of Broadcast Journalism*. Boston: Houghton Mifflin, 1996, p. 260.

42. Ibid.

43. Edison Records had marketed a microgroove vertically recorded disc with 20 minutes' playing time per side in the 1920s but they were a commercial failure.

44. *The Great Radio Sitcoms*, pp. 165–166.

45. Smith, pp. 290–291.

46. Ibid., p. 268.

47. Ibid., pp. 268–269.

48. *Business Week*, July 21, 1951.

49. Smith, p. 269.

50. Ibid.

51. Eugene Lyons, *David Sarnoff: A Biography*. New York: Harper and Row, 1966, p. 275.

52. Smith, p. 269.

53. Lyons, p. 277.

54. Smith, p. 281.

55. Until the early 1930s, the networks supplied almost everything heard on the air. Afterward, until the

late 1940s, the webs relinquished much of that investment to ad agencies.

56. Peter Baida, "A Legendary Chairman." *American Heritage Magazine*, July–August 1987.

57. Ibid.

58. Raymond William Stedman, *The Serials: Suspense and Drama by Installment*. Norman, Okla.: University of Oklahoma Press, 1971, p. 393.

59. *Gunsmoke* breathed its last as an aural mainstay on June 18, 1961. Bing Crosby and Rosemary Clooney prevailed to September 28, 1962. *Suspense* left the air on November 27, 1960, only to return on June 25, 1961, surviving alongside *Yours Truly, Johnny Dollar* to September 30, 1962. Art Linkletter's *House Party* bit the dust on October 13, 1967. *Arthur Godfrey Time* persisted to April 30, 1972. Lowell Thomas said his last "so-long" on May 14, 1976.

60. This transitional period is detailed in Chapter 13.

61. Perhaps ironically, both stations (WINS, WCBS-AM) would find themselves under the same corporate umbrella three decades later, and both would still be competing fiercely with all-new formats in the same metropolitan market.

62. Himan Brown was born in New York City on July 21, 1910. He was still living in July 2008, having turned 98. E. G. Marshall (nee Everett Eugene Grunz) was born June 18, 1914, at Owatonna, Minnesota. He died August 24, 1998, at Bedford, New York.

63. Elliott Lewis was born in New York City November 28, 1917, and died at Gleneden Beach, California, on May 20, 1990.

64. In a compelling sidebar, Charles T. Ireland, Jr., gave up his job as senior VP of International Telephone and Telegraph Corporation to succeed Frank Stanton as CBS president. He was a "surprise choice" for the post, an outsider moved in over no less than two heirs-apparent: John A. Schneider, president of the CBS Broadcast Group, and Richard W. Jencks, Washington CBS corporate VP. (Both men were passed over for the presidency a second time. By 1978, Schneider left the company, having "fallen into personal disfavor with Mr. Paley," a newspaper account observed.) Meanwhile, Ireland said—when tapped for the post—he knew little about broadcasting and seldom watched TV. "I guess you can say I'm starting out with a clean slate of ignorance," he allowed. In less than six months he was hospitalized with an illness diagnosed as "acute gastronomic disturbance that triggered a heart spasm." He returned to work within two weeks, aides reported, in good health. He learned of the death of his father, 77, on June 6, 1972; during the night of June 7–8, 1972, the younger Ireland, 51, died in his sleep. Ireland's successor as CBS president, named a month following his death, was another outsider who was quick to also admit to no broadcasting background and, until approached by CBS, he "knew no one there." Arthur R. Taylor, 37, had been executive vice president-CFO at International Paper Company.

65. Sally Bedell Smith, p. 22.

66. Holcomb B. Noble, "Frank Stanton, Broadcasting Pioneer, Dies at 98." *The New York Times*, December 25, 2006.

67. The new video trademark was credited to CBS-TV creative director William Golden of the advertising and sales promotion department. He was asked by Stanton to develop an identifying symbol for the video network.

68. A number of historiographers have mistakenly referenced Arthur R. Taylor as "Arthur B. Taylor," which is not the case. Fired by Paley on October 13, 1976, Taylor was replaced by John D. Backe, president of the CBS publishing division, on the same date. Backe was forced to resign on May 8, 1980; the resignation of Wyman, who had earlier been vice chairman of Minneapolis-based Pillsbury Company, was requested on September 10, 1986, by CBS. In his "afterlife," Taylor helped develop the Entertainment Channel (now A&E) and devoted much of his career to educational administration. For eight years he was dean of the grad school at New York's Fordham University; in July 2002, he was forced to step down from a decade-long tenure as president of Muhlenberg College, Allentown, Pennsylvania, the result of "abrasive behavior" toward faculty that had threatened him with a no-confidence vote. Students, on the other hand, reportedly admired him while his accomplishments were assessed as substantial. After departing CBS, Backe formed The Backe Group at Wayne, Pennsylvania, managing global broadcast, communications, technology and publishing interests. He subsequently owned and operated a mass marketing paperback publishing enterprise and a magazine publisher in New York, plus a Philadelphia advertising agency. Concurrently, he was general partner in a New York investment outfit in communications properties. Wyman, born November 30, 1929, at St. Louis, died in Boston on January 8, 2003.

69. Peter Baida, "A Legendary Chairman." *American Heritage Magazine*, July–August 1987.

70. In 2007, the umbrella included Paramount Pictures and Paramount Home Entertainment, plus cable ventures MTV, MTV2, mtvU, Nickelodeon, BET, Nick at Nite, TV Land, NOGGIN, VH1, Spike TV, CMT, Comedy Central, Showtime, The Movie Channel, Flix and Sundance Channel, along with other interests.

Chapter 5

1. "M. B. S." *Time*, January 4, 1937.

2. WOR went on the air February 22, 1922—George Washington's birthday—with a de Forest transmitter on the sixth floor of Bamberger's Department Store at 131 Market Street, Newark. The furniture department had added a line of radio apparatus and owner Louis Bamberger launched the station to improve sales, a fairly common practice among vendors of that embryonic radio epoch.

3. Gerald Nachman, *Raised on Radio: In Quest of The Lone Ranger, Jack Benny, Amos 'n' Andy, The Shadow, Mary Noble, The Great Gildersleeve, Fibber McGee and Molly, Bill Stern, Our Miss Brooks, Henry Aldrich, The Quiz Kids, Mr. First Nighter, Fred Allen, Vic and Sade, The Cisco Kid, Jack Armstrong, Arthur Godfrey, Bob and Ray, The Barbour Family, Henry Morgan, Joe Friday, and Other Lost Heroes from Radio's Heyday*. New York: Pantheon, 1998, p. 201.

4. Francis Chase, Jr., *Sound and Fury: An Informal History of Broadcasting*. New York: Harper and Brothers, 1942, p. 45.

5. Numerous historiographers have written McClelland's surname *McLelland*. It is spelled *McClelland* on multiple ship manifests, census records in 1910 and 1930, and in New York City death records, however.

6. http://jeff560.tripod.com/mutual.html.

7. *The Chicago Tribune*, October 10, 1944, p. 14.

8. Adapted from Dick Perry, *Not Just a Sound: The Story of WLW*. Englewood Cliffs, N.J.: Prentice-Hall, 1971.

9. "In 1934, four powerful stations ... banded together to form 'The Quality Group,' which later changed its name to the Mutual Broadcasting System." Leonard Maltin, *The Great American Broadcast: A Celebration of Radio's Golden Age.* New York: Penguin Putnam, 1997, p. 15.
10. http://www.spiritus-temporis.com/mutual-broadcasting-system/origins.html.
11. Texas Quality Network's member stations were all affiliated with NBC. See entry under this sobriquet in Chapter 7.
12. "M. B. S." *Time,* January 4, 1937.
13. WXYZ was jointly owned by Trendle and John H. Kunsky, although Trendle managed the station. They bought the property in 1929; in 1936, Kunsky legally changed his surname to King.
14. Don Lee Broadcasting System had been composed of 13 stations through November 1936 when the five members owned by McClatchy Newspapers departed to join NBC and California Radio System. The Hawaii stations linked by shortwave brought the number to 10. Don Lee launched into major expansion in 1937, picking up numerous new affiliates along the Pacific coast.
15. MBS's first transcontinental show, originating at WOR, featured live music by Morton Gould of the WOR staff plus sundry guests that included George M. Cohan.
16. *Report on Chain Broadcasting,* Federal Communications Commission, May 1941, Sec. IV B.
17. http://jeff560.tripod.com/mutual.html.
18. *Report on Chain Broadcasting,* Federal Communications Commission, May 1941, Sec. VII E.
19. After this change the total issued MBS capital stock consisted of 100 shares held as follows: WGN, WOR and Don Lee, 25 shares each; Colonial, United, *Cincinnati Times-Star* and Western Ontario, 6 shares each; Fred Weber, MBS general manager, 1 qualifying share.
20. *The New York Times,* November 1, 1941, p. 32.
21. *Report on Chain Broadcasting,* Sec. IV B.
22. Ibid., Sec. VII A 1.
23. Charles Hull Wolfe, *Modern Radio Advertising.* New York: Printers' Ink, 1949, p. 365.
24. http://jrff560.tripod.com/mutual/html.
25. Bill Jaker, Frank Sulek, and Peter Kanze. *The Airwaves of New York: Illustrated Histories of 156 AM Stations in the Metropolitan Area, 1921–1996.* Jefferson, N.C.: McFarland, 1998, p. 153.
26. Mary Jane Higby, *Tune in Tomorrow: Or How I Found The Right to Happiness with Our Gal Sunday, Stella Dallas, John's Other Wife, and Other Sudsy Radio Serials.* New York: Cowles Education Corporation, 1968, p. 172.
27. While Lum and Abner may never have been credited as Mutual's foremost performers during its formative years, they were the most widely recognized recurring artists on the web in that period.
28. Includes *The Bell Telephone Hour, The Cities Service Band of America, The Railroad Hour,* and *The Voice of Firestone.*
29. Sportscasters Red Barber of WLW, Bob Elson and Quin Ryan of WGN covered the games in the early days.
30. Erik Barnouw, *The Golden Web: A History of Broadcasting in the United States, 1933–1953.* New York: Oxford University Press, 1968, p. 127.
31. Kevin L. Goldman, "Radio's Latest Boom: Late-Night Talk Shows." *The New York Times,* May 2, 1982.
32. A separate outfit operated the National Black Network, which began airing on July 2, 1973.
33. Beginning in the World War II years, General Tire gradually ceased to exclusively manufacture and market tires. It entered the entertainment business, followed by tennis ball, wrought iron and soft drink production, chemicals and plastics manufacturing, motion picture and video fabrication (in the latter instance, acquiring RKO Radio Pictures in 1955).
34. Other regional chains had been folded into MBS earlier, including the Allegheny Mountain Radio Network and the InterMountain Network, the latter in the Mountain Time zone.
35. "General Tire Buys Yankee Network," *The New York Times,* December 17, 1942, p. 60.
36. According to "Lee Rites Set for Tomorrow" in *The Los Angeles Times,* September 1, 1934, p. A3, the senior Lee died on August 30, 1934, of a heart attack at 53 in Los Angeles. Surprisingly, more than one authoritative scholar references his death as 1936; more than one also certifies his son's death as 1948, although it occurred in 1950. (See following endnote.)
37. Thomas S. Lee, 45, sole heir to the $9 million vehicle and broadcasting fortune left by his father 16 years earlier, jumped to his death from the 12th floor of a Wilshire Boulevard office building in Los Angeles on Friday, the 13th of January 1950. (Adapted from "Thomas Lee Dies in Fall." *The New York Times,* January 14, 1950, p. 6.)
38. On January 1, 1951, television station KTSL in Los Angeles passed from the hands of the Don Lee estate to CBS. CBS had previously owned 49 percent of KTTV, another local video outlet, which it sold to *The Los Angeles Times.* The sale of KTSL ended liquidation of the Don Lee network and other properties. (Adapted from "Coast Video Station Bought by Columbia," *The New York Times,* January 2, 1951, p. 23.)
39. Adapted from "Radio-TV Merger Approved by F. C. C.," *The New York Times,* January 18, 1952, p. 33.
40. The Don Lee operations ceased to exist in 1967. See Christopher H. Sterling and John M. Kittross, *Stay Tuned: A Concise History of American Broadcasting,* 2nd Ed. Belmont, Calif.: Wadsworth Publishing, 1990, p. 385.
41. Adapted from "General Tire Gets Control of M. B. S.," *The New York Times,* April 2, 1952, p. 49.
42. Adapted from "Macy's and General Tire to Merge Coast-to-Coast TV-Radio Interests," *The New York Times,* October 11, 1951, p. 69.
43. Erik Barnouw, *The Image Empire: A History of Broadcasting in the United States; Volume III, from 1953.* New York: Oxford University Press, 1970, pp. 127–128.
44. Ibid.
45. http://en.wikipedia.org/wiki/Mutual_Broadcasting_System.
46. "Mutual generally had the weakest program lineup of all networks, and WOR had built a strong local personality, so the transition did not leave it unsure of its future." Jaker, Sulek, Kanze, p. 155.
47. This figure appeared in *The New York Times* on July 21, 1987. There is a multiplicity of vintage radio historians who state that the sales price was $39 million, which hasn't been substantiated.
48. http://indopedia.org/Mutual_Broadcasting_System.html.
49. *Funding Universe* website, Westwood One company history, http://www.fundinguniverse.com/company-histories/Westwood-One-Inc-Company-History.html.
50. "Company News: Westwood One Completes Purchase of Unistar Radio," *The New York Times,* February 5, 1994.
51. James P. Lucier, "Jim Bohannon on Air—Radio Talk Show Host," *Insight on the News,* February 9, 1998.

52. Cox, *Say Goodnight, Gracie*, 178–179.
53. Founding stations WGN and WOR now have radio webs of their own. WGN's Tribune Radio Networks, a division of Tribune Broadcasting, airs Orion Samuelson and Max Armstrong's farm reports and Chicago Cubs baseball games. WOR Radio Network syndicates general interest material and established personalities (Dr. Joy Browne, the Dolans, the Frommers, et al.). WLW syndicates many of its in-house hosts through parent company Clear Channel Communications. Mutual Broadcasting System LLC, Spokane, Washington, applies Mutual nomenclature to its dual stations, KTRW–AM 970 in Spokane and KTAC–FM 93.9 in Ephrata, Washington. The outlets have no ties to the original chain. They present adult standards, nostalgia and Christian shows using the Mutual name as part of their vintage branding.

Chapter 6

1. *Report on Chain Broadcasting*, Federal Communications Commission, May 1941, Sec. VII E.
2. Ibid., Sec. VII F.
3. George Ansbro, *I Have a Lady in the Balcony: Memoirs of a Broadcaster in Radio and Television*. Jefferson, N.C.: McFarland, 2000, p. 123.
4. Bill Jaker, Frank Sulek, and Peter Kanze, *The Airwaves of New York: Illustrated Histories of 156 AM Stations in the Metropolitan Area, 1921–1996*. Jefferson, N.C.: McFarland, 1998, p. 105.
5. Erik Barnouw, *The Golden Web: A History of Broadcasting in the United States; Volume II, 1933 to 1953*. New York: Oxford University Press, 1968, p. 187.
6. *The New York Times*, July 28, 1943, pp. 187–188.
7. Jim Cox, *This Day in Network Radio*. Jefferson, N.C.: McFarland, 2008, p. 142.
8. Alfred Balk, *The Rise of Radio: From Marconi Through the Golden Age*. Jefferson, N.C.: McFarland, 2006, p. 258.
9. Barnouw, 1968, p. 188.
10. "Asks FCC Approval to Buy Radio Chain," *The New York Times*, August 13, 1943, p. 36.
11. Barnouw, 1968, p. 188.
12. Ibid.
13. Jaker, Sulek, and Kanze, p. 105.
14. Balk, p. 258.
15. Jaker, Sulek, and Kanze, p. 105.
16. Balk, p. 258.
17. The following year (1944), Edgar Kobak resigned from the Blue network to cast his lot with MBS.
18. "Noble Explains ABC Stock Plan," *The New York Times*, July 10, 1946, p. 36.
19. "Network Without Ulcers," *Time*, April 21, 1947.
20. James C. Petrillo was president of the American Federation of Musicians, 1940–1958, and a tough bargainer. He called multiple strikes against radio, TV and recording firms in attempts to strengthen the union against technology that didn't require the actual presence of musicians.
21. http://www.museum.tv/archives/etv/A/htmlA/americanbroa/americanbroa.htm.
22. Jaker, Sulek, and Kanze, p. 103.
23. Jim Cox, *Say Goodnight, Gracie: The Last Years of Network Radio*. Jefferson, N.C.: McFarland, 2002, p. 70.
24. Frank Buxton and Bill Owen, *The Big Broadcast, 1920–1950*. New York: Viking, 1972, p. ix.
25. Gerald Nachman, *Raised on Radio: In Quest of The Lone Ranger, Jack Benny, Amos 'n' Andy, The Shadow, Mary Noble, The Great Gildersleeve, Fibber McGee and Molly, Bill Stern, Our Miss Brooks, Henry Aldrich, The Quiz Kids, Mr. First Nighter, Fred Allen, Vic and Sade, The Cisco Kid, Jack Armstrong, Arthur Godfrey, Bob and Ray, The Barbour Family, Henry Morgan, Joe Friday, and Other Lost Heroes from Radio's Heyday*. New York: Pantheon, 1998, p. 347.
26. Thomas A. DeLong, *Quiz Craze: America's Infatuation with Game Shows*. New York: Praeger, 1991, p. 118.
27. Only one minor daytime drama returned across a long dry spell, *Sweet River*, lasting just 10 months (1943–1944).
28. During the summer of 1983, ex–Beatle Ringo Starr began hosting a series of weekly one-hour shows over the ABC FM network. The programs traced the history of the famed vocal entourage and were branded *Ringo's Yellow Submarine: A Voyage Through Beatles Magic*.
29. http://en.wikipedia.org/wiki/American_Broadcasting_Company.
30. http://www.museum.tv/archives/etv/A/htmlA/americanbroa/americanbroa.htm.
31. Ibid.
32. ABC's relationship with Disney dates to 1953, when Leonard Goldenson pledged enough money that the Disneyland theme park could be completed. ABC continued to hold Disney notes and stock until 1960 and had first call on the *Disneyland* TV series in 1954. The new relationship brought cross promotions with attractions based on ABC shows at Disney parks and an annual soap festival at Walt Disney World. Ex-president Robert Iger of ABC, Inc., left to head Disney. Many more obvious and subtle ties have linked the parent firm and its subsidiary.
33. *Paul Harvey News and Comment* debuted on ABC on December 3, 1950. While the celebrated newsman was frequently absent from the microphone long before 2008, his series persisted, easily the most enduring continuous news program of its type on the air. In recent years Harvey was often replaced by Paul Harvey, Jr., and other visiting electronic journalists.
34. http://en.wikipedia.org/wiki/ABC_News_%26_Talk.

Chapter 7

1. Erik Barnouw, *The Golden Web: A History of Broadcasting in the United States, 1933–1953*. New York: Oxford University Press, 1968, p. 32.
2. Christopher H. Sterling and John M. Kittross, *Stay Tuned: A Concise History of American Broadcasting*, 2nd Ed. Belmont, Calif.: Wadsworth Publishing, 1990, p. 156.
3. "Yankee Network is Being Formed," *The New York Times*, February 9, 1930, p. X20.
4. Some of the figures and data in this entry are adapted from *Report on Chain Broadcasting* issued by the Federal Communications Commission, May 1941. Specific references are drawn from Appendix D, Section G.
5. Adapted from *Report on Chain Broadcasting*, FCC, May 1941, Appendix D, Section A.
6. Adapted from *Report on Chain Broadcasting*, FCC, May 1941, Appendix D, Section B.
7. Sterling and Kittross, p. 385.
8. Chapter 5 provides greater detail about these transactions.

9. Adapted from *Report on Chain Broadcasting*, FCC, May 1941, Appendix D, Section C.
10. Adapted from *Report on Chain Broadcasting*, FCC, May 1941, Appendix D, Section H.
11. Adapted from *Report on Chain Broadcasting*, FCC, May 1941, Appendix D, Section I.
12. "The Old Scotchman," *Time*, September 4, 1950.
13. Ibid.
14. http://www.powerset.com/explore/semhtml/Liberty_Broadcasting_System?query=Liberty...
15. "Watch Liberty Grow," *Time*, August 20, 1951.
16. "End of Liberty," *Time*, June 9, 1952.
17. http://www.powerset.com/explore/semhtml/Liberty_Broadcasting_System?query=Liberty...
18. Jim Cox, *Say Goodnight, Gracie: The Last Years of Network Radio*. Jefferson, N.C.: McFarland, 2002, p. 57.
19. http://en.wikipedia.org/wiki/Liberty_Broadcasting_System.
20. "IDT Media Announces the Formation of Liberty Broadcasting System; Broadcast Radio System Will Provide News, Information and Entertainment Programming," Business Wire Web site, November 4, 2003.
21. Adapted from *Report on Chain Broadcasting*, FCC, May 1941, Appendix D, Section E.
22. Adapted from *Report on Chain Broadcasting*, FCC, May 1941, Appendix D, Section D.
23. Sterling and Kittross, p. 107.
24. Adapted from *Report on Chain Broadcasting*, FCC, May 1941, Appendix D, Section J.
25. http://www.powerset.com/explore/semhtml/Progressive_Broadcasting_System?query=Lib...
26. "The Old Scotchman," *Time*, September 4, 1950.
27. http://www.tshaonline.org/handbook/online/articles/RR/ebr1.html.
28. "New Plant, Tower at Antenna Area," *The San Antonio Express and News*, December 7, 1958, p. 3-H. This substantiates that the Texas Quality Network was still alive and functioning more than two dozen years after it premiered, very late in the golden age of radio and after most regional radio tieups had long ago bit the dust.
29. Adapted from *Report on Chain Broadcasting*, FCC, May 1941, Appendix D, Section K.
30. Adapted from *Report on Chain Broadcasting*, FCC, May 1941, Appendix D, Section F.
31. "The $200,000 Deal," *Time*, October 8, 1945.
32. Jim Cox, *Radio Speakers: Narrators, News Junkies, Sports Jockeys, Tattletales, Tipsters, Toastmasters and Coffee Klatch Couples Who Verbalized the Jargon of the Aural Ether from the 1920s to the 1980s—A Biographical Dictionary*. Jefferson, N.C.: McFarland, 2007, pp. 244–248; also Jim Cox, *This Day in Network Radio: A Daily Calendar of Births, Deaths, Debuts, Cancellations and Other Events in Broadcasting History*. Jefferson, N.C.: McFarland, 2008, entry for September 23.
33. Adapted from *Report on Chain Broadcasting*, FCC, May 1941, Appendix D, Section L.
34. "The one and only reason for the proposed sale of the Yankee network and the Colonial network to the General Tire and Rubber Company of Akron, Ohio, was future inheritance tax problems," noted John Shepard III in an Associated Press article appearing in *The New York Times* on December 17, 1942. His father, John Shepard, Jr., who owned the networks, was to turn 86 on January 2, 1943, although he didn't die until December 21, 1948. No "material changes" were expected in the webs' operation under General Tire including personnel, said Shepard III, who signed a five-year contract with General Tire to continue as president and general manager.
35. Sterling and Kittross, 1990, p. 385.
36. Adapted from *Report on Chain Broadcasting*, FCC, May 1941, Appendix D, Section B.
37. Inventor Edwin H. Armstrong had successfully demonstrated his experimental FM station, W3XMN, at Alpine, New Jersey, in 1938. It became the first permanent FM outlet to conduct low power testing. Armstrong won Federal Communications Commission approval for his experiments in 1936.
38. Sterling and Kittross, p. 144.
39. http://www.powerset.com/explore/semhtml/Yankee_Network?query=Yankee+Network.
40. Ibid.
41. Adapted from "Allowed to Acquire the Yankee Network," *The New York Times*, January 1, 1943, p. 11.

Chapter 8

1. The liner *Republic* collided in 1909 with the *Florida* in fog off the U.S. East Coast. An unidentified radio operator on the sinking vessel stayed at his post, issuing a call for help that resulted in saving almost all persons on board. That same year passengers and crew on 18 other ships with similar radio installations were also saved while those on many more ships without radio perished. (Adapted from Christopher H. Sterling and John M. Kittross, *Stay Tuned: A Concise History of American Broadcasting*. 2nd ed. Belmont, Calif.: Wadsworth Publishing, 1990, p. 34.)
2. http://en.wikipedia.org/wiki/Wireless_Ship_Act_of_1910.
3. More about Marconi and its impact on American broadcasting is in Chapter 3.
4. The Navy had bought units of the Federal Telegraph Company plus some coastal Marconi outlets and also acquired installations in all American seagoing vessels.
5. Sterling and Kittross, p. 88.
6. George H. Douglas, *The Early Days of Radio Broadcasting*. Jefferson, N.C.: McFarland, 1987, p. 94; Erik Barnouw, *A Tower in Babel: A History of Broadcasting in the United States; Volume I, to 1933*. New York: Oxford University Press, 1966, pp. 179–180.
7. Susan J. Douglas, *Listening In: Radio and the American Imagination, from Amos 'n' Andy and Edward R. Murrow to Wolfman Jack and Howard Stern*. New York: Random House, 1999, p. 63.
8. Alfred Balk, *The Rise of Radio: From Marconi Through the Golden Age*. Jefferson, N.C.: McFarland, 2006, p. 68.
9. Fritz Messere, associate professor of broadcasting and mass communications, State University of New York, Oswego, writing for http://www.oswego.edu/~messere/FRCpage.html.
10. Ibid.
11. Commissioner John F. Dillon died October 8, 1927, and chairman W.H.G. Bullard died November 24, 1927—both in the year in which the commission was established. Some reporters say President Calvin Coolidge forced a third member, Henry Adams Bellows, to quit October 31, 1927, while others claim Bellows merely resigned. Whatever the reason, it left just two commissioners and an agency in disarray. Neither Bellows nor Orestes H. Caldwell, a fourth member, had been confirmed before Congress recessed, leaving them to perform without pay. Caldwell was barely reconfirmed in March 1928 (on a 36–

35 vote) and resigned less than a year later (February 23, 1929). Only Eugene Octave Sykes of the original five appeared to prosper; he was the sole survivor nominated for membership on the successor Federal Communications Commission formed in 1934.

12. For a succinct yet comprehensive overview of the difficult challenges facing the Federal Radio Commission, spelling out some of the deplorable conditions under which those appointees labored, see Barnouw, *A Tower in Babel*, pp. 211–219.

13. The U.S. Supreme Court held in *National Broadcasting Co. Inc. et al. v. United States et al. 319 U.S. 190* on May 10, 1943, that the FCC had the right to issue regulations pertaining to associations between broadcasting networks and their affiliated stations. The opinion of the Supreme Court was not unanimous, however, at 5–2.

14. http://en.wikipedia.org/wiki/FCC.

15. Balk, p. 257.

16. For more detail on this topic see Chapter 3.

17. In the modern age the FCC's principal regulatory weapon is revoking licenses. Otherwise, its leverage is limited. Less than one percent of station renewals aren't granted immediately; only a small fraction of the remainder is ultimately denied.

18. Christopher Sterling and John Kittross, writing in *Stay Tuned: A Concise History of American Broadcasting*, offer an objective treatise that adequately defines the history of governmental regulation of the airwaves in this country through the 1970s. (See 2nd edition, pp. 575–580.) One wonders what their assessment might be now if given the advantage of another three decades to observe what has transpired in that arena.

19. Gerald Nachman, *Raised on Radio: In Quest of The Lone Ranger, Jack Benny, Amos 'n' Andy, The Shadow, Mary Noble, The Great Gildersleeve, Fibber McGee and Molly, Bill Stern, Our Miss Brooks, Henry Aldrich, The Quiz Kids, Mr. First Nighter, Fred Allen, Vic and Sade, The Cisco Kid, Jack Armstrong, Arthur Godfrey, Bob and Ray, The Barbour Family, Henry Morgan, Joe Friday, and Other Lost Heroes from Radio's Heyday*. New York: Pantheon Books, 1998, p. 498.

20. Ibid., p. 487.

Chapter 9

1. Adapted from Erik Barnouw, *A Tower in Babel: A History of Broadcasting in the United States; Volume I, to 1933*. New York: Oxford University Press, 1966, p. 154.

2. Financing by states, not suggested by the magazine, was more easily realized. Some of the most stable educational outlets were founded by states, in fact, often situated on state university campuses.

3. Adapted from Gleason L. Archer, *History of Radio to 1926*. New York: American Historical Society, 1938, p. 329.

4. Adapted from Robert J. Landry, *This Fascinating Radio Business*. Indianapolis: Bobbs-Merrill, 1946, p. 46.

5. Bruce Bliven, "How Radio is Remaking Our World." *Century*, June 1924.

6. Susan Smulyan, *Selling Radio: The Commercialization of American Broadcasting, 1920 to 1934*. Washington, D.C.: Smithsonian Institution Press, 1994, p. 103.

7. Christopher H. Sterling and John M. Kittross. *Stay Tuned: A Concise History of American Broadcasting*. 2nd ed. Belmont, Calif.: Wadsworth Publishing, 1990, p. 566.

8. Alfred Balk, *The Rise of Radio: From Marconi Through the Golden Age*. Jefferson, N.C.: McFarland, 2006, p. 63.

9. Barnouw, 1966, p. 200.

10. Adapted from *Historical Dictionary of American Radio* edited by Donald C. Godfrey and Frederic A. Leigh. Westport, Conn.: Greenwood Press, 1998, p. 81.

11. Barnouw, 1966, p. 244.

12. These figures appear in Barnouw, 1966, p. 239.

13. Sterling and Kittross, pp. 211–212.

14. Charles A. Siepmann, *Radio, Television and Society*. New York: Oxford University Press, 1950, pp. 44–45.

15. Charles A. Siepmann, *Radio's Second Chance*. Boston: Little, Brown, 1947, p. 62.

16. Ibid., p. 65.

17. Ibid., p. 134.

Chapter 10

1. More of the organizational history is detailed in Chapter 3.

2. Many of the unidentified quotes appearing here, though not all, are attributed to memoirs on the two individuals who are the subjects of this chapter: Eugene Lyons, *David Sarnoff: A Biography*. New York: Harper and Row, 1966; Sally Bedell Smith, *In All His Glory: The Life of William S. Paley, The Legendary Tycoon and His Brilliant Circle*. New York: Simon and Schuster, 1990.

3. More details on an imperiled Columbia network are included in Chapter 4.

4. http://en.wikipedia.org/wiki/Jack_Benny.

5. Adapted from Jim Cox, *Music Radio: The Great Performers and Programs of the 1920s through Early 1960s*. Jefferson, N.C.: McFarland, 2005, p. 112.

6. While well wishers from all over the nation applauded Sarnoff and NBC on the triumph, the network's stockholders found little to cheer about. The orchestra's launch, including the creation of Studio 8H in Radio City to host it, cost about $250 million, no small change in 1937. There was little prospect that any of the outlay could be reclaimed. Some of the investors murmured, "Really, this time the man [Sarnoff] was overdoing it."

Chapter 12

1. Wesley Hyatt, *The Encyclopedia of Daytime Television: Everything You Ever Wanted to Know About Daytime TV but Didn't Know Where to Look! From American Bandstand, As the World Turns, and Bugs Bunny, to Meet the Press, The Price Is Right, and Wide World of Sports, the Rich History of Daytime Television in All Its Glory!* New York: Billboard Books, 1997, pp. viii–ix.

2. Hyatt states that the NBC station in New York went on the air in 1928. While the government granted a permit for such a station that year, it appears that it was July 1930 before there was any successful transmission (initially a fuzzy image of Felix the Cat). See Sally Bedell Smith, *In All His Glory: The Life of William S. Paley, The Legendary Tycoon and His Brilliant Circle*. New York: Simon and Schuster, 1990, p. 186.

3. Some of this material is adapted from Jim Cox, *The Daytime Serials of Television, 1946–1960*. Jefferson, N.C.: McFarland, 2006, pp. 24, 25.

4. Sally Bedell Smith, p. 269, quoting David Adams.

5. *Business Week*, July 21, 1951.

6. Sally Bedell Smith, p. 269, quoting William S. Fineshriber, Jr.
7. F. Leslie Smith, *Perspectives on Radio and Television: An Introduction to Broadcasting in the United States*. New York: Harper and Row, 1979, p. 50.
8. Christopher H. Sterling and John M. Kittross, *Stay Tuned: A Concise History of American Broadcasting*. 2nd ed. Belmont, Calif.: Wadsworth Publishing, 1990, p. 262.
9. Ibid.
10. Ibid., p. 271.
11. Ibid., p. 262.
12. According to John Chancellor, who was to eventually become a major news presence on NBC-TV, the majority of sets until that time were situated in the nation's saloons. Programs were often slanted toward the bars' clientele, Chancellor affirmed, including "wrestling and ladies with large bosoms on variety shows."
13. David Halberstam, *The Fifties*. New York: Villard Books, 1993, p. 181.
14. Ibid., pp. 184–185.
15. Charles A. Siepmann, *Radio, Television and Society*. New York: Oxford University Press, 1950, pp. 343, 346.
16. Some of these dynamics are examined in Chapter 13.
17. Halberstam, p. 185.
18. F. Leslie Smith, p. 52.
19. *Variety*, July 28, 1948, p. 41.
20. J. Fred MacDonald, *Don't Touch That Dial! Radio Programming in American Life from 1920 to 1960*. Chicago: Nelson-Hall, 1991, p. 84.
21. Frank Buxton and Bill Owen, *The Big Broadcast, 1920–1950*. New York: Viking Press, 1972, p. ix.
22. Gerald Nachman, *Raised on Radio: In Quest of The Lone Ranger, Jack Benny, Amos 'n' Andy, The Shadow, Mary Noble, The Great Gildersleeve, Fibber McGee and Molly, Bill Stern, Our Miss Brooks, Henry Aldrich, The Quiz Kids, Mr. First Nighter, Fred Allen, Vic and Sade, The Cisco Kid, Jack Armstrong, Arthur Godfrey, Bob and Ray, The Barbour Family, Henry Morgan, Joe Friday, and Other Lost Heroes from Radio's Heyday*. New York: Pantheon Books, 1998, p. 347.
23. In addition to hundreds of "now playing" features, some of which would extend for several more years after the "passing" of Allen, new shows premiering in the 1950s would be headlined by Eddie Fisher, Rosemary Clooney, Stan Freberg, Steve Allen and others. Beyond those would be scores of new series, e.g.: *The Amos 'n' Andy Music Hall, The Big Show, Biography in Sound, Bob and Ray, Cathy and Elliott Lewis Onstage, The CBS Radio Workshop, City Hospital, The Crime Files of Flamond, Dimension X, Dragnet, Gunsmoke, The Halls of Ivy, Have Gun—Will Travel, Hopalong Cassidy, The Lineup, Mark Trail, Meet Millie, Monitor, My Little Margie, The NBC Radio Theater, The Roadshow, Twenty-First Precinct, The Six Shooter, Weekend, What's My Line?, Whispering Streets, Wild Bill Hickok, The Woman in My House* and *X-Minus One*.
24. Editors of Time-Life Books, *This Fabulous Century: Volume VI, 1950–1960*. Alexandria, Va.: Time-Life Books, 1970, p. 250.
25. Halberstam, p. 180.
26. Ibid., p. 183.
27. Ibid., p. 182.
28. Jim Cox, *Say Goodnight, Gracie: The Last Years of Network Radio*. Jefferson, N.C.: McFarland, 2002, p. 43.
29. *Variety*, January 9, 1946, p. 7.
30. Halberstam, pp. 202–203.
31. Nachman, p. 404.
32. Ibid., p. 252.
33. Ibid., p. 287.
34. Ibid.
35. Editors of Time-Life Books, *Our American Century: The American Dream, the 50s*. Alexandria, Va.: Time-Life Books, 1998, p. 150.
36. Alfred Balk, *The Rise of Radio: From Marconi through the Golden Age*. Jefferson, N.C.: McFarland, 2006, p. 275.
37. Ibid., p. 267.

Chapter 13

1. Nevertheless, when a Philadelphia radio station began airing records in the mid 1920s as part of its accustomed everyday format, not quite everybody was amused. Several New York music publishers and a few dance band impresarios, including Paul Whiteman, sued the station, claiming the venture diminished their livelihoods. On the contrary, a judge ruled: "A recording purchased from a proper source is no longer the property of the manufacturer or the performer. The buyer may use it in any way he sees fit, including broadcasting its contents." Did it ever cross anybody's mind that exposing tunes to legions of listeners might increase demand for same, thereby lining the pockets of performers, publishers, manufacturers and sellers? Helllooooo. (Adapted from Jim Cox, *Music Radio: The Great Performers and Programs of the 1920s through Early 1960s*. Jefferson, N.C.: McFarland, 2005, p. 144.)
2. Adapted from J. Fred MacDonald, *Don't Touch That Dial! Radio Programming in American Life from 1920 to 1960*. Chicago: Nelson-Hall, 1991, pp. 86, 89.
3. Ecclesiastes 3:1. *The Message: The Bible in Contemporary Language*. Colorado Springs, Colo.: NavPress Publishing Group, 2002.
4. *Variety*, February 12, 1958, p. 49.
5. Walker, Leo. *The Wonderful Era of the Great Dance Bands*. New York: Da Capo Press, 1990, p. 155.
6. Ibid, p. 157.
7. Employed concurrently by WABC Radio and WNEW-TV, New York DJ Alan Freed was dumped by both in November 1959. He may have been the most visible "payola" poster boy to take a hit. Freed never recovered, dying "both broke and broken-hearted" in 1965 at 42.
8. Wes Smith, *The Pied Pipers of Rock 'n' Roll Radio Deejays of the 50s and 60s*. Marietta, Ga.: Longstreet Press, 1989, p. 9.
9. Gerald Nachman, *Raised on Radio: In Quest of The Lone Ranger, Jack Benny, Amos 'n' Andy, The Shadow, Mary Noble, The Great Gildersleeve, Fibber McGee and Molly, Bill Stern, Our Miss Brooks, Henry Aldrich, The Quiz Kids, Mr. First Nighter, Fred Allen, Vic and Sade, The Cisco Kid, Jack Armstrong, Arthur Godfrey, Bob and Ray, The Barbour Family, Henry Morgan, Joe Friday, and Other Lost Heroes from Radio's Heyday*. New York: Pantheon Books, 1998, p. 180.
10. Ibid., p. 497.
11. Ibid.

Chapter 14

1. This is not to say that music went away from the dial. It persisted but it was not only reduced in the 1960s,

that which still aired was most often specialized—concentrated in ethnic-oriented, country-western, rock, middle-of-the-road, golden oldies, classical, gospel, progressive jazz, beautiful music, etc. The DJ was often downplayed if he existed at all.

2. WINS and WCBS-AM would be under the same corporate umbrella three decades later, both still aggressively competing with dissimilar formats.

3. A companion service is offered by the same distributor (NPR), *Morning Edition*, focusing on hard news that is reportedly "the most popular morning news program in America," NPR publicists claim. Both *Morning Edition* and *All Things Considered* regularly appear in research polling among the top five programs favored by listeners in the U.S.

Epilogue

1. Some words adapted from "Twinkle, Twinkle, Little Star," a popular English nursery rhyme by Jane Taylor, first published in 1806 in *Rhymes for the Nursery*, a collection of poems by Taylor and her sister Ann. It is often sung to the tune of the French melody "Ah! vous diraije, Maman," originally published in 1761.

2. A nursery rhyme believed to be of late 19th century American origin.

3. Opening words of *X-Minus One* fictional sci-fi dramatic radio series on NBC, 1955–1958, 1973–1975.

Bibliography

This register lists the principal sources consulted for the main text. It should not be construed as utterly complete. While the majority of published references are recorded here, hundreds of added online resources were examined, mostly for verifications. Painstaking effort was made for accuracy. Data was frequently corroborated through multiple online and published suppliers as well as through material provided by several competent informants.

Publications

Allen, Steve. *Bigger Than a Breadbox.* New York: Doubleday, 1967.

American Heritage Magazine, July–August 1987.

Ansbro, George. *I Have a Lady in the Balcony: Memoirs of a Broadcaster in Radio and Television.* Jefferson, N.C.: McFarland, 2000.

Archer, Gleason Leonard. *Big Business and Radio.* New York: American Historical Company, 1939.

_____. *History of Radio to 1926.* New York: American Historical Society, 1938.

Balk, Alfred. *The Rise of Radio: From Marconi through the Golden Age.* Jefferson, N.C.: McFarland, 2006.

Barnouw, Erik. *The Golden Web: A History of Broadcasting in the United States; Volume II, 1933 to 1953.* New York: Oxford University Press, 1968.

_____. *The Image Empire: A History of Broadcasting in the United States from 1953.* New York: Oxford University Press, 1970.

_____. *A Tower in Babel: A History of Broadcasting in the United States; Volume I, to 1933.* New York: Oxford University Press, 1966.

Business Week, July 21, 1951.

Business Wire (Web site), November 4, 2003.

Buxton, Frank, and Bill Owen. *The Big Broadcast, 1920–1950.* New York: Viking, 1972.

Campbell, Robert. *The Golden Years of Broadcasting: A Celebration of the First 50 Years of Radio and TV on NBC.* New York: Charles Scribner's Sons, 1976.

Cantril, Haley, and Gordon W. Allport. *The Psychology of Radio.* New York: Harper and Brothers, 1935.

Century, June 1924.

Chase, Francis, Jr. *Sound and Fury: An Informal History of Broadcasting.* New York: Harper and Brothers, 1942.

The Chicago Tribune, October 10, 1944.

Cloud, Stanley, and Lynne Olson. *The Murrow Boys: Pioneers on the Front Lines of Broadcast Journalism.* Boston: Houghton Mifflin, 1996.

Collier's, April 17, 1948.

Columbia Broadcasting System, Inc. *The Sound of Your Life.* New York: CBS 1950.

Cox, Jim. *The Daytime Serials of Television, 1946–1960.* Jefferson, N.C.: McFarland, 2006.

_____. *The Great Radio Audience Participation Shows: Seventeen Programs from the 1940s and 1950s.* Jefferson, N.C.: McFarland, 2001, 2008.

_____. *The Great Radio Sitcoms.* Jefferson, N.C.: McFarland, 2007.

_____. *The Great Radio Soap Operas.* Jefferson, N.C.: McFarland, 1999, 2008.

_____. *Historical Dictionary of American Radio Soap Operas.* Lanham, Md.: Scarecrow, 2005.

_____. *Music Radio: The Great Performers and Programs of the 1920s through Early 1960s.* Jefferson, N.C.: McFarland, 2005.

_____. *Radio Crime Fighters: Over 300 Programs from the Golden Age.* Jefferson, N.C.: McFarland, 2002.

_____. *Radio Speakers: Narrators, News Junkies, Sports Jockeys, Tattletales, Tipsters, Toastmasters and Coffee Klatch Couples Who Verbalized the Jargon of the Aural Ether from the 1920s to the 1980s—A Biographical Dictionary.* Jefferson, N.C.: McFarland, 2007.

_____. *Say Goodnight, Gracie: The Last Years of Network Radio.* Jefferson, N.C.: McFarland, 2002.

_____. *Sold on Radio: Advertisers in the Golden Age of Broadcasting.* Jefferson, N.C.: McFarland, 2008.

_____. *This Day in Network Radio: A Daily Calendar of Births, Deaths, Debuts, Cancellations and Other Events in Broadcasting History.* Jefferson, N.C.: McFarland, 2009.

DeLong, Thomas A. *Quiz Craze: America's Infatuation with Game Shows.* New York: Praeger, 1991.

Douglas, George H. *The Early Days of Radio Broadcasting.* Jefferson, N.C.: McFarland, 1987.

Douglas, Susan J. *Listening In: Radio and the Amer-*

ican Imagination, from Amos 'n' Andy and Edward R. Murrow to Wolfman Jack and Howard Stern. New York: Random House, 1999.

Dunning, John. *On the Air: The Encyclopedia of Old-Time Radio*. New York: Oxford University Press, 1998.

Editors of Time-Life Books. *Our American Century: The American Dream, the 50s*. Alexandria, Va.: Time-Life Books, 1998.

_____. *This Fabulous Century: Volume VI, 1950–1960*. Alexandria, Va.: Time-Life Books, 1970.

Godfrey, Donald C., and Frederic A. Leigh, eds. *Historical Dictionary of American Radio*. Westport, Conn.: Greenwood Press, 1998.

Grams, Martin, Jr. *Radio Drama: American Programs, 1932–1962*. Jefferson, N.C.: McFarland, 2000.

Halberstam, David. *The Fifties*. New York: Villard Books, 1993.

Harvey, Rita Morley. *Those Wonderful, Terrible Years: George Heller and the American Federation of Television and Radio Artists*. Carbondale: Southern Illinois University Press, 1996.

Hickerson, Jay. *The Third Ultimate History of Network Radio Programming and Guide to All Circulating Shows*. Hamden, Conn.: Presto Print II, 2005.

Higby, Mary Jane. *Tune in Tomorrow: Or How I Found the Right to Happiness with Our Gal Sunday, Stella Dallas, John's Other Wife, and Other Sudsy Radio Serials*. New York: Cowles Education Corporation, 1968.

Hyatt, Wesley. *The Encyclopedia of Daytime Television: Everything You Ever Wanted to Know About Daytime TV but Didn't Know Where to Look! From American Bandstand, As the World Turns, and Bugs Bunny, to Meet the Press, The Price is Right, and Wide World of Sports, the Rich History of Daytime Television in All Its Glory!* New York: Billboard Books, 1997, pp. viii–ix.

Jaker, Bill, and Frank Sulek and Peter Kanze. *The Airwaves of New York: Illustrated Histories of 156 AM Stations in the Metropolitan Area, 1921–1996*. Jefferson, N.C.: McFarland, 1998.

Lackmann, Ron. *Same Time, Same Station: An A–Z Guide to Radio from Jack Benny to Howard Stern*. New York: Facts on File, 1996.

Landry, Robert J. *This Fascinating Radio Business*. Indianapolis: Bobbs-Merrill, 1946.

The Los Angeles Times, September 1, 1934.

Lyons, Eugene. *David Sarnoff: A Biography*. New York: Harper and Row, 1966.

MacDonald, J. Fred. *Don't Touch That Dial! Radio Programming in American Life, 1920–1960*. Chicago: Nelson-Hall, 1991.

Maltin, Leonard. *The Great American Broadcast: A Celebration of Radio's Golden Age*. New York: Penguin Putnam, 1997.

McNeil, Alex. *Total Television: The Comprehensive Guide from 1948 to the Present*. 4th ed. New York: Penguin Books, 1996.

The Message: The Bible in Contemporary Language. Colorado Springs, Colo.: NavPress Publishing Group, 2002.

Nachman, Gerald. *Raised on Radio: In Quest of The Lone Ranger, Jack Benny, Amos 'n' Andy, The Shadow, Mary Noble, The Great Gildersleeve, Fibber McGee and Molly, Bill Stern, Our Miss Brooks, Henry Aldrich, The Quiz Kids, Mr. First Nighter, Fred Allen, Vic and Sade, The Cisco Kid, Jack Armstrong, Arthur Godfrey, Bob and Ray, The Barbour Family, Henry Morgan, Joe Friday, and Other Lost Heroes from Radio's Heyday*. New York: Pantheon Books, 1998.

NBC History Files. Folders 299, 431, 784, 998. Library of Congress archives.

The New York Times, June 23, 1927; February 9, 1930; November 1, 1941; December 17, 1942; January 1, 1943; July 28, 1943; August 13, 1943; July 10, 1946; January 14, 1950; January 2, 1951; October 11, 1951; January 18, 1952; April 2, 1952; December 9, 1955; May 2, 1982; July 21, 1987; October 8, 1988; February 5, 1994; March 18, 2002; December 25, 2006.

The Oakland Tribune, September 13, 1926.

Perry, Dick. *Not Just a Sound: The Story of WLW*. Englewood Cliffs, N.J.: Prentice-Hall, 1971.

Radio and Education, 1936.

Radio Broadcast, June 1929.

RCA Annual Report, 1924.

Report as to Social and Economic Aspects of Allocation Hearings. Washington, D.C.: Federal Communications Commission, 1937.

Report of Federal Trade Commission on the Radio Industry. Washington, D.C.: Federal Trade Commission, 1923.

Report of the Federal Radio Commission in Reply to Senate Resolution 129. Washington, D.C.: Federal Radio Commission, January 7, 1932.

Report on Chain Broadcasting. Washington, D.C.: Federal Communications Commission, 1941.

Report on Social and Economic Data Pursuant to the Informal Hearing on Broadcasting. Washington, D.C.: Federal Communications Commission, 1936.

Robinson, Marc. *Brought to You in Living Color: 75 Years of Great Moments in Television and Radio from NBC*. New York: John Wiley and Sons, 2002.

The San Antonio Express and News, December 7, 1958.

Schulberg, Bob. *Radio Advertising: The Authoritative Handbook*. Lincolnwood, Ill.: NTC Business Books, 1989.

Siepmann, Charles A. *Radio, Television and Society*. New York: Oxford University Press, 1950.

_____. *Radio's Second Chance*. Boston: Little, Brown and Co., 1946.
Singer, Arthur J. *Arthur Godfrey: The Adventures of an American Broadcaster*. Jefferson, N.C.: McFarland, 2000.
Smith, F. Leslie. *Perspectives on Radio and Television: An Introduction to Broadcasting in the United States*. New York: Harper and Row, 1979.
Smith, Sally Bedell. *In All His Glory: The Life of William S. Paley, the Legendary Tycoon and His Brilliant Circle*. New York: Simon and Schuster, 1990.
Smith, Wes. *The Pied Pipers of Rock 'n' Roll Radio Deejays of the 50s and 60s*. Marietta, Ga.: Longstreet Press, 1989.
Smulyan, Susan. *Selling Radio: The Commercialization of American Broadcasting, 1920 to 1934*. Washington, D.C.: Smithsonian Institution Press, 1994.
Stedman, Raymond William. *The Serials: Suspense and Drama by Installment*. Norman, Okla.: University of Oklahoma Press, 1971.
Sterling, Christopher H., and John M. Kittross. *Stay Tuned: A Concise History of American Broadcasting*. Second Ed. Belmont, Calif.: Wadsworth, 1990.
Summers, Harrison B., ed. *A Thirty-Year History of Programs Carried on National Radio Networks in the United States, 1926–1956*. New York: Arno Press and *The New York Times*, 1971.
Time, January 4, 1937; October 8, 1945; April 21, 1947; February 21, 1949; September 4, 1950; August 20, 1951; June 9, 1952.
U.S. Communications Act of 1934.
Variety, January 9, 1946; July 28, 1948; December 19, 1948; February 12, 1958.
Walker, Leo. *The Wonderful Era of the Great Dance Bands*. New York: Da Capo Press, 1990.
Waller, Judith C. *Radio: The Fifth Estate*. New York: Houghton Mifflin, 1946.
The Washington Post, March 18, 2002.
Wolfe, Charles Hull. *Modern Radio Advertising*. New York: Printers' Ink, 1949.

Web Sites

http://en.wikipedia.org/wiki/ABC_News_%26_Talk
http://en.wikipedia.org/wiki/American_Broadcasting_Company
http://en.wikipedia.org/wiki/Blue_Network
http://en.wikipedia.org/wiki/FCC
http://en.wikipedia.org/wiki/Jack_Benny
http://en.wikipedia.org/wiki/Liberty_Broadcasting_System
http://en.wikipedia.org/wiki/Mutual_Broadcasting_System
http://en.wikipedia.org/wiki/Wireless_Ship_Act_of_1910
http://indopedia.org/Mutual_Broadcasting_System.html
http://www.museum.tv/archives/etv/A/htmlA/americanbroa/americanbroa.htm
http://www.oswego.edu/~messere/FRCpage.html
http://www.powerset.com/explore/semhtml/Liberty_Broadcasting_System?query=Liberty...
http://www.powerset.com/explore/semhtml/Progressive_Broadcasting_System?query=Lib...
http://www.powerset.com/explore/semhtml/Yankee_Network?query=Yankee+Network
http://www.spiritus-temporis.com/mutual-broadcasting-system/origins.html
http://www.tshaonline.org/handbook/online/articles/RRebr1.html

INDEX

The A&P Gypsies 125
ABC Family Channel 193
ABC News & Talk Radio 186, 191
ABC News Radio 100
Adams, Bill 154
Adams, David 63
Adams, Franklin P. 32
The Adventures of Ozzie and Harriet 29, 38, 63, 95, 96, 135
The Adventures of Philip Marlowe 159
The Adventures of Sherlock Holmes 163
The Adventures of Superman 82, 152
The Adventures of the Falcon 82, 163
Advertising: agencies 5, 126, 129–130; policies 11
Affiliates: contracts 26, 65; rebellion 179–180
Against the Storm 97, 141
Agronsky, Martin 95
Air Features, Inc. 164, 166
The Aldrich Family 29
Alexander, Ben 159
Alexander, Joan 166
Alexander, Tom 200
Aley, Albert 154
All Star Game 83
All Star Radio Theater 41
All Things Considered 186, 187
Allen, Fred 29, 30, 42, 44, 95–96, 124, 136, 141, 145, 171, 173–174, 188
Allen, Gracie 38, 62, 125, 135, 144, 173
Allen, J. Roy 92
Allen, Steve 181
Alsop, Joseph W., Jr. 94
Amahl and the Night Visitors 35
Amalgamated Broadcasting System 191–192
Amanda of Honeymoon Hill 165
America Overnight 198–199
American Broadcasting Company (ABC) 20, 25, 26, 32, 38, 39, 40, 43, 56, 62, 63, 71, 78, 79, 80, 81, 82, 83, 84, 86, 89–100, 101, 111, 120, 129, 135, 139, 141, 142, 143, 144, 149, 150, 152, 153, 154, 155, 156, 201, 157, 158, 159, 173, 174, 177, 179, 180, 181, 185, 186, 191, 192, 196, 198, 199, 200, 202
American Broadcasting System, Inc. (Storer) 75, 76, 91
American Magazine 133
American Marconi Company 18, 19, 28, 46, 117, 132–133

American Newspaper Publishers Association 126
American Public Media (APM) 186
The American School of the Air 184
American Society of Composers, Authors and Publishers (ASCAP) 45, 119
American Telephone & Telegraph Company (AT&T) 6, 9, 10, 11, 12, 13, 14, 15, 16, 17, 21, 23, 24, 27, 46, 47, 48, 49, 54, 74, 76, 93, 110, 115, 117, 123, 188
American Tobacco Company 34, 158
American Urban Information Radio 197
American Urban Radio Networks 197, 200
America's Town Meeting of the Air 184
Amos 'n' Andy 22, 30, 33, 38, 42, 48, 49, 55, 62, 135, 136, 146, 181
The Amos 'n' Andy Music Hall 65, 146, 181
Amway Corporation 42, 87
Anderson, Arthur 154
Anderson, Eddie (Rochester) 145
Anderson, Jack 194
The Andrews Sisters 56
Ansbro, George 90
Anthony, John J. 83, 184
Antonini, Alfredo 56
Applause meter 140
Arbitron audience measuring service 84, 198
Archer, Gleason L. 73, 74
Arden, Eve 56, 148
Arenstein, Howard 71
Arms, Russell 158
Armstrong, Edwin H. 3, 115
Armstrong of the SBI 153
Armstrong Theater of Today 58
Arness, James 160
Arnheim, Gus 55
Arnold, Frank 23
Arrowhead Network 102
The Art Linkletter Show 139
Art Linkletter's House Party 139–140
Arthur Godfrey and His Friends 57, 140
Arthur Godfrey and His Ukulele 140
Arthur Godfrey Time 57, 65, 140, 179
Arthur Godfrey's Digest 57, 140
Arthur Godfrey's Talent Scouts 140–141

Artist bureaus 5, 45, 54–55, 75, 115, 120
As the World Turns 66
Asimov, Isaac 150
Ask Mr. Anthony 83
Ask President Carter 61
Associated Press 31, 201
At Home with Faye and Elliott 113
Atlantic Broadcasting Company 51
Atwater Kent 47, 121
Audience measurement systems 5, 67–68, 80
Audimeter 68
Automated format 183
Autry, Gene 56
Ayers, Jack 154
Aylesworth, Merlin Hall ("Deac") 15, 18, 19–20, 21, 29, 43, 137

Baby Snooks 146–147
Backe, John David 69
Backstage Wife 82, 164–165
Backus, Jim 162
Bagnato, Barry 71
Bailey, Bob 164
Bailey, Jack 142
Baird, John 169
Baker, Phil 33, 141
Baker, "Wee" Bonnie 158
Ball, Lucille 56, 161
Baltimore Radio Shows, Inc. 78
L. Bamberger & Company 51, 72, 74
Bamberger Broadcasting Service, Inc. 74, 83, 114
The Band of America 29, 57
Band remotes 66
Bankhead, Tallulah 38, 43, 136
Banquet Foods 37
The Baptist Hour 184
Barber, Red 75
Barlow, Howard 5, 47, 157
Bartell, Harry 159
Bartlett, Tommy 49
Baruch, Andre 181
Bauer, Charita 154
The Beach Boys 201
The Beatles 201
Beatty, Morgan 31, 43
Beaudin, Ralph 98–99
The Bee Gees 201
Beech-Nut Packing Company 93
Bell, Alexander Graham 16
Bell System 16
The Bell Telephone Hour 29, 57
Bennett, Tony 140
Benny, Jack 22, 29, 30, 38, 62, 96,

124, 125, 135, 136, 142, 144–145, 161, 173, 175
Bergen, Edgar 29, 38, 62, 96, 135, 136, 143–144
Berle, Milton 5, 29, 172–173
Berlin, Irving 156
Bernie, Ben 5, 20
Beulah 148
The Big Show 38, 136
Biggs, E. Power 57
Billboard 170, 202
The Bing Crosby Show 155–156
Biography in Sound 32, 38
Biscayne Television Corporation 33
Black Enterprise 200
"Black Rock" 65–66
"Blacklisting" 59–60, 61
Blackwell, Elizabeth 149
Blackwell, H.M. 10, 43
Blaine, Martin 160
Blattner, Bud 107
Bleyer, Archie 56
Bloch, Irwin H. (Sonny) 194
Block, Martin 180–181
Bloom, Sol 124
Blue and Red Network affiliate numbers 25; origins/features 21–22
Blue Book 120
Blue Network Company, Inc. 91, 192
Bob and Ray 81, 143
The Bob Hope Show 22
Bobby Benson and the B-Bar-B Riders 82
Bogart, Humphrey 161
Bonanza 175
Boone, Pat 140
Bosley, Tom 67
Bow, Clara 142
Bowes, Major Edward 5, 57, 141
Bradbury, Ray 150
The Breakfast Club 29, 95, 98
Bremer, Frank 94
Breneman, Tom 95
Brice, Fanny 147
Briem, Ray 186, 191
Briggs, Donald 166
Brinkley, David 201
British Broadcasting Company (BBC) 83
British Marconi 117
Broadcast Center (CBS) 66, 87
Broadcast Music, Inc. (BMI) 29
Broadcasting 126
Broadcasting & Cable 194
Broadcasting Company of America (BCA) 14, 15, 17
Broadway Is My Beat 58, 159
Brokenshire, Norman ("Broke") 46
Brothers, Joyce 41, 184
Brown, Himan 66–67
Brown, Les 29
Brown, Ted 43
Brownell, Lalive 147
Browning King Orchestra 9
Brunswick-Balke-Collander Company 28

Buka, Donald 154
Burns, George 38, 62, 125, 135, 144, 147, 173
Busch, Ed 199
Business Radio Network 192
Business Week 198
Business Wire 108

California Radio System 102–103, 105
Cantor, Eddie 29, 33, 44, 125
Capital Cities/ABC, Inc. 99
Capital Cities Communication 99
Carnegie, Andrew 122
The Carpenters 201
Carrington, Elaine Sterne 49
Carroll, Carroll 125
Carroll, Madeleine 54
Carter, Jimmy 61
Casey, Crime Photographer 162
Casey, Press Photographer 162
Catholic Family Radio 192
The Catholic Hour 184
Catholic Radio Network 192
The Cavalcade of America 149
CBN Northeast 193
CBS Corporation 70
CBS Evening News 67, 71
CBS MarketWatch.com Radio Network 43, 70–71
CBS News on the Hour 71, 98, 180
CBS RADIO 70, 71
The CBS Radio Adventure Theater 67
The CBS Radio Mystery Theater 67
CBS Radio News 70, 71
The CBS Radio Workshop 58
CBS World News Roundup 61, 71
Chain broadcasting 4
The Challenge of the Yukon 76, 109, 152
The Chamber Music Society of Lower Basin Street 29
Chambers, Robert William 163
Chaplain, Charlie 74
Chenango and Unadilla Communications 199
Chicago Symphony Orchestra 81
The Chicago Theater of the Air 81
The Chicago Tribune 72, 74, 76, 130–131
Chick Carter, Boy Detective 82
Children's Broadcasting Corporation 192, 198
Chimes (NBC) 23–25, 43
The Chordettes 56, 140
Christian Broadcasting Network (CBN) 193, 199
The Christmas Channel 201
Churchill, Winston 32
Cincinnati Times-Star Company 77, 78
The Cisco Kid 82
Citadel Broadcasting Corporation 100, 191, 201
Civic Concert Service, Inc. 26, 93
CKLW 76
Clara, Lu 'n' Em 97
Clark, Buddy 158

Clark, Dick 181, 201
Clark, Roy 140
Clarke, Everett 161
Clear Channel Communications 200
Cliburn, Van 140
The Cliquot Club Eskimos 125
Clooney, Rosemary 49, 56, 65, 140, 155
CNNRadio 43, 71, 87
Coast to Coast on a Bus 141
Coats, George A. 45, 46–47, 201
Code of Ethics 119, 127
Collingwood, Charles 31
Collins, Dorothy 158
Collins, Fred (announcer) 40
Collins, Frederick L. (author) 159
Collins, Peter B. 194
Collins, Ted 156
Colmes, Alan 43
Colonial Network, Inc. 76, 77, 78, 85, 101, 103–104, 114, 115, 193, 202
Columbia Artists, Inc. 45, 54–55
Columbia Broadcasting System (CBS) 17, 25, 26, 29, 31, 33, 35, 37, 38, 39, 40, 43, 45–71, 72, 73, 74, 75, 77, 78, 79, 80, 81, 82, 83, 84, 86, 87, 89, 91, 94, 95, 96, 98, 101, 103, 105, 106, 111, 112, 120, 128, 129, 132–138, 139, 140, 141, 142, 143, 144–145, 146, 148, 149, 150, 151, 153, 155, 156, 157, 158, 159, 160, 161, 162, 163, 164, 165, 166, 167, 169–171, 172, 173, 175, 177, 179, 180, 181, 184, 186, 191, 193, 201
Columbia Concerts Corporation 45, 54–55
Columbia Concerts Service 55
Columbia Phonograph Broadcasting System, Inc. (CPBS) 47, 48, 55, 133, 201
Columbia Phonograph Company 5, 133, 201
Columbia Records 45, 47, 55, 57
The Columbia Workshop 58
Comment on the News 41
Communications Act of 1934 120
Companionate Radio 83
Congress Cigar Company 50
Conley, Eugene 157
Conrad, Anthony 41
Conrad, Frank 3, 178
Conrad, William 58, 160
Continuity acceptance 128
Coolidge, Calvin 12–13, 29, 30, 118, 146
Corbet, Lois 147
Coronet carpets 37
Correll, Charles 30, 38, 62, 135, 146, 181
Cosby, Bill 140
Cotsworth, Staats 162
Couric, Katie 71
Courtney, Del 181
Couzens, James 128
Cowles Publishing 36
Cox, H.C. 48, 55

Index

Cox, Wally 140
Coxe, George Herman 162
Crawford, Joan 54
Crime Photographer 162
Crocker, Betty 184
Cronkite, Walter 61, 67, 68–69, 201
Crooks, Richard 157
Crosby, Bing 38, 49, 55–56, 62, 65, 71, 125, 135, 155–156
Crosley, Powel, Jr. 72, 75, 76
Crosley Radio Corporation 72, 75
Cross, Milton J. 90, 96, 157
Crossley, Archibald 80
Crowley, Matt 162
Cullen, Bill 43, 181
Cullen, Hugh Roy 107, 108
Culligan, Matthew J. 39, 180
Cummings, Irving 151
Curry, Ann 43
Curtain, Joseph 162
Customized recordings 26
CW Network 70

The Daily Dose 200
Daly, John 61
Damone, Vic 140
Damrosch, Walter 5, 20, 22
Dan Rather Reporting 67
A Date with Judy 29
The Dave Ross Show 71
Davenport, Judith 199
Davenport, Ronald R., Sr. 199, 200
David Harum 82
Davies, Gwen 154
Davis, Elmer 95
Davis, Janette 56
Davis, Mark 100
Day, Dennis 29, 145
Day, Doris 158
DB Communications 202
Dear Abby 66
Dearborn, Bob 199
Declaration of Independence 124
de Forest, Lee 3, 94, 130–131
DeLeath, Vaughn 5
DeMille, Cecil B. 151
Dempsey, Jack 142
Denning, Richard 162
The Des Moines Register and Tribune 36
Desmond, Johnny 158
The Detective Story Hour 164
Diamond, Neil 201
Diaz, Ray 90
Dick Clark's Rock, Roll & Remember 201
Dietrich, Marlene 54
Dimension 40, 66
Dimension X 150, 174
Disc jockey (DJ) impact 178–179, 180–183, 184, 199
Dr. Christian 58
Dr. Paul 97
Dr. Sixgun 58, 160
Doggett, Jerry 107
Domingo, Placido 96
Don Lee Hollywood studios 85, 105, 193

Don Lee Network 54, 76–78, 84, 85, 101, 104–106, 109, 110, 114, 193
Donellan, Nanci 200
Dorsey, Tommy 181
Downey, Morton 56
Downs, Bill 176
Dragnet 29, 38, 58, 159, 174
Dragonette, Jessica 5
Drake, Galen 184
Dreier, Alex 43
Dreyfuss, Michael 154
The Drive 200
DuMont, Allen B. 170, 195
DuMont Broadcasting Corporation 195
DuMont Television 98, 195
Dunning, John 30, 49, 82, 159, 161
E.I. du Pont de Nemours Company 149
Durante, Jimmy 29
Durocher, Leo 32
Durr, Clifford J. 115

The Early Show 66
The Ed Sullivan Theater 66
The Edgar Bergen and Charlie McCarthy Show 143–144
The Edge of Night 166
Edison, Thomas A. 93, 132
Edward J. Noble Company 92
Edwards, Douglas 31, 167
Edwards, Ralph 141–142
E.I. du Pont de Nemours Company 149
Eidson, Ruth Googins Roosevelt 113
8XK 178
Eisenhower, Dwight David 134–135
Elder, Larry 100
Eleanor and Elliott Roosevelt 113
Elliott, Bob 49, 81, 143
Ellis, Herb 159
Emerson, Faye 113
Emmis Broadcasting Corporation 42
Emphasis 40
Empire State Network, Inc. 106
Enterprise Radio Network 193–194
Eskridge, Michael 194
ESPN Radio 100, 193, 200
Eternal Word Television Network 192
Etting, Ruth 5
Evans, W. Leonard, Jr. 197
The Evening Herald Publishing Company 102–103
The Eveready Hour 9
Excelsior Radio Networks 200
"Exclusivity" clauses/contracts 52, 78–79, 104, 114

Face the Nation 71
Faith, Percy 56, 57
The Family Channel 193
Family Life Network 193
Family Theater 82
Famous Jury Trials 97

The Fat Man 97
Father Knows Best 29
Faye, Alice 29, 136–137
The FBI in Peace & War 58, 159–160
Feather, Leonard 181
Federal Communications Commission 22, 26, 32, 52, 62, 78–79, 85, 89, 90, 91, 92, 98, 99, 100, 101, 115, 119, 120, 121, 170, 171, 192
Federal oversight 116–121
Federal Radio Commission (FRC) 8, 27, 118–119, 120, 126, 128
Federal Trade Commission (FTC) 14
Ferrall, Scott 200
Fessenden, Reginald 3
Fibber McGee & Molly 22, 29, 33, 82, 147–148, 161, 188
Fidler, Jimmy 184, 187
Fields, W.C. 144
Financial impact of networks: on communities 6; on radio industry 6
Financing broadcasting 122–131
Fineshriber, William S., Jr. 63
First "network" aircast 12
Fistell, Ira 186, 191
The Fitch Bandwagon 29
Fitzgerald, F. Scott 32
F.L. Jacobs Company 86
Flair Reports 40
Flashgun Casey 162
Fletcher, Lucille 160
Fonda, Henry 161
Forman, Bill 161
Fort Laramie 58–59
Fortune 50
Foster, Cedric 83
Fox Broadcasting Company 195
Fox Family Channel 193
Fox News 43, 71, 87
Fox Sports Radio 200
Fraim, John P. 87
Francis, Arlene 184
Francis, Connie 140
Fraser, Jack Gordon 90
The Fred Allen Show 95–96, 173–174
Frederick, Pauline 31, 43
Freeman, Florence 167
Frequency Modulation (FM) 28, 85, 115
Fridell, Vivian 165
Froman, Jane 75
Front Page Farrell 82
Frontier Gentleman 59
Frost, Alice 162
Fudderman, Steve 71
Fuss, Bob 71

Gallaher, Eddie 181
Gallup, George 80
Game of the Day 83
Gangbusters 159
Garagiola, Joe 184
Garden, Mary 20
Gardiner, Don 95

Gardner, Erle Stanley 166
Garland, Judy 161
Gaylord Entertainment 70
General Electric Company (GE) 9, 11, 12, 14, 15, 17, 18, 21, 24, 25, 27, 28, 41, 42, 43, 70, 100, 132, 169, 198
General Foods Corporation 129, 147
General Mills Corporation 153, 177
General Mills Radio Adventure Theater 67
General Motors Building 66
General Teleradio 84, 104, 114, 115
General Tire & Rubber Company 84, 85, 86, 103–104, 105, 114, 115, 193, 196, 202
The George Burns and Gracie Allen Show 144
Gershwin, George 32
Gibbs, Georgia 158
Gibson greeting cards 37
Gluskin, Lud 56
Goddard, Paulette 54
Godfrey, Arthur 49, 56, 57, 71, 95, 140–141, 179, 181
The Gold Dust Twins 125
Goldenson, Leonard 94, 98, 99
Goldman, Edwin Franko 20
Goldmark, Peter Carl 61–62
Goodman, Benny 181
The Goodrich Silver Masked Tenor 42, 125
The Goodwill Hour 83
Goodyear, Charles 149
Gordon, Gale 148, 161
Gordon Baking Company 73
Gorin, Igor 81, 157
Gosden, Freeman 30, 38, 62, 135, 146, 181
Gould, Jack 37
Goulding, Ray 49, 81, 143
Goulet, Robert 140
Grable, Betty 144
Grand Central Station 58, 150–151
Grand Ole Opry 29
Grant, Cary 161
Grauer, Ben 90
Great Day in Sport 107–108
Great Depression 30, 55, 67, 126, 128, 129, 169
The Great Gildersleeve 29, 62, 135, 148
Grebe, A.H. 51
The Green Hornet 76, 95, 109, 152–153, 159, 163
Greene, Lorne 67
Griffin, Ken 165
Griffith, Andy 67, 148
Grimes, Michael 154
Gross, Ben 20
The Groucho Show 142
Guedel, John 139–140, 142, 143
Gunsmoke 58, 59, 65, 71, 160, 161, 174
Guterma, Alexander 86
Gygi, Ota 191

Haines, Connie 111, 198
Hal Roach Studios 86
Hale, Barbara 162
Hall, Juanita 197
Hall, Radcliff 90
Halop, Florence 154
Hammer, Armand 86
Hannity, Sean 100
The Happiness Boys 125
Harbord, James 94
Harding, Warren G. 12, 117
Harding-Cox election 12, 178
Hare, Ernie 5
Harlow, Jean 54
Harris, Arlene 147
Harris, Phil 29, 44, 145
Hartge, John 71
Hartmann, Thom 194
Harvey, Paul 95, 100
Haskins, Virginia 81
Hatch, Wilbur 56
Have Gun, Will Travel 59, 65, 160, 176
Hawkins Falls 97
Hawthorne, Nathaniel 10
Hayes, Arthur Hull 65, 180
Hayes, George 90
Haymes, Dick 158
Haymond, Carl E. 109
HD Radio 70
Head of the Lakes Broadcasting Company 102
Hearst, Jack 134
Hearst, William Randolph 103, 134
Hearst Radio, Inc. 22, 102, 103
Heatter, Gabriel 83
Heinl, R.D. 125
Hemingway, Ernest 32
The Herb Jepko Show 84
Here's Morgan 81
Hertz, Heinrich 3
Hertz Rent-A-Car 37
Hewitt, Don 176
Hicks, George 90
Hightower, Jim 194
Hilltop House 58, 82
Hines, Jerome 96, 157
Hitler, Adolf 61
HMS *Pinafore* 13
Holmes, Betty Fleischmann 46, 48, 50, 201
Holt, Lester 43
Home 35
Hooper, C.E. 80
Hoover, Herbert 53, 117, 118, 123, 125, 131
Hoover, J. Edgar 152, 159
Hopalong Cassidy 82, 176
Hope, Bob 29, 30, 124, 136
Hopper, Hedda 184
Hottelet, Richard C. 176
Houdini, Harry 74
The Hour of Decision 184
House Party 65, 139–140, 142
The Howard Miller Show 181
Howdy Doody 143
The Human Side of the Record 181
Hummert, Anne 49, 163, 164–165, 166, 167

Hummert, Frank 49, 163, 164–165, 166, 167
Husing, Ted 5, 46, 53, 107

I Looked and I Listened 20
IDT Media 208
I.E. (Information Entertainment) America Radio Network 194
Iger, Robert 100
Imus, Don 43
Independent Broadcasters Network (IBN) 194
Indianapolis 500 stock car race 83
Infinity Broadcasting 43, 70, 71, 87, 198
Information, Please! 22, 184–185
Inglis, Elizabeth 35
Ingram, Dan 98
The Ink Spots 75
Inner Sanctum Mysteries 67, 188
Inter-City Broadcasting System 106
International News Service 31, 201
Interstate Commerce Commission 120
The Interwoven Pair 125
The Ipana Troubadours 125
It's Sports Time 66
Ivy Broadcast Company 199
Ivy Broadcasting Network 199

Jack, Wolfman 43
Jack Armstrong, the All-American Boy 153
The Jack Benny Program 22, 38, 144–145, 161
Jackson, Allan 31
Jackson, Eugene D. 196
F.L. Jacobs Company 86
J.C. Studios 66
Jeff Regan, Investigator 159
Jeff 2x 200
Jenkins, Charles Francis 169
Jenkins, Gordon 29
Jensen, Mike 41, 184
Jepko, Herb 84
Jessel, George 79
Johnny Madero 159
Johnson, Edward 157
Johnson, Lyndon Baines 94
Johnstone, William 82, 161
Jolson, Al 5, 29, 33
Jonas, Howard 108
Jones, Billy 5
Jordan, Jim 147, 161
Jordan, Marian 147, 161
Joseph, Mike 98
Joyce Jordan, M.D. 97
J.T. the Brick 200
Judson, Arthur 45, 48, 49, 50, 52, 54, 201
Judson, O'Neill & Judd 45–46
Judson Radio Program Corporation 46, 47
Juke Box Jury 181
Just a Minute with Harry Smith 71

KABC 98
Kahn, Otto 137

Kaltenborn, H.V. 31, 43, 74
Kaplan, Scott 200
Kaplow, Herbert 31
The Kate Smith Show 156
Katie Couric's Notebook 71
Kaufman, Stefan 71
KDB 77, 104, 105
KDKA 12, 13, 21, 22–23, 27, 116, 178
KDPM 13
Kearns, Joseph 161
KECA 98
Keech, Kelvin 90
KEHE 103
Keighley, William 151
Kelk, Jackie 154
Kelly, Pat 90
Kennedy, John F. 61
Kentucky Derby 49
KERN 103, 104
Kesten, Paul 68
Keystone Broadcasting Company 195
Keystone Broadcasting System (KBS) 194–195
KFBK 103, 104
KFOX 103
KFPY 104, 105
KFRC 54, 77, 85, 104
KFWB 103
KFXX 13
KGA 109
KGB 77, 85, 104
KGO 23, 27, 32, 91, 98, 110
KGY 109
KHJ 54, 77, 85, 104
KHQ 109
Kids Say the Darndest Things 140
Kilgallen, Dorothy 184
King, John H. 108
King, Larry 84, 186, 191, 199
King-Trendle Broadcasting Corporation 72, 92, 108, 109
The Kingston Trio 188
Kintner, Robert E. 93–94
Kirby, Durward 181
KIT 109
Kittross, John 126
KLIF 107
KLOS 99
Kluge, John 195
KMJ 103, 104
KMO 109
KMOX 47, 53
Knight Rider 153
Knoller, Mark 71
KNX 53
KOA 27
Kobak, Edgar 92
KOH 103, 104
KOIL 47
KOIN 104, 105
KOL 104, 105, 109
KPLT 112
KPO 12, 23, 27, 110
KPRC 111
KQV 98
Kraft Foods Company 156
Kraft Music Hall 155

Kramer, Mandel 164
KRLD 112
KSD 13, 21
KTAC 108
KTMS 103
KTRW 108
KTSL 105, 193
Kunsky-Trendle Broadcasting Corporation 72, 108, 109
KVI 104, 105
KWG 103, 104
KYA 103
KYW 12, 21, 27

Lamour, Dorothy 144
Lanson, Snooky 158
The La Palina Smoker 50
Larkin, John 166
LaRoche, Chester J. 92
The Late Show with David Letterman 66
Lauck, Chester 81
Law, Bob 197
Lawrence, Gertrude 32
Lawrence, Steve 140
The Lawrence Welk Show 98
Lazer, Joan 154
Leave It to the Girls 83
Ledoux, Leone 147
Lee, Don 54, 55, 104, 105, 106, 193
Lee, Thomas Stewart 85, 105
Lekas, Bill 200
Lescoulie, Jack 181
LeSueur, Larry 31
Let George Do It 82
Let's Pretend 58, 153–154
Lever Brothers, Inc. 129, 151
Levine, Irving R. 31, 43
Levy, Blanche Paley 49
Levy, Isaac D. (Ike) 46–47, 49, 50
Levy, Leon 46–47, 49
Lewis, Elliott 67
Lewis, Fulton, Jr. 83
Lewis, Robert Q. 49, 57, 95, 181
Lewis, Sinclair 32
Lewisohn Stadium 45
Liberty Broadcasting System (LBS) 107–108, 111, 195
Life Can Be Beautiful 141
The Life of Mary Sothern 82
Life Savers Corporation 91, 92, 93
Life with Luigi 64
Light Crust Doughboys 112
Lindbergh, Charles 29
The Lineup 58, 159
Linkletter, Art 49, 57, 95, 139–140
Lipton, Bill 154
Litzinger, Sam 71
Livingstone (Benny), Mary 145
Lockridge, Frances 162
Lockridge, Richard 162
Loews Corporation 69
Logan, Laura 71
Lone Journey 97
The Lone Ranger 73, 76, 80, 82, 95, 109, 152, 154, 163
The Longines Symphonette 57
Look 36
Lopez, Vincent 5, 8, 20, 42

Lora Lawton 165
Lorre, Peter 161
Louchheim, Jerome H. 49, 50
Louis, Joe 32
Love of Life 97
Lowe, Don 90
Lowe, Jim 181
Luce, Henry R. 92
Luke Slaughter of Tombstone 59, 160
Lum and Abner 33, 81
Lund, John 164
Lux Radio Theater 58, 71, 151, 161
Lux Video Theater 151
Lydon, Jimmy 154
Lynch, Christopher 157
Lynch, John 192

Ma Perkins 33, 58, 65, 75, 165–166, 180
MacFarlane, Wilbert Ernest 74, 76
Mack, Connie 32
Mack, Nila 153, 154
MacKenzie, Gisele 158
R.H. Macy & Company 72, 85, 105
Maer, Peter 71
Major Bowes' Original Amateur Hour 141
Major League Baseball (MLB) 107, 195
Make Believe Ballroom 180
Malloy, Mike 194
Malone, Ted 184
The Man Called X 96
Management contracts with licensees 27
Mandeville, Betty 160
March, Frederic 161
Marconi, Guglielmo 3, 117
The Mariners 56
Mark Trail 82
Marketplace 186
Marketplace Money 186
Marriage for Two 97
Marsh, Daniel 176
Marshall, E.G. 67
Marshall Field Company 91
Martin, Mary 35
Martino, Al 140
Marx, Groucho 29, 38, 62, 63, 135, 142–143
The Mary Tyler Moore Show 168
Massey, Curt 49
Mathes, J.M. 9
Matinee with Bob and Ray 143
Matthews, Grace 82
Maxwell House Presents Good News 147
Mays, David 200
McBride, Mary Margaret 95, 184, 187
McCarthy, Charlie 29, 62, 135, 143–144
McCarthy, Jack 90
McCarthy, Joseph R. 59, 60, 61, 94
McClatchy Broadcasting Company 102, 103, 105
McClatchy Newspapers 102, 103, 104, 105
McClelland, George 73, 74

McConnell, Smilin' Ed 75
McCormick, Cami 71
McCormick, Robert 43
McCosker, Alfred Justin 74, 76
McDaniel, Hattie 56–57
McDonald, Eugene 134
McGraw, James H. 91
McGraw-Hill Publishing Company 91
The McGuire Sisters 56, 140
McLendon, Gordon 107, 195
McLeod, Elizabeth 73, 74, 75
McMahon, Ed 43
McNamee, Graham 21, 46
McNeill, Don 49, 95
McPherson, Aimee Semple 118
Meet Millie 64
Meet the Press 29, 34, 41, 83, 185
Meighan, James 165
Melchior, Lauritz 81, 96
Mellon Bank 91
Melton, James 81
Meltzer, Bernard 41, 186, 197
Memories 201
Menotti, Gian Carlo 35
Mercer, Johnny 158
The Mercury Theater on the Air 58, 82, 151–152
Metromedia Radio 195
Metropolitan Broadcasting Corporation 195
The Metropolitan Opera 29, 57, 81, 95, 96, 137, 138, 156–157
The Metropolitan Opera Auditions on the Air 157
Metropolitan Opera Company 47, 95, 97, 156–157
Meyers, Joseph O. 32
Michigan Radio Network 73, 101, 108–109
Mickelson, Sig 64, 172
Middleman, Sharon 71
Mike Wallace at Large 66
Miliano, Lou 71
Miller, Howard 181
Miller, Marvin 161
Mills, Billy 29
The Mills Brothers 75
Milner, Martin 159
Miner, Jan 166
Les Miserables 82
Mr. and Mrs. North 58, 162
Mr. Keen, Tracer of Lost Persons 58, 163
Mr. President 97
Modern Romances 97
Mohr, Gerald 164
Monday Night Football 83
Monitor 29, 32, 35, 37, 38, 40, 53, 64, 83, 98, 99, 136, 147, 179, 197
Monroe, Vaughn 56
Moore, Garry 95
Moore, Mary Tyler 168
Moorehead, Agnes 82, 160
Moran and Mack 48
Moraweck, Lucien 161
Morgan, Frank 147
Morgan, Henry 81, 96, 174
Morrison, Bret 82, 164

Morrow, Bruce 43, 98
Morse, Samuel F.B. 117, 149
Morse Code 117
Motorola 121
MSNBC 24, 43
Mudd, Roger 41
Mueller, Merrill 31
Mullen, Frank 23, 36
Munchausen, Baron 5
Munsel, Patrice 96
Murrow, Edward Roscoe 31, 60, 61, 69, 175
"Murrow Boys" 60, 61, 175–176
Mutual Black Network (MBN) 84, 195–195, 199
Mutual Broadcasting System (MBS) 25, 26, 29, 31, 39, 42, 43, 67, 70, 71, 72–88, 91, 95, 98, 101, 103, 104, 105, 106, 107, 109, 110, 111, 112, 113, 114, 129, 143, 152, 153, 154, 155, 156, 164, 165, 177, 179, 181, 186, 191, 192, 193, 195, 196, 199, 202
Mutual Broadcasting System (Washington State) 108
Mutual Cadena Hispanica Network 84, 196
Mutual Lifestyle Radio 196
Mutual Lifestyle Reports 196
The Mutual Radio Theater 67, 83
Mutual Spanish Network 196
"Mutual Television" 83
My Favorite Husband 64
My Friend Irma 64
My Little Margie 64, 176
My True Story 82, 97
The Mysterious Traveler 81

Nally, Edward Julian 18–19, 43
National Amusements 70
National Association of Broadcasters (NAB) 45, 119, 127, 130–131
National Association of Regional Broadcast Stations (NARBS) 101
National Black Network (NBN) 196–197
National Broadcasting Company (NBC) 4, 6, 9, 11, 13, 14, 15, 16–44, 45, 47, 49, 51, 52, 53–54, 55, 56, 57, 58, 59, 62, 63, 64, 66, 70, 71, 72, 73, 75, 76, 77, 78, 79, 80, 81, 82, 83, 84, 86, 87, 89–90, 91, 93, 94, 95, 96, 97, 98, 99, 100, 101, 103, 105, 109, 110, 111, 112, 113, 114, 115, 119, 120, 128, 129, 132–138, 140, 141, 142, 143, 144, 145, 146, 147, 148, 149, 150, 151, 152, 153, 154, 155, 156, 157, 158, 159, 162, 163, 165, 169, 170, 171, 173, 174, 177, 179, 180, 181, 185, 186, 191, 192, 197–198, 199
The National Farm and Home Hour 29, 185
National Football League (NFL) 107, 195
National Independent Broadcasters (NIB) 101
National Negro Network (NNN) 197

National Public Radio (NPR) 108, 186–187, 196
National Vespers 185
NBC Blue Network, Inc. 32
NBC News and Information Service (NIS) 197
NBC News on the Hour 40, 41, 98, 197
NBC News Radio 43
NBC Red Network, Inc. 32
The NBC Symphony Orchestra 57, 96, 136, 138
NBC Universal, Inc. 42
Neal, Harold L. 98
Neal, John 192
Nebel, Long John 84
Nelson, Harriet Hilliard 29, 38, 62, 95, 96, 135, 161
Nelson, Lindsey 107
Nelson, Ozzie 29, 38, 62, 95, 96, 135, 161
Nelson, Willie 40
New Sounds 83, 99
The New York Daily News 73
The New York Herald-Tribune 93–94
New York Oratorio Society 20
New York Philharmonic Symphony 20, 45, 47–48, 57, 96, 137, 138
The New York Times 34, 48, 64, 92, 125, 169
The New York World 13, 31, 53
The New York World-Telegram 20
New York World's Fair (1939) 28, 134, 169, 170
The New Yorker 162
News and Information Service (NIS) 37, 40
News format (local stations) 66, 98
News programming 30–32, 39–40, 43–44, 64, 65, 71, 83, 84, 86, 95, 97–98, 172
Newspaper Guild Press Club 35
Nick Carter, Master Detective 82, 163
Nielsen, A.C. 38, 62, 80
Nielsen audience measurement system 38, 62, 136
Niesen, Claire 165
Night Talk (NBN) 197
Nighttalk (NBC) 40–41, 84, 99, 185–186, 191, 197
Nimoy, Leonard 67
Noble, Edward John 32, 91, 92–93, 94, 100, 192
Noble, Robert P. 92
Notre Dame football 83
NPR.org 187

O'Brien, Edmond 164
Official Detective 82
Olbermann, Keith 200
Olsen, George 20
Olsen, Johnny 95
On a Sunday Afternoon 57, 181
One Man's Family 29
One on One Sports 200

Index

O'Neil, T.F. 85
O'Neil, William 85
Orange Network 23, 110
The Original Amateur Hour 141, 176
Ortega, Santos 166
Osgood, Charles 71, 184
The Osgood File 71
Our Gal Sunday 165
Our Miss Brooks 64, 148–149
Owned and Operated Stations (O and Os) 26–27, 98

Pacific Broadcasting Company 104, 105, 109–110
Pacific Coast Network 23, 53–54, 110
Paine, Thomas 7
Paley, Samuel 49–50, 133, 201
Paley, William S. 29, 35, 37–38, 39, 45, 49, 50–51, 52, 54, 55, 56, 57, 59, 60, 61, 62, 63, 64, 65, 67, 68, 69, 106, 132–138, 170–171, 177, 179, 201
"Paley's Comet" 38, 62, 63, 135
The Palmolive Hour 125
Paramount-Famous-Lasky/Paramount-Publix/United Paramount Pictures 47, 54, 91, 93
Parks, Bert 95, 96, 141
Parsons, Louella 95, 184
Participating sponsorship 130, 177
Pat Novak for Hire 159
Pattiz, Norman J. 87
Paul Harvey News and Comment 100
Payne, Virginia 16
Payola scheming 181–182
Peabody, George Foster (awards) 43, 68
Pearce, Al 22
Pearl, Jack 5
Peary, Harold 38, 62, 135, 148
Pennsylvania Broadcasting Company 78
Pennsylvania Network 111
People Are Funny 140, 142
Peoples Radio 194
Pepper-Uppers 112
Performance Today 186
Perrin, Vic 159
Perry Mason 58, 166
Pete Kelly's Blues 159
Peter Pan 35
Petrillo, James C. 93
The Phil Baker Show 141
Philadelphia Symphony Orchestra 45, 48
Philco 121
Philco Radio Time 155
Phillips, Barney 159
Phillips, Irna 49
Picard, John 168
Pier 23 159
Pierpoint, Robert 31, 61, 176
HMS *Pinafore* 13
Pinza, Ezio 96
Platterbrains 181
Police drama subgroup 58

Poole, Bob 181
Poole's Paradise 181
Postmaster General 120
Potter, Peter 181
Powell, Dick 164
Powell, Jane 144
A Prairie Home Companion 186
Pressman, Gabe 43
Price, Leontyne 96
Price, Vincent 67
Printer's Ink 124
Procter & Gamble Company 129, 159, 166
Progressive Broadcasting System 111, 198
Prokofiev, Sergei 159
The Providence Journal 31
Provo, Frank 168
Public Broadcasting System (PBS) 143

Quality Network 75, 80
Queen for a Day 83–84, 142
Queensboro Corporation 10–11, 43
Quinn, Carmel 140
Quinn, Don 147
Quiz show scandals 176

Radio AAHS 192, 198
Radio Act of 1912 116–117, 118
Radio Act of 1927 8, 27, 118, 119, 121, 127
Radio and Television Mirror 170
Radio Broadcast 48, 122–123, 124, 125
Radio City 23, 42, 91, 94
Radio City Music Hall 24, 81
Radio Corporation of America (RCA) 8, 9–10, 11, 12, 13–14, 15, 17, 18, 19, 21, 23, 24, 25, 26, 27, 28, 29, 32, 33, 35, 36, 37, 39, 41, 42, 43, 46, 47, 51, 62, 63, 70, 91, 94, 100, 110, 115, 121, 132–133, 134, 136, 137, 169, 170, 177, 198
The Radio Dealer 124
Radio Disney 100, 198
Radio Group 9, 12, 13, 14, 15, 16, 17, 21, 22
Radio Guide 75, 158
Radio-Keith-Orpheum Corporation (RKO) 20, 24, 28
Radio Mirror 170
Radio News 124
RadioRadio 67
Radio set manufacturing/sales 5–6, 12, 28
The Railroad Hour 29, 57, 81
Railway Express Agency 23, 110
Randall, Vischer 10
Random House 37
Ranger, Richard H. 24
Rangertone Company 24
Raphael, Sally Jessy 41, 186, 197
Rasmussen, Bill 193
Rasmussen, Scott 193, 194
Rather, Dan 61, 67
Raviv, Dan 71
Rayburn, Gene 181

RCA Manufacturing Company 26
RCA Photophone 28
RCA Victor radio/phonograph services 28, 121
Readick, Bob 154, 164
Red and Blue Network affiliate numbers 25
Red and Blue Network origins/features 21–22
The Red Skelton Show 145–146
Redfield-Johnstone advertising agency 79
Redstone, Sumner 70
Reed, Alan 147
Reed, B. Mitchell 99
Regional networks 101–115
Reichman, Joe 181
Report on Chain Broadcasting 120
The Return of Nick Carter 82
R.H. Macy & Company 72, 85, 105
Riddle, Nelson 67
Riding with the Texas Rangers 112
The Right to Happiness 65
The Rise of the Goldbergs 97
Rizzuto, Phil 57, 66, 184
RKO Radio Network 198–199, 200, 201
Roach, Hal, Jr. 86
The Road Show 32
Robertson, Pat 193, 199
Robin Hood Dell East 45
Robinson, Bartlett 166
Robinson, C. Terry 200
Robinson, Hubbell, Jr. 173
Robinson, Marc 158
Rockefeller Center/Plaza ("30 Rock") 23, 24, 36, 66, 81, 94
Rockline 99
Rogers, Ginger 54
Rogers, Will 5, 20
Rolfe, B.A. 20
The Romance of Helen Trent 166–167
Ronstadt, Linda 201
Roosevelt, Eleanor 113
Roosevelt, Elliott 112, 113
Roosevelt, Franklin Delano (FDR) 43, 92, 112, 113, 115, 120
Roper, Elmo 80
Rose Bowl 21
Rosenberg, Sid 200
Ross, Dave 71
Ross, Lanny 158
Rountree, Martha 83
Royal, John Francis 33, 138
Ruben, Harvey 41, 186, 187
Ruffo, Titta 20
Rural Radio Network (RRN) 193, 199
Russell, Charles 164
Russo, Chris 200
Ryan, Tim 200

The Saint 82
The Salt Lake City Tabernacle Choir 56
Saltzman, Charles McK. 128
Sam 'n' Henry 30, 146
Sam Spade 96

Samuel Paley & Company 133
Sandburg, Carl 32, 126
Sarnoff, David 16, 18, 19, 29, 30, 32, 35, 36, 37, 38, 39, 41, 42, 43, 44, 46, 51, 57, 62, 63, 84, 91, 94, 95, 132–138, 169, 170, 177
Sarnoff, Robert W. 33, 35, 36–37, 41, 42, 94
Satellite Music Network (SMN) 199
Satellite technology 84, 120, 121, 185, 188–189, 195, 198, 199, 200
SBN Sports Network 200
Scanlan, Dan 71
Schechter, Abraham A. 31–32
Schoenbrun, Daniel 61, 176
Scott, Ray 200
Scott, Willard 41
Scripps-Howard Corporation 20
Search for Tomorrow 97
The Sears Radio Theater 67, 83
The Second Mrs. Burton 65
Second Sunday 40, 41
See It Now 60, 175
Self-regulation of the industry 117–118
Sergeant Preston of the Yukon 109
Serling, Rod 83
Settipani, Frank 71
Sevareid, Eric 31, 201
The 700 Club 193
The Shadow 82, 163–164
Shalit, Gene 41, 184
Sharbutt, Del 43
Shearer, Norma 54
Shepard, John, Jr. 103, 114
Shepard, John, III 103, 114
Shepard, Robert F. 103, 114
Sheridan Broadcasting Corporation 84, 186, 197, 199
Sheridan Broadcasting Network (SBN) 196, 199–200
Shore, Dinah 158, 161
Shortwave transmission 13
Showtime cable network 70
Shutta, Ethel 5
Siepmann, Charles 172
Sillerman, Michael 194–195
The Silver Masked Tenor 42, 125
Simms, Ginny 158
Simms, Lu Ann 140
Simon, Carly 201
Simon and Schuster 70
Sinatra, Frank 158
Singin' Sam 75
The Six Shooter 38, 59, 160
60 Minutes 71, 176
The $64,000 Question 176
Skelton, Red 38, 62, 75, 96, 135, 136, 145–146, 173
Sky King 82, 155
Small, Sidney L. 196
Smith, Al 53
Smith, Buffalo Bob 43
Smith, Harry 71
Smith, Howard K. 176
Smith, Jack 49, 56
Smith, Kate 56, 62, 95, 124, 156
Smith, Robert "Wolfman Jack" 181

Smith, Sally Bedell 68, 106
Sony BMG Music Entertainment 42
Sorel, Guy 165
Sounds of the City 196
Source (magazine) 200
The Source Radio Network 40, 42, 200
The Source Street Beat 200
Speaking of Faith 186
Speaks, Margaret 157
Spier, William 161
Spivak, Lawrence 83
The Splendid Table 186
SPM Radio Network 200
Sports Fan Radio Network 200
Spot advertising 80
Stafford, Hanley 147
Stanton, Frank Nicholas 57, 59, 60, 63, 64, 65, 67–69, 70, 135, 177
Stardust 201
Stars Over Hollywood 58
Steber, Eleanor 157
Stella Dallas 165
Stephan, Doug 194
Sterling, Christopher 126
Sterling, Jack 181
Stern, Bill 29, 44, 184
Stevens, Connie 144
Stevens, Leith 56
Stevens, Risë 96, 157
Stop the Music! 96, 141, 173–174
Storer, George B. 75, 91, 192
Storer Broadcasting 84
The Story of Mary Marlin 97
The Story of Ruby Valentine 197
Storz, Todd 182
The Strange Romance of Evelyn Winters 97
Straus, Nathan 92
Striker, Fran 154
STRZ Entertainment Network 200
Stubblefield, Nathan 3
Subscription Television, Inc. 36
Sullivan, Brian 96
Sullivan, Ed 144–145
Summerall, Pat 57, 184
Sun Radio 194
Superman 152
Supreme Court 32, 90, 119
Suspense 58, 65, 71, 81, 160–161
Swarthout, Gladys 96, 157
Swing, Raymond Gram 83
"Syndicate style" advertising sales 79
Syndicated formats 183
System cue 51

Taft, Archie G. 109
Taft, William Howard 132
Talent bureaus 5, 26, 28
Talent Scouts 57, 140–141
Talk format 87, 98, 183, 184–187, 189
Talknet 41, 42, 84, 99, 186, 191, 197–198
Talkradio 84, 99, 186, 191
Talmadge, Norma 54, 79

Taylor, Arthur R. 69
Taylor, Deems 34, 48
Taylor, Henry J. 43
Taylor, James 201
Taylor, Mary Lee 184
TDI 70
Teagarden, Jack 181
Telecommunications Act of 1996 100
Telephone Group 9, 12, 13, 14, 16, 17, 22
Television Broadcasters Association 134, 169
Television's impact on radio 130, 169–177
Telstar 188
Terry and the Pirates 95
Tetley, Walter 154
Texas Quality Network 75, 111–112
Texas Rangers 113
Texas State Network 77, 101, 112–113
Thesaurus transcribed library 26
Thibault, Conrad 81
Thirty Minutes in Hollywood 79
This Day in Network Radio 47–48
This Is Your FBI 97, 159
This Is Your Life 142
Thomas, Lowell 31, 65
Thomas, Thomas L. 81, 157
Thomas S. Lee Enterprises 105
Thomson SA 42
3M Company 80, 87
Tibbett, Lawrence 158
Tilton, Martha 49, 158
Time 18, 57, 72, 73, 92, 93, 113, 192
Time-Warner Corporation 70
Timeless 201
Timeless Classics 201
Timeless Favorites 201
Tisch, Laurence Alan 69–70
RMS *Titanic* 116, 132
Today 31, 35
Toll stations 11, 12
Tom Corbett, Space Cadet 176
Tom Mix 82
Tonight 35
Top 40 music format 114, 182
Torme, Mel 111, 198
Toscanini, Arturo 30, 43, 57, 137, 138
Tovrov, Orin 165
Town Hall Tonight 141
Townsend, Dallas 31
Tracy, Arthur 56
Trammell, Niles 33, 171
Transcription: ban 156; services 26, 28, 55
Transtar Radio Network 200, 201
Trendle, George Washington 73, 76, 108
Trendler, Robert 81
Trent, Sybil 154
Trout, Robert 31
True Detective Mysteries 82
Truman, Harry S 171
Truth or Consequences 29, 141–142
Tucker, Tommy 79
Turner, Allyson 200

Turner, Ted 69
Twenty-First Precinct 58, 159
Tyson, Cicely 67

Uggams, Leslie 140
Under Arrest 82
Underwriting methods 122–123, 124–125, 126
Unforgettable Favorites (UF) 200–201
Unistar Communications 198, 200, 201
United Auto Workers 194
United Broadcasting Company 77, 78
United Broadcasting Network 194
United Independent Broadcasters Association (UIB) 46, 47, 48, 49, 50, 51, 133, 201
United Paramount Theaters 94, 98, 99
United Press 31
United Press International Network 201
U.S. Department of Commerce 117, 118
U.S. Navy 116, 117
U.S. Office of War Information 31
U.S. Patent and Trademark Office 24
U.S. Securities and Exchange Commission 194
United Stations Radio Network 198, 200, 201–202
The University of Chicago Roundtable 185

Valiant Lady 97
Vallee, Rudy 29, 31, 42, 44, 125
Valli, June 158
Van Buren, Abigail 66, 184, 187
Vandercook, John W. 43
Van Patten, Dick 154
Van Voorhis, Westbrook 83
Variety 113, 124, 169, 170, 171
Vendig, Irving 166
Verbitsky, Nick 200, 201
Viacom, Inc. 70, 198
Vic and Sade 141
Victor Talking Machine Company 28, 47, 133, 146
Virginia Broadcasting System, Inc. 113
The Voice of Firestone 29, 57, 97, 157–158

WAAB 103, 104
WABC 4, 48, 51, 53, 80, 94, 98, 99, 100
WABY 106
WADC 47
Wain, Bea 158
WAIU 47
Waldorf-Astoria Hotel 20, 94, 133
Waldrop, Bob 90
Walker, Jimmy 74
Walker, Paul A. 115
Wallace, Mike 66
Waller, Judith 48, 55

Walsh, George 160, 161
Walt Disney Company 99, 100, 198
Walter Cronkite Reporting 67
Walton, Sidney 184
The War of the Worlds 58, 151
Waring, Fred 29, 49
Warner, Gertrude 82, 164, 166
Warner Brothers 70
Warwick, J.R. 93
WASH 108, 109
Washington News Desk 202
Wasmer, Louis 109
Waterman, Willard 148
WATR 103, 114
Waxworks 181
WBAP 111
WBAY 10, 16, 42
WBBM 53
WBCM 108
WBNY 106
WBT 53
WBTM 113
WBZ 21, 27
WBZA 21, 27
WCAE 21, 78
WCAO 47
WCAP 12, 21
WCAU 46, 47, 49, 111
WCBM 106
WCBS 51, 66, 94, 184
WCCO 21, 53
WCFL 84
WCHV 113
WCLE 77, 78
WCOU 103, 114
WCSH 21, 114, 115
WDAF 21
WDEL 106
WDY 46
WEAF 4, 6, 9, 10–11, 12, 13, 14, 15, 16, 17, 21, 22, 23, 27, 42, 80, 90, 93, 94, 123
WEAN 47, 85, 102, 104, 114, 115
Weaver, Sylvester Laflin (Pat), Jr. 33–36, 39
Webb, Jack 159
WEBC 102
Weber, Cynthia 71
Weber, Fred 76
Weber, Henry 81
Weber and Fields 20
WEEI 21, 53
Weekday 35
Weekend 32
Weems, Ted 181
Weigner, Steve 194
Welk, Lawrence 98
WELL 108
Welles, Orson 58, 82, 151, 160
Wells, H.G. 58, 151
Wendy and Me 144
Wendy Warren and the News 58, 167–168
WENR 27, 32, 91, 98
Werbe, Peter 194
West, Mae 42–43
Western drama subgroup 58–59
Western Electric (WE) 9, 11, 12, 16

Western Ontario Broadcasting Company, Ltd. 76, 77, 85
Western Union 13, 16, 18, 21, 22, 94
Westinghouse Electric and Manufacturing Company (WEM) 8, 9, 11, 12, 13, 14, 15, 21, 25, 27, 28, 66, 70, 94, 184
Westwood One 42, 43, 70, 71, 87, 196, 198, 200, 201
WFAA 111, 112
WFAN 43
WFBL 47
WFBR 78
WFDF 183
WFEA 10, 114, 115
WFI 21
WFIL 98
WGAL 106
WGH 113
WGHP 47
WGN 21, 30, 72, 73, 77, 86, 146
WGR 21
WGY 12, 27
WHAI 103, 114
What's My Line? 176
WHB 123
WHDH 143
When a Girl Marries 97
Whispering Streets 97
The Whistler 58, 159, 161
White, Major James Andrew 46, 49, 52, 201
Whiteman, Paul 5, 74, 181
Whiting, Margaret 158
Whitney, Bill 71
WHK 77, 78
WHKC 77, 78
WHLB 102
WHN 84, 106
WIBM 108
WIBX 106
WICC 104, 114, 115
Wide Wide World 35
Widmark, Richard 67
Wikipedia 198
Wilcox, Harlow 147
Wild Bill Hickok 82
Williams, Brian 31, 43
Williams, Bruce 40, 186, 197
Willkie, Wendell L. 92
Willson, Meredith 29
Wilson, Don 145
Wilson, Eileen 158
Wilson, Woodrow 18, 117
Winchell, Walter 31, 86, 95, 184
WINS 66, 184
Winter Street Corporation 103
WIP 78, 106
Wireless Age 46
Wireless Ship Act of 1910 116, 118
Wireless Telegraph and Signal Company 117
Wireless Telegraph Company, Ltd. 117
The Witch's Tale 81–82
WJAR 9, 21
WJAS 47
WJAZ 118

WJIM 108
WJSV 53
WJY 10, 94
WJZ 4, 8, 9–10, 11, 13, 17, 21, 22, 23, 27, 32, 46, 80, 91, 92, 94, 98
WKRC 47, 53, 77, 78
WKZO 108
WLAW 106
WLBZ 103, 114, 115
WLIB 21
WLIT 21
WLLH 103, 114
WLNH 103, 114
WLS 75, 98, 100
WLVA 113
WLW 72, 73, 74, 75, 76, 77
WMAF 12
WMAK 47
WMAL 27
WMAQ 27, 30, 47, 48, 146
WMBO 106
WMCA 92, 106
WMEX 106
WMFG 102
WNAC 12, 47, 85, 102, 114, 115
WNBC 42, 43, 94
WNBF 106
WNBH 103, 114
WNBT 134
WNEW 195
WNLC 103, 114
WNYC 122
WOAI 111

WOC 21
WOIC 83
WOL 106
Wolfe, Miriam 154
Wolfe, Thomas 188
WONS 85
WOOD 92, 108, 109
Woods, Mark 90, 91, 92, 93, 100
Woods and Warwick, Inc. 93
WOR 4, 47, 48, 51, 72, 73, 75, 76, 77, 80, 83, 85, 86, 87
WORK 106
World Music Festivals 57
World News Roundup 71
World News Roundup Late Edition 71
World Series 22, 78–79, 83, 107, 171
WOWO 47
WPRO 106
WRC 10, 27, 46
WRCA 42, 94
WRDO 103, 114, 115
Wright, Robert C. 42
WRKO 114
WRNL 113
WSAI 21
WSAR 103, 114
WSAY 106
WSB 24
WSYR 22
WTAG 114, 115
WTAM 21, 27, 33

WTIC 21, 114, 115
W2XAB 170
WWJ 21
WWTC 198
WXYZ 72–73, 74, 75, 76, 77, 92, 98, 108, 109, 152, 154
Wyman, Thomas Hunt 69
Wynn, Ed 5, 29, 33, 125, 191–192

X-Minus One 29, 39, 40, 150

Yankee Network, Inc. 85, 102, 103, 104, 114–115, 193, 202
Yarborough, Barton 159
You Bet Your Life 63, 142–143
Young, Loretta 54
Young, Nick 71
Young, Owen D. 15, 17–18, 19, 20, 23, 43
Young & Rubicam advertising agency 34
Young Doctor Malone 65
Young Widder Brown 82, 165, 167
Young Widder Jones 82
Your Hit Parade 158, 181
Yours Truly, Johnny Dollar 58, 65, 71, 164

Z-Rock Radio Network 202
Zenith Corporation 118, 121, 134
The Zero Hour 83
Ziegfeld Follies 147

www.ingramcontent.com/pod-product-compliance
Lightning Source LLC
Chambersburg PA
CBHW081553300426
44116CB00015B/2861